Bottled Poetry

Bottled Poetry

*Napa Winemaking
from Prohibition
to the Modern Era*

James T. Lapsley

UNIVERSITY OF CALIFORNIA PRESS

Berkeley / Los Angeles / London

University of California Press
Berkeley and Los Angeles, California

University of California Press, Ltd.
London, England

© 1996 by
The Regents of the University of California

Library of Congress Cataloging-in-Publication Data

Lapsley, James T.
    Bottled poetry : Napa winemaking from Prohibition to the
modern era / James T. Lapsley
        p.   cm.
    Includes bibliographical references and index.
    ISBN 0-520-20272-4 (alk. paper)
    1. Wine and wine making — California — Napa
Valley — History.   I. Title.
    TP557.L35   1996
    641.2'2'0979419 — dc20   96-7072
                                                              CIP

Printed in the United States of America
9 8 7 6 5 4 3 2 1

This book is dedicated with great respect to the memory of three "winemen" and one wine historian:

JIM BEARD
printer, St. Helenan, and tireless partisan of Napa wine

LOU GOMBERG
observer, quantifier, and promoter of California wine

ANDRÉ TCHELISTCHEFF
enologist, educator, and experimenter

RUTH TEISER
preserver of a generation's history

Wine in California is still in the experimental stage; and when you taste a vintage, grave economical questions are involved. The beginning of vine-planting is like the beginning of mining for precious metals: the wine-grower also "prospects." One corner of land after another is tried with one kind of grape after another. This is a failure; that is better; a third best. So, bit by bit, they grope about for their Clos Vougeot and Lafite. Those lodes and pockets of earth, more precious than the precious ores, that yield inimitable fragrance and soft fire; those virtuous Bonanzas, where the soil has sublimated under sun and stars to something finer, and the wine is bottled poetry: these still lie undiscovered; chaparral conceals, thicket embowers them; the miner chips the rock and wanders farther, and the grizzly muses undisturbed. But there they bide their hour, awaiting their Columbus; and nature nurses and prepares them. The smack of California earth shall linger on the palate of your grandson.

Robert Louis Stevenson, "Napa Wine,"
in *The Silverado Squatters* (1880)

Contents

Acknowledgments

Bottled Poetry was conceived long ago, but actual work on it, as a doctoral dissertation in history at the University of California at Davis, only began in 1989. Any writer receives help and support from family, friends, and professional colleagues, but as a full-time academic employee split between two jobs, with a small winery to operate on weekends, I have received more than my share. I would like to take this opportunity to acknowledge and thank the following individuals and institutions.

First, my love and thanks to my wife Carol, my daughter Grace, and my son Jake for their support, patience, and understanding. Much of the time spent in writing this book was taken from them. Second, my thanks to Charles Lacy, dean of University Extension and friend, for his constant and unwavering support. A "late bloomer" himself, Charles knows all too well the additional problems engendered in completing a dissertation later in life when fully employed. Third, my thanks to Mort Rothstein, my dissertation adviser, for his willingness to take on a superannuated graduate student, and, more important, for his gentle encouragement that, yes, this could be done.

Historians seem to collect librarians, and I have special relations with three: my thanks to Axel Borg, wine librarian at the Shields Library at the University of California at Davis; to John Skarstad, head of Special Collections at the Shields Library and keeper of the Bureau of Alcohol, Tobacco and Firearms archives and oral histories; and to Vicki Herrmann, BATF librarian in Washington, D.C., who sent me the transcript of the Napa Valley Appellation Hearings.

The following industry members have given me time, resources, and encouragement and deserve thanks: Louis Martini, Peter Mondavi, Roy Raymond, and the late André Tchelistcheff for interviews; John Wright for making available the Arthur D. Little study; Jon and Eileen Fredrikson for sharing Lou Gomberg's industry statistics, as well as Gomberg's minutes of the meetings of the Premium Wine Producers of California; Zeke Oman and the board of the Napa Cooperative Winery for allowing me to review and use the co-op's minute books; and the Napa Valley Vintners' Association's board of directors for allowing me to review the Association's minutes.

The first three chapters were written while I enjoyed a three-month research leave funded by Academic Affairs of the University of California at Davis but created at the urging of the Academic Federation, a counterpart to the Academic Senate for non-senate academic employees. That leave allowed me to concentrate fully on the project and was crucial in convincing me that the dissertation was feasible. I thank the Academic Federation and encourage the continuation of the research leave program so that other academic staff members may experience the same chance for professional growth that I have enjoyed. Finally, my thanks to my colleagues in the Department of Viticulture and Enology and to my friends in the California wine industry, whose support and enthusiasm for the project convinced me that it was worth undertaking. Whether or not my winemaker friends are located in Napa, *Bottled Poetry* is their history too, since it is as much a history of the emergence of quality wine in California as it is a history of a region. To that end, I hope it edifies as well as entertains.

Preface: Why *Bottled Poetry*?

In the late afternoon of a spring day in 1977, I chanced to meet Cary Gott unloading his pickup truck in the parking lot at Corti Brothers, a fine wine and food shop in Sacramento. Cary was the winemaker, general manager, and founder of Monteviña, a winery funded by his father-in-law, an investment banker. In those days, wineries were popping up across the state like mushrooms after some vinous rain, but unlike most vintners, Cary had chosen Amador County in the Sierra foothills, rather than the more popular Napa County to the west. My home-winemaking mentor, Dutch Martinich, had worked the 1976 crush for Cary and had introduced us earlier, but it was still a thrill to meet a "real" winemaker. I asked Cary what brought him "down the hill" to the "flatlands." He grinned and his arm described an arc as he pointed to the cases of wine in the bed of his truck: "Delivering bottled poetry," he replied.

"Bottled poetry." It was a delicious phrase that rolled off the lips. I knew it was not original to Cary, but could not place its origin and tucked it away in the back of my mind for further study. That summer, while traveling to my wife's family's ranch in the hills east of St. Helena, I took Highway 29 rather than the Silverado Trail and passed the sign erected by the Napa Valley Vintners' Association that welcomes visitors to the "world famous" Napa Valley. There, at the bottom of the sign, was the phrase, in quotation marks, "and the wine is bottled poetry."

On asking at several wineries, I was informed that the quotation came from Robert Louis Stevenson's *The Silverado Squatters*, and that, as all valley residents knew, the phrase was Stevenson's estimation of Napa wine, one of the first testimonials to its quality. Carol's grandmother had the collected works of Stevenson at the ranch, and so one evening I sought out *The Silverado Squatters* and turned to the chapter "Napa Wines." The language was beautiful, written by a man who obviously knew and loved fine wine, but it was equally obvious that the phrase "and the wine is bottled poetry" referred, not to Napa wine, but to wines produced from the elite vineyards of France. So why was the Stevenson quotation on the Napa Vintners' sign?

The Napa Valley has become America's best-known wine region for two basic and interrelated reasons. First, its leading vintners and growers have relentlessly pursued a vision of excellence. In the early years, they often fell short of that vision, but they moved forward, and in the pursuit, they have helped to define what quality American wine might be. Second, they have not been shy in telling fellow Americans about their region and their quest. Napa's leading vintners have pursued excellence, but they have also effectively organized a cooperative program of regional promotion, in addition to individual brand development. In short, they have been dogged salesmen of the Napa Valley.

Most successful salespeople share an incurable optimism, coupled with a capacity for minor levels of self-deception. They believe what they want to believe, and that, through "positive thinking," such belief can actually create the desired outcome. They may be right. Diligence and perseverance can wear down most buyers, and as Legh Knowles, the master salesman of Beaulieu, once noted, most sales are made after the third call. With that in mind, I see in the use of the Stevenson quotation an illustration of the sales mentality par excellence, a concrete example of how and why the Napa Valley has become the best-known wine region in the United States. There was no deliberate misrepresentation when the Napa Vintners' Association placed the Stevenson quotation on the sign. Rather, they assumed the quotation to be about Napa because it came from a chapter referring to their valley and fitted with their self-image. Over a half century of acting upon that self-image has ultimately made the quotation functionally true. If Stevenson were with us today and could taste some of Napa's best, I doubt he would ask for his words to be removed from the sign — although he might ask for some formal attribution!

Bottled Poetry is a study of the formative years of Napa winemaking. Although the concluding chapter, "Harvest," places the wine boom of the 1970s in a social context and explains Napa's place in it, the main emphasis is on the period between Repeal in 1934 and 1967, when table wine, which is wine containing less than 14 percent alcohol, finally out-sold fortified wine nationally. The book has three levels or foci. As the title suggests, the primary focus is on the production and marketing of premium wine from the Napa Valley. The names Beaulieu, Beringer, Charles Krug, Christian Brothers, Louis Martini, and Inglenook will all be familiar to wine drinkers, and they receive the majority of attention. But premium wine was such a small segment of the total wine indus-try — perhaps 1 percent of all California sales for many years — that other premium producers from outside the Napa Valley are also included when relevant.

A second focus is on regional history. For at least the first two and a half decades following Repeal, the majority of Napa grapes were trans-formed into inexpensive bulk wine by such large wineries as the two co-ops, Napa Wine Company, and Sunny St. Helena. They are ignored or forgotten now, relics of the past, but they were important parts of the valley's economy, providing "homes" for what would otherwise have been surplus grapes. And, of course, there are the wineries that were unsuccessful. During its first twenty-five years after Repeal, Napa expe-rienced two boom-and-bust cycles, the first following Repeal and the second during World War II, in which wineries entered and went out of business. Some of these "losers" are included here too, object lessons that winemaking is a business as well as a romantic endeavor.

A final focus, entertained somewhat reluctantly, is on the broad his-tory of California wine. Before the wine boom of the 1970s and the emergence of a significant larger market for fine wine, Napa was simply part of a state wine economy dominated by the dessert wine producers of the Central Valley. As necessary, the politics and history of the Central Valley producers is included here, but that is more appropriately another history, still waiting to be written.

The two major themes, the pursuit of excellence and the collective promotion of the Napa Valley have already been alluded to, but may need further explanation. Perhaps owing to its narrow shape, relatively short length, and the fact that it is Napa County's main avenue of com-merce, the Napa Valley is unusual in its concentration of winemaking enterprises and strong personalities. Even more atypical of other wine regions is the fact that Napa's strong-willed and competitive vintners found ways to work cooperatively to promote the Napa Valley as a re-gion and to share knowledge and technology for improvement of wine quality. Napa winemakers were at the forefront in promoting varietal wine production. They developed and adopted technology that dramatically improved wine quality, and through the Napa Wine Technical Group shared their knowledge with one another. The owners, through the Napa Valley Vintners' Association, were also innovators, developing a program to promote their region at least a decade prior to other premium areas. Combined, these two forms of cooperation made the Napa Valley the best-known wine region in the United States and helped define the possibilities of fine wine production in California.

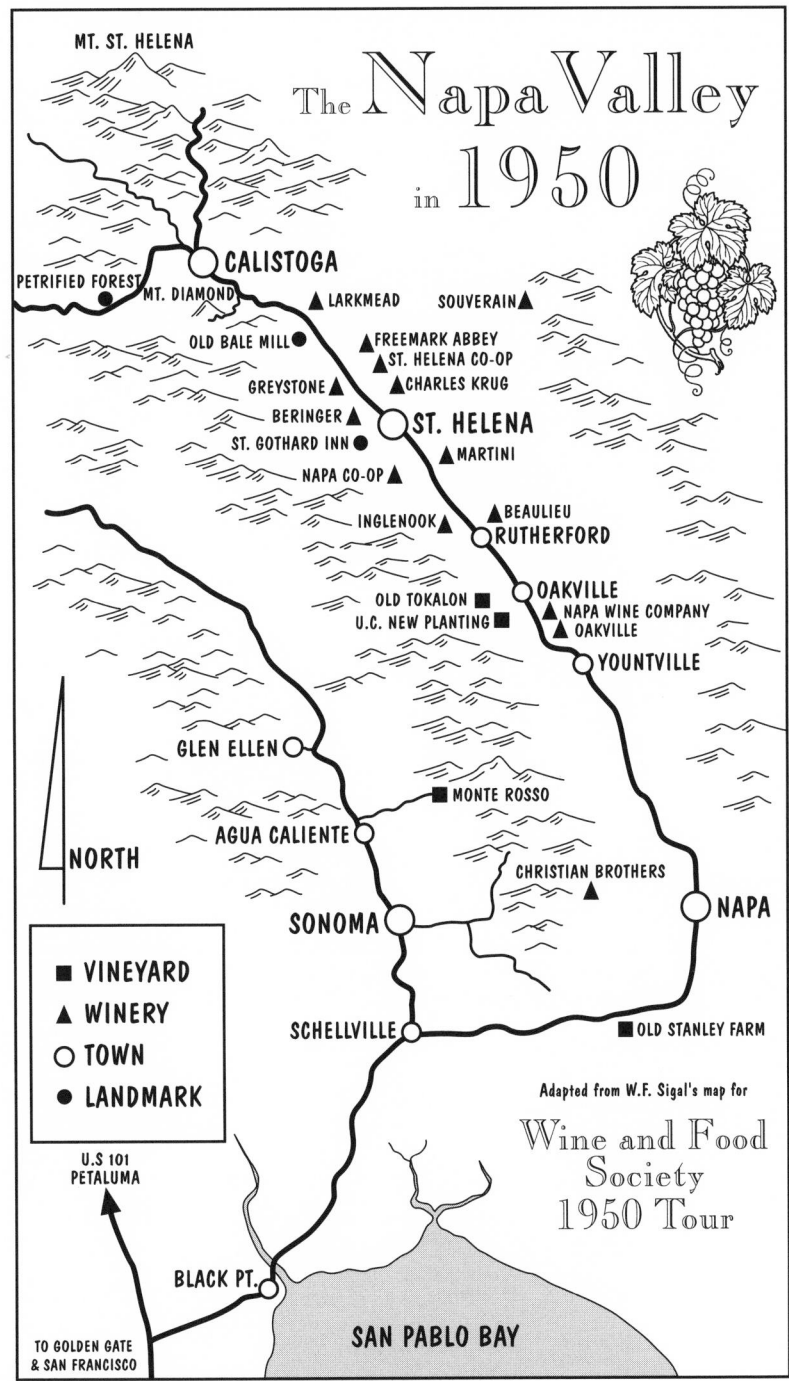

The relatively small market for finer California wines following World War II is reflected in this map adapted from a guide produced for the Wine and Food Society Tour of 1950. A similar map produced in 1995 would include almost 200 listings. Cartography by Dino Gay, 1996.

Introduction: Napa and the Notion of Wine Quality

Americans' notion of quality wine — indeed, their very idea of what "wine" was or should be — changed dramatically during the five decades that separated Repeal of Prohibition in 1933 from the introduction of geographic appellations of origin in the 1980s. Put starkly, the public's expectation of "wine" shifted from a fortified, often oxidized or spoiled beverage, produced from indistinct grape varieties, to a table wine possessing distinct flavor attributes derived from varietal grapes and from processing. If the transformation was dramatic, it was not abrupt. Fifty years is, after all, a fairly long time in human terms, more than the average American's working career. The alteration in Americans' conception of wine was gradual and incremental, the result of a series of interactive efforts on the part of California producers to increase wine quality through the adoption of technology and varietal grapes, while attempting to build a market for such wine through brand and generic education. No one individual or company led this change, it was rather the result of individual efforts, coupled at times with collective action. However, one area can be identified as the locus of the change.

Today, the Napa Valley is the nation's best-known premium wine district, an American Bordeaux and Burgundy, compressed into a relatively small valley. Roughly thirty-five miles long, it ranges from a few miles wide at its southern terminus on San Pablo Bay to perhaps a mile wide at its northern end at Calistoga. It is this area that has become synonymous with quality for U.S. wine lovers.

Other viticultural regions may chafe at Napa's dominance in the public's mind, but the reality of American wine drinkers' equation of Napa with wine quality is a cold marketing fact of life for all California producers. The primacy of the Napa address in the minds of wine consumers is evidenced in two representative statistics. First, just under one quarter of all of California's more than eight hundred wineries are located in Napa County, creating a concentration of wineries per square mile unrivaled anywhere else in the nation. Second, reflecting the marketing cachet of the Napa appellation, Napa Valley grapes routinely sell for 10 to 20 percent more than the same varieties grown in neighboring Sonoma or Lake counties. How did this region, representing roughly 5 percent of all California's winegrape vineyard acreage, become synonymous with wine quality and achieve such dominance?

The short answer is that Napa producers were leaders in defining wine quality and creating a market for such wine. As leaders they expended the initial energy—planting the vineyard, so to speak—and as leaders they have reaped the harvest. The individual and group activities of Napa winemakers in promoting brand and region, in introducing varietal wines, and in adopting new technology and science are thus the main focus of this book. One result of these cumulative activities was the evolution and introduction to Americans of a new type of wine. A second result was the transformation of Napa from a poor, backwater county whose economy was based on cattle to a cosmopolitan leader in wine production.

The change in Napa is easily documented, but the notion that a new type of wine, or at least a new definition of what quality wine should be, was introduced may seem overreaching, especially to a generation of wine enthusiasts who have come to wine in adulthood as individuals, rather than growing up with wine in a family or social context. Wine was, and to some degree still is, a "foreign" beverage in the United States. Even now, only about 5 percent of Americans who consume alcoholic beverages describe wine as their drink of choice. Most U.S. consumers thus have no basis to know what wine was like, and taking present wine quality as a given, today's critical wine lover may be forgiven for assuming that California's best wines have always been varietal, intensely flavored, and complex. Such is not the case, and a discussion of the notion of wine quality, along with a brief review of the realities of wine production in the years immediately following Repeal, will supply the necessary background for appreciating the magnitude of the changes in California wine production and quality.

Wine quality is difficult to define for several reasons. First, the word *quality* is used in two different but interrelated ways: it is generally used to mean "degree of excellence," yet it also can mean "attribute." The potential for linguistic confusion is compounded in that it is the collection and interaction of "qualities" (meaning attributes) that the consumer responds to in judging wine "quality" (meaning degree of excellence). Linguistic difficulties aside, the notion of quality is inherently subjective and depends upon the past experience and personal likes and dislikes of the evaluator. For someone with no real experience with wine, like most Americans at Repeal, a judgment about wine quality is practically impossible. Finally, the very idea of what constitutes "wine" has changed over time, making the definition of quality wine a continually moving target. To understand the extent of the change in the dominant paradigm, we must thus briefly review the cultural milieu in which wine quality was judged and examine the attributes associated with wine at Repeal.

The dry varietal table wines that were to make Napa famous did not exist in any appreciable quantity at Repeal. The dominant commercial California wine types for the first twenty-five years following Repeal were fortified wines, what the industry referred to as "sweet" wines, produced in the Central Valley, often from raisin varieties. Following Repeal, the newly revitalized industry had expected a "tremendous boom in sales," which, in the words of Roy Raymond, who had worked in the cellar at Beringer at the end of Prohibition, "just didn't materialize."[1] Instead, the California industry was surprised to find that 18 percent fortified wines identified as "port" or "sherry" were outselling dry table wines three to one, a reversal of pre-Prohibition drinking habits.

To some degree, the commercial predominance of dessert wines following Repeal was a result of Prohibition, which had discouraged the moderate use of alcohol. Americans who drank alcohol during Prohibition tended to drink to get drunk, and this attitude carried over after Repeal and was reflected in the market for fortified wine. A second aspect was that the market for commercial table wine — that is, unfortified wine with less than 14 percent alcohol — was artificially low, because immigrant Americans continued to produce their own wine at home from grapes shipped from California. During Prohibition, immigrants from Mediterranean countries, for whom wine was as necessary a commodity as bread or cheese, had been forced to vinify their own to assure an adequate supply. Following Repeal, they continued to make their own wines, thus escaping high state taxes. One economist concluded that almost 25 million gallons of dry wine was produced in 1934 for home consumption, about as much as was produced by commercial wineries.[2] The lack of a significant market for dry table wines, quality or otherwise, severely inhibited the development of Napa and North Coast wineries.

Moreover, for a number of reasons, the table wines shipped from California in the years immediately following Repeal were frequently of poor quality. Almost 80 percent of California wine was sold in bulk to out-of-state bottlers, who blended and cellared the wines and then bottled them under their own labels, not the winery's. This system encouraged California wineries to relinquish responsibility for the quality of the bottled wine and to view their product as an unbranded commodity. Furthermore, the early post-Repeal California wines were produced by untrained winemakers in unsanitary conditions, and the new wines were often stored in old, infected cooperage. These wines were then shipped in bulk to wholesalers and retailers who were equally unprepared to maintain the wines in sanitary, anaerobic conditions. The predictable result was wines spoiled by oxidation or by acetic and lactic bacteria, resulting in a sullied reputation for California wines. Such quality problems did not disappear quickly. Three years after Repeal, A. R. Morrow, the president of the Wine Institute, speaking at the first Dry Wine Institute held at St. Helena, complained that the emphasis on "quantity rather than quality" had retarded sales, and that "confusion is still the order of the day."[3] In a similar vein, an out-of-state buyer said in 1934: "Some [California wines] are as fine as can be purchased anywhere in the world, but as for some of the others, they can only be described as terrible. It is most detrimental . . . that such vintages are permitted on the market."[4]

Another reason for poor wine quality lay in the choice of grape varieties. The Eighteenth Amendment and its enforcing legislation, the Volstead Act, had a curious, and certainly unintended, effect on the grape-growing and winemaking industry in California. Because the Volstead Act allowed the home production of "nonintoxicating cider and fruit juices," an unanticipated but extremely strong demand for grapes suitable for shipping to urban ethnic communities or to bootleggers followed the enforcement of Prohibition. Grape growers who had assumed that there would be no market for the fruit of the vine following Prohibition were surprised to be offered $60 to $70 a ton for grapes that a year earlier had brought at most $20 to $25 a ton from commercial wineries.

Such demand had two results for the California industry and Napa until World War II. First, many farmers grafted their vines to poorer-quality varieties with thicker skins that could withstand shipping, or to varieties with deeper pigmentation or astringency, such as Alicante Bouschet or Petite Sirah, that could stand dilution with water.[5] Second, the temporary profitability of vineyards caused an influx of almost $100 million in the period between 1920 and 1923 and led to plantings of new vineyards all over California.[6] Although most of these plantings were in the San Joaquin Valley, when they came into production three to four years later, they created a chronic statewide oversupply of poor-quality grapes, which reduced grape and wine prices for years to come.

In a slightly different context, the famous University of California professor of enology Maynard Amerine once argued that "a high quality product cannot exist in a vacuum," and in the case of California wines following Repeal, he was undoubtedly correct.[7] Produced predominantly from non-wine-grape or non-distinct varieties, California dry table wines after Repeal would at best have had faint flavors and aromas. Most often even this neutral level of quality was not achieved. Overripe grapes fermented warm in unsanitary cooperage by inexperienced wine-makers resulted in wines whose main "qualities" were those of bacterial spoilage. It should come as no surprise that California wines, sold in bulk as an unbranded commodity to regional bottlers, who then offered the resulting blends to a non-wine-literate public, received a cool reception from immigrants, who could usually make similar wine more cheaply at home; from connoisseurs, who continued to drink European wines; and from the U.S. public in general, who saw wine as foreign and thought it tasted unpleasant.

This, then, was the milieu in which Napa wine producers found themselves at Repeal. They shared with other North Coast producers the advantage of a comparatively cool climate in which to grow grapes. The North Coast allowed the development of more flavorful, more colorful, and better-balanced grapes than did the growing conditions of the San Joaquin Valley. But the potential for improved wine quality was counter-balanced by a lower yield per acre, resulting in increased costs per gallon. For the Napa growers and winemakers to succeed, they would have to earn a premium for their wines, and to do that they would have to educate themselves and consumers about wine quality. This process of education spanned several decades of individual and group promotion and created a new definition of quality table wines as wines possessing distinct positive attributes derived both from the grapes themselves and from careful processing. Ultimately, a new class of wines was created. The new wines were varietally distinct, flavorful, and complex, wines that could compete with their European ancestors. The result of a marriage of climate, technology, science, and the purposeful pursuit of excellence by a handful of California winemakers in the Napa Valley, these wines, the "festive" wines predicted by Albert Winkler, professor of viticulture at the University of California, redefined the notion of quality wine and, in so doing, placed the Napa Valley firmly in the minds of American wine drinkers as the leading wine region in the United States. This campaign took almost a half century, and *Bottled Poetry* is its history.

CHAPTER ONE

The Quality Producers, 1934-1940

The Napa Valley clearly had the climate needed to produce grapes of high quality, but its reputation would ultimately be based on the products of its wineries, not those of its vineyards. Grapes are not bottled and aged, opened and savored, reviewed and remembered; wine is. Napa County has enjoyed a rich viticultural history, but so have Sonoma and Santa Clara counties. Napa's post-Repeal status depended upon the commitment and skill of its winemakers, upon their ability to produce and market a superlative product that would promote the Napa Valley and stand out in the consumer's mind. Immediately following Repeal, that ability and commitment seemed questionable.

The wineries of the Napa Valley after Repeal were an odd group of businesses. Some were large, others small; some produced only quality wines, others were interested only in profits. Some winery owners aspired to create their own brands, a difficult undertaking when most wine was sold in bulk to be bottled elsewhere under someone else's label. Others were content to produce bulk wine, considering it a commodity to be pumped into tank cars immediately following fermentation and sent east. Some viewed wine as a symbol of culture, an item with intrinsic worth, while others saw it simply as a way to preserve the vintage.

This diverse group did have common concerns and problems. Most producers were undercapitalized and could be counted on to support the New Deal industry codes and policies designed to stabilize the new industry. All shared marketing problems associated with myriad new state regulations regarding licensing, taxation, and retail sales of wine. But

beyond these basic factors, not all Napa winemakers seemed to understand the core economic truth that the coastal counties in general, and
Napa in particular, could only flourish by emphasizing quality. Frederic
Bioletti of the University of California had recognized this prior to Prohibition, when he wrote in his introduction to *Winemaking on a Small
Scale* that "the small scale operator cannot compete profitably with the
large wineries except on the score of quality," and that "the only reason
in California for making wine on a small scale . . . is to obtain a wine of
exceptional quality."[1] Seen from the perspective of total wine production in California, even the largest Napa Valley wineries were small producers, and ultimately they would survive and prosper by producing and
promoting a high-quality branded product rather than a mass-produced
commodity sold by the tank car.

During the 1930s, at least sixty or more wineries operated in the Napa
Valley, but only a handful of these were responsible for most of the production.[2] Four were also the established leaders in quality production.
André Tchelistcheff, a Russian-born, French-trained enologist who came
to work at Beaulieu in 1938, recalled four "outstanding wine processing
plants: Inglenook, Beaulieu, Larkmead, and Beringer." Robert Mondavi, who preceded Tchelistcheff in the Napa Valley by one year, was
"tremendously impressed by what I called the big four of the California wine industry . . . Inglenook, B.V. [Beaulieu Vineyards], Beringer
Brothers, and Larkmead" and bowed his head when he drove past the
first two.[3] By the end of the decade, two new wineries had joined the
"big four" in establishing the Napa Valley as the center of fine wine production: the Christian Brothers at the southern end of the valley, and
L. M. Martini in St. Helena. Of these six enterprises, Beaulieu Vineyards
was clearly the dominant winery in the valley in 1934.

Beaulieu Vineyards, or "B.V." as it became known to American wine
drinkers, was primarily the effort of one man, Georges de Latour, a native of Bordeaux who emigrated to San Francisco in 1883 at the age of
twenty-six. Descended from a grape-growing family, de Latour received
a classical early education from the Jesuits, a connection that proved important during Prohibition. He then got strong technical training in
chemistry at the Ecole centrale in Paris. After an ill-fated mining expe-
dition in Nevada left him penniless, de Latour started the American
Cream of Tartar Company, serving as both chief chemist and president.
The company specialized in refining the "argols," or bitartrate crystal
deposits that accumulated on the inside of wine tanks, processing it for
cream of tartar, a compound important in the baking industry. The job

brought de Latour into intimate contact with the California wine industry of the 1890s, where he saw firsthand the devastation wrought by *Phylloxera vastatrix*, a root louse that destroyed the vines of the *Vitis vinifera* grapes used in commercial winemaking. In the early 1900s, taking advantage of his viticultural ties in France, de Latour began importing and selling Rupestris St. George rootstock, a phylloxera-resistant selection. He became famous for his cuttings, importing them by the millions and employing agents throughout California's wine regions. When Prohibition came, he continued his importation business, but instead of bringing in rootstocks, he imported heavily colored varieties such as Grand noir and Alicante Bouschet for sale to California growers, who were grafting vineyards to fill the East Coast demand for intensely colored grapes.[4] According to Tchelistcheff, the vine-importation business was significantly more lucrative than the winery in the early 1900s and constituted a major source of de Latour's income.

De Latour acquired four acres and a home in the Napa Valley near Rutherford in 1900, and later claimed that year as the start of his winery, although there is no direct evidence of winemaking activities until 1904, when he leased a cellar. Certainly he did not have a commercial vineyard until after 1903, when he bought a 125-acre parcel and began planting fine varietal grapes of all kinds, including Cabernet Sauvignon from his native Bordeaux, Pinot noir, Muscat de Frontignon, Gray Riesling, White Riesling, Petite Sirah, and the Pinot noir clone that was to become known in California as "Napa Gamay."[5] For de Latour, it was a period of experimentation, when he tried to determine what varietals would create the finest wines in the Rutherford climate. It was also the period when he began cultivating his relationship with the Catholic Church by supplying altar wines for dioceses across the United States. That Beaulieu was purchasing grapes from the St. Joseph's Agricultural Institute in Rutherford, a Catholic school for boys, certainly did not hurt his case with the archbishops. Father Crowley, who ran the school, also supervised the manufacturing and distribution of the altar wines, and later the de Latours built a guest house for visiting priests interested in viewing the production of their altar wines.[6] When the Volstead Act became law, it allowed for production of sacramental wines, and Beaulieu was positioned to dominate this market with the strong backing of the Catholic Church.

During Prohibition, Beaulieu grew dramatically. By 1925, the winery was writing to federal Prohibition administrators on stationery identifying Beaulieu as "The House of Altar Wines" to request permission to treat three separate wineries used by Beaulieu for storage as one winery, in order to "avoid the present trouble incidental on the removal of wines from one winery to another," all of which had to be reported to the government monthly. Total storage had grown to 900,000 gallons, and Beaulieu requested permission to expand to a million gallons.[7] In 1926, de Latour entered into an agreement with the Wentes in the Livermore Valley under the terms of which the Wentes produced high-quality white wines for Beaulieu under the Beaulieu federal permit. This arrangement continued until Repeal, and many of the fine white wines sold under the Beaulieu label (then miscalled "Sauternes" after the Bordeaux district of that name) were actually produced by Wente in the Livermore Valley rather than in Napa County.[8] At a time when other wineries were shutting their doors, de Latour expanded production each year. Ironically, while other growers in California and the Napa Valley were planting or grafting to lower-quality shipping grapes, supplied by de Latour, he himself was planting fine varietals. At Repeal, Beaulieu thus not only enjoyed the benefits of an operating winery with aged wine on hand, but its five hundred acres of vineyards also accounted for much of the fine varietal production in the Napa Valley.

Perhaps as important as access to fine grapes, de Latour had also built a marketing network during Prohibition that stressed the Beaulieu name, even when the majority of the wines were sold in bulk. In New York, de Latour had established the Beaulieu Vineyard Distributing Company, a corporation separate from Beaulieu but wholly owned by de Latour, to distribute Beaulieu wines. Beaulieu also had marketing arrangements with local beverage distributors in Cleveland, Milwaukee, Omaha, Chicago, and Cincinnati, while distributing wine in San Francisco and Los Angeles direct from the winery.[9] As was typical before, during, and after Prohibition, the wine went in barrels to licensed wholesalers, who then resold it in smaller containers or, in some cases, bottled it. In every case, because Beaulieu was the permitted producer, the Beaulieu name was prominently featured, even on bulk containers, to distinguish the wine from "bootleg" product. Sometimes bulk shipment created problems. In at least one case, Christ's miracle of the wedding at Cana was reversed: barrels of wine shipped from Rutherford arrived in Milwaukee as water. In explaining to the Prohibition commissioner, de Latour commented, "If the package is very small, it is stolen altogether, but if the package is large, they cannot take out wine so easily; that is why I advise priests to buy a larger quantity at a time."[10]

Still, even with brand recognition and the beginnings of a distribution system, in the first years following Repeal, it was difficult to sell bottled wine in the depths of the Great Depression. Although Beaulieu had a storage capacity of over two million gallons and could produce at least half a million gallons annually, its sales of bottled wine were considered by Tchelistcheff to be "limited, very limited." He estimated that most case sales of Beaulieu wine were limited to California, amounting to about 3,000 cases a year in 1935 and 1936. Bulk sales to bottlers out of state, bulk sales of sacramental wine, and the sale of so-called "industrial wines" (that is, aromatic wines such as Muscat, used to flavor tobacco products) remained Beaulieu's bread and butter.[11] It was not until 1937, when Beaulieu signed with Park & Tilford, an old importing house in New York, that Beaulieu bottled wines became available nationally.[12] The wine bottled was obviously of high quality for the time. From 1934 through the end of the decade, Beaulieu won more medals in California judgings than any other California winery, perhaps hitting its peak at the Golden Gate Exposition in 1939, when de Latour walked away with three of the ten gold medals awarded, including the grand prize for red wine, a "Burgundy."[13] The Cabernet entered, also awarded a gold medal, was released after de Latour's death in 1940 as the first de Latour Reserve Cabernet, becoming the benchmark against which other Cabernets would be measured for at least the next forty years.

By the time of Repeal, de Latour was seventy-eight, a financial success, a power in the Napa Valley and San Francisco, and a founding member of the Wine Institute. Tchelistcheff's first impression of him when they met in France was of "a gentleman impeccably dressed with a beautiful London made suit, polished fingernails, with an expression of tremendous self confidence and self respect." Louis M. Martini referred to de Latour as "an elegant, patrician man . . . capable, honest, ethical, a gentleman in every way. . . . He knew wine, He had a good palate."[14] And he could afford to pursue only the best, in both personal consumption and in wine production. Each spring, the de Latour family traveled from San Francisco to their country home in Rutherford, Beaulieu, "The Beautiful," where Mrs. Fernande de Latour had planted extensive gardens, and where the de Latours lived as landed nobility in France might have lived prior to the French Revolution: with its trout and crayfish ponds, small animals and poultry (including, of course, pheasant), and gardens, the estate was almost self-sufficient.[15] Generally, once a year, the de Latours traveled to France, where de Latour renewed friendships, ordered winemaking supplies, such as barrels, and arranged for shipments of rootstocks and varietal cuttings to Beaulieu. It was while visiting the

Paris Viticultural Experimental Station in 1937 that he met and hired a new winemaker for Beaulieu, André Tchelistcheff.[16]

Tchelistcheff's odyssey from a prerevolutionary Russian estate to the Napa Valley is a microcosm of the European upheavals of the early twentieth century. Born in 1901, descendant of landed gentry and the son of a liberal lawyer who served in the ill-fated Kerensky government, Tchelistcheff fought with the White Russians, and in the 1920s, as a stateless person, received agronomic training at Brno in Czechoslovakia. Arriving in France in the early 1930s, he held a series of jobs in the French wine industry and the national department of enology and viticulture, all the while taking graduate courses in microbiology at the Pasteur Institute. When de Latour arrived at the Paris Viticultural Experiment Station looking for a replacement for the newly retired Léon Bonnet, a former University of California professor who had guided Beaulieu wines since Repeal, he found Tchelistcheff, a technically trained and experienced winemaker and scientist, whose influence ultimately extended beyond Beaulieu into the Napa Valley and throughout California.[17]

Although de Latour was interested in improving Beaulieu wines and later allowed Tchelistcheff to refurbish the winery in pursuit of improved quality, Beaulieu was essentially a business designed to produce income for the de Latour family. The situation was different across the road, and as Tchelistcheff later remarked, "I always personally considered Inglenook the first Château, not Beaulieu," primarily because Inglenook pursued a policy of selling bottled wine, and only bottling wine worthy of the Inglenook label.[18] Inglenook rarely sold bulk wine to the retail trade; wine that was not up to its standards was sold in bulk to other wineries.[19] In this sense, Inglenook was the first "estate" winery, producing wine predominantly from its own vineyards and following the path laid out by its founder, Gustave Niebaum, in the late 1800s.

There is an old joke that in order to make a small fortune in the wine business, one needs to start with a large fortune. Gustave Niebaum had both the large fortune and the desire to produce the best wines in California when he began Inglenook in the early 1880s. Niebaum was an achiever. Born in Finland in 1842, when it was still part of Russia, he studied at the Nautical Institute in Helsinki, receiving his master's papers at the age of nineteen. By the age of twenty-one, he was captain of his own ship, sailing for Alaska, where he explored what was left of Russian America, especially the Pribilof Islands, and traded for furs. In 1868, following the United States's purchase of Alaska, Niebaum sailed into San Francisco at the ripe age of twenty-six with a cargo worth over

$600,000. Within two years, he had helped found the Alaska Commercial Company, obtained exclusive fur-sealing rights off the Pribilof Islands, and was well on his way to amassing the large fortune necessary for starting a winery. Private wealth is difficult to measure for the period prior to the income tax, but it is a matter of record that the Alaska Commercial Company paid the United States government over $9.7 million dollars during the next twenty years for the fur-sealing rights, $2.5 million more than "Seward's Folly" had cost the government.[20]

Why or how Niebaum caught the "wine bug," is unclear. During the 1870s, he spent a good deal of his time in Europe negotiating fur sales for his company. Fluent in five languages, he traveled throughout the prime vineyard areas of Europe, later collecting soil samples and vines, and creating an enormous library on viticulture and winemaking. Married in 1873 to a woman who did not share his love of sailing, he abandoned a personal dream of building his own yacht in which to circumnavigate the world; instead, he apparently decided to build a château modeled on the great wine estates in Europe. In 1879 he acquired land at Rutherford, part of it already in vineyards, and began expanding the plantings.

Niebaum's first crush was in 1881, and the following year, construction began on the winery, a huge, three-story edifice, built into a hill for temperature control, complete with steam-powered machinery (and steam for sanitation), concrete floors, and oak cooperage. With the goal of matching the best wines of Europe and no pressing financial needs, Niebaum insisted on a level of sanitation and grape quality that his neighbors considered both unnecessary and extraordinary. In addition, he experimented with grape selection, wine aging, and blending. In 1887, he took another unprecedented step: henceforth he only shipped Inglenook wines in bottles, rather than in bulk, thus eliminating any possibility of adulteration. The result was that from 1890 up to Prohibition, Inglenook achieved a level of admiration and respect generally reserved only for the best foreign wines.

At Repeal, Gustave Niebaum had been dead for twenty-six years, but his widow was alive, wealthy, and determined to reopen the winery and to recapture its past reputation for quality. To direct the reopening, production, and marketing of Inglenook wines, and to serve as a guide for her grand-nephew, John Daniel, Jr., who would become owner at her death in 1936, Mrs. Niebaum hired Carl Bundschu. "Born in a wine barrel," Bundschu had grown up in Gundlach, Bundschu and Company, the family-owned winemaking and marketing firm in San Francisco. At fifty-five, Bundschu combined appreciation of fine wines with an understanding of marketing and public relations. A showman who loved center stage, he was a tireless organizer and promoter of fine wines, always willing to attend a meeting of wine producers or speak before any audience to promote Napa and Inglenook wines.[21]

Bundschu's skill at marketing was displayed at Repeal, on December 5, 1933. While other Napa wineries loaded trucks or tank cars for shipment to market, Bundschu hosted a day-long party at Inglenook for three hundred people, most of them from San Francisco society, at which older Inglenook vintages were brought up from the cellar, displaying the promise of aged wines, in sharp contrast to the three-month-old 1933 vintage, which was also served.[22] Rather than capitalize on the new market, Bundschu and Mrs. Niebaum preferred to hold their new wines. This had been their plan from the beginning.

In August 1933, prior to crush, Bundschu had outlined a three-year program to a *St. Helena Star* reporter, claiming that it would "take that long to get results from the efforts and expenditures," and that Inglenook would produce 100,000 gallons of wine, most of it from grapes grown on the Inglenook estate.[23] Later Bundschu reiterated, "Here at Inglenook, we will do no marketing until we are able to furnish a product that will be comparable with the best."[24] Inglenook introduced its "I.V.Y." brand, used for standard quality wines, in late 1934, and the "Cabinet" Inglenook label, used only for special lots of reserve varietal wine, in 1935.[25] Although some of the I.V.Y. wines occasionally bore generic names, both brands prominently featured the Napa Valley as the source of the grapes, and the Cabinet wines were some of the earliest post-Repeal varietal labelings in California. At the first State Fair wine judging since Prohibition in 1934, Inglenook received a gold medal and best of class for red wine, probably a Cabernet.[26] Emphasizing the themes of quality, history, and scarcity, Bundschu built the Inglenook brand to where, at $2 a bottle during the 1930s, its varietal wines were the most expensive in the state. Demand for high-quality varietal wine was not nearly strong enough for Inglenook to bottle and label all of its production, and the winery sold excess wine in bulk to other wineries.[27] Based on a strictly dollars-and-cents analysis, Inglenook could not be considered a financial success, because it continued to require subsidizing by Niebaum wealth. But by the late 1930s, Inglenook had reestablished its reputation as one of a handful of fine wine producers in the state.

Just north of St. Helena and across the road from the defunct Charles

Krug winery was the third of Mondavi's and Tchelistcheff's "big four": Beringer Brothers. Established in 1877 by Jacob Beringer, the winemaker for Charles Krug, with his brother Frederick, Beringer quickly became one of the valley's showpieces. The three-story winery, built against a steep hill, allowed for wagons full of grapes to be brought to the third floor by horsepower. Crushing operations took place there, and the crushed grape juice and skins were directed to fermenting tanks on the second floor. New wine then flowed by gravity to the first floor and into casks or barrels stored in one of three one-hundred-foot-long by seventeen-foot-wide tunnels carved into the hillside. When finally completed, the winery had a storage capacity of 600,000 gallons. The idea of such a gravity-flow winery was not new, but the Beringer Brothers winery, with its tunnels carved into stone, was the most elegant expression of the concept and was copied throughout the valley.[28]

During Prohibition, Beringer Brothers continued to produce medicinal and altar wine, but on a much reduced scale, and, like most wineries with vineyards, to sell grapes to home producers. Roy Raymond, who was cellarman during the 1930s, recalled that Beringer had roughly three hundred acres of producing vineyards at Repeal, which should have produced between 600 and 800 tons or between 100,000 and 120,000 gallons.[29] The *Star* noted that in 1932, Beringer had 300,000 gallons in storage and had produced 50,000 gallons of new wine from its own vineyards.[30] Almost all of the wine was generic rather than varietal, a result of both the grafting to shipping varietals such as Alicante and Grand noir during Prohibition and of the rather common pre-Prohibition practice of intermixed plantings. For example, the 40-acre block between the winery and the highway was a mixture of "Cabernet Sauvignon, Petite Sirah, Carignane, Zinfandel, and some Pinots."[31] Wine from such a vineyard was a logical candidate for "California Burgundy," if bottled, and more likely to be sold in bulk.

In 1933, in the flush of optimism over Repeal, Beringer bought outside grapes and expanded production. The following year, Beringer followed the market trend, producing more "sweet" wine—the term used in the California industry for fortified "dessert" wine—than dry.[32] Such wines were sweet because residual sugar remained in the wine; more important, owing to fortification, they were higher in alcohol, at 17 to 20 percent, as opposed to 12–14 percent for "dry" wines. In 1935, the winery expanded, adding storage for 300,000 gallons, a new bottling room, and a distillery. The distillery allowed the production of both the "high proof" spirits used to fortify the sweet wine and of brandy, which

Beringer began marketing in 1937. Although the market preference for fortified sweet wines did not help the dry wine producers, the distilling of spoiled wine into neutral spirits did provide an outlet for wines that had become acetic during Prohibition, or that had been poorly made following Repeal. According to Raymond, by 1935, Beringer was selling perhaps 15,000 cases of bottled wine, primarily in California, of which 80 percent was sweet, fortified wine. He estimated that by 1938, Beringer's output had increased to 40,000 cases, including brandy.[33] Such numbers were impressive during the depression, but still represented only 10 percent of Beringer's total storage capacity, or perhaps 30 percent of its annual production. Obviously, most of the wine produced by Beringer was sold in bulk, either in tank cars or in barrels, to be blended and rebottled elsewhere under other labels.

Three miles north of Beringer, on the valley floor toward the Napa River, was the Larkmead Winery, owned by the Salmina family. The smallest of the "big four" wineries, Larkmead was originally built of wood by a local cooper, who then leased and later sold the property to the Salmina family in 1892. The Salminas were Swiss and had come in the 1860s to the valley, where Battista Salmina purchased the William Tell Hotel in St. Helena and acquired real estate and vineyards. In partnership with his nephew, Felix Salmina, who had learned winemaking in Switzerland, they began operation as F. Salmina and Company. In 1906, they expanded, building a massive stone winery 33 feet high and 66 feet square *around* the existing wooden winery, which was dismantled *after* the new winery was completed.[34]

Larkmead eked out an existence during Prohibition, selling grapes from its 100-acre vineyard and producing sacramental wine. The *California Grape Grower*, in its Repeal issue, commented that Salmina and his sons, F. W. Salmina and Elmer Salmina, were thus in a position to offer "the very choicest aged wines made exclusively from Napa Valley grapes."[35] Unfortunately, like many wineries with wine in storage but little sales activity during Prohibition, most of the 300,000 gallons of wine was exceedingly high in volatile acidity and needed blending with new wine to meet government limits. Seventy out of eighty-four tanks sampled by government inspectors in 1932 had volatile acidity above the legal limit of .12 percent.[36] Much of this wine was apparently blended with new wine and sold in bulk to other wineries or to out-of-state bottlers. Government inventory records indicate that on average Larkmead produced about 80,000 gallons annually through 1937, but sold about 150,000 gallons each year in bulk, gradually reducing its inventory of spoiled wine.

During the 1930s, Larkmead produced and bottled wine under its own label, renewing its reputation as a high-quality producer, probably averaging between 5,000 and 10,000 cases in the late 1930s, a total comparable to Beaulieu's sales in California.[37] As was typical of the period, most of the Larkmead bottled wine was labeled generically as "White Chianti," "Burgundy," "Chablis," or "Moselle." However, Larkmead also offered varietal wines, including Cabernet and Zinfandel, for which it took two "firsts" at the 1937 California State Fair. For Larkmead, the 1937 judging was a high-water mark, as it won four first places and three second places, beating out Inglenook and Beaulieu in both the Cabernet division and in the "Burgundy."[38] The same year, Larkmead, along with Beringer and Inglenook, received a *diplôme d'honneur* from the Paris Exposition in 1937, creating excitement in St. Helena that Napa wines could compete with French wines on their own soil, or, as the *Star* editorialized, "that our area is second to none in the production of the world's best."[39] The California wines entered must have been varietally labeled, since France would not allow importation of wines bearing French appellations such as "Burgundy." Probably most of the Larkmead "Burgundy" came from Petite Sirah grapes, since Larkmead had been known for the variety prior to Prohibition.[40]

Although Larkmead was not a leader in varietal labeling, the Salminas did keep some varietals separate. The 1936 government summary shows grape varieties such as Zinfandel, Cabernet, and Barbera mixed with tanks labeled "Burgundy," Sauterne," "Chablis," "Riesling," and "Claret." Given the nomenclature of the day, it is difficult to know if "Riesling" was considered a wine type or a variety. Three years later, in its report to the government to substantiate vintage claims on labels, Larkmead listed Cabernet, Mondeuse, Semillion, Traminer, Gütedel, Zinfandel, and Johannisberg Riesling in tanks. Although Larkmead may have kept some wine lots separate as varietals, most of the wine it produced was generic. The government report showed that over two-thirds of the volume of wine stored was still simply called "Burgundy."[41]

The Salminas were not only leaders in the production of high-quality Napa wines. They were also leaders in the organization of the Napa wine industry. It is not an exaggeration to say that if there was a meeting involving wine production in the Napa Valley during the 1930s, a Salmina, either Felix or one of his sons, along with Carl Bundschu, was there, probably acting as the host or chair. Prior to Repeal, Felix Salmina served for two years as vice president of the Napa County Association for Prohibition Reform. In 1934, F. W. Salmina was the Napa and Solano representative to the NRA-backed Western Wine Code Committee.

During the revival of the St. Helena Vintage Festival, Felix Salmina headed up the winery exhibits. He was founding president of the Napa Valley Wine Industry group (also known as the Napa Valley Wine Producers' Association), a county chapter of the Wine Institute, while serving, along with Carl Bundschu, as a delegate to the Wine Institute, later becoming a director in 1936 and 1937. When the 20–30 club, Rotary, or the Chamber of Commerce needed a speaker on wine, the call was directed either to Inglenook or to Larkmead.[42] Larkmead may have been smaller than either Beringer or Beaulieu during the 1930s, and it was certainly less well financed than Inglenook, but it had definitely earned its place among the "big four" in the Napa Valley.

Conspicuous in their absence in the Tchelistcheff/Mondavi quality ranking were two newcomers to the Napa Valley: Christian Brothers in Napa and the Martini Winery in St. Helena. One winery was the creation of a religious brotherhood, the other the result of one man's dream. Although both wineries were established in the valley prior to Repeal, they were perhaps overlooked by Mondavi and Tchelistcheff because neither winery really started selling commercial bottled wine with a Napa appellation until the late 1930s. Ultimately, both would become indelibly associated with the Napa Valley in the mind of the American wine-drinking public.

The Christian Brothers located their winery in the hills ten miles west of Napa in 1932. A teaching order, they had produced sacramental and commercial wine at their novitiate in Martinez starting in 1884, using the income to help underwrite their teaching efforts, including St. Mary's College in Moraga. In 1931, with the city of Martinez creeping up around the novitiate, the order acquired the old Gier Winery and vineyard northwest of Napa and moved "lock, stock and barrel," including 240,000 gallons of wine, to the new site. Built of stone into a hill, the winery was the typical three-story design articulated so well by Beringer, with crushing operations at the top, fermentation on the second floor, and storage and aging on the first floor. The vineyard consisted of 150 acres, replanted in the 1900s on phylloxera-resistant rootstock, and included finer varietals such as Cabernet, Sylvaner, Johannisberg Riesling, and Pinot St. George, usually referred to as "Red Pinot." In Martinez, the brothers had used a label called "La Salle Products," named after the founder of their order, St. Jean-Baptiste de La Salle. After moving to the hills, they refined the label to "Mont La Salle" for their first commercial wines.[43]

The Christian Brothers, like so many other producers, had expected a wine boom following Repeal, but were disappointed. As Brother Timothy, the cellar master, dryly put it, "the wine business seemed to be a little harder business to make money in than the Brothers had initially expected . . . it was discovered that a lot of the wine in the tanks was not really saleable right away."[44] It is unclear whether Brother Timothy was alluding simply to young wine or to older, spoiled wine with high volatile acidity, but certainly the demand was not overwhelming. In 1934, the Brothers announced plans to crush 500 tons of grapes and to produce approximately 40,000 gallons each of dry and sweet wine, although they ended up crushing 400 tons and producing 60,000 gallons.[45] Two years later, they planned to produce 110,000 gallons of wine, but over 75 percent was to be sweet wine rather than dry. By 1937, production had expanded to 230,000 gallons, with the overwhelming preponderance of it sweet wine.[46] Although the Brothers had expanded their original plantings, to meet the demand for sweet wine, they trucked Muscats from Fresno and Missions and Palominos from Lodi for sherry production. This importation of what Napa growers often referred to as "foreign" grapes was a touchy subject, involving labeling issues and economics, but was clearly a response to the market.

Although the Christian Brothers sold bottled wine after Repeal, the volume was small, and as with the other Napa wineries, most of their production was sold in bulk. In 1937, this began to change when they entered into a marketing arrangement with Alfred Fromm, a young Jewish wine merchant from Germany, whose family had been making and exporting wine for four generations, but who had decided it was time to leave the Third Reich. Fromm had first come to the United States in 1934, immediately following Repeal, to work with the importing firm of Picker-Linz, which distributed his family's wines in the United States. He was a dynamic individual, and his sales amounted to "almost 26 percent of all wine imports from Germany" between 1934 and 1936. In 1937, Fromm toured California, seeking a quality producer in need of marketing expertise and eventually finding the Christian Brothers.[47]

The notion of a Catholic religious order producing wine to be marketed by a Jew did not seem odd to Fromm, since in Germany many monasteries owned vineyards. If it seemed odd to the Brothers, they quickly gained respect for Fromm and his knowledge of wine. That fall he lived with them at the novitiate, sharing their life, rising with them (not so much for prayers, he confided, as to be sure that he got breakfast) and helping them make the wine that vintage. At his urging, a new die-cut label in the shape of gothic cathedral arches was designed and the brand name "The Christian Brothers" adopted, with Mont La Salle relegated to use on sacramental wines. Sales began on the East Coast in 1938, and the following year, the Brothers announced that in-bond shipments to other wineries and commercial bulk shipments would be discontinued, and that all future sales would be bottled at the winery.[48] Christian Brothers was probably the first winery in the state to make a commitment to bottle and market its entire production. That it could live up to that commitment spoke equally well of the quality of its wine and of Fromm's marketing capability.

Just south of the town of St. Helena was the L. M. Martini Grape Products Company, better known as the Martini winery, which would burst on the scene at the end of the decade, when it released a full line of varietally labeled, vintage-dated wines. In 1933, Louis M. Martini was already well known throughout the California wine industry when he purchased ten acres south of St. Helena and announced plans to build the first new winery in the valley since Prohibition.[49] Born near Genoa in 1887, he had immigrated to San Francisco in 1900, where he worked in his father's shellfish business. In 1906, the family started a small winery at Hunter's Point, with the plan of producing wine that could be sold in the North Beach area of San Francisco, along with the shellfish harvested from the bay. When the entire vintage turned out "sour," young Louis was sent back to Italy to study winemaking for a year at the University of Alba, returning in time to oversee the 1907 vintage, which turned out fine. He later recalled the parting words of a professor of enology when Martini had announced that he would be returning to California to make wine: "Wine has four enemies: High temperature, too much sulfurous acid, metal, and air," his professor cautioned. "Keep away from them and ferment it cool and you're going to make wine despite everything."[50] Martini took those words to heart, and they served as the basic operating principles for his production of fine wine.

Shortly after the onset of Prohibition, Martini and two silent partners bought the old Italian Swiss Colony Winery in Kingsburg, establishing the L. M. Martini Grape Products Company, where they produced sacramental and medicinal wines and a grape concentrate, appealingly named "Forbidden Fruit," for home wine production. As Martini put it, they produced "sweet wines, dry wines, brandy, concentrate, syrup, everything"; with a rabbi living on the grounds, they even produced kosher wine.[51] During Prohibition, the Martini operation grew in size until, just prior to Repeal, his firm was one of the dominant producers in California, ranking with Italian Swiss Colony, Colonial Grape Products, and Beaulieu, all of which joined with Martini in late 1932 to establish the Grape Growers' League of California, the precursor to the Wine Institute.

San Joaquin Valley grapes were then fine for the production of alcoholic "sweet" wines, but not suitable for high-quality dry wines. Martini later commented that "at Kingsburg, I wanted to make good dry wine . . . [but] I recognized that you can't make good dry wine out of the local grapes in Fresno . . . I had to settle in a winery up North to make good dry wine."[52] He was familiar with the Napa Valley, having bought grapes from the Wheeler ranch south of St. Helena prior to Prohibition. In 1932, realizing that repeal of Prohibition was simply a matter of time, he began scouting the Napa Valley and arranged for the production of 40,000 gallons of wine at the Covick facility in Oakville.[53] A practical man, Martini first explored existing facilities in the St. Helena area, including the Krug Winery, Greystone, and the Lombarda Winery on Tychson Hill, owned by the Fornis. Each of these locations had problems, and by 1933, he decided to buy land and build a new winery from the ground up.

The new Martini Winery was, in 1933, state-of-the-art in its use of building materials, insulation, and refrigeration. Built on the flat valley floor, it was quite large by Napa Valley standards: 204 feet long by 144 feet wide, with a 26-foot-high ceiling and an excavated basement. The *St. Helena Star*, always a fountain of enthusiasm, referred to the building as "immense." The Treasury inspectors sent to review the Martini application were equally impressed, writing in their inspection report: "The winery building is in a class by itself as a building for the production and storage of wine. It is new and is now practically complete, sufficiently so as to permit the crushing of grapes. It is constructed of steel frame for the strengthening portions of the walls, with the walls themselves of hollow tile. It is being fitted out in the most modern manner."[54] The space between the double walls, which were built of hollow tile, was filled with cork and redwood for insulation, and the entire structure was covered with a metal roof "from a dog racing track in Southern California."[55] Inside the building was a large cold room, cooled by mechanical refrigeration, for the fermentation of white wines. Outside was a tower for cooling water used in controlling fermentation temperatures in red wines.[56] Until the 1960s and the start of the "wine boom," the Martini Winery remained the most technically advanced winery in the valley.

The original intent for the facility was the production in quantity of

North Coast dry wines to ship by rail to Kingsburg for blending and bottling under the Martinis' Royale label. Treasury inspection reports and correspondence demonstrate that this was done. With a total storage capacity of over a million gallons, the Martinis annually produced over a half million gallons of wine from 1934 through 1940, most of which was shipped out in tank cars to Kingsburg as bond-to-bond transfer. Throughout the 1930s, Kingsburg remained the center of the Martini winemaking operations, and at least once Louis M. Martini wrote to the Treasury Department: "We again ask you to please communicate with us direct here at Kingsburg instead of mailing any requests or communications to Rutherford for the simple reason that our office is conducted from here."[57] In a 1936 inspection report, the Treasury inspector commented, "All wine is shipped on written orders from office in Kingsburg, except that wine may be shipped to Kingsburg upon verbal instructions."[58]

Still, Martini was drawn to the valley for more than just dry wine production. In March 1934, the *Star* reported that he had "purchased the fine J. Y. Eccleston farm three miles south of St. Helena." Covering 250 acres, 70 of which were vineyards, the property included "a fine old residence," and the *Star* announced that although "Mr. Martini will continue to make his home at Kingsburg," he would "divide his time between that place and this."[59] Six years later, the Martinis moved to St. Helena to stay. On March 12, 1940, Martini sold the Kingsburg Winery to a new conglomeration, Central California Wineries, for a reported $1,000,000.[60] "The sweet wine business was getting to be a bit of a rat race," Louis P. Martini remembered, and Louis M. Martini asked the family "whether they would rather live down there or come up here and have a smaller business . . . and we all voted to do that."[61] That same year, he introduced the L. M. Martini brand of varietally labeled and vintage-dated wines, and according to Leon Adams, "He became famous overnight as one of the coast counties' premium table-wine producers."[62] "I was the first in this county to produce varietals in quantity," Martini subsequently asserted. "Nobody else did. And I put the vintage on. Each year's crop is different."[63] His claim has merit. Members of the "big four" all produced some varietally labeled wine, but none except Inglenook emphasized only varietal wine, and Martini easily eclipsed Inglenook in quantity. Later, Martini did produce generic wines too, but cleanly made, cool-fermented varietals were his emphasis and had been from the start of operations in 1933.

One of the government inspectors found the Martini emphasis on varietals unusual enough to remark in the 1936 inspection report that "tanks in general show kind of grapes from which produced" and the report details thirteen separate varieties in storage. The list literally went from *A* to *Z*, starting with Alicante and ending with Zinfandel, and listing such varieties as Cabernet, Barbera, Folle Blanche, Mondeuse, Gamay, Charbono, and Petite Sirah in between.[64] By 1941, just prior to crush, a Treasury inventory report showed over twenty-four varieties being kept in separate tanks, including four tanks of "W. Zinfandel," one of the earlier references to White Zinfandel in the California wine industry.[65] No other winery in the Napa Valley could come close to the Martinis' diversity of varietal production. In 1938, Tchelistcheff and Mondavi could be excused for overlooking the Martini winery, since it was primarily a crushing and processing facility for wines that would be shipped in bulk to Kingsburg. But the emphasis on varietal separation in conjunction with state-of-the-art processing equipment ensured that when the Martinis moved to St. Helena, they would quickly join the handful of fine wine producers in the valley.

Although the "big four" plus Christian Brothers and Martini were the dominant quality producers in the valley, in the 1930s they did not use even one-third of the grapes grown in the Napa Valley and the majority of their production came from their own vineyards. This was in part a result of the lack of premium varieties such as Cabernet, Pinot Noir, and Semillon; primarily, however, it was because of relatively low demand for quality wines. Production records for each winery are not available, and we must estimate the tons of grapes crushed in the 1930s by each winery. However, a 1943 Treasury report of an investigation of appellation labeling did review the major wineries' grape crush and indicates that in 1943, a prosperous period for the Napa Valley, the quality producers used only about 30 percent of the grapes grown in the valley. Beringer was listed as crushing 2,000 tons; Beaulieu, 2,000; Christian Brothers, 1,400; and Martini 1,050.[66] Larkmead and Inglenook are not mentioned, but probably accounted for about 600 tons each. The quality producers would thus have used at most less than 8,000 tons each year during the 1930s, while from 1934 through 1940 the valley's average total production was just under 28,000 tons.[67] Although production of high-quality varietal wine represented the future of the Napa Valley, the realities of the 1930s demanded either the establishment of large-scale wine factories that could produce wine as a bulk commodity or the export of grapes from the county.

CHAPTER TWO

Bulk Producers and Failures, 1934-1940

If Napa's future lay with the quality producers, it was a future dimly seen by only a handful of dreamers or visionaries. The cold reality at Repeal was that winemaking in California was a poorly organized, highly competitive, and undercapitalized industry attempting to meet the unknown demand of a fragmented national market from an oversupply of low-quality grapes, all in the depths of the depression. Immediately following Repeal, hundreds of small producers rushed to begin production throughout the state, assuming that a thirsty America would swallow all the wine they could produce. Few would be successful in creating a branded bottled product; most quickly turned to the sale of bulk wine as a way of staying in business.

Bulk wine production was a tough, low-margin business that placed a premium on efficiency of production and marketing. All of the wineries in the Napa Valley, including the quality producers, sold wine in bulk during the 1930s. The question was whether they could sell it for a profit or not, and the answer depended primarily on personal contacts within the California industry and with franchise bottlers out of state. Anyone could make wine once; the difficult part was selling it. Ultimately, four major bulk producers emerged in St. Helena as successes: Lou Stralla's Napa Wine Company, the two co-ops, and the Mondavis' Sunny St. Helena Winery. Each was unique and successful during the 1930s, but only the Mondavis would successfully accomplish the transition from bulk production to the making of branded wine.

The Napa Valley Cooperative Winery was established in 1934, although as early as 1932, Farm Advisor Herman Baade had submitted a proposal to the Farm Bureau suggesting that a winemaking and marketing cooperative be organized. The Napa co-op was a child of the New Deal, a time when basic questions about social organization and the role of capital were being asked. As the *St. Helena Star* put it in reporting on a growers' meeting in November 1932, would the grape grower of the future "make up the wine and market it collectively, or will private individuals buy the grapes from him, make up the wine and make the majority of the profits?"[1] By early 1934, the *California Wine Review* reported "a lively tendency toward the development of co-operative wineries designed to handle the output of the vineyardists."[2] The time was right. The New Deal fostered a cooperative attitude, and the Bank of Cooperatives in Berkeley was designed to encourage such enterprises.

In July 1934, Napa grape growers surveyed the empty cooperage available in local wineries, anxiously eyed the large crop on their vines, and decided that almost 8,000 tons of Napa grapes would be surplus unless a new winery were opened.[3] With the harvest only a few months off, local growers banded together, subscribed the required 3,000 tons of grapes necessary for loans, and bought a winery in Calistoga run by the Petri organization in 1933. By mid September, the Napa co-op was crushing grapes, producing close to a half million gallons of wine and relieving pressure on the Napa grape market.[4]

The 1934 crush was so successful that growers at the southern end of the valley who had not joined decided that they, too, would create a cooperative venture near Napa. After initial efforts, they did not sign the necessary minimum tonnage, so the Napa co-op acquired a second winery from Petri, two miles south of St. Helena, with local growers subscribing over 3,000 tons and promising to contribute $5 for each ton processed to defray the purchase cost.[5] Known as the "big co-op," the two units together could handle 8,000 tons, roughly a third of the average Napa Valley harvest in the 1930s. The grapes crushed were generally common shipping varieties rather than premium varietals, and most of the wine produced was sold in bulk rather than bottled, but the co-op was successful in creating a market for its growers' grapes and helped stabilize prices in the Napa Valley.

Co-ops were responses to general economic adversity, but a triggering event was often needed to move growers to action. In the case of the Napa co-op, it had been the importation of San Joaquin Valley grapes in 1933, which had filled all the local cooperage, not leaving room for the 1934 vintage. In the case of the St. Helena Cooperative Winery, or "little co-op," the impetus was the 1938 "prorate" requiring that 45 percent of the state's grape crop be distilled.

The prorate was primarily a response to the chronic overproduction in the San Joaquin Valley, which affected grape prices throughout the state. Since the effect of overproduction in the San Joaquin Valley was statewide, the answer was necessarily industrywide. Although the quality difference between "valley" and North Coast grapes was acknowledged by a slight price differential between valley and North Coast dry wines, the demand for quality wines had not advanced enough to insulate the North Coast from industrywide problems. A surplus in Fresno or Kern counties was felt as lower prices in Santa Rosa and St. Helena. A. "Soxs" Setrakian, president of California Growers' Winery of Cutler in the San Joaquin Valley correctly claimed that "the welfare of the vineyardist growing grapes in Ukiah suitable for the finest type of dry wines is dependent upon the welfare of the grape grower in Kern county whose grapes can be used for wine or fortifying material."[6]

That the California wine industry was interdependent did not mean that "one size fit all." For a Fresno grower whose irrigated vineyard produced ten tons to the acre, $12 a ton for 45 percent of his crop was not bad. For a St. Helena viticulturist with dry-farmed grapes bearing two to three tons per acre, the $12 a ton provided by the prorate was ruinous. George Edmonstone, who had helped lead the growers in 1934 and 1935, and who had tried to establish a second cooperative winery in Napa, declared that "the prorate had done what he had been trying to do for twenty years, organize growers for their own interests."[7] Although the Napa growers did vote in favor of the prorate, they apparently soon had second thoughts. A meeting in early September 1938 designed to answer questions regarding the administration of the program "developed into a protest session instead," as three hundred growers began "a heckling session which at times reached considerable heat as questions were shot at the speaker."[8] A new organization quickly appeared, the Napa County Dry Grape Growers' Protective Association. As its president, Edmonstone filed for injunctions to halt the prorate in Napa County. The reaction was too late, but in conjunction with protests from Sonoma, it ensured that the prorate would be a one-time solution, rather than an annual mechanism.

The Napa County Dry Grape Growers' Protective Association served as the nucleus for the new St. Helena Cooperative. By early summer 1939, Edmonstone announced that the proposed new co-op had contracted enough tonnage to go forward, and that it had bought the Navone Winery north of town, where it planned to crush at least 2,000 tons.[9] With thirty members, the St. Helena Cooperative was not as large a force in the valley as the big co-op, but it did take excess grapes off the market and helped further stabilize prices.

From the perspective of quality wine production, the co-ops were throwbacks to an earlier time in wine history when growers had processed their crops simply as a way of preserving them. Co-op wine was produced from standard grapes and sold in bulk to be blended with cheaper wine from California's Central Valley. The transformation of a perishable crop into wine gave the growers some breathing room each harvest and prevented the market from being flooded with surplus grapes at harvest. But ultimately the solution of crushing grapes was temporary at best: at some point, the wine had to be sold. It was this problem that would plague both co-ops throughout their existence.

Still, socially and economically, both co-ops were important and progressive steps forward. Although in one sense they resembled earlier organizations, their scale and scope were far removed from the small wineries of the era before Prohibition. With over 140 members, the big co-op generally crushed around 8,500 tons of "standard" varieties, taking about 40 percent of the valley's annual production off the market and helping to stabilize prices. Marketing of the co-op's wine was handled by Fruit Industries, a cooperative sales agency run by the ten member wineries, with blending and sales branches in New York, Chicago, New Orleans, Los Angeles, and San Francisco. Participation in the Napa co-op profited its members, who generally received seven to ten dollars more a ton than growers who sold nonvarietal grapes on the open market.[10] Of course, as members of a cooperative, the growers normally waited at least one year until initial payments were made on their "pool," and in some cases growers might wait three to four years for the last payment as a "pool" was closed out. Still, waiting and receiving 30 to 50 percent more income was preferable to barely covering the cost of production. Neither co-op would ever successfully market its own branded wine, but they did provide a more assured livelihood and economic return to between 30 and 40 percent of Napa's growers through market power that none could have achieved individually.

Both co-ops were supported by government loans and represented an aggregate of many members. In contrast, Lou Stralla's winery was the work of one individual, who gives us new definition to the words *leverage* and *nerve*. Stralla was a stranger to the Napa Valley and the wine business when he and his wife arrived in Calistoga in early 1933, looking for some sort of business to start. After meeting the grape growers and shippers Adam Bianchi and Charles Forni, he was convinced that a tremendous demand for wine would exist following Repeal. Upon inspecting the old Charles Krug Winery, he made an appointment in San Francisco with the owner, Charles Moffitt, the owner of the Blake, Moffitt and Towne Paper Company. Stralla's oral history describes the interview best:

I went in to the fellow and I told him who I was and what my name was and said I had no knowledge of this business at all. I said that I was 32 years old, and have a lot of ambition, and a lot of nerve. I said that I thought I could work and work hard enough that I thought I could do something with this plant, but I had no money. I said that I'd like to go into the plant and start it going, but I told him there were two or three things that I needed. One of the things I needed was for him to let me move in there without any money.[11]

Stralla must have impressed Moffitt, who told him to go ahead and try.

Next, Stralla looked for a winemaker and succeeded in enticing Rufus Buttimer, the winemaker before Prohibition for the Ewer and Atkinson Winery, but now long retired. Following Buttimer's directions, Stralla hired knowledgeable local people and supervised the dismantling, cleaning, and recoopering of the long-vacant fermentation tanks at Krug. As Stralla put it, "Buttimer was running the place and all I did was listen to what he said and did exactly what he told me to do."[12] By August, everything was ready, and on September 5, the grapes arrived for crushing. Stralla's Napa Wine Company produced 400,000 gallons of wine that first season, crushing over 2,000 tons. "It was an amazing thing to me when it came the month of November," he recalled, "and here we had made 400,000 gallons of wine . . . I couldn't quite understand what happened."[13]

The next urgent step was to sell the new wine, since he owed 110 farmers for the grapes they had supplied. He had borrowed money to advance the growers cash to pay the pickers, and with the crush over, the thought hit him, "Now wait a minute, I've got to start moving this stuff, or we're not in business."[14] The Napa Wine Company might very easily have failed at that point, but Stralla went back east, where he sold his wine in tank-car loads, competing with the Gallos and the Petris, and somehow managed to bring in enough money to pay his growers and keep the business afloat. Paying $15 a ton for grapes, Stralla figured his cost for the wine was about 10 cents a gallon, and he sold the wine for 12 to 13 cents that first year. He preferred Petite Sirah, because his market wanted tannic red wines, but he'd take most reds and didn't discriminate much in the first few years. Cabernet or Alicante, Zinfandel or Grand Noir, as long as the grapes were red, he'd pay $15 a ton. In retrospect, he admitted, "Sure it was rough on the farmers. It was rough on the winemaker; it was rough on the man that operated a winery." [15] But he stayed in business, playing the angles, trying new ideas, and increasing production.

In 1934, Stralla added cooperage and started to bottle wine under the "Betsy Ross" brand. Even in bottling, Stralla thought like a bulk producer: Betsy Ross Sauterne and Burgundy were packaged in twelve-ounce bottles and designed to retail at 15 cents a bottle.[16] It is unclear whether the Betsy Ross brand was successful, but the vast majority of Stralla's business in any case remained bulk wine sold at low prices. In 1934, he initiated what would prove to be a long relationship with John Cella of the Roma Wine Company, and increasingly through the decade, the Napa Wine Company became a processing winery for Roma, although Stralla continued to sell to East Coast bottlers. Throughout the decade, Stralla was one of the major grape buyers in the valley. As he recalled it, he bought on average about one-fifth of all grapes grown in Napa each year, or about 6,000 tons.[17]

It was a tough business, but Stralla was successful enough to purchase the Covick Winery in Oakville for $14,500 at a foreclosure sale, and in 1940, he moved the Napa Wine Company from Charles Krug. Originally built in the late 1870s, the Covick Winery was very large and filled with small oak cooperage useful in the production of small lots of fine wine. Stralla stripped the building, selling most of the oak cooperage to Larkmead and Cresta Blanca in order to raise cash. He had no use for small cooperage, since his "prime interest in the plant was to produce a bulk red good wine for cheap home consumption on the East coast." [18] Stralla's business grew in size to an annual production of over a million gallons before he sold out to the Roma Wine Company in 1945. He had never made wine for the romance of it, but to make money, and the bulk end of the wine business had become more difficult after the distillers entered the industry during World War II. As usual, Stralla, the hard-nosed businessman, described his reasons for leaving the business colorfully and directly:

At that time the wine business was very, very rough. There was a very short mark-up on a large investment. Companies the size of Roma, Schenley, National Distillers were making it real tough in the wine business, and I figured, if they want to buy me out, let them get tough with one another. . . . I got out of the wine business from the standpoint of bulk commercial red wine, but I never lost my liking for wine or liking the making of it or raising grapes for it or anything else. It's merely that I didn't want that kind of competition. I wasn't interested in building a business of making varietals or fancy bottled wines. I had no family to make it for or leave it to. . . . I didn't feel that I wanted to spend the years and time to develop a business of that kind to make a living out of it. I didn't have to, I didn't want to, and I didn't do it, that's all.[19]

Stralla had seen the writing on the wall, that bulk Napa wine could not compete in price with wine produced in the San Joaquin Valley, and that industry consolidation would eventually squeeze the independent bulk producers. During his twelve vintages of operation, he built the Napa Wine Company into the largest independent winery in the valley, and if the prices he paid for grapes were not high, they were sufficient to cover the grower's cost of production in good years. His winery provided a home for grapes that would otherwise have been surplus in the valley.

A family that would prove interested in fine bottled wine, although not before World War II, were the Mondavis, who operated the Sunny St. Helena Winery just south of St. Helena. For Stralla, the Napa Wine Company was a business, not a way of life. He correctly foresaw the amount of effort that would need to be invested to create a branded commodity and, not having children to whom he could pass on the fruit of such effort, he chose to get out of the bulk business. For the Mondavis, the bulk business at Sunny St. Helena was a transitional enterprise, the middle step in a logical, if apparently unplanned, progression, as the family moved from grape buying and shipping in the 1920s, through bulk wine production in the 1930s, and finally into the marketing of bottled wine in the 1940s. It was fitting, if perhaps ironic, that it would be the Mondavis who would resurrect the wines of Charles Krug, the winery where Stralla had been baptized into the business.

The Sunny St. Helena Winery was originally established by Gioachino "Jack" Riorda as the "Sunny Hill Winery" in 1934 and provides a clear lesson in the importance of marketing to the success of a winery. A native of Bra, Italy, Riorda emigrated to San Francisco in 1911, eventually locating in 1924 in the Napa Valley, where he worked for various companies that shipped wine grapes east to the immigrant market.[20] In 1934, he built a new winery on Main Street, north of Charter Oak Avenue. Forty feet wide by one hundred and thirty feet long, the structure was well insulated and could handle one hundred tons a day, with total storage capacity of 175,000 gallons.[21] Crushing grapes and making wine was one thing, however; selling wine was another. For three years, Riorda struggled, producing between 50,000 and 70,000 gallons a year and buying and blending bulk wine for resale.[22] The margins, sales, and gallonage were small. By 1937, Riorda recognized that he needed to increase volume, which would entail capital infusion and marketing help, and he sought a partner, Cesare Mondavi of Lodi. In May 1937, the Riorda Winery was incorporated as Sunny St. Helena, with Cesare Mondavi as president and Jack Riorda as vice president and winemaker.[23]

Cesare Mondavi, the father of Robert and Peter, was born in Italy but had immigrated to Minnesota, where he and his wife ran a boarding-house and saloon for Italians working in the iron mines. In 1918, foresee-ing Prohibition, the local Italian Club sent Cesare Mondavi to California to buy grapes. There he entered the grape-shipping business, moving to Lodi in 1923 with his family and creating business relationships with Italian communities across the United States. Cesare Mondavi's style stressed a personal relationship between buyer and seller. As Robert Mondavi put it, "They [the buyer and his father] understood that they would do business with each other and that they would try to be reason-able. There seemed to be a lot of good faith. . . . The price would be dependent on whether you had big or small crops."[24] The result was a profitable business and a web of personal friendships with fellow immi-grants outside California, many of whom would move into the wine business after Repeal by purchasing California wine in bulk and bottling it under their own brands for sale in their locales.

In 1935, when Robert Mondavi was a junior at Stanford University, his father asked him and his brother Peter about their plans following graduation, suggested that there might be a future in the table wine busi-ness, and commented that he believed that the Napa Valley was "the outstanding wine-growing region for table wines."[25] In his senior year, Robert Mondavi took chemistry. Following graduation, he studied for three months with Vic Enriques, a research chemist at the University of California in Berkeley, who taught him wine chemistry and analysis. In March 1937, young Robert moved to St. Helena to work with Jack Riorda and to represent Cesare Mondavi in the new business.[26]

Cesare Mondavi's contacts allowed an immediate increase in sales, and the winery was expanded to accommodate annual production and storage of half a million gallons, making it one of the largest in the valley. At the 1939 annual stockholder's meeting, Cesare Mondavi reported that "although the wine industry suffered a set back during the fiscal year ending July 1939, the corporation was able to increase . . . sales more than forty percent over the previous year." Everyone agreed that the year had proved successful, and the company retired to the Hotel St. Helena for dinner, where they toasted Jack Riorda "who has been ill and was unable to attend the affair."[27]

Riorda died on October 1, 1939, and Robert Mondavi assumed the title of assistant treasurer, essentially becoming the corporation's manager and winemaker, filling out government applications and forms, and handling the day-to-day business of Sunny St. Helena.[28] He had plenty to keep him busy. Continued growth in bulk wine sales created the need for more tank space, and Sunny St. Helena rented the former Di Marco Winery on Spring Street in 1939, and leased the Gagetta Winery in Rutherford for additional storage in 1941.[29] In its annual coverage of the harvest, the *St. Helena Star* reported that Sunny St. Helena planned to crush between 2,500 and 3,000 tons in 1940. In 1941, the winery again increased production, producing 700,000 gallons from what must have been about 4,000 tons of grapes, ranking it behind the Napa co-op and Stralla, but well ahead of Beaulieu and Beringer.[30] By the eve of World War II, Sunny St. Helena was clearly the fastest-growing bulk winery in the valley, and its 28-year-old manager, Bob Mondavi, had become well known in the small community of St. Helena.

Although large bulk producers such as Stralla's Napa Wine Company, the Mondavis' Sunny St. Helena, and the two co-ops did little to further wine quality or Napa's reputation among consumers, they played an important role in the economic life of the valley. They maintained Napa's acreage, kept the growers employed, and allowed a slow transition to varietal wines as consumption of fine wine slowly grew in the 1940s and 1950s.

Between the quality producers on one hand and the bulk producers on the other, there was a group of individual businesses lured by the promise of a booming wine market following Repeal. The excess of grapes, the availability of old winery locations, and the potential market for wine all created an opportunity for undercapitalized producers and speculators to enter the wine business, promising a "home" for uncontracted grapes. Some of these entrepreneurs planned to bottle the wine they produced. Others were strictly bulk producers, selling the new wine to other wineries or to out-of-state franchise bottlers, with no intention of developing a brand. A few were out-and-out frauds, attempting to capitalize on low grape prices and new markets. In the first three years following Repeal, many small producers entered the market. Only a handful survived. Most ended in bankruptcy or messy litigation.

A classic case of fraud occurred at the Tokalon Winery in Oakville. Founded by Henry Crabb in the early 1870s, the Tokalon (sometimes written To Kalon) Winery quickly became one of the largest and most famous quality producers in the valley.[31] At Crabb's death in 1899, E. S.

Churchill and his wife, Mary, bought the property. She operated the farm after her husband's death in 1903. Surrounded by 250 acres of bearing vines, the winery was capable of producing 350,000 gallons of wine, but by the tail end of Prohibition, the aging Mary Churchill informed a government inspector that "every effort was being made to make legal disposition of all wine on hand," and that "she would be glad to discontinue operation of the winery, as well as sell the vineyard and property."[32] In November 1933, just prior to Repeal, she got her wish, selling the property on an installment basis to A. F. Kauth and O. F. Kellstrom, who announced plans to expand production, replant vineyards, and market wine on the East Coast.[33]

By March 1934, Mary Churchill was writing to the Treasury Department. Kauth and Kellstrom had not only not made the required payments, they had sold nonexistent wine to out-of-state bottlers by issuing fraudulent warehouse receipts. Bonded warehouses had been established in many states to receive alcohol in bond, thus relieving the requirement of immediate payment of government excise taxes. In several cases, Kauth and Kellstrom had received payment in exchange for warehouse receipts for nonexistent wine, a quick way to turn a profit, but not one that encouraged repeat business. The most damaging instance was the sale of 20,000 gallons of "Blend 6" Burgundy for $17,000 to A. C. King of Citrus Products Inc. in Chicago. Although "Blend 6" was not in the Chicago warehouse, it did exist at the winery. Unfortunately, it was exceedingly high in volatile acidity, "making it unfit for beverage use," and it was later removed for distilling. The Treasury inspector, E. C. Mosby, concluded his report by noting that "Messrs. Kauth and Kellstrom are being sought by Napa County authorities to face court litigation in connection with their activities at the winery."[34] After fighting a lawsuit filed by the Citrus Products Company, Mary Churchill turned the winery over to her son, Edward Churchill, who produced between 50,000 and 60,000 gallons of wine annually, which he sold in bulk to other wineries.[35] By 1937, the tanks were empty, and Crabb's famous winery was essentially out of business. The fire that destroyed the building on Sunday morning, May 29, 1939, was anticlimactic.

Winery ventures that started with high hopes often ended in litigation or bankruptcy even when fraud was not the intent. Sometimes the operation struggled on for years; in other cases, the duration was measured in months. One that lasted several years was the Napa Cantina Winery, started by two "wealthy residents of Crockett," Patrick Murphy and James Mahoney.[36] Foreseeing the end of Prohibition, they bought the old Lombarda Winery on Tychson Hill north of St. Helena and announced plans to make wine that season. By early 1934, the *Star* was reporting on the "tangled affairs of the Napa Cantina winery." Murphy had brought suit against Mahoney, seeking recovery of $11,290.[37] Mahoney countersued, and in late August, he announced that the winery was "in the market for 3,000 tons of grapes, which will be purchased exclusively from Napa county vineyards."[38] In 1934, 3,000 tons would have made Napa Cantina one of the largest processors in the county, and there is no record of how much actually was bought, although most purchases would not have been for cash, since litigation was continuous during 1934 and much of 1935. By the harvest of 1935, Mahoney had won in court and announced that "all creditors will be paid their claims in full."[39] In retrospect this promise may have been premature, since two years later Mrs. Forni, the original property owner, filed suit against the ill-fated venture, seeking $16,000 on the mortgage note due her.[40] Eventually, she foreclosed, selling the winery in 1940 to the Ahern family, who established Freemark Abbey at the site.[41]

The Lombarda Winery had been founded at the Tychson site by Antonio Forni, an immigrant from the Lombardy region of Italy. Forni leased the property from Josephine Tychson in 1895 and built a new winery on the site in the 1900s. This new building was later used by Napa Cantina and eventually became the home of Freemark Abbey.[42] In 1932, Joseph Gagetta produced wine at the facility, appropriating the name "Lombarda" when Mrs. Forni sold the site to Napa Cantina. Gagetta had made wine in the valley prior to Prohibition, and in February 1934, he and Walter Martini created a corporation to buy and make wine to sell in bottle and in bulk. Gagetta had his own facility in Rutherford, and perhaps the intention was to move Lombarda there, but soon after incorporation, he died, leaving his half ownership in Lombarda to his estate, to be managed by his son, Dennis.[43] Walter Martini became president, assumed management of the Lombarda Winery, and moved it to a new location north of St. Helena on Lodi Lane. Dennis Gagetta became winemaker at the Joseph Gagetta Winery on the family property in Rutherford.

From 1934 through 1941, rather than producing its own wine, the Lombarda Winery eked out an existence as a bonded storeroom, buying young wine in the valley and reselling it in bottle and bulk. There were plenty of small wineries from which to buy. George Deuer of Inglenook recalled that "there were quite a few real small wineries. They just crushed their own grapes from their own places and they had maybe

5,000 up to 10,000 gallons and they sold to bigger places."[44] Small wineries run by growers such as J. Butale and Valentine of St. Helena, or the Haus Winery in Pope Valley regularly sold to Martini.[45]

Walter Martini was definitely aiming for quality, however, and his stationery letterhead proudly proclaimed, "Producers of Fine Dry Wines of the Famous Napa Valley since 1885," cautioning at the bottom: "Wine is not a competitive price commodity, Wine is a competitive quality commodity."[46] Lombarda's wines won awards at the State Fair in 1934 and 1935, but much of its business was nonetheless in bulk wine. When label approval was required by the federal government, Martini submitted the stencils he applied to barrels used for bulk shipment.[47]

The Lombarda Winery did not prosper. Some time in 1937, the corporation reorganized, with Martini buying the Gagetta stock. In June that year, Charles O'Conner, the vice president of sales for the company since its inception in 1934, sued the Gagettas, "claiming payment for services in connection with reorganization of the Lombarda Wine Company and the sale of wine at the time of reorganization."[48] By 1941, the winery was in poor financial condition. The inspection on the "Report on Application" showed that Martini had mortgaged his home on Spring Street for half its value. Neighbors interviewed as character references considered Martini "a good winemaker and citizen, with financial integrity, but do not rate his business ability very highly."[49] Martini attempted to move Lombarda to Calistoga, where he proposed to reorganize it as a new corporation with an infusion of fresh capital and new stockholders. The proposed reorganization floundered and Lombarda closed its doors.[50]

The Lombarda Winery was atypical of many of the small wineries in the valley in that it had tried to create a branded commodity in bottle. Most of small wineries were the by-products of grape growing, operated by grape growers who were trying to make a living, not from processing grapes, but from growing them. For these growers of a prior generation, the production of wine was almost an afterthought. Lombarda was also atypical in that it stayed in business much longer than most operations that entered the Repeal era with the the idea of selling wine to a society hungry for alcohol. Most of these marketing ventures started out undercapitalized, misread the demand for their new product, and quickly went out of business. Two examples of firms that did not last a year are the Metropolitan Fruit Distilling Company in St. Helena and Montelena Winery in Calistoga.

Strictly speaking, the Metropolitan Fruit Distilling Company was not a winery, but it was fueled by the same optimism that motivated many wineries following Repeal. Initiated in May 1934 by Benjamin Finkelstein, the distillery was located at the old Borhorst Winery on Dowdell Lane in St. Helena. The idea behind the business, besides the obvious notion of meeting America's perceived thirst for ethanol, was to manufacture alcohol from off-grade prunes and raisins. The distillery promised to be a definite boon to the valley, employing a crew of twenty-five local men, putting up to fifty tons of otherwise unmarketable prunes and raisins to use, and marketing its output under the Mont St. Helena brand.[51] Within a month of commencing operations, however, two of the partners had brought suit against a third, Abraham Schorr, citing fiscal mismanagement and "extravagance."[52] By October that year, the partnership had been dissolved and the property sold by court order.[53]

The Montelena Winery outlasted the Metropolitan Fruit Distilling Company by a few months, but ultimately ended in bankruptcy. In 1888, Alfred Tubbs, a wealthy San Francisco businessman, had built the magnificent stone winery called Château Montelena in Calistoga and planted vineyards on the property. The winery became inactive during Prohibition, although it held a permit to crush grapes as necessary to salvage the crop. Only a small amount of wine was stored, and federal inspectors declared it all unfit for consumption just prior to Repeal.[54]

With a 55-acre vineyard and neighbors with grapes, Tubbs's son, Chapin Tubbs, became a leader in the fight for Repeal, serving as president of the Napa County Association for Prohibition Reform. By September 1933, it was obvious to him that Repeal was imminent, and he applied to reopen his winery on September 11, 1933. On November 1, he requested permission to increase his production from 50,000 to 60,000 gallons, saying, "On account of the recent rains in this section I find that numerous growers will have additional grapes which they cannot dispose of and which they offer to me."[55] By the end of November, he again requested permission to increase production, this time to 80,000 gallons, in order to salvage rain-damaged grapes. Again, permission was granted.

The rain may have been fortuitous, for Tubbs had obviously been planning a major change at his winery. In early January 1934, Montelena Winery was incorporated with Chapin Tubbs as president and William Malm as vice president. Two articles in the *California Wine Review* described the modern laboratory installed at Château Montelena and the corporation's plans to recondition the winery and produce 250,000 gallons the following vintage.[56] In July, the *Wine Review* reported that

Montelena would market "a full line of sweet as well as dry wines," and that the winery had "added a line of dry wines in 6 oz. packages."[57]

It is surprising, then, to find Tubbs writing to the district supervisor of the Bureau of Internal Revenue in September 1934 for permission to take over the bonded winery premises "formerly operated by Montelena Wineries, Inc." and requesting quick action as "the grapes in this section are now ready for crushing . . . [and] I am very anxious to manufacture wine this season."[58] In a later letter to the Alcohol Tax Unit of the Bureau of Internal Revenue, Tubbs wrote "that in August 1934, Montelena Wineries, Inc. became involved in financial difficulties, and in September of that year went into bankruptcy."[59]

Tubbs was a wealthy man, who owned vineyards and a winery, and it is puzzling that he would have allowed the corporation to go into bankruptcy. Perhaps he had difficulties with his partners, although if so there is no sign of these in print. For the remainder of the decade, Tubbs operated his winery as the Chapin Tubbs Winery, crushing his own and his neighbors' grapes and selling the wine on the bulk market, generally to the large Napa Valley wineries. In the 1940s, he entered into a "crushing deal" with the Mondavis, providing new wine for Sunny St. Helena Winery and Charles Krug until 1945, when Tubbs was "declared incompetent" and his wife, as guardian of the estate, discontinued the winery.[60]

The examples of Lombarda, Tokalon, Napa Cantina, and Château Montelena could easily be multiplied. Circumstances naturally differed, but many other wineries also failed because of poor management, undercapitalization, and lack of marketing expertise. Wineries were seductively easy businesses to start, especially if the principals had access to grapes. Immediately following Repeal, everyone assumed that sales would follow, but by the time the wine was ready for market, the initial capital had generally been exhausted, law suits were filed, and the business dissolved voluntarily or by court order.

The 1941 *Wines and Vines Yearbook of the Wine Industry* listed thirty-seven operating wineries in Napa County, but only ten were of major significance. Ranked in terms of storage capacity, which may be mislead ing, since cooperage was not always full, they were:[61]

Winery	Storage Capacity in Gallons
Napa co-op	2,000,000
Central California Winery	2,000,000
Martini	1,600,000

distillation—roughly half the inventory at Beaulieu.[2] Yet the same system of winemaking produced limited amounts of stunning wine: Beaulieu's 1936 Cabernet, bottled in 1938, was awarded the grand prize for best red wine in the 1939 Golden Gate International Exposition, after Georges de Latour's death, became the first Georges de Latour Private Reserve wine offered by Beaulieu.[3] How do we reconcile this seeming contradiction?

A flippant, but partially valid, explanation is a variation on the thesis that "even a blind pig finds an acorn occasionally," or, in this case, that given enough good grapes, most wineries can produce a superlative wine some of the time. But the real question is, if the goal is quality, how often will a given system of production yield fine wine? For California in the 1930s, the simple answer was "very rarely." In the first years following Repeal, California winemakers were untrained and unscientific, often not understanding the process of fermentation, and they lacked the technology to control it even if they did. As a whole, the California industry was primitive and backward. Winemakers worked with antiquated equipment in undercapitalized enterprises at a time of cut-throat competition. It was not an environment conducive to the pursuit of quality.

Fine wine is rarely the result of accident, but rather of conscious effort. High-quality wine that could compete with Europe's best was the goal, perhaps a dream, of only a handful of California producers, the majority of whom were located in the Napa Valley. Economic reality for most Napa quality producers dictated that only a small portion of their output could be devoted to high-quality production until market demand grew. The process of technological change and adoption of science over the next thirty years in California slowly resulted in the elimination of unsound wine and led gradually to large-scale production and marketing of varietal wines, helping to expand the market for truly fine wines from California. But until the wine boom of the late 1960s, the lack of market demand limited both investment in and the amount of high-quality wine produced in Napa. During the 1930s, Napa wineries continued to bring forth small volumes of fine wines, but were confined by their production methods, by the marketplace, and by a lack of high-quality varietal grapes.

In 1934, Frank Schoonmaker and Tom Marvel co-authored *The Complete Wine Book*, designed to introduce a generation of Americans to the pleasures of wine. Written in a sprightly fashion and direct in its opinions, the book's candid descriptions of California wine engendered ill feeling in many California producers. "The main reason why fully nine-tenths of the wine from California for the next seven or eight years will necessarily be of second rate quality," Schoonmaker and Marvel wrote, "is because it will necessarily come from vines that can produce only second rate wine grapes."[4] In fact, it was kind of Schoonmaker and Marvel to ascribe the poor quality of most California wine primarily to poor grapes—they could easily have pointed to careless winemaking and obsolete technology. In any case, they were essentially correct. Fine wines could not be produced without fine wine grapes. If Marvel and Schoonmaker were overly optimistic that better varieties would be planted and brought to bearing during the next decade, it was simply because they assumed that the cost of replanting would easily be compensated for by the increased revenue from superior varietals. For decades, however, this did not transpire. Grape growing was a business like any other, and, like most businesses in the depression, it did not pay particularly well.

Napa viticulture had experienced several boom/bust cycles and, by Repeal, it had undergone at least three and perhaps four waves of plantings. Vineyards based primarily on the Mission grape, a prolific low-quality producer, were established by viticultural pioneers in the late 1850s and throughout the 1860s. By 1868, Titus Cronise commented in *The Natural Wealth of California* that two-thirds of the vines in the state "are of the native Los Angeles grape."[5] A versatile vine, the Mission could be used to produce red wine, white wine (if lightly pressed), and brandy, all of which was mediocre at best. The main virtue of the Mission grape was its availability, but its shortcomings were many and serious. Throughout the 1860s and early 1870s, winemakers imported other varieties from eastern and European nurseries in search of improved wine quality. Henry Crabb, the founder of Tokalon winery, became so enthusiastic about this viticultural quest that in 1878, two years after moving to Oakville, he claimed a vineyard with over 250 varieties, including "Crabb's Black Burgundy," a popular black grape later identified as Refosco.[6] By the mid 1870s, varieties such as Zinfandel, Charbono, Burger, Golden Chasselas (Palomino), Muscat, and Riesling were all planted and their relative merits debated by Napa winemakers.

The global economic downturn of 1873 and the glut of poor wine from new plantings temporarily stalled vineyardists for the remainder of the decade, but by 1880 a new planting boom had commenced. Phylloxera was devastating the vineyards of France, creating the possibility of the end of European viticulture and opening new opportunities for California and Napa wine. *Frenzy* may be a better word than *boom* to describe Napa's response: vineyard acreage increased from 3,500 acres in 1880 to almost 12,000 in just two years.[7] By 1887, according to the state viticultural commissioners' *Annual Report*, there were 16,611 acres of vineyard, of which roughly a third was Zinfandel. Red Bordeaux varieties such as Cabernet Sauvignon, Cabernet franc, Merlot, Malbec, and Petite Verdot together comprised 779 acres. Other red varieties totaled 1,608 acres. Rieslings of all types were lumped together and accounted for 2,636 acres, while 412 acres were planted in "Sauternes," probably meaning Sauvignon vert, later identified as Colombard. The valley still contained 2,031 acres of Mission grapes, but they were exceeded by such white grapes as Chasselas and Burger, which grouped together came to 2,597 acres.[8] Even with the dominance of Zinfandel, Napa showed an astonishing diversity of grape varieties planted in commercial quantities.

There is generally a three-year lag between planting and first harvest, and new red wine is generally held for two years prior to blending for sale. The fruit of the massive planting of the mid 1880s came to market in the early 1890s, coinciding with the depression of 1893 and the emergence of phylloxera in the Napa Valley. Growers had known that phylloxera existed in the southern end of the valley by the early 1880s, but Viticultural Commissioner E. C. Priber's *Report* on phylloxera made clear just how far the root louse had spread throughout the valley. Those viticulturists with enough funds and a desire to remain in the business began a frantic search for rootstocks resistant to the pest, finally settling on Rupestris St. George. Most growers, disgusted by the low prices for grapes and the damage done to their vineyards, simply walked away. By 1897, Napa grape acreage had fallen to a low of 2,000 acres. The true believers then began the third wave of planting, this time on resistant rootstocks.[9]

The replanting of the Napa Valley in the early 1900s afforded an excellent opportunity to improve grape variety selection, but the chance was quickly lost with the passage of the 18th Amendment to the U.S. Constitution in 1918 and the advent of Prohibition. A. J. Winkler of the University of California, who was to play a seminal role in the movement for improved wine quality through the matching of grape varieties with climatic regions during the 1930s and 1940s, recalled that "Prohibition placed a premium on certain poor varieties . . . that would ship well and, above all that would serve as a source of material to color and doctor up the wines made from cheap table grapes."[10] The fourth wave of planting and grafting, fueled by Prohibition, carried through the first half of the 1920s, until the demand for red varieties that were thick-skinned, highly colored, or astringent had been met and surpassed. The first casualties to the grafting knife were fine white varieties such as Sauvignon blanc, Semillon, and the Rieslings. Thin-skinned and white, they were unwanted. Varietal red grapes such as Cabernet, Pinot noir, and Pinot St. George suffered a similar fate. Although red, they were shy bearers compared with standard varieties such as Carignane or Zinfandel when those vines were pruned for maximum production. The grower was, after all, paid by the ton, and during Prohibition, few buyers offered premiums for fine varietals.

By the time the grafters' knives were still, almost two-thirds of Napa's approximately 11,000 acres were planted to just two varieties: Petite Sirah and Alicante Bouschet.[11] Neither was a premium variety, but both were excellent for the purposes of home winemakers or bootleggers. Alicante Bouschet was a vinifera cross developed by Professor Henri Bouschet in the late nineteenth century for the purpose of supplying color to wines grown in the south of France. Alicante and another "coloring" variety, the Grand noir, were so intensely pigmented that bootleggers could add sugar and water to the skins to make a second, and sometimes a third, "wine" from the grapes. Petite Sirah, or "Pets" as it was known to valley growers, was also a darkly pigmented grape, but with a high level of tannin and astringency. A heavily extracted Petite Sirah wine added body and color to any blend, allowing a bootlegger to stretch a wine with 20 percent water. Neither grape variety was particularly suited for the production of fine wine.

At Repeal, even if Napa wineries had had trained employees and new technology, they would not have produced fine wines in any quantity because they did not have access to high-quality grapes. In 1934, the *California Wine Review* devoted most of its August issue to Napa Valley and dry wine production. The *Review*'s listing of the valley's grapes exposed the limited possibilities for fine wine production. Napa's 11,000 acres included:

Variety	Acres
Petite Sirah	4,400 (40%)
Alicante	2,720 (25%)
Zinfandel	1,650 (15%)
Carignane	1,210 (11%)
Palomino	220 (2%)[12]

This was a sad comparison to the vineyards described in 1887, when almost 800 acres were planted to Bordeaux red varieties, and over 2,500 acres of various Rieslings prospered. It did not represent progress toward quality.

Still, there was scattered acreage of fine wine varieties that had survived Prohibition and the grafter's knife. De Latour's Beaulieu had
500 acres of vines and included both Cabernet and Pinot noir in the
home vineyard, as well as Gray and White Riesling and Gamay. The old
Gier vineyard, purchased by the Christian Brothers, included Cabernet
Sauvignon, Riesling, and Pinot St. George. Inglenook, immediately following Repeal and before replanting or grafting, had roughly sixty acres
of varietals, mostly white, including Chenin blanc, Traminer, and Johannisberg Riesling, as well as such reds as Cabernet, Pinot noir, and Pinot
St. George. The Doak vineyard adjoining Far Niente contained Cabernet franc, Sauvignon blanc, and Semillon, all sold to Beaulieu.[13]

Many vineyards were mixed plantings of several varieties, and it was
possible to find small amounts of premium varietals. But out of a total
bearing acreage of 10,227, the 1936 California Fruit and Nut Acreage
Survey prepared for the Agricultural Adjustment Administration listed
only 326 acres of "Misc. Varieties" after naming such standard cultivars
as Alicante, Carignane, Petite Sirah, and Zinfandel.[14] Those 326 acres
would have included all of the better varieties mentioned above, and
even if Cabernet and Pinot noir predominated, it is doubtful whether
more than 100 acres of either variety existed in Napa in 1934. No wonder
Harry Caddow of the Wine Institute commented that the new federal
Alcohol Administration varietal labeling standards requiring that wine
contain at least 51 percent of the named variety would "reduce greatly the
quantity of Cabernet and several other wines on the market" because of
limited acreage.[15] Such a reduction would have had little impact in the
1930s, since varietally labeled wines made up only a small fraction of
wine sales in the United States.

Even if a demand had existed for fine wine grapes, few Napa viticulturists could have afforded to replant or graft over immediately to better
wine varieties. From Repeal to World War II, wine grapes were not a
profitable crop for Napa growers if depreciation and family labor were
included in the cost of production. In most years, grapes prices were
sufficient to cover the actual cash expenses associated with cultivation
and harvest, but little remained for vineyard improvement.

A three-tier grape-price system emerged during the 1930s. Scarce
white grapes fetched the highest prices, followed by standard red varietals such as Petite Sirah and Zinfandel, while the coloring grapes, Alicante and Grand noir, were discounted 10 to 15 percent. Filled with optimism over the coming Repeal, wineries offered their highest prices in
1933, and the Napa County Farm Advisor Herman Baade reported prices
of $50 a ton for "choice white grapes" and $40 a ton for "the better qual-

ity of colored grapes."[16] For the remainder of the decade, prices averaged closer to $20 a ton for white varietals, $17 for standard reds, and $15 for Alicante and Grand noir. Prices fluctuated somewhat for each vintage, and by 1941 and the emergence of a war economy, white grapes fetched $30 a ton, Zinfandels and Petite Sirahs brought $20 a ton, and coloring varieties received $17.50, up $5 from the year before.[17]

In a presentation made to the local Rotary Club in 1937, Felix Salmina reminded St. Helenans of the importance of wine grapes to their community's economy. Napa's 811 vineyards supplied over one ton of grapes for each of the county's 23,000 inhabitants, but, more important, one-sixth of the county's population were "dependent upon . . . grape production for their incomes," and at harvest from 6,000 to 8,000 people were employed to bring in the crop.[18] Viticulture certainly played a crucial role in the local economy, but at $17 to $20 a ton for standard grapes, just what kind of living did grape growing provide?

The University of California produced two statewide cost studies of grape production during the 1930s and determined, not surprisingly, that the key to making or losing money in the grape business was yield. Farm Advisor Baade reported that "those vineyardists who produced five or more tons per acre realized a profit," and he suggested to his readers that they "should give attention to increasing tonnage of quality grapes."[19] This was welcome, if obvious, advice, but since the unirrigated Napa vineyards averaged from two-and-a-half to three tons per acre during the 1930s, the cost studies implied that the majority of growers had lost money during the decade.[20]

The University of California cost surveys placed the full cost of production of an acre of dry farmed grapes at about $50 in 1934 and in 1939.[21] Of course, some expenses, such as picking, varied with production, while others, such as cultivation and taxes, remained constant, no matter the yield. The 1934 cost survey assumed that a vineyard producing three tons to the acre had a full cost of $19.32 a ton, while at two tons per acre expenses jumped to $27.36 a ton. The 1939 cost survey included fewer man-hours per acre in its calculation of costs than had the earlier survey, thus reducing the costs per ton of a vineyard yielding three tons per acre to $17.50, which climbed to $21.53 per ton for one yielding just two tons per acre. These estimates of cost of production were just at or slightly above the typical prices paid for standard grape varieties and included such accounting formalities as depreciation and interest. Few growers were sophisticated enough to include depreciation of assets or the opportunity cost of money tied up in vineyards in their own accounting, but most implicitly knew that they were not gaining ground. In an effort to cut costs wherever possible, Napa growers minimized all inputs, and the University of California enologist Maynard Amerine commented: "The vineyards were not terribly well taken care of . . . there were weeds in many of the vineyards . . . you would see vineyards that were not pruned or very sloppily pruned."[22]

Still, working on a strictly cash accounting basis and with family labor, a family could survive on thirty acres of grapes. Both surveys assumed between 36 to 40 hours of cultural labor per acre, excluding actual picking, although the 1934 survey assumed a wage rate of 25 cents an hour, while the 1939 report increased the rate to 30 cents. The university economists figured total cash and labor costs at between $12 and $14 a ton, depending upon yield, but of that labor, perhaps $6 dollars worth could be performed by family members, reducing actual cash expenditures to between $6 and $8 a ton. Assuming a $10 difference between minimum cash expenditures and grape price per ton, and estimating a yield of two-and-a-half tons per acre, a thirty-acre vineyard could produce $750 after subtracting actual cash expenses. For small producers, viticulture was essentially a form of peasant agriculture. As Roy Raymond said, "A thirty acre ranch would probably develop enough to raise a family on . . . [although] the standard of living was a lot different."[23]

The depressed economy of the 1930s, coupled with low grape prices, meant that few growers could afford to improve their vineyards. Both cost surveys spoke of "horse labor" rather than of tractors, and the only chemical used in the vineyards on a routine basis was sulfur dust, twice a season, to control mildew. The sulfur was applied by hand, directly from the bag, rather than by machine. At Beaulieu, Tchelistcheff was amazed to see "thirty or forty men going in the rows . . . shaking the burlap sacks . . . there was no control of the sulfur volume and there was a tremendous sulfur burn on the vineyard."[24] Little, if any, fertilizer was applied to North Coast vineyards. The 1934 cost survey provided for application of half a ton of manure per acre, while the 1939 cost report excluded any provision for fertilizer. Nor were vineyards irrigated after establishment, although work by Winkler showed that "irrigated vines produce more and in many cases better grapes, while the quality of wines is not adversely affected."[25] Unfertilized and unirrigated, the Napa vineyards were also heavily infested by viruses, which turned the grape leaves red "from one end of the valley to the other" in October.[26] All in all, the typical Napa vineyardist was lucky to average two-and-a-half tons to the acre and to eke out a meager existence for his family.

The low-income agriculture of the Napa Valley did not provide fertile ground for the gospel of variety improvement. But from the mid 1930s on, the enology and viticulture professors of the University of California preached the text to whomever would listen. Led by Winkler and Amerine, the university initiated an exhaustive series of experiments on variety selection and improvement of wine quality in 1935. Viticultural and enological research had been a major thrust of E. W. Hilgard and F. T. Bioletti at the University of California prior to Prohibition, but in 1916, the Regents of the University of California prohibited research on alcoholic fermentation, and all applied research on wine and wine grapes was discontinued until 1933. Following Repeal, the university had no real basis for making recommendations, and Winkler and Amerine "plunged into work to improve quality."[27]

For the next several years, Winkler and Amerine identified and harvested varietal grapes from all of the state's viticultural regions, producing small separate lots of wine in order to establish the effects of climate and variety on wine quality. "We made over five hundred lots [of wine] a year," recalled Winkler, "and everyone [*sic*] of those was true to name and came from a given region." The grape juice and wines were subjected to the usual chemical analyses as to percentage of soluble solids, titratable acidity and pH, tannin and color, but the wines also underwent sensory analysis and were rated as to general quality. These quality scores were then correlated with climate as expressed by heat summation, the number of degree-days above 50° F from April 1 through October 31, the growing season for most grapevines.[28]

Everyone in the wine industry knew that Fresno was hotter than St. Helena, and that wines made from the same varieties grown in those two locations would differ significantly. Heat summation expressed as degree-days allowed Winkler and Amerine to quantify climate, to describe more precisely just how much difference there was between Fresno and St. Helena, or for that matter, between St. Helena and Calistoga. Data from chemical or sensory analysis could then be correlated with climate to express how particular grape varieties responded to different environments. These experiments became the basis for the preliminary division of California into five viticultural regions based on temperature, and for recommending specific grape varieties for each region. The results were published in 1944 as *Composition and Quality of Musts and Wines of California Grapes*, which was ultimately recognized as one of the most important and groundbreaking works in the history of California winemaking. Recognition did not come overnight, and Winkler ruefully commented that the recommendations for quality improvement "didn't take a hold until in the late 1950s."[29]

If Winkler and Amerine's suggestions for varietal selections were not immediately embraced by Napa growers, it was not for lack of effort on the university's part. Winkler authored a series of articles on varietal selection and the effect of climate for the popular wine journals from 1936 through 1938. Articles such as "Grape Varieties for Dry Wines," "What Climate Does," "Factors Determining Wine Quality," and "The Effect of Climatic Regions" all detailed the importance of the interaction between climate and variety in determining wine quality.[30] Amerine, Winkler, and Harold Olmo, who headed the university's grape-breeding program, all penned short pieces designed to introduce important fine grape varietals to the California wine industry. These university researchers also took their message to the growers in person — "missionary work," Amerine called it — through a series of meetings or "schools" throughout the state, St. Helena always being a popular venue for such programs.[31]

Changing the old adage to "tasting is believing," the Division of Viticulture even invited growers to travel to Davis to sample the results of the variety experiments. In 1937, Herman Baade alerted readers of his column to a "wine tasting demonstration" involving 450 lots of wine to be "inspected by the vintners" at the Viticultural Field House at Davis. "We believe that this division has some very important things to demonstrate to the wine makers of Napa County," he wrote, "and we therefore urge as many as possibly can to attend."[32] A similar offer was repeated in 1940.[33] There was little more that Davis could do. You could lead a winemaker to quality, but you couldn't make him drink.

In arguing for increased quality production, the university faculty picked up in the 1930s where Hilgard and Bioletti had left off. They knew that the coastal counties could never compete in quantity with the San Joaquin Valley, and that they thus had to concentrate on quality. In 1936, Winkler spoke directly to this point when he put forth the notion of "table wines" and "festive wines," the latter being "wines which possess a delicacy of flavor, bouquet, smoothness and balance approaching perfection . . . wines of such quality as to maintain and extend our markets," wines "so good that it will be recognized as a privilege and a treat to set them before guests."[34] Such festive wines could only be produced in relatively cool growing areas, such as Napa and Sonoma. But a cooler climate was not in and of itself sufficient to ensure quality.

When Winkler spoke of "festive wines," he had in mind wines that possessed "a marked flavor of aroma and bouquet-producing properties," wines that derived "their most outstanding quality — varietal characteristics — from the principal variety used in their production."[35] From this it was just a short jump to an idea that would take decades to be realized: varietal labeling as a mark of quality. Winkler noted that under the present system of nomenclature, wines such as California "Burgundy" were impossible to define, leading to a wide variation in quality. "The use of variety names for the wines made of grapes possessing sufficiently pronounced characteristics to be recognized in their wines," he argued, "may well be made to serve as the basis for the standardization of these quality wines." [36] But if that were to occur, varietal distinctiveness would have to be maintained and emphasized.

Two years later, at a Dry Wine Conference at St. Helena, Winkler again impressed the importance of the interaction between climate and varietal selection upon his audience. After reviewing the degree-day concept and assuring his cool-climate listeners that "under warmer climatic conditions the aromatic qualities of the grapes lose some of their delicacy and richness and the other constituents of the fruit are not so well balanced," he moved to his main point, the need for specialization. [37] Noting that most wineries attempted to produce everything "from Angelica to Reisling," he decried the "unsound practice of producing everything everywhere." Such practice encouraged the interregional movement of grapes, and beside putting "all regions in conflict with each other," it prevented "the establishment of a reputation for a given region." [38] If that point was too abstract, he woke his audience up with his concluding comment that reputation meant money:

If you want your wine to sell for 25 cents, 50 cents, or $1.00 a gallon more than that of another region, you will have to put that much more quality into your bottles. You have the conditions in the North Coast for the production of quality dry wines, but the only way for you to convince the buying public of the superiority of the wines of your region is to grow the right varieties, pick them at the proper maturity, and convert them, without dilution of their quality, into really fine wines . . . until you have something distinctive of your region you have no basis for asking for protection. [39]

By 1936, Winkler was making preliminary varietal recommendations for geographic areas based on heat summation, although he noted that "the number of varieties recommended should be further reduced," and that the suggestions represented "a compromise of the opinions of today." [40] For the Oakville area, Winkler listed such red varieties as Cabernet Sauvignon, Charbono, Pinot Noir, Mondeuse, Verdot, and Zinfandel. The white varieties he recommended included Rieslings, Gewürztraminer, and, for the first time, Chardonnay, which Winkler described as "superior to Pinot blanc in bearing and in the superior aroma, delicacy, and smoothness of its wine."[41] Somewhat surprisingly, Sauvignon blanc and Semillon were suggested for the slightly warmer coastal valleys such as Livermore and Ukiah. Among the reds, Cabernet Sauvignon, which "by common consent is given first place among red wine grapes," and Pinot Noir, whose "smoothness and character . . . warrant its place in this list of varieties," were the most praised by Winkler.[42] Eight years later, the university would remove Zinfandel from its list of recommended varieties because of statewide overplanting of the variety. As Amerine warned, "It is already the most extensively planted red-wine grape variety, and only occasionally will its new plantings be as profitable" as other, less planted varieties.[43]

By the end of the decade, the road to quality improvement had been clearly marked by the university. The role of climate in wine quality had been measured and partially explained. Specific varietals had been recommended for each climatic region. The university had even gone so far as to suggest that varietal wine labeling could prove the key to raising consumer acceptance of quality wine, allowing regional specialization and higher returns for growers and wineries.

Some varietal replanting did occur. The 1936 California Fruit and Nut Survey showed almost 800 acres of nonbearing wine grapes, up from 110 acres in 1932.[44] Between 1934 and 1936, Petite Sirah declined from 4,400 to 2,022 acres, and Alicante fell from 2,720 to 898 acres, while Zinfandel and Carignane remained constant.[45] Well-financed wineries led the way in the grafting and replanting. Beaulieu grafted Chardonnay and Pinot Noir onto Palomino and Petite Sirah; Inglenook pulled out prunes and planted "close to 60 or 100 acres," while grafting over standard varieties to Cabernet and Pinot Noir; and Beringer removed a thirty-acre mixed standard red vineyard and replanted in Cabernet and Pinot Noir.[46] Amerine even reported one "Rutherford vineyard that was in white grapes and was grafted to Petite Sirah during Prohibition and after Prohibition was grafted back to white grapes again."[47] By 1940, most of the replanting and grafting had taken place, and the nonbearing acreage reported by the Napa agricultural commissioner fell to just 160 acres.[48]

Napa growers and wineries were slow to adopt university suggestions for viticultural improvement — the time would be measured in decades rather than in years. Viticulture in the valley, like the rest of Napa agriculture, was a marginal business, producing enough income for survival, but little for improvement. Aside from the labor cost, grafting took a vineyard out of production for at least a year, and most growers did not have the economic strength to fallow their vineyards. Planting was even more expensive and took longer, requiring rootstocks and grafting, and then a three-year wait without income, but with the cultural costs associated with training a vineyard. Even if a grower made the required economic commitment, the market for the new varietal grapes was unsure. Only a handful of Napa wineries showed any interest in attempting to make fine wines, and most of those owned their own vineyards. Throughout the 1940s and 1950s, growers and wineries upgraded by grafting or replanting on a case-by-case basis as vineyards aged and production fell. The massive planting of varietal winegrapes had to await the wine boom of the late 1960s and early 1970s.

The wines should have been better. Even the wines produced from standard varieties should have proved commercially sound. Instead, as W. V. Cruess of the University of California's Fruit Products Laboratory reminded a St. Helena audience at the 1937 Napa County Wine Institute meeting, "After Repeal, the outstanding characteristic of our wines was instability."[49] He then went on to list the problems of cloudiness, tartrate and metal instabilities, and microbial spoilage found in the early wines. At the same meeting, Harry Caddow, secretary-manager of the Wine Institute, said of the first years following Repeal, "We all know that some vinegar was shipped out of the wineries as dry wine . . . [but] aside from a few seizures of 1934 and 1935, your dry wines in the Napa valley are less of a problem for the state health inspector now than they have been at any time since Repeal."[50] Caddow implied improvement, but even in 1937, low-quality wine was being produced in quantity.

The factors contributing to poor wine quality were obvious, interactive, and predictable. Prohibition and the depression had almost ensured that the first post-Repeal wines would be poor at best and at worst spoiled. Prohibition had removed from the California wine industry the trained personnel who understood the science and practice of winemaking. It had cut short the dissemination of knowledge about the basis and control of fermentation and wine spoilage just when such information was becoming available to the industry. Had Prohibition come ten years later, a scientific understanding of winemaking would have had time to spread and take hold throughout the industry; instead, most winemakers with pre-Prohibition experience based their practice on information derived from peasant agriculturists, the *vignerons* of Europe. Of course, the alternative was a winemaker with no experience at all, but

European experience did not always fit well with California conditions. A more subtle, but just as important, effect of Prohibition for both the industry and consumers was the lack of knowledge and appreciation of quality wine. Without an understanding of what quality wine should be, it was difficult for any new winemakers to pursue and improve quality in their products.

The terrible economic conditions of the depression also took their toll on wine quality. Most wineries in the 1930s were undercapitalized, forced to employ obsolete technology and equipment. Five years after Repeal, André Tchelistcheff was so shocked by conditions at Beaulieu that he seriously considered returning to France. Considering only such consumer goods as radios or automobiles, he "had always thought the American technology was far ahead of French technology," he remembered, but in California he "faced a situation . . . which existed only in the lower sections of Italy and Spain."[51] The direct consequence of poor equipment and obsolete technology was wine often spoiled by high fermentation temperatures and contact with infected cooperage, or unstable wine resulting from severe metal contamination and oxidation. In the struggle for survival, the temptation to ship wine with high levels of volatile acidity — which is to say, wine containing acetic acid (vinegar) — must have been very strong for many wineries, especially if the immediate alternative was bankruptcy. The tragedy was that so much of the spoilage could have been avoided.

The elements necessary for the commercial production of sound wine were well identified by progressive California winemakers by the early 1910s. In the last decades of the nineteenth century, Eugene Hilgard had undertaken and reported upon a series of experiments involving methods of fermentation. His successor, Frederic Bioletti, had continued this work, writing short circulars on pure yeasts, white wine production, and must cooling. In 1911, Bioletti integrated the previous research into one bulletin, *The Principles of Wine-Making*, with the intention of explaining the causes of wine spoilage and detailing the steps that California winemakers could take to ensure healthy fermentations and sound commercial wines. "Some of our wine is good, some of it very good, but much of it is indifferent, and too large a portion, frankly bad," wrote Bioletti in the introduction. "There is no reason, except lack of skillful winemaking, why any California wine should be bad."[52]

The same year Rudolf Jordan, Jr., a Napa County winemaker of some fifteen years' experience, published *Quality in Dry Wines through Adequate Fermentations*, a detailed account of five vintages in which he had employed Bioletti's methods. Jordan's book, subtitled *A Manual for Progressive Winemakers in California*, was intended to bridge the gap between traditional cellar practices and scientific theory, which many winemakers felt was "not always applicable to a larger scale in the open."[53] Both books contained practical, step-by-step advice for improving wine production. Both would have proved important in raising industry standards if Prohibition had not curtailed commercial wine production.

Both Bioletti and Jordan advocated specific steps to ensure a complete, clean fermentation. First, grapes should be clean and, although ripe, of moderate sugar content, preferably below 23 percent by weight. Second, a measured amount of sulfur dioxide, generally in the form of potassium metabisulfite, should carefully be added to the freshly crushed grapes to inhibit spoilage bacteria and wild yeast. The suggested amount depended upon the temperature and condition of the grapes — warmer grapes would need more — but generally six to eight ounces per ton of grapes, roughly equivalent to 150 parts per million sulfur dioxide.[54] Third, juice intended for white wine production should be "defecated" (settled) for twenty-four hours, allowing gross solids to fall from the juice, and the clear juice should then be racked off the settled lees prior to fermentation. Fourth, enough vigorous pure yeast starter culture should be added to initiate immediate fermentation. Fifth, the fermentation should be monitored for temperature and cooled when necessary through the use of a heat exchanger. Bioletti recommended 75° to 80°F for white wines and between 85° to 90°F for reds. Temperatures much higher would result in "stuck" fermentations, in which the yeast died off. "Such wines," he wrote, "remain sweet on account of the failure of the yeast to do its work, and become unpleasantly sour owing to the volatile acids produced by the bacteria." Jordan was more direct: "It is far better to have a cooler for the prevention than a pasteurizer for the correction of the defects and diseases of wine."[55] These steps would ensure a clean and commercially sound wine that, with reasonable cellar treatment, would remain pure until bottling.[56]

Had California wineries followed Bioletti's advice immediately following Repeal, much less spoiled wine would have been produced. Stability problems are generally divided into two groups, those caused by microbiological organisms and those owing to such elements in the wine as protein or metal hazes, or tartrate or pigment precipitation. California and Napa wines experienced the full range of stability problems, but immediately following Repeal, two forms of microbiological spoilage caused the most immediate and irreversible damage to wines. The most prevalent and easily identified spoilage was acetification, the presence of high levels of acetic acid caused by acetobacter or, as they were known, vinegar bacteria. A second group of bacteria, known in the 1930s as "Tourne," lurked in the wooden cooperage so prevalent in the 1930s. Both spoilage organisms could have been controlled through proper and timely use of sulfur dioxide.

Tourne was a generic name given lactic-acid-producing bacteria, some of which metabolized sugars left over from incomplete fermentations, and others of which consumed the malic acid naturally present in grapes and wine. Both types produced lactic acid and generally resulted in off odors and flavors as well. The damage done by Tourne bacteria can perhaps best be appreciated by realizing that they were part of the same group of bacteria used to create sauerkraut and pickles. Decades later, in the 1950s and 1960s, the controlled use of desirable bacteria to perform the malolactic fermentation was introduced, but in the 1930s, with the organisms then prevalent in wineries, Tourne bacteria were definitely a class of spoilage organisms.

Wines containing high levels of acetic acid were a common problem in Napa and throughout the California industry. Some degree of spoilage was understandable in wines stored in wooden tanks for the fourteen years of Prohibition. All of the Napa wineries that had attempted to keep wine during Prohibition had large amounts of spoiled wines on hand. Beringer, Fawver, Larkmead, Tubbs, and Beaulieu together had more than a million gallons of wine spoiled by high volatile acidity.[57] There was enough spoiled wine in 1932 for Charles Forni, who was later to manage the Napa co-op, to start a vinegar factory south of St. Helena to convert over 300,000 gallons of wine, which was "for the most part unfit for beverage purposes because of its long storage in wood," into vinegar.[58] Vinegar production or distilling was the logical end of such wines. These wines often became the source of infection for newly made wines, since economic pressure forced most wineries to continue to use infected cooperage, leading to predictable spoilage of new wines.

Worse, though, was the common practice of blending spoiled wines with new wines to reduce the volatile acidity to just under the legal limit. Amerine recalled that wineries had only three options for economically disposing of wine with high volatile acidity: sell it for vinegar stock, distill it for fortifying material for dessert wines, or "blend it down with low-acetic acid wine and get it out." In the process of blending, wineries "transferred the bacteria to the new wine, so it was important to get it out very fast. So they just bottled the next day after they had made the blend . . . [and] some wines had to be bottle pasteurized" because the bacterial count was so high.[59]

One result of such practices was a vigorous debate among California winemakers over the proposed California state levels for maximum volatile acidity, initially set below federal standards. Both the proposed state and federal levels were quite high. California had suggested .11 and .12 percent for white and red wines, while the federal standards were .12 and .14 percent respectively. According to Léon Bonnet, a former University of California professor and André Tchelistcheff's predecessor at Beaulieu, the proposed California standards were unnecessarily low and would "impose a hardship on wine producers, condemning large amounts of fine wines."[60] Bonnet's position was understandable, if self-serving. As Tchelistcheff was to discover in 1938, Beaulieu owned roughly 300,000 gallons of wine damaged by high volatile acidity. Eventually, most was distilled as part of the prorate distillation agreement, which Tchelistcheff called "a lifesaver. . . . I liquidated all this wine of old inventory and sent it to the distillery."[61] That Beaulieu, a quality producer with an academically trained winemaker, still had large amounts of spoiled wine in storage toward the end of the decade suggests that throughout the 1930s, volatile acidity and microbiological spoilage were common and partially accepted aspects of winemaking.

Much of the post-Repeal wine would have spoiled rapidly even if the vast reservoirs of acetic wine had not infected new vintages. In 1934 and 1935, few wineries employed winemakers with a scientific understanding of fermentation. Consequently, only a minority of wineries used pure yeast cultures, measured amounts of sulfur dioxide, or cooling systems to control fermentations. At the 1934 University of California short course on wine analysis, W. V. Cruess of the Fruit Products Laboratory suggested that wineries "employ permanently some of the promising graduates of the University," arguing that "if one of these should save a 10,000 gallon tank each year, the savings would pay his salary several times over."[62]

This was no doubt true. Tchelistcheff, a trained enologist, came to Beaulieu in 1938 for a monthly wage of $150.[63] At 15 cents a gallon, a 10,000-gallon tank represented a $1,500 investment, probably more than a recent graduate could expect in the depths of the depression. Still, there were few jobs for university-trained enologists, and much wine was made in the centuries-old peasant agricultural tradition, which sometimes worked under European conditions, but was not generally applicable to the hot, dry summers of California.

Many winemakers held to the European peasant belief that the higher the sugar at harvest, the better the resulting wine. In California, this often led to fermentation of grapes with excessively high sugar, which in turn produced high fermentation temperatures. At Christian Brothers immediately following Repeal, the Brothers "let the grapes get as ripe as possible," resulting in years when they "crushed grapes all the way up to 28 or more degrees sugar."[64] At Beringer's winery, the intermixed vineyards created a dilemma for the winemaker, since the varieties would usually be at various stages of ripeness when the vineyard was harvested. Often the resulting musts were too high in sugar, and the uneven ripening did not allow the winery to extract "the maximum amount of quality out of the varieties."[65] George Deuer, the winemaker at Inglenook, used grapes from four locations to balance the must for his Cabernet, but he rarely checked sugars during the 1930s.[66] Reliance on the "art" of the individual winemaker succeeded in some instances, but more often it resulted in spoiled wine.

Following Repeal, few wineries used pure yeast culture to initiate fermentation. In part this failure to employ science was the result of faith in the traditional system, which assumed the presence of sufficient natural yeast to produce a healthy fermentation. In part it was the result of the difficulty in building a pure yeast culture. Both Jordan and Bioletti gave detailed instructions that explained, step by step, how a yeast "slant" could be grown into sufficient quantity for use in the winery. The process may have been intimidating to untrained agriculturists; it was certainly time-consuming and put a premium on a level of sanitation unusual in most wineries of the period.

The University of California did what it could to encourage the use of pure yeast cultures. In September 1934, W. V. Cruess and George Marsh lectured about forty winemakers at a meeting held at Inglenook on the use of such cultures, explaining about types of yeasts and demonstrating "various methods of preparing cultures." The Star urged "all wine cellar men" to attend and to "bring with them a container in which they can take home a supply of pure yeast culture."[67] The following year, the university gave the Salminas "a quantity of yeast culture to be used in the fermentation of grapes," which Larkmead propagated and then distributed to local winemakers.[68] Whether many local wineries actually maintained a pure culture during the fermentation season is doubtful. Wineries that used a yeast culture probably inoculated the first tank with the culture and then inoculated subsequent tanks with actively fermenting juice from the first tank. Most wineries, like Christian Brothers, still "depended upon the yeast cultures that were present on the skins [of the grapes]." According to Brother Timothy, it was not until the end of the decade that they "began to consider and talk about an experiment with pure yeast cultures."[69]

Sulfur dioxide in the form of potassium metabisulfite was widely available from companies that supplied winery chemicals. Advertisements and testimonials for it appeared in most issues of *Wines and Vines* and *Wine Review*, along with articles by university faculty and industry spokesmen recommending and explaining its use.[70] Study after study showed that fermentation with pure yeast and treatment with moderate amounts of sulfur dioxide produced sounder wines, with volatile acidity levels half those of wines fermented without sulfur dioxide and pure yeast cultures.

Generally, however, sulfur dioxide was either not used at all or overused. In many of the wineries where it had been adopted, it was inconsistently or inappropriately employed. At Beaulieu in 1938, Tchelistcheff was shocked to observe buckets of dry potassium metabisulfite added directly to musts without first dissolving the chemical in water to allow complete mixing in the tank. Cellar workers were "throwing salts in the fermenting tank empirically by saying 'Well the chemist recommends to put, let's say, six ounces per ton, but to be sure, put 25 to 30 ounces per ton.'"[71] According to Tchelistcheff, the same technique was in use across the highway at Inglenook, and he claimed to have shown George Deuer the importance of first mixing the metabisulfite in water to create a 5 or 6 percent solution. Too much sulfur dioxide was bad, but what was worse was not to use any. Many wineries did not make any addition, preferring to ferment their wines on the "let it alone" principle. "By the Grace of God," Cruess commented, "good wine sometimes results, but it is a risky method and often proves costly."[72]

The shortcomings of the "let it alone" method were most obvious with high-sugar grapes in the three hot summers of 1934, 1935, and 1936. Yeast metabolism of sugar produces three main end products: alcohol, carbon dioxide, and heat. High-sugar musts always run the risk of generating high enough temperatures during fermentation to kill the yeast, leaving the partially fermented must open to attack by aerobic spoilage bacteria. Secondly, wild yeasts generally have low tolerance for alcohol and may die off before all the sugar in a must is fermented. This is especially true in high-sugar musts, which produce a correspondingly higher degree of alcohol than musts made from grapes harvested at lower sugar levels. In both cases, high temperature and high alcohol, the result is often a "stuck" fermentation, in which the yeast dies off before all the sugar is converted to alcohol.

Such stuck fermentations were common throughout California in hot years. In early October 1934, at about the middle of the harvest, the Napa farm advisor wrote in his weekly column that "owing to high sugar content of grapes and to excessively high temperatures reached during fermentation, many wine makers are having trouble with stuck fermentation."[73] He advised adding at least three hundred to four hundred gallons of actively fermenting juice from another tank to each one thousand gallons of stuck wine in an attempt to revive the failed fermentation. Cruess, in arguing the case for the employment of enologists, pointed out that simple measurements of sugar with a hydrometer would have predicted future problems and would have allowed "proper adjustment" (meaning addition of water to dilute the must) "to prevent sticking with danger of subsequent spoilage."[74]

A third and technological component in the control of fermentation was cooling. Unlike the use of sulfur dioxide or pure yeast, which could be bought incrementally on an as-needed basis and required no addition to a winery's physical plant, cooling systems represented a permanent investment. At its simplest, a cooling system consisted of a supply of cold water and a coiled copper pipe that could be dropped into a fermenting tank, and through which cold water could be circulated. Slightly more sophisticated were counterflow tube-in-tube heat exchangers in which fermenting juice flowed in one direction through a small tube, while cold water was pumped in the opposite direction through a surrounding tube. The greater the difference in temperature between the cold water and the must, the greater the efficiency of the system. Such cooling systems worked tolerably well as long as an adequate supply of cold water was available. Unfortunately, most wineries then had no efficient way to cool water.

The predominant method of cooling water was through the use of a cooling tower. Warm water that had passed through the cooling coil in the fermenting must was pumped to the top of a tower, whence it flowed by gravity through cooling fins, while fans blew air over them, pulling heat from the water. Depending upon the humidity and dew point, such a system could cool water to below the ambient temperature. During the summer, a system operating at night could cool water to about 60° F. But once daytime temperatures started to climb, cooling towers became less efficient. Most wineries had standing orders with the ice company. Louis P. Martini remembers buying ice "five tons at a time and [dump-

ing] it in the cooling tower," while at Beaulieu "the winery had daily delivery of tons of ice to keep control of fermentation."[75]

A more expensive but effective method of cooling was mechanical refrigeration, in which a gas, generally ammonia, was compressed into a liquid, cooled, and then run through a heat exchanger, pulling heat from the must, causing the compressed refrigerant to boil back into a gas again. Much more heat could be absorbed during the change from liquid to gas than was possible with a water system, and mechanical refrigeration was thus capable of significantly greater efficiencies of cooling and temperature differentials than the cooling-tower system. But mechanical refrigeration also required much more energy in the form of electricity for motors and much higher costs for equipment than a cooling-tower system.

The Martini Winery was probably the first winery in the Napa Valley to invest in mechanical refrigeration, used to cool air in a large room for fermenting white wines at 50° F.[76] Other wineries brought in mechanical refrigeration on a much smaller scale, generally to augment their cooling-tower systems. In 1936, the *St. Helena Star* reported that the Frigidaire Corporation was equipping two 18,000-gallon tanks with cooling coils at Greystone Cellars, and that the installation was "the second of its type here, Beringer Brothers having installed similar coils last year."[77] By 1938, Beaulieu had "a little freon refrigerator with coil refrigeration set in two 10,000 gallon tanks," and just before World War II, Inglenook acquired a "5,000 gallon tank of water and a refrigeration unit," allowing Deuer to cool the fermentation enough "so it wouldn't go over the top."[78] Such systems were small and primitive. They helped guide fermentations, but generally were not adequate to control them. As Deuer put it years later, "My refrigerator [at home] does better work now than that [system] did."[79]

In the absence of sufficient cooling capacity, most wineries experienced short high-temperature fermentations. One technique to minimize stuck fermentations was to ferment in small-volume tanks, so that there was less mass for heat buildup and more surface area for heat dissipation. At Beringer, the redwood fermenting tanks were only 1,000 to 1,200 gallons in size, while at Inglenook the fermenters ranged in size from 1,600 to 2,600 gallons.[80] If small tank size was not sufficient to prevent heat buildup, the fermenting musts could be physically manipulated. "Pumping over," the pumping of the fermenting juice from the bottom of the tank onto the "cap" of skins buoyed to the top of the tank by the evolution of carbon dioxide, was used to dissipate heat, as

was the more physical "punching down" of the skins into the fermenting juice.

Wines of the period exhibited much higher levels of phenolic extraction than wines in the 1960s and later. This was no doubt partly owing to the heat of the fermentation, allowing greater extraction of pigments and tannins, and to the grape varieties used, such as Petite Sirah and Alicante, both of which have high levels of pigmentation. Roy Raymond commented that "Pets [Petite Sirah] were a pretty good source throughout the whole valley, and they made a pretty gutty red wine."[81] Surprisingly, in the only description of premium red wine production, George Deuer of Inglenook claimed that in Cabernet production, he generally only punched down once a day, in the evening, and that the must was pumped over in the morning only if such pumping over was needed to cool it; otherwise it was left alone. Under modern fermentation temperatures, such a regime would not have been adequate to extract color, but it seems to have worked at Inglenook, which rarely needed to add press wine to improve its Cabernets.[82]

The typical production techniques and facilities used in Napa in the 1930s were barely suitable for quality red wine production, and they were woefully inadequate for producing delicate or aromatic white wines. White wines, which made up approximately 20 percent of the dry wine produced in the Napa Valley, were generally fermented warm in open-top tanks, like reds, and as a result of variety selection, fermentation temperature, and style of production, they were coarse, containing more pigments and tannin than are found in present-day white wines.[83] The two most widely grown white varieties were Burger and Palomino, neither of which was noted for aromatic characteristics or delicacy. This was perhaps just as well, since few wineries were prepared to emphasize inherent grape aromas through low-temperature fermentations.

In the late 1930s, Cruess conducted a series of experiments at Berkeley on small lots of juice fermented in rooms maintained at various temperatures and showed that 45° to 50°F seemed to maximize wine quality.[84] Such cold fermentation was, with the exception of the Martini Winery's cold room, a practical impossibility during the 1930s. At Beaulieu, white wine fermentations were often cooled by the direct addition of ice, diluting the must and resulting wine.[85] Few if any wineries had facilities to cool, settle, and rack the white juice, the "defecation" described by Jordan and Bioletti, prior to fermentation. Thus most wineries fermented their white wine juice with high levels of solids, further reducing the fruitiness of the resulting wines.[86] Some wineries did not even press the grapes prior to fermentation. At Beringer, according to Roy Raymond,

white grapes of about 21 percent sugar were crushed into fermenters, the fermentation started, and the fermenting juice was pulled off the skins when sugar had dropped to 16 to 17 percent. The resulting heavily extracted white wines were often stored in large tanks for three to five years prior to bottling, creating "straw colored" wines with low fragrance.[87] Although both red and white wines later benefited from improved technology, the white wines improved most in the 1960s with the introduction of stainless steel and cold fermentations.

Ignorance on the part of producers and primitive technology were interactive. Much of the high volatile acidity associated with early vintages immediately following Repeal was, however, primarily owing to a lack of understanding of basic microbiology. Good sanitation and use of pure yeast cultures and sulfur dioxide would have improved the average wine even without the use of cooling systems. Some Napa winemakers recognized their need of education, and in early 1934, the county librarian reported an "active demand" for "books on winemaking," going so far as to comment that "one winery which has [had] a shipment [of wine] returned as unsatisfactory . . . was not the winery which had all the books on wine making."[88] By the harvest of 1934, several free publications were available from the University of California at the Napa farm advisor's office. Pamphlets such as *Principles of Wine Making, Control of Fermentation, Sulfur Dioxide and Metabisulfite in Wine Making, Aging and Stabilizing Wine, Notes on White Wine Making, Notes on Red Wine Making, Diseases and Defects of Wine*, and *Clarification and Filtration of Wine*, were printed by the university and distributed without charge to anyone interested.[89]

Such University of California publications were reinforced by a series of short courses and training programs, taught at first by the members of the Fruit Products Laboratory in Berkeley, later augmented by the Department of Viticulture at Davis. The need for such training was evident, and the *Wine Review* reported in February 1934 that "a number of winemakers" had asked the university to hold a course on wine analysis.[90] The first of what would prove to be annual meetings was held in Berkeley, April 19–23, 1934, providing "practical advice based on sound theory" according to the *California Grape Grower*.[91] Later, just prior to harvest, the faculty held a series of evening lectures on three consecutive Fridays in Healdsburg, drawing 150 "interested men and women" and providing, in the words of the Napa farm advisor, "a great deal of valuable information that our wine makers will be able to make use of during the coming vintage."[92]

In reporting on the Healdsburg "school," Farm Advisor Baade also

expressed his desire to hold a similar class in Napa County in the near future.[93] The first such program was held on Friday evening, March 29, 1935, featuring W. V. Cruess, George Marsh, and L. G. Saywell, who spoke on the need for cooling coupled with pure yeast and the measured use of sulfur dioxide, with Saywell making a preliminary report on a new product, bentonite, for use in clarifying wines.[94] The following year, a full day was scheduled on Saturday, April 4, 1936, at the Hotel St. Helena. Attended by seventy-two "winemen," the program included technical speakers from the university, politicians, and tours of local wineries. Those in attendance decided the event should become "an annual one," and that St. Helena, "as the center of the dry wine area," was the "logical place to hold it."[95] Similar one-day educational meetings were held the next two years, bringing the gospel of cooling, pure yeast, and sulfur dioxide to any St. Helena winemaker willing to travel a few miles and devote a day to education.[96] However, understanding the need for improved facilities was one thing; paying for them was another.

During the 1930s, California wineries slowly upgraded their processing equipment, but even by the end of the decade, the technology was primitive, required hand labor, and was a cause of physical instability in wines. At the second wine conference in Berkeley in 1934, Marsh described the importance of cooling fermentations, and *Wines and Vines* characterized the meeting as "a field day for the refrigeration men as report after report was given . . . showing the excellent results secured by the use of refrigeration equipment."[97] Three years later, at the meeting in St. Helena, Marsh commented that "cooling during fermentation has increased," with the result that the university had "fewer calls for help from wineries faced with bacterial spoilage." Instead, he noted, "calls are now for methods to improve quality."[98] Adoption of the use of pure yeast cultures, sulfur dioxide, and cooling had increased the percentage of sound new wine being removed from the fermenters. But it did not necessarily ensure that the aged and bottled wine would remain uninfected and stable.

Throughout the 1930s and 1940s, the major causes of instability in finished wines were metal contamination, tartrates, protein instability in white wines, and refermentation in the bottle. Although all were common, metal instability was probably the most prevalent, owing to the use of iron and copper piping and equipment in most wineries. Wine is an acidic liquid that reacts with most metals, pulling into solution metal ions that may later complex with other compounds in wine to produce a haze, or "casse," as it was known. Such casses were particularly trouble-

some in white wines, which "after filtering and bottling" often became "cloudy because of casse."[99] At Beaulieu, the machinery and piping were made of "cast iron, copper and brass." One of Tchelistcheff's first actions at Beaulieu was to disconnect the iron grape crusher from the iron must line, where he discovered a "thickness of one half to one inch of pure iron oxide—rust—in the must line." Testing showed that new wines fresh from the Beaulieu fermenters were routinely showing between forty and eighty parts per million of iron, resulting in illegal use of ferrocyanide, the so-called "blue fining," to reduce the iron content.[100]

Beaulieu's problem was common, and the permanent solution was expensive: elimination of reactive metals from any contact with wine. In many cases affordable alternatives did not exist. In 1938, Dr. Emil Mrak of the University of California conducted a series of tests on forty-six different metals and alloys to determine reactions in wines. Not surprisingly, stainless steel proved "the most resistant," but stainless steel was relatively expensive and did not become generally used in most wineries until the 1960s. Least resistant were pure metals such as iron and copper.[101] Certain metal alloys held up fairly well in contact with wine, especially phosphorus bronze, which gradually became the metal of choice for pumps and valves during the 1930s. At Beaulieu, Tchelistcheff took a different tack, replacing all metal must lines with Pyrex glass, a sanitary and inert material.[102] Pyrex was, however, expensive. Few other Napa wineries had Beaulieu's financial strength, and none duplicated Beaulieu's investment.

Two other common instabilities in white wines were clouding, caused by protein haze, and precipitation of potassium bitartrate crystals. In a sense, these were cosmetic problems, as neither affected the taste of the wine if it was carefully decanted. Cosmetic or not, both were real problems to overcome, since, as Marsh noted, Americans placed "an unwarranted demand for clarity and brilliance upon the manufacturer of bottled beverages . . . in order for the products of any winery to meet with general consumer acceptance, they must be clear."[103] Inexpensive wine sold in bulk out of the barrel to the housewife in her own container could perhaps be allowed some instabilities; bottled wine had to be brilliantly clear and stable, requiring a higher degree of processing and knowledge than was common in many wineries in the 1930s.

Of the two problems, the bitartrate crystals were better understood and more easily cured. Bitartrate crystals, or cream of tartar, are a natural by-product of winemaking; indeed, Georges de Latour had started his career in California by processing the "argols" from wine tanks. Potas-

sium bitartrate is a naturally occurring compound, formed when the tartaric acid in wine combines with potassium. Barely soluble in grape juice, potassium bitartrate is even less so in the alcoholic medium of wine and decreases in solubility as temperature declines. Under normal cellar conditions and aging regimes, most bitartrate drops out of solution in wine if exposed to winter temperatures over several years. However, the California industry in the 1930s often rushed wines to market, selling unstable wines so early that the tartrates deposited when cooled. The simple technical answer was to refrigerate the wine in bulk to just above freezing as part of the processing prior to bottling, thus forcing precipitation in the tank rather than in the bottle.[104] Cooling was an effective solution for those wineries with adequate mechanical refrigeration, and it became more prevalent in the Napa Valley as wineries added cooling systems to their processing technology.

Protein instability was not as well understood as bitartrate crystallization and was a problem in bottled wines in the 1930s. Proteins are essential constituents of grapevine metabolism and thus a natural residual component in wines. In red wines, proteins combine with pigments and tannins to create stable compounds. Because white wines possess less tannin and fewer pigments than do red wines, most white wines have an excess of proteins, which, if subjected to warmer temperatures, may be denatured by heat and combine, causing a haze in the wine or a deposit at the bottom of the bottle. Such haze was primarily a problem in young white wines that had been fermented from clarified or settled juice. White wines produced in the manner described by Raymond at Beringer possessed more phenolic material, which could combine with proteins, and longer storage allowed more time for the proteins to combine during bulk storage and settle to the bottom of the tank. Heat treatment, such as pasteurization in bulk, was an effective method both to sterilize the wine and to achieve protein stabilization. In-bottle pasteurization was not recommended, since if the wine was not completely protein-stable prior to pasteurization, a considerable protein deposit would result in the bottled wine. Bulk pasteurization was effective, but at a severe cost to wine flavor and freshness, and it was thus not the method of choice for stabilizing premium wines.

The standard method of attempting to achieve protein stability during the 1930s and into the 1940s was to add more phenolic material, generally tannin, to the fermenting white wine, thus encouraging a complexing of tannin and protein. Treasury inspection reports indicate that the Martini winery routinely added one-fourth of a pound of tannin to each thousand gallons of fermenting white juice "to assist in later clari-

fication," and Cruess commented in a short article in 1935 that most white wines "were improved in flavor when .05 per cent (about four pounds per thousand gallons) of good quality tannin was added."[105] Many winemakers believed that tannin possessed antimicrobial properties, and that tannin addition would not only help stabilize wines and improve taste, but would deter spoilage organisms. Cruess and other university researchers found this to be true, but only at extraordinarily high levels, and did not recommend tannin addition as a method of controlling spoilage organisms.[106] Tannin additions could help to achieve protein stability, but generally at some cost to flavor in white wines.

During the 1930s, L. G. Saywell of the university's Fruit Products Laboratory introduced bentonite, a volcanic clay, which would ultimately become the winemaker's first choice in the protein stabilization of white wines. During Prohibition, Saywell had worked with bentonite in helping clarify fruit juices and vinegars. Following Repeal, he recommended the use of bentonite to speed clarification of both red and white wines and to help reduce iron and copper levels in wines.[107]

Initially, bentonite was considered a clarifying aid rather than a stabilizing agent. Saywell suggested that the wine to be clarified be tested on a small scale to determine what level of bentonite addition resulted in the "most brilliantly clear wine with a minimum of sediment."[108] Increasing amounts of bentonite slurry were added to given volumes of wine, allowed to settle, and the resulting samples evaluated for clarity and sediment. In the 1950s, this test would be revised to check for the absence of protein by heating the clear wine, thus precipitating any remaining protein. Saywell recommended test levels of bentonite in increments of four pounds of rehydrated bentonite per thousand gallons of wine, which was probably sufficient to stabilize proteins in most instances.[109] Although bentonite was actively recommended by the university during the 1930s, it does not seem to have been employed as a stabilizing agent in the Napa Valley until much later. The Martini Winery continued to rely on tannin additions until after World War II, and Beaulieu did not begin to experiment with bentonite until the 1950s.[110]

Assuming that a winery could ferment a wine cleanly with little spoilage and then stabilize it, the wine still needed to be filtered and bottled. Efficient filters and automatic, high-speed bottling lines were expensive and only used by large wineries in the Central Valley. Throughout the Napa Valley, everything was done by hand, with primitive equipment. Bottles were not always available, and thus had to be ordered far in advance of bottling and stored, necessitating hand cleaning prior to use.[111] At Beaulieu, wine was pumped to the second floor, run by gravity through asbestos filters, and siphoned by hand into a bottle, which was then passed on to another worker to be corked.[112] Siphon fillers in which the bottles were put on and off by hand were the rule rather than the exception in most Napa wineries, as were hand corkers. Louis Martini recalled that until 1958, his winery used a hand corker, and that an employee would then "hand clean it [the bottle], hand wipe it. . . . It would be shoved down the table to the next person who would set it on a little stand and put one label on it. It would be shoved down to the next person who would set it on a stand and put the back label on."[113] A similar procedure was followed at Beaulieu, Inglenook, and Beringer. Most wineries did not even have a machine for applying glue to labels; instead, glue was spread on a plate and the label applied to the glue, and then to the bottle.[114] Tchelistcheff dryly commented that "the efficiency of this operation was very slow."

Once bottled, wine was generally stored for at least a few weeks prior to shipping, allowing time for problems to emerge. The university recommended testing bottled wine by "storing some bottles at 90 degrees F. in an incubator and some at 32 degrees in a refrigerator" in order to hasten any changes, warning, "It is extremely hazardous to 'bottle wine today and ship it tomorrow.'"[115] Of course, after bottling was a bit late to discover that a wine was unstable, although certainly preferable to such discovery after bottling and shipping. The implication is that bottling unstable wine was relatively common in the 1930s, and that Beaulieu's experience with the wine bottled for Park & Tilford in 1937 was unfortunately not an aberration.

In retrospect what is surprising is, not that most wines were coarse, unstable, or spoiled, but that so many lots of fine wines were successfully produced and bottled. Prohibition had stolen fourteen years from a young industry, necessitating a total reeducation of producers in the science of enology. The depression had limited capital expenditures, obliging wineries to employ obsolete machinery and infected cooperage while battling in the marketplace. By the end of the decade, the general quality of California wine had improved, in part owing to the efforts of the university to educate growers and winemakers in the science of grape growing and winemaking, in part owing to the stabilization of the industry as early producers fell by the wayside. By 1940, the basic tools were in place, if not universally employed, and the advent of World War II was creating a period of calm on the home front, with protected markets and prices, allowing producers the opportunity to apply the university's lessons about quality wine and grapes at their wineries and vineyards.

CHAPTER FOUR

Building a Market for Napa Wines

Brand Development from Repeal to World War II

The idea for a public relations coup was clever: use sparkling wine from St. Helena to christen the new Grace Lines steamship *St. Elena*. Although Repeal was still a year away, the St. Helena Chamber of Commerce hoped that the media, interested in the growing movement to end Prohibition, would capture the moment on newsreel footage and in national magazines, catapulting St. Helena into the forefront of the minds of America's potential wine consumers. In cooperation with the Grace Steamship Lines, the St. Helena Chamber of Commerce held a contest to determine which St. Helena maid would represent the city at the christening in New York, finally selecting Arlene Bassford, an 18-year-old high school senior, who made the transcontinental trip accompanied by a chamber of commerce chaperone. On a cold, gray, rainy day in November, Bassford broke the bottle of sparkling wine over the bow of the *St. Elena*, but caught a cold, which quickly turned into pneumonia. Within a week, the *Star* reported her untimely death in New York.[1] It was not an auspicious beginning for a campaign to promote Napa Valley wines. The marketing of Napa wines was to prove an uphill battle for most of the 1930s, a struggle that was to require unceasing efforts on the part of individual wineries and the local community.

At Repeal, Napa possessed a few specific advantages in the promotion of its wines. In Napa's favor was a recognition among drinkers of fine wines that Napa had been the quality leader prior to Prohibition. Although wines from the California Wine Association had dominated the marketplace in the early 1900s, smaller Napa wineries such as Inglenook,

Charles Krug, Beringer, and Salmina (Larkmead) had consistently taken awards and had bottled their best wines in glass with labels displaying "Napa" as their appellation.[2] The legacy of quality was augmented by the existence of several wineries that had operated during Prohibition, most notably Beaulieu and Beringer. St. Helenans assumed that Napa Valley would quickly reclaim its place as the leader of quality dry wine production, and the local chamber of commerce was eager and willing to promote the valley's premier product.

The need for generic promotion of dry wines in general, and of Napa wines in particular, quickly became obvious following Repeal, when the expected boom in sales failed to appear. Prior to Prohibition, dry wine had outsold sweet fortified wine by about 50 percent. In 1934, the dry wine industry was shocked to discover that sweet wine outsold dry wine by almost three to one. Analysis of grape shipments showed that the change was in sales, not in production or consumption, since home wine production of dry wines had flourished during Prohibition and continued after Repeal.[3] To succeed, the dry wine industry had to win over three groups of consumers: those who produced their own wines, those who associated quality in dry wines with foreign wines, and those who assumed that "wine" meant fortified wine. A fourth group of potential consumers, who did not think of wine at all, would remain a tantalizing target for the next half century. To win over the three groups that did consume wine, taxes and other state barriers to California wines had to be fought, wine quality had to improve, and the image of Napa wines had to be raised.

If they expected to get premium prices for their wines — which was, after all, the key to local prosperity — the task at hand for Napa's winemakers was not just to create excellent wines, but to differentiate them from the mass of other, indifferent California wines. A quality product had to be produced and promoted, both by brand and by region. A. R. Morrow, chairman of the Wine Institute's board of directors, addressed the issue squarely at the 1938 Dry Wine Conference at St. Helena when he told the Napa audience: "Your problem is to identify your wine and to educate the consumer and the trade to recognize your dry wine because yours is better."[4]

Quality improvement and definition, regional identification and promotion, and brand development are never-ending jobs, but it is possible to distinguish stages within the progression. The first phase of Napa's post-Repeal identification with wine quality extended to 1938–39, when the outbreak of war in Europe caused American wine marketers on the

East Coast to reexamine California wines. The years 1938–39 also coincided with the advent of industrywide promotion underwritten by the Wine Advisory Board; with the 1939 Golden Gate International Exposition, which focused national attention on California; and with a general improvement in wine quality in an industry that had undergone a five-year "shakeout" period. During that initial period, Napa winemakers joined together with local business to promote the image of Napa Valley as the home of domestic fine wine production. Together, they successfully linked Napa and quality wine production in the minds of wine buyers for years to come.

In the first years following Repeal, the Napa winemakers joined with the St. Helena Chamber of Commerce to promote Napa Valley wines in myriad ways, most of which were chronicled by the *St. Helena Star*. Tours, tastings, brochures, parade floats, and window displays were all employed to keep Napa in the news. As the *Star* put it, "Our prosperity is so largely dependent upon a fair price for grapes, which is in itself dependent upon sufficiently wide consumer acceptance . . . that the means used to promote sales are of direct financial interest to us all."[5] By the end of the decade, new techniques such as public tastings and newsreel footage would be used to promote the Napa Valley, but in 1934, the chamber of commerce turned to the past to involve the entire community of St. Helena in a public celebration of the rebirth of the wine industry: the vintage festival.

The vintage festival was essentially an extravagant "open house" on the part of St. Helena. Held over the three-day Labor Day weekend, just prior to the start of harvest, the festival drew over forty thousand visitors each year—more than the entire population of the county—and promoted St. Helena as the center of quality wine production.[6] The first Vintage Festival had been held in 1912, and festivals were held each following year until Prohibition made the commercial sale of the festival's main product illegal.[7]

Even prior to Repeal, the St. Helena Chamber of Commerce discussed reviving the festival as "a civic celebration" to be "participated in by all local organizations."[8] The festival's purpose was clearly stated by the chamber of commerce, which underwrote its initial costs: "The festival will serve to advertise the community and to impress upon the generation which has grown up since the advent of Prohibition that St. Helena is the center of the nation's wine industry."[9]

St. Helena spared no expense in mounting its first festival since Prohibition. As Director-General A. G. Haskell put it: "Every detail is being carefully arranged so as to make this year's Festival bigger and better than ever. It will constitute St. Helena's celebration in honor of the repeal of the 18th Amendment, and the return of prosperity to the Napa Valley. In addition, it is the effort of a small but wide-awake community to show wine, vineyard, orchard and farm products."[10] Committees were established, tasks parceled out, and the chamber of commerce even hired two consultants: an engineer to "handle placing and decorations of the huge exhibit tent" and a musical producer to script and direct the festival play or "allegory."[11] The planners included all the trappings they could think of: two large parades, one industrial and one floral; a contest to choose a queen to reign over the festival; the queen's grand ball; sporting events, including barrel-rolling contests; and even a "kiddie pet revue."[12] The entire town participated, decorating buildings and turning "Main street, from bridge to bridge" into "a gala boulevard with a beautiful grape arch over Sulphur creek bridge at the entrance to town."[13] The total effort was impressive, especially considering that St. Helena and its environs only had some three thousand inhabitants.

The two most labor-intensive and important features of the festival were the vintage play and the winery exhibits. For the play, or "allegory," as it was referred to by the *Star*, the chamber of commerce hired Arthur Kinney, who had staged a similar event in San Juan Bautista earlier that year. Drawing on its Old World heritage, St. Helena titled the play in Italian, "Il Sogno di Sant'Elena," or "The Dream of St. Helena." Involving over two hundred local folk, the play was elaborate, and the *Star* enthusiastically described the plot:

The play . . . depicts the dream of an early day vintner who dreams asleep in his chair after a hard day's toil. The dream is a prophetic one, covering the early day history of wine making in Napa valley. It includes the arrival of the German, Swiss, and Italian vintners and their selection of Napa valley because of its resemblance to their native lands, the phylloxera plague, the subsequent revival of the wine industry, only to be destroyed by Prohibition, and finally the joyous celebration of repeal. A delightful romance is entwined in the story of the play, and the native costumes and folk songs of the vintners form a colorful background of song and dance.[14]

Reports do not indicate whether the pageant was presented only once, or if it was repeated throughout the festival. Complete with music composed for the occasion, the allegory represented an enormous outpouring of time and money on the part of St. Helena, an expense that was apparently appreciated by the more than forty thousand people who attended the three-day festival.

If the main purpose was to establish Saint Helena as the capital of the state's dry wine production, the main product to be promoted was its wine. The exhibit tent included other agricultural displays, but center stage was given over to elaborate displays arranged by the leading Napa wineries. Dominating the middle of the area was the Beaulieu exhibit, a raised square set on a base of barrels and topped with a circular pyramid of wine bottles, extending twelve to thirteen tiers high to a peak roughly twenty feet from the floor. Larkmead, L. M. Martini, Inglenook, Beringer, Greystone Cellars (Bisceglia Brothers), Lombarda, and Christian Brothers all participated as well. The most novel display was that of the new Napa Valley Cooperative Winery, which created "an elaborate replica of the Golden Gate bridge, built entirely of white and black grapes" spanning "a Golden Gate in which red wine replaced salt water."[15] The wineries also capitalized on the crowds to hold open houses at individual wineries, encouraging tourism and tasting. As the editor of *Wines and Vines* commented a year later in describing the second vintage festival, "Inviting the public to inspect a winery is a phase of merchandising that could well be made a regular affair," although his idea was not acted upon in a coordinated manner until the end of the decade.[16]

When the weekend was over and the visitors had gone, the community paused to catch its breath prior to harvest and to review the accomplishments of the festival. By all measures, it had been a stunning success. The chamber of commerce reported a profit of $1,500 for the festival, aside from the increase in the business of all the local merchants. The festival had attracted a huge crowd and, perhaps more important, had created national publicity for St. Helena and Napa Valley wines: one St. Helena merchant filled a large shop window with "newspaper clippings and pictures taken from newspapers all over the country. New Jersey, Florida and all states in between were among those represented."[17] It was hardly "free" publicity, in that an enormous amount of community effort had gone into the festival, but it was a type of generic promotion that no individual winery could have undertaken, and it helped position the Napa Valley in the minds of potential consumers across the United States.

The 1935 vintage festival was again scheduled for the Labor Day weekend, with initial plans that it was to be on a "bigger and better scale" than the previous season's. A new vintage play, "The Ruby in the Vine," was created and staged. Dances, flower shows, parades, and carnival attractions were included, all in honor of "the great God Bacchus and King Grape."[18] Again, the festival drew over forty thousand visitors and received national publicity. Immediately following its conclusion, the festival's directors announced that it had been a financial success.[19] But the accounting proved premature. By the time all the bills had been paid, the 1935 festival had run a $2,000 deficit, or, as the *Star* reported, "the $1,500 nest egg from the 1934 Festival was wiped out and Chamber funds to the tune of another $500 were required to stage the 1935 celebration."[20]

Debate over the fate of a festival in 1936 continued throughout the remainder of 1935 and into the new year. The *St. Helena Star* editorialized that the two festivals should be considered in aggregate, that the total loss for two years was thus only $500, or $250 per festival. In return for this, "Advertising worth thousands and thousands of dollars was realized. St. Helena wines were publicized by every known method, in all sections of the country. . . . If the purpose of the Festival is kept in mind, the intention to make St. Helena wines household commodities everywhere, the actual cost of $250 a year is not important," concluded the *Star*.[21] The *Star* was correct about the value of the publicity derived from the festival, but the real question was, who should underwrite future fairs?

The obvious answer was the local wineries. In February 1936, the St. Helena Chamber of Commerce sent out cards to all local wineries to canvass support for a 1936 festival. The response was underwhelming: only four cards were returned. The chamber of commerce therefore decided to throw its support to the County Fair in Napa, to be held a week prior to the Labor Day weekend, on which St. Helena vintage festivals had traditionally been held. As the *Star* reported, "The apparent lack of interest in the Festival by those for whom it was given played a large part in the decision not to hold it this year."[22] It was not that the Napa wineries were uninterested, rather that in the depths of the depression, with wine sales slow and extremely competitive, few wineries could afford the time or money needed to underwrite a festival. Carl Bundschu, the manager of Inglenook, attempted to rally the local wineries to go forward with a festival and to seek funding from the Wine Institute, which had promised to contribute an unspecified amount.[23] But the funding fell through, and the task was too great for just a few core individuals. The 1936 harvest thus came and went without a vintage festival.

The passing of the 1936 festival was remarked upon in the editorial column of *Wines and Vines*, one of the two major industry magazines. "To let [the festival] lapse is a pity and a slur on the whole industry," *Wines and Vines* said; "the industry as a whole" should support "this typically California celebration that glorifies the grape and shows in such an effective way how wine contributes to the health and happiness of the state and the nation."[24] Clearly, the festival was an effective promotional vehicle for California wines in general and Napa wines in particular. But as is so often the case with generic promotion, the immediate dollars and cents value to local producers could not be quantified.

In late fall 1936 and throughout the first months of 1937, the chamber of commerce reconsidered support for a 1937 festival. Two changes were proposed. First, the festival should be made simpler and easier to stage. "There would be no carnival and no exhibit tent"; instead, wineries would use "Main street windows for their displays."[25] An elaborate pageant would not be staged, since "the huge cost of such a production" made "success too much of a gamble" and offered "little that cannot be obtained in larger quantities in the city." Instead, the *Star* argued for a "jewel-like show, small in scale" more suited to the size of St. Helena.[26] Second, state funding would be sought through the support of State Senator Frank Gordon, who proposed that a second agricultural district be created for the "up-valley" portion of Napa County, thus making the vintage festival in essence a second County Fair and eligible for state horse-racing funds.[27] By spring, Senator Gordon had given up on his legislation, however, and the chamber of commerce turned to the local community to raise the $3,000 needed to ensure a 1937 festival. Finally, in mid-May, the chamber announced that because "there was still too large a gap between the minimum amount required and money pledged," there would be no festival.[28]

Arguably, the vintage festival fell victim to the depression and slow wine sales, but the festival was just one expression of St. Helena's belief that it was the "center of the dry wine industry of the country" and would ultimately be recognized as such.[29] Throughout the 1930s, the local community worked with Napa wineries to promote Napa County as the home of quality dry wines. In some cases, the chamber of commerce took the lead; in others, it aided representatives from the local wineries. The *Star* always acted as a booster, reporting and commenting on any event that brought St. Helena to the fore.

The local chamber of commerce, on its own and through its connections with the state chamber of commerce, rarely missed an opportunity to promote St. Helena and its wines. It coordinated business tours of the county, lobbied the regional Redwood Empire Association to feature local wineries in an association-sponsored newsreel, and fought to assure prime coverage in the state chamber's business magazine, *California*, whenever that magazine mentioned California wine.[30] The chamber sponsored floats in most regional parades, with grapes and wine always the motif. St. Helena's award-winning entry in the 1934 Santa Rosa Rose Carnival parade "portrayed Bacchus . . . riding on a huge cask," and the Napa County float in the 1936 parade marking the opening of the San Francisco Bay Bridge featured giant grape clusters and a ten-foot-high wine glass, the work of St. Helena winemakers.[31] At the suggestion of the Napa industry, the chamber adopted the slogan "Serve Famous Napa Valley Dry Wines" and urged members to include the phrase on all business stationery. Two years later, the chamber took the idea one step further, arranging for a special cancellation as part of the postal service's celebration of "Air Mail Week." Consisting of a rendering of two men operating a wine press, the cancellation boldly proclaimed "St. Helena, California — the Dry Wine Center of the World."[32] Local boosters believed in the supremacy of Napa wines and took every opportunity to promote their community's product.

Claiming the title of "dry wine center of the world" was perhaps extreme, but St. Helena could point to the results of wine judgings throughout the 1930s to substantiate its assertion that it was the center of quality dry wine production in the state. Beginning in 1934, when the California State Fair reintroduced a commercial wine competition, Napa producers dominated the dry wine categories. In part this was because a relatively large number of dry wine producers in Napa bottled their best wines, rather than selling all wine in bulk to eastern bottlers. This led to a larger number of entries in the dry wine category from Napa than from Alameda or Sonoma counties. But the weight of numbers did not assure awards, and the preponderance of both entries and awards attested to the inherent quality of Napa grapes, as well as to the pursuit of quality on the part of Napa's wineries.

Although other wine competitions were held, most notably in Orange County, the State Fair was preeminent and received the most attention. Wineries awarded top honors were not shy about announcing the fact, since a third-party validation of quality not only helped sales of the award-winning wine but also bolstered the entire product line. Unlike current judgings, which may have over two hundred entrants in one category and will thus often award multiple "gold" medals, the State Fair competition was based on the time-tested "win, place and show" formula. In each category, first, second, and third places were recognized. At times this created a problem, not owing to an excess of quality, but rather because of the reverse. A. R. Morrow, chairman of the 1936 judging, commented that the judges had recommended that "gold, silver and bronze medals be reserved for the really superlative wines," rather than awarded simply to "the leaders of the class in which they are entered."[33] However, the rules of the State Agricultural Society provided that entries only be judged in relation to other entries, rather than in relation to a subjective standard of quality, and the judges complied. The judging was also made complex by the existence of generic categories such as "Burgundy," "Claret," "California Hock," "California Red Chianti," "California Sauterne," and even a "California Chateau Yquem," alongside such varietal categories as "Cabernet" and "Zinfandel."

Whatever the category was called, Napa County wineries dominated in the dry wine competition. In the five years between 1935 and 1939, *Wines and Vines* reported a total of fourteen awards in most categories. During that period, Napa reigned predominant. Half the awards, seven of fourteen, went to Napa in such dry wine categories as "Dry Sauterne," "Chablis," and "Claret." Nine of fourteen awards went to Napa in the "Burgundy" category during the same period. And in the varietal category of Cabernet, Napa wineries took twelve of fourteen possible awards, with a Napa winery taking the gold medal each year.[34] The awards won by Napa were perhaps a testament more to the existence of limited acreage of fine varietals such as Cabernet and Pinot Noir than to careful winemaking. W. V. Cruess of the University of California, who headed the judging team at the 1937 competition, commented that the "dry wines that were made from fine varieties of grapes stood out in no uncertain manner," constituting "proof of what can be done."[35] For the most part, the medal-winning wines represented special bottlings of small lots of wine, only a small portion of Napa's annual production. The award-winning Napa wineries were still producing most of their wines from indifferent varieties and selling the result in bulk to out-of-state bottlers. There was, after all, a very limited market for fine wines. The awards clearly indicate that Napa was capable of producing high-quality wines. The question that remained to be answered was, did a market for them exist?

Napa winemakers certainly attempted to capitalize on state fair awards and to expand the market for their wines through displays, tours, and tastings. In most instances, they aimed at individuals already interested in fine wine and food. Thus in September 1936, Beringer, Inglenook, and Beaulieu joined together to host some fifty members of the Los Angeles branch of the Wine and Food Society, determined to impress on these gourmets that California could match the fine wines of Europe. After spending a day in the Napa Valley visiting and tasting, the society's members returned to the Palace Hotel in San Francisco for a "superb California dinner" served, fittingly, "in the French room." A. R. Morrow of the Wine Institute presided at the table, eliciting comments from the visitors, who admitted that the trip "had made them realize the fine wines that are being made in California."[36]

The next month, these same wineries participated in a novel event, a public wine tasting held in the Palm Court of the Palace Hotel, San Francisco, under the auspices of the Wine Institute. Intended for "epicures and socialites interested in fine wines," the tasting included twenty wineries and drew from three to four thousand participants. The first public tasting since Repeal, the event gave the city's upper class the opportunity to "learn at first hand" which wineries produced "the fancy wines of California." Although the audience was not as specifically defined as that of the Food and Wine Society, most winery representatives agreed that the tasting was "one of the most effective methods of interesting the public in the finer wines."[37]

Although direct interaction with potential consumers was probably the best way to spark interest in wines, Napa wineries participated in more general methods as well. Following the triumph of the county's wineries in the 1937 State Fair, the St. Helena Chamber of Commerce arranged for a "spectacular and colorful exhibit" in the windows of the downtown Emporium, then one of San Francisco's leading department stores. The display consisted of a wine press and crusher, grape cutouts, bottled wines from the major producers, and all sixty-five awards garnered by Napa at the State Fair. Lasting a week, the exhibit extolled "Napa Valley—Land of Abundant Vineyards" to an estimated ten thousand San Franciscans and tourists.[38]

Regional promotion provided a backdrop for the success or failure of Napa wineries. While the identification of Napa with quality wine production in the minds of potential consumers helped all Napa producers, ultimately the responsibility and rewards for brand development lay with the individual wineries. At Repeal, Napa winemakers were faced with the dual task of brand and commodity development. The existing U.S. market for fine wines was minuscule and dominated by European producers. To succeed, Napa wineries had to expand the domestic market for fine wine through education, and they had to produce a consistently high-quality product that would come to be recognized as competing with European imports in quality and prestige. Such brand development was a long, slow process, depending not only on wine quality but upon the personalities of key individuals, strategy, and positioning in the marketplace. Ernest Wente, who with his brother Herman faced a similar struggle in the Livermore Valley, remembered being advised by a friend of his father's that it would take "at least twenty years to build up a good, reputable, honest-to-goodness label."[39]

The prediction was accurate, perhaps optimistic. Not all Napa producers succeeded. Immediately following Repeal, Beaulieu clearly emerged as the marketing leader of the "big four." Although both Beringer and Larkmead had produced sacramental wine during Prohibition, it was Beaulieu that had prospered and expanded, creating a dynamic business organization, staffed by professionals, which allowed for specialization of function. Beaulieu was clearly George de Latour's creation, but by the mid 1920s, it had grown beyond the scope of any one individual to control all facets of production and marketing, and de Latour, who did not have brothers or sisters, like the Beringers, to help manage the business, relied on hired expertise. His son was born deaf, and, as was common in the early twentieth century, was institutionalized throughout his life. His daughter had married a French nobleman, Marquis de Pens, and neither she nor her husband expressed interest in becoming actively involved in the management of Beaulieu while de Latour lived. As Beaulieu expanded, de Latour hired the best available—generally French-speaking—staff to oversee production and sales, creating a business structure that dwarfed those of other Napa wineries and that survived his death in 1940.

Joseph Ponti, an immigrant vineyardist hired prior to Prohibition, eventually became the day-to-day overseer of winemaking operations throughout the 1920s and into the 1930s.[40] Just prior to the advent of Prohibition, de Latour hired Charles Fay as vice president, and the latter managed marketing and sales at Beaulieu until his death in 1938. Fay, who was prominent in San Francisco society and politics, having served as secretary to the mayor and later done an eight-year stint as postmaster of San Francisco during the Wilson administration, presided over the Beaulieu headquarters in San Francisco. Toward the end of Prohibition, he and Ponti were joined by Léon Bonnet, graduate of a research institute at Montpellier in the south of France, who had become a University of California faculty member in enology prior to World War I.[41] Although ill health made Bonnet's tenure at Beaulieu relatively short, he brought with him a level of scientific understanding of winemaking that was rare for the period, which was continued by his French-trained successor, André Tchelistcheff, who joined Beaulieu in 1937.

Beaulieu started from a position of strength and added to it. As a major supplier of altar wine for the Catholic Church, Beaulieu enjoyed a natural market among upper-class Catholics in most cities across the United States. Having produced wine continuously during Prohibition, the winery claimed to have "set aside" "choice white and red wines . . . for aging purposes," which could now be released.[42] As a major supplier of rootstocks and grape cultivars, de Latour had planted five hundred acres of choice varieties in his own vineyards, a fact he was not shy of publicizing. Most of the wine produced from these vineyards was sold as altar wine, used for industrial flavorings, or shipped in bulk to out-of-state bottlers. This arrangement allowed Beaulieu to pick the best lots for bottling and supplied the cash flow necessary for building a market for bottled wines. Given Beaulieu's scientifically trained wine-maker, choice grapes, and strong management, it is not surprising that the *California Wine Review* commented in 1935 on the winery's "extensive distribution of cased wines to Eastern markets" and the "steadily widening outlets for the Beaulieu products."[43]

Success begets success. In 1936, de Latour made two more key hires: Jack Stanton, a traveling representative for Beaulieu, and Leon Munier, a writer, editor, and publicist for the wine industry, who had worked with both Italian Swiss Colony and the dominant California Wine Association as an "advertising and publicity man" prior to Prohibition.[44] In Stanton, de Latour recruited youthful energy, a road salesman who traveled throughout the United States conducting classes on wine sales-manship and promoting Beaulieu. Such classes for retailers and wine stewards became an integral part of Beaulieu's brand-development strat-egy, educating key individuals who would in turn relate to the consumer. In Munier, de Latour acquired a mature publicist with over thirty years of connections throughout the U.S. wine industry. Hired in late Decem-ber 1936, Munier moved quickly, producing a new promotional booklet by February 1937 that gave "ten good reasons why [Beaulieu] wines are popular among discriminating wine lovers everywhere."[45]

In January 1938, following the death of the 74-year-old Charles Fay, de Latour made his final major hire, setting Beaulieu on a course that it kept to after his own death in 1940. For his new general manager, de Latour picked the 35-year-old, Italian-born assistant manager of San Francisco's Palace Hotel, L. M. Fabbrini. A cultured man, trained in ho-tel management in Europe, Fabbrini had a true love of wines and was at home in the upper-class surroundings where Beaulieu's products would be sold. He thus fitted in perfectly with Beaulieu's marketing strategy, and he successfully managed the winery until his death in 1946, when his brother, Aldo, who had been in charge of sales in New York, became general manager, a position he held until he retired in 1962.

Nine months prior to the hiring of L. M. Fabbrini, *Wines and Vines* had asserted that "the best listed California bottled wines in the United States are undoubtedly the Beaulieu Vineyard wines," going on to say that Beaulieu wines were named in "over 400 wine lists of the most exclusive and representative hotels, restaurants and clubs in all the leading cities."[46] Placements in such image-building accounts put Beaulieu's offerings on a par with imported wines and built brand awareness. Fabbrini also helped American restaurateurs to better merchandise wines in general by drawing on his experience at the Palace Hotel, where he had introduced a program of wine education and service that had raised "wine orders" to "the highest percentage in any American hotel."[47]

By the late 1930s, Beaulieu was clearly the leader in California premium wines. In 1937, it had acquired distribution on the East Coast through Park & Tilford, an old importing firm, and the Midwest was opened up to it the following year by D. Richeter and Co. of Chicago, which noted, "The demand for better quality wines is steadily increasing."[48] Nonetheless, although the combination of managerial talent, winemaking skill, high-quality grapes, promotional energy, and aggressive salesmanship marked Beaulieu as the leader, not just in the Napa Valley, but throughout California, it was of a very small market segment. Most Beaulieu wine was sold in bulk to out-of-state bottlers, and sweet fortified altar wine remained a significant portion of its product mix. Thinking back to his arrival at Beaulieu in 1937, Tchelistcheff said out-of-state distribution of its bottled wine was "sporadic" and sales in San Francisco were "negligible," while those in Los Angeles were "ridiculous" and "microscopic."[49] Clearly, there was room for growth and for other producers of premium wines.

The other three members of the big four were at best junior partners, much smaller organizations than Beaulieu. In the case of Inglenook, size was primarily the result of a focused ideal originally articulated by Gustav Niebaum and reinvigorated by his widow: the estate winery, growing and vinifying its own grapes. Necessarily limited in size by vineyard holdings and concentrating on the production of high-quality wines only, Inglenook neither required nor could have supported the massive sales and management organization of Beaulieu. Immediately following Repeal, Mrs. Niebaum hired Carl Bundschu as general manager, who in turn brought in John Gross, an experienced pre-Prohibition winemaker, to direct cellar operations.[50] Bundschu served as general manager from

1933 through 1939, helping to reestablish Inglenook as a top quality producer and, from 1936 through 1939, training Mrs. Niebaum's grand-nephew, John Daniel, Jr., who inherited the winery following her death in 1936.

Bundschu was an excellent choice, both for Inglenook and Napa Valley.[51] Born into the wine trade, he was a tireless promoter of quality in wines, whether entertaining society leaders from San Francisco with pre-Prohibition wines from the Inglenook cellar, which he employed to display the continuity of quality from past to present, or representing Napa winemakers at Wine Institute meetings. He continued the pre-Prohibition Inglenook tradition of vintage dating wines released under the main Inglenook label, and many of the wines produced during his six years as manager were varietally identified, including releases of Traminer, Riesling, Charbono, and Cabernet Sauvignon.[52] When John Daniel, Jr., took over day-to-day management of Inglenook in 1939, he assumed control of a well-positioned company with a clear market niche as the top Napa producer. Beaulieu may have been more profitable, selling larger amounts of more types of wine, but Inglenook consistently received the highest prices. The Niebaum fortune had allowed Bundschu the luxury to concentrate on quality, and Bundschu had performed admirably in helping to fulfill Gustav Niebaum's dream. For almost the next three decades, Inglenook remained identified as one of the top quality producers in the Napa Valley.[53]

To the north, Beringer Brothers, faced with its own set of problems and opportunities, developed a distinctive marketing strategy and market position by combining efficient bulk production of sweet and dry wines with retail sales of bottled wine at the winery. With 350 acres of its own vineyards, Beringer was almost as large as Beaulieu and over three times the size of Inglenook. However, unlike those of Beaulieu and Inglenook, the majority of its plantings were of nonpremium varietals that had been set out or grafted during Prohibition.[54] Without access to premium varieties, Beringer could not really compete at the highest quality level in the dry wine categories.[55] Its major assets were a large, historic, and picturesque winery and sufficient quantities of medium-quality grapes. It is not surprising, then, that the Beringers and their winemaker, Fred Abruzzini, chose to emphasize both bulk wine sales to out-of-state bottlers and retail sales of bottled wine to tourists.

Beringer was owned by the sons and daughters of Jacob Beringer, who had founded the winery with his brother Frederick. But at the tail end of Prohibition, Jacob Beringer, Jr., the eldest son and winery manager, left Beringer, trading his shares in Beringer to his siblings for vine-yard land. In 1932, the remaining brothers and sisters hired Fred Abruz-zini, an experienced winemaker who had worked through Prohibition for Cribari and Sons producing altar wines, as winemaker and general manager. Sales and general financial matters were handled by Charles Beringer, Jacob Sr.'s youngest son, out of the Beringer sales office in San Francisco, but day-to-day management rested firmly in Abruzzini's hands. Although a third generation of Beringers, most notably Otto Beringer's son and son-in-law, worked in production under Abruzzini's direction, it was Abruzzini and Charles Beringer who set the winery's course until Charles Beringer's death in 1954 and Abruzzini's retirement in 1956.[56]

Abruzzini and the Beringers quickly recognized that the post-Repeal market was for sweet fortified wines rather than table wines. In 1935, rather than go on buying brandy to fortify Beringer wines, Abruzzini erected his own still and began producing both brandy and fortifying alcohol from the wines spoiled by high volatile acidity that were in stor-age at Beringer and throughout the valley.[57] Fortified wines predomi-nated in the Beringer sales mix, accounting for an estimated 80 percent of its bottled wine sales, with the remaining percentage split between sweet white table wine and dry red and white table wines.[58] The still proved an excellent investment, providing a source of income through custom distillation for other wineries and allowing Beringer to intro-duce its own line of brandy in 1937. By then, Beringer more resembled a small version of a large Central Valley winery, selling most of its wines in bulk, and with fortified wine presiding over a wide-ranging product line, than it did a North Coast dry table wine producer.[59]

If Abruzzini and Beringer produced sweet fortified wines, it did not mean that they had turned their back on their Napa Valley heritage. They were simply meeting the demands of the majority of contemporary wine drinkers. Abruzzini and Beringer realized, too, that they had history, location, and romance to sell along with their wines. The Beringer win-ery was the oldest continuously operated winery in the valley; the beau-tiful multistoried Rhine House adjoined the winery grounds and was easily visible from Highway 29; and the caves dug into the hillside adja-cent to the winery provided a unique tourist attraction.

Starting in 1934, when he opened the winery to the public during the St. Helena vintage festival, Abruzzini pursued an aggressive policy of tours and retail sales at the winery. He recognized that he had "to intro-duce people to buy wines so I started inviting people to come to the winery."[60] In a 1937 piece on Beringer, *Wines and Vines* commented that although the winery had been modernized, "care has been taken not to destroy any of the old-world atmosphere which lends charm to this sixty-year-old establishment," concluding, "Visitors are welcome at all times."[61] During the 1939 Golden Gate International Exposition at Treasure Island, while other Napa wineries were content with participating in a static display, Abruzzini traveled to the Napa exhibit almost every night, inviting fair visitors to visit Beringer the following day, and even providing maps with directions on how to get to Beringer.[62] Abruzzini's efforts paid off in brand development and sales. While other wineries opened for private groups by appointment, Abruzzini established a retail salesroom, encouraged informal visits, and by 1940 almost one-third of Beringer's 40,000 cases of bottled wine were sold at the winery.[63]

The personal connections and concomitant opportunities for brand development inherent in a policy of tours were probably best exemplified by Abruzzini's interaction with Carole Lombard and her husband, Clark Gable. In 1940, Lombard visited Beringer while filming *They Knew What They Wanted*, a comedy set in the Napa Valley. Abruzzini personally guided Lombard and Gable through Beringer, selling them sixty-one cases of wine, which Gable distributed to friends in the Hollywood community. More important than the sale though, was the connection. Lombard invited Abruzzini and the Beringers to attend the film's San Francisco premiere and to use the opportunity to promote Beringer wines by bringing barrels and pictures to the theater.[64] Such associations were important for brand development, even if the dollar value was hard to quantify.

Consumers who could not visit Beringer were nonetheless encouraged to identify the winery with Old World romance. In 1937, Beringer introduced a full-color folding display panel, designed to "dominate any [retailer's] floor space or store window," depicting

in full natural color photography, six sharply detailed Beringer Bottled Wines, which stand out from a cleverly blended composite background of Napa hillside vineyards, luscious grape clusters and a glimpse of the underground wine tunnels, looking down a long vista between rows of oval casks. Everything that produces quality is suggested visually and instantly—the fine grapes, the sloping vineyards warmed by the sunny blue California sky, and the wine being aged under ideal cellar conditions.[65]

Across the top of the display were the words "Beringer Bros. Inc., Napa County Wines Since 1876. St. Helena, Calif." The bottom of the center panel boasted in smaller type: "Owners of Famous Underground Tunnels." The display was impressive, suggesting quality, tradition, and romance. All six bottles pictured were of generic wines — Sherry, Burgundy, Riesling, Sauterne, and two carbonated wines, a Moselle and a Burgundy — but these were not wines for connoisseurs; they were moderately-priced wines for consumers just being introduced to wines.[66] The Beringer wines were not of as high a quality as those of Inglenook or the best of Beaulieu, but they were as good or better than the wines coming from the Central Valley. For many consumers, Beringer wines served as a first introduction to Napa Valley wines, and the imagery of sunlit hillside vineyards and tunnels filled with wine barrels reinforced the notion of Napa Valley as the home of hand-crafted quality wines.

By 1938, then, a few wineries had emerged as Napa's quality producers: Beaulieu, Inglenook, Beringer, and Larkmead in the heart of the valley; the Christian Brothers' Mt. La Salle to the south; and, waiting in the wings to release its first wines, L. M. Martini. Their status as industry leaders was confirmed by their participation in the 1939 Golden Gate Exposition at Treasure Island. The large bulk producers, such as Mondavi's Sunny St. Helena, Lou Stralla's Napa Wine Company, and the Napa Valley Cooperative Winery, chose not to spend the money on what was basically a form of brand promotion. With no brand to promote, why participate? The handful of other Napa producers that had survived the initial post-Repeal years had essentially become small processors of wine from specific vineyards, eking out an existence by selling their wine in bulk to large producers in California or niche markets back east.

The Golden Gate Exposition ran from February 18 to December 2, 1939. Planning for wine industry participation had begun in mid 1937. Led by Carl Bundschu, a special committee of the Wine Institute investigated the costs of establishing a "Wine Temple" within the proposed Food and Beverage Palace and determined that at least $50,000 would be required.[67] Using the organization of the 1915 Panama-Pacific International Exposition as a model, Bundschu's committee recommended that a nonprofit corporation, Viticultural Industries, be created to establish the temple, selling exhibit space to individual producers to raise the necessary funds. Proponents claimed that collective action would allow "publicity and promotion of California wine on a scale far beyond anything that could be attempted by a few producers exhibiting independently," and that the inner Wine Temple would "be devoted to promoting California wines, without reference to brands." Exhibitors would be

allocated space for individual winery displays in the courtyard surrounding the educational display. The planners encouraged "producers who
have no products to sell to the public under their own names" to contribute too, since they would "reap equal benefits from the educational
accomplishments of the industry exhibit."[68]

The response from the wine industry was underwhelming. The goal
of $50,000 was met, and an impressive two-story, 3,400-square-foot
Wine Temple erected, but only 38 of the state's approximately 560 bonded
wineries participated as sponsors or exhibitors.[69] Of these, five were
from Napa. Beringer, Inglenook, Larkmead, and Beaulieu combined
dollars to create one large exhibit lauding Napa's "four points of superiority . . . soil, climate, proper varieties of grapes, and proper aging."[70]
The final participating Napa winery, Mt. La Salle, joined with another
wine-producing Catholic order, Novitiate of Los Gatos, in a separate
display. L. M. Martini Grape Products Company took part as well, but
as a sweet wine producer from the Central Valley rather than as a dry
wine producer from Napa. It was estimated that twenty million people
attended the fair, although not all passed through the Wine Temple.
Clearly, the Wine Temple was a necessary statement from the producers
of California's second largest agricultural commodity, and probably an
effective promotional aid for California wine. Participation by Napa producers was not solely a tool for brand development; it was also a statement that they were among the industry leaders, that in this instance
they were on par with Roma, Petri, Shewan-Jones, or Italian Swiss
Colony.[71]

The failure of over 90 percent of California's wine industry to participate in the Wine Temple was partially a result of the economic climate,
but it clearly shows the problem inherent in organizing voluntary action
by individual firms for their common good — in this case, promotion of
California wine. Despite the avowed intentions of its promoters, the
Wine Temple was not simply a concrete form of generic advertising. It
was also a venue for brand development. Even if the Wine Temple had
been devoted solely to the generic promotion of California wine, in all
probability it would have been the brand owners, rather than the bulk
producers, who would primarily have benefited. Although most wine
left California in bulk tank cars, it was generally sold to consumers in
glass containers after being bottled by one of the approximately 1,500
out-of-state bottlers.[72] Raw bulk wine was a commodity, subject to sav-
age price competition. Bottled and labeled wine was a branded good,
in a competitive environment to be sure, but generally capable of com-

manding significantly higher profit margins than bulk wine. It was the brand owners, the producers of bottled wine, who gained the most from an increase in wine consumption. Generic advertising was clearly needed, but who should pay for it?

The establishment and funding of generic market development had been a major goal of the Wine Institute since its inception in 1934. Voluntary support of past programs had proved inadequate, and the institute saw in the California Marketing Act of 1937, which allowed the development of agricultural commodity marketing boards, a mechanism to force 100 percent participation and funding of a new marketing order dedicated to increasing consumption of California wines. The Wine Institute, a voluntary organization, thus enthusiastically backed the creation of a new marketing order, the Wine Advisory Board, which would collect gallonage assessments from California producers, .75 of a cent per gallon for dry wine and 1 1/2 cents per gallon for sweet wines, to be used for market development.[73] At a time when average-quality dry wine was available in bulk at under 20 cents a gallon, such an assessment amounted to about 5 percent of value.

Under the law, 65 percent of producers had to vote in favor of the proposed marketing order, and its proponents used the logic of "a rising tide lifts all ships" to urge the marketing order's passage. Harry Caddow of the Wine Institute argued that the potential U.S. wine market had "scarcely been scratched," and that wine had "the greatest marketing opportunity ever opened to an American farm product."[74] Clearly, an oversupply of grapes existed, as evidenced by the 1938 prorate, which forced distillation of 45 percent of the grape crop. Did the industry want to control production or expand consumption? "All the pro rates, all the legal measures whereby quantities are regulated are, to our belief, not a fraction so important as intelligent means of stimulating consumption," the *St. Helena Star* editorialized.[75] The industry was convinced and voted overwhelmingly in favor of the Wine Advisory Board, which officially came into existence on October 24, 1938.

It is impossible to determine the actual effectiveness of the Wine Advisory Board's work in increasing consumption of California wine in general, and its effect on the sales of Napa wineries in particular. In its early years, roughly half the board's funds went into an advertising campaign that targeted middle-class consumers, urging them, for example, "Come dinnertime enjoy some wine from California grapes."[76] Advocates of the marketing order pointed to a 20 percent increase in wine shipments when the first quarter of 1940 was compared with the first quarter of 1938. But by 1940, the United States was already entering a wartime economy, and comparing 1940 with the recession year of 1938 perhaps gives a misleading estimate of the effectiveness of generic advertising. Still, such advertising could not hurt, even if it probably differentially benefited those producers emphasizing bottled wine sales.

From the perspective of California's bottled wine producers and marketers, the other 50 percent of the Wine Advisory Board's allocations, which were split between dealer education and trade barrier removal, were more important.[77] The industry analyst Lou Gomberg, who worked for the Wine Institute at the time, recalled that the "purpose of the Wine Advisory Board from its inception was to provide funds for lobbying. They didn't call it lobbying . . . the term they used . . . is 'trade barrier' work. . . . It provided funds that otherwise would have had to be raised by dues of Wine Institute members."[78] In 1937, Harry Caddow, secretary-manager of the Wine Institute, had commented that of the forty-eight states, only six were really open for wine sales, and that "many of the remaining forty-two States are still closed to wine by obstacles comparable in some instances to foreign embargoes."[79] Lowering taxes on wines, which in some cases were twice the cost per gallon of standard bulk wine, reducing license fees, and pushing to allow wine sales in grocery stores, where it would be "accessible to the housewife who might include healthful wine among the daily articles of food she buys for her table," were all examples of "trade barrier work" benefiting bottled wine producers.[80]

Probably most important to the quality Napa wineries was the Wine Advisory Board's educational work with wholesalers and retailers. Prior to the board's creation, the Wine Institute had produced a sixteen-page booklet, *California Wines*, to familiarize the wine trade with California regions, wine types, production methods, and service. This work was expanded by the Wine Advisory Board, which contracted with the Wine Institute to hire, train, and support a "crew of dealers' service men" who were to be responsible for "direct personal contact with dealers in wine" in most U.S. markets.[81] Gomberg recalled that "forty-five or fifty" individuals were "sent around the country to talk to wholesalers and key retailers."[82] Their mission was to encourage the sale of California wine, but the natural tendency was to emphasize wine bottled by California producers rather than California bulk wine bottled by out-of-state producers. For the Napa wineries, which, with the possible exception of Beaulieu, really could not afford extensive sales teams, the institute's field men became a surrogate sales force, supplementing each winery's individual efforts. While the institute's employees were not partisans of one brand or another, the actual number of higher-end California producers was so limited that Napa wines were generally included when the institute field men "brought out their best" for tastings. Napa wineries clearly got their money's worth from this facet of the Wine Advisory Board's activities.

Starting in 1938, Napa producers entered into a new stage of brand development, one marked by increasing product differentiation and, at least in the case of some successful Napa brands, a continued emphasis on quality, defined in terms of varietally labeled and vintage-dated wine. Although the 1938 prorate program was indicative of a statewide surplus of grapes, quality dry wine producers that had established brand recognition through the sale of bottled wine saw a gradual increase in interest in California wines on the part of eastern wholesalers, especially those who had previously handled only imported wines. Partially, this was the result of an overall improvement in California wine after the five-year shake-out period that followed Repeal. Partially, it reflected increased public attention paid to California wine owing to the combined effects of the Wine Advisory Board's generic advertising campaign and the national media's emphasis on California resulting from the 1939 Golden Gate Exposition at Treasure Island. Primarily though, the interest in higher-quality California wine was fueled by a realization on the part of importers that war was coming to Europe, war that would at best interrupt shipment of fine wine and at worst would end all commerce with the European continent.

For the California industry as a whole, dominated as it was by sweet wine producers from the Central Valley, the U.S. market for fine wines was not terribly important, amounting to perhaps 5 percent of all wine sold.[83] But for Napa wineries producing quality dry wines, the market portion controlled by European wines was the exact niche desired. In the lead article in the January 1938 issue of *Wines and Vines*, E. M. Sheehan reviewed the past year's wine sales, saying that makers of premium California wines "felt as if they have not been making a great deal of headway, and one of the particular reasons . . . is that imported European wines of unknown quality and yet bearing the imported label are being sold in the United States very often at prices lower than the domestic high-class wines. Naturally this has curtailed the avenues of distribution for the domestic classy wines."[84]

During 1938, "avenues of distribution" opened to "domestic classy wines" as East Coast importers began to search for higher-quality California wines to augment their line of imported European wines. Being selected by a prominent East Coast importer generally meant immediate access to key national markets for California wineries. It also meant listening to and taking marketing advice from the importer, who in some cases insisted upon varietal-specific labeling in lieu of European place-name appellations such as "Sauterne" and "Burgundy." Such labeling requests renewed identity and status questions for the California wine industry, sparked a continued debate in 1940 and 1941, and, ultimately, set the California industry in a new direction in defining quality in wine.

The post-Repeal California wine industry suffered from an inferiority complex with regards to European wines, while at the same time exacerbating its problem by its continued use of European place-names to describe its own products. Throughout much of the United States, and especially on the East Coast, imported wines were considered by many consumers and members of the trade to be superior to California wines. Quite possibly the prejudice was correct. Much of the California wine shipped immediately following Repeal was of poor quality, a blend of just-fermented wine and high-volatile-acid wine stored too long during Prohibition. Although some members of the California industry were willing to admit this truth in private, the public voice of the industry, as represented by such publications as the *Wine Review* and *Wines and Vines*, declared that California wines were just as good as imports, that European producers were exporting poor-quality wines at inflated prices, and that the U.S. public, chasing the "will-o'-the-wisp lure of the fanciful word 'imported' " was being deliberately misled by East Coast importers and wine snobs interested only in high profits.[85]

The California industry's voice grew particularly strident whenever the European producers, or their importers, raised the vexing issue of California's use of European place-names. At the Madrid Convention of 1891, representatives of the major European wine-producing regions had agreed not to trade in wines that had misappropriated specific European place-names. However, the United States had never signed the treaty, and U.S. winemakers had continued to use names such as "Burgundy," "Sauterne," "Port," "Sherry," "Moselle," and the ever-popular "Champagne."[86] Following Repeal, U.S. winemakers reintroduced these terms, arguing that they represented generic types of wines, well known to consumers. Importers demurred, suggesting that California find its own distinctive names. In 1933, the *California Grape Grower*, which subsequently became *Wines and Vines*, commented: "It is rather amusing these days to read the suggestions of importers that California winemen refrain from using European wine district names on their wine labels."[87]

The amusement disappeared two years later in 1935, when new labeling requirements and new standards of identity for U.S. wines were proposed as part of the Federal Alcohol Administration Act, which was introduced after the Supreme Court declared the National Industrial Recovery Act unconstitutional. Marion DeVries, the Wine Institute's legal counsel in Washington, D.C., reported menacingly:

Great foreign forces are moving through various channels by treaties between foreign nations and by every device known to deny vintners of the United States the use of the very common names such as "Port" and "Sherry" and other well-known wine names. It takes no argument to emphasize the fact that any such inhibition in its fulfillment would entirely destroy our wine markets for our domestic products and turn them over to the foreign importers.[88]

The eventual compromise was to allow U.S. winemakers to use European appellations as descriptive of a particular "type" of wine but to require California producers to place the adjective "California" in direct conjunction with the wine type in lettering "substantially as conspicuous and emphatic."[89] California wineries were thus able to go on using European place-names, but the general antagonism in the industry to European wines and their representatives, the importers, increased.

The Federal Alcohol Administration's Regulation No. 4, promulgated on January 3, 1936, did more than deal with the issue of California's use of European appellations. It codified standards of identity and nomenclature for wines and required that every producer who shipped wine in interstate commerce possess a certificate of label approval for that wine. It demanded that certain information appear on all labels, dictating the type size, and in some cases the location, of the information. A confusing and legalistic twenty-four pages of text, requiring the submission by domestic producers and importers of an estimated 60,000 labels by December 15, 1936, it amounted to what *The Wine Review* called "a veritable revolution in the labeling of California wines." Expensive and troublesome though this was, it provided "definite, nationally enforceable nomenclature, quality and labeling requirements for wine" for the first time, Harry Caddow noted.[90]

This was small solace to winemakers forced to submit labels for approval in an attempt to meet the December 15 deadline. Larkmead's experience was typical. In early April 1936, Felix Salmina wrote the Federal Alcohol Administration saying that he had forwarded labels for approval in February but had not yet had a reply. Larkmead was now almost out of labels and wanted to print new ones, but "since it is necessary to have these labels printed in large quantities we are most desirous of knowing if our label in its present form . . . meets with the requirements of the labeling regulations." Salmina was no doubt disheartened to learn that his label needed to be redone, since his phrase "from selected grapes" required "the amount in percent by volume of the grapes used which are, in fact, selected grapes."[91] Hundreds of producers and importers experienced similar frustrations, to the point that the Wine Institute issued a series of specimen labels, including one that illustrated "the seventeen most common errors to be avoided in labeling."[92]

Although the California industry was focused primarily on the issue of European place-names, far-reaching other definitions were made. Wines named for varieties henceforth had to contain at least 51 percent of the named variety, vintage-dated wines had to be produced entirely from the stated vintage, and wines were permitted to be given geographical names, such as those of counties or towns, providing that 51 percent of the grapes came from the stated region.[93] Some producers argued that Zinfandel and Riesling should be considered wine "types" as well as varieties, but by and large, few were concerned with these regulations, since only a handful of California wineries were producing varietally labeled wines. However, it was this small group that would, to some degree inadvertently, cause the question of European appellations to once again rear its head.

In early 1937, the *St. Helena Star* commented in an editorial about a group of East Coast importers who had traveled to France after the tariff on French wines had been reduced: "Of all the ridiculous junkets, that of Eastern wine merchants to France to learn something of winemaking is the cream of the crop. . . . The idea of turning their back on California, where the world's best wines are now made would be funny if it did not indicate serious French attempts to capitalize on the lowered tariff on their products."[94]

The overblown rhetoric masked the California industry's sense of inferiority, but the *Star* would no doubt have been surprised to know that within two years, eastern wine merchants would travel to California to sample, select, and buy California wines. Even in 1937, the first crack in the monolith of importers' wine lists had become visible when Wildman and Company, a San Francisco importer of fine wines, experimented with California wines by adding a red and a white wine "labeled under their own geographical names" to its list. Wildman chose a white wine produced by Wente Brothers from the Livermore Valley and a red wine from Inglenook, labeled "Rutherford Red," with the description "Dry and Full Bodied." The wines were selected by Wildman in the cask and specially bottled and labeled, since Wildman, like most importers, believed that "no California wine should have a European name, but rather should be designated by its own geographical locality."[95] The crack widened the following year when the old and respected New York importer Park & Tilford announced that it would handle distribution of Beaulieu wines on the Atlantic coast as well as in Pennsylvania, Texas, Louisiana, and Missouri. Declaring that the quality of most domestic wine had "improved tremendously," Park & Tilford expressed certainty that a new market for domestic wine was "bound to develop." But hidden in the middle of the announcement was a cautionary note: "There will always be a certain class of people who will demand foreign wines of excellent character."[96] The improved California wines could not, in other words, be expected to displace fine European wines entirely.

In spring 1939, in what might be akin to the devil visiting the Vatican, the wine writer and importer Frank Schoonmaker made an extended trip through California's dry wine districts, ultimately selecting several wines to supplement his company's portfolio of imported wines. Schoonmaker was infamous among California winemakers for his 1934 publication of *The Complete Wine Book*, a candidly written text that emphasized European wines and "slightly disparaged" California wines.[97] Schoonmaker's book proved influential, but in the opinion of many in the California wine industry, it was a classic of wine snobbery, perpetuating the "myth" of the superiority of foreign wines at the expense of the domestic product. In California winemakers' eyes, Schoonmaker's bias toward French wines was confirmed in 1935 when he started Frank Schoonmaker and Company with his co-author Tom Marvel and Alexis Lichine and began importing European wines to the East Coast. The California industry's reaction to Schoonmaker was more an example of its own provincialism and insecurity than an accurate perception of reality, but for many winemakers, Schoonmaker was the enemy incarnate, the archetypal importer intent on depriving the industry of its use of European place-names, while disparaging its products.[98] Schoonmaker's visit to California was considered an overdue acknowledgment of the quality of the state's wine, but it was also viewed with suspicion.

Schoonmaker traveled throughout California, just as he did in France, visiting wineries, meeting the winemakers, and tasting from the barrel. As his partner Tom Marvel explained, "We have never bought and listed a bottle of wine from a person we did not know personally, nor a bottle of wine from a vineyard that we have never seen."[99] In December 1939, after considering over five hundred wines, Schoonmaker made selections from five producers: Wente Brothers of Livermore, Fountain Grove of Santa Rosa, Paul Masson of Saratoga, and Inglenook and Larkmead in the Napa Valley, giving these wineries immediate access to the twenty-four states in which his firm operated.[100] The following year, he added two more wineries: the sparkling wine producer F. Korbel in Sonoma County and L. M. Martini of the Napa Valley, which had just sold its Central Valley operation, allowing concentration on dry wines.[101]

Schoonmaker promoted his new selections in his spring bulletin, offering a candid appraisal of the sixteen California wines, presented in the form of an inter-office memo that his company's "executives would turn in if they had tasted these wines for the first time, and if the wines were not ours."

As a group, these are the best American wines that we have tasted since Prohibition. . . . They are all, in our opinion, honest, clean and sound. The better wines have excellent balance and a certain amount of distinction, the less expensive ones are of the more ordinary table-type wines. . . . The older and finer red wines have plenty of body and flavor [but] lack . . . softness coupled with fullness. . . . Had they been kept in small oak cooperage they . . . would have been ready for bottling sooner and would now have more of the polish and bouquet which a wine only acquires in glass. . . . The white wines are also pretty full, and apparently made from grapes picked too late. . . . The alcoholic content of the wines is, as a result, fairly high and the acidity is too low. The wines, as a result, like the white wines of southern Italy and the Rhône Valley and Spain, have a slight tendency to "go yellow." Such technical questions aside, these are good wines, vastly better than the ordinaires which the average Frenchman drinks. They are, it seems to us, American wines in which we can take honest patriotic pride and which anyone can serve without apology to his friends.[102]

The description was objective, gentle, and damning with faint praise. What Schoonmaker described as "the best American wines" that he "had tasted since Prohibition" were wines that could be served "without apology to friends." California's best wines, although better than the *vins ordinaires* of Europe, were clearly not in the same league as the first growths of France. Schoonmaker's judgment was no doubt accurate. But accuracy did not make the assessment especially palatable to the California industry as a whole.

Particularly bothersome to many California producers was Schoonmaker's requirement that his selected wines eschew European place-name appellations in favor of specific geographic and varietal information. As

Schoonmaker's catalog put it, "the labels give specific information con-
cerning their [the wines'] origin—where they were made, by whom,
when and from what grape."[103] His initial offering included an Inglenook Napa Cabernet and a Livermore Valley Zinfandel. The following
year, he introduced a wide range of vintage-dated, varietal-specific wines
from L. M. Martini, including a 1937 Pinot Noir, a 1935 and a 1938 Cabernet from Napa, a Sonoma Sylvaner, and a Santa Cruz Folle Blanche.
Promoted under the slogan, "American Names for American Wines,"
the wines were well received in the eastern market. Schoonmaker was
well connected with the "carriage trade," advertised in the *New Yorker*
and *Town and Country*, and even sold a mail-order "California Sampler"
direct to consumers.[104]

By mid 1940, most quality producers recognized that the European
war presented a golden opportunity for brand development. In the December issue of the *Wine Review*, Hal Marquis commented:

We would be depraved indeed if we found satisfaction in profiting from
another's misfortune. Nevertheless, there are some in the American wine
industry who are benefiting. . . . The small U.S. market for choice and fancy
wines, previously dominated to a large extent by foreign products, is now
suddenly opened to the wine producers of our own country. . . . Now, as a
direct result of the war and the stoppage of French and Italian imports, the
carriage folk are turning to the fine wines of our own country. . . . Long
established wholesale and retail wine firms . . . are now scurrying about frantically trying to line up supplies of the best California wines. . . . California
growers who have invested much time and money in producing only wines
of high quality have a seller's market.[105]

The St. Helena Chamber of Commerce also recognized the opportunity
to promote the Napa Valley, and conferred with the Napa and Calistoga
chambers of commerce to buy advertising in "a swanky Eastern journal,"
since the valley was "in the most favorable spot of any region in the entire
country to benefit from the removal of French wines from competition,
leaving a market ready to capture."[106] But one cost of capturing the new
market was the reopening of the labeling and appellation controversy.

In July 1941, in an editorial with the martial title "Defense Program
for U.S. Wines," the *Wine Review* declared: "A major effort has been
made to convince the wine consuming public that wine labeling in this
country is dishonest," asserting that importers who "formerly did a
highly profitable business in foreign wines . . . wish to preserve their
profits by keeping alive the myth that the wines of this country are inferior to those of Europe."[107] In case readers were wondering just who

they were referring to, the *Wine Review* fired a shot across Schoonmaker's bow, claiming, "Only those American wines which are handled by a small group of importers have escaped resounding condemnation and even those have occasionally been belittled in order to keep wide open the market for foreign product when it once more becomes available."[108]

The strategy that kept premium California wines from claiming a permanent spot in eastern markets, the *Wine Review* argued, was certain importers' insistence on varietal labeling, which created an artificial distinction between French and California wines, implying the latter's inferiority. Over the next several issues, the *Wine Review* trotted out industry warhorses such as Leon Munier and Carl Bundschu to pen pieces defending the sanctity of California's use of European place-name appellations and threatening dire consequences if varietal and American geographic appellations were pursued. It was entertaining reading, even if it shed more heat than light. The core argument was articulated by Munier in an ominously titled article, "Wine Men Are Warned." "While certain wineries are now enjoying a nice business in wines bearing varietal names," he wrote, "they have created a stepping-stone to legislate the California wine-type out of existence." He concluded with the question: "Gentlemen: are you going to sacrifice the California wine-business by espousing the idea of adopting grape-varietal names to suit the needs of persons who have no regard or sentiment for California wines?"[109] Marvel responded for Schoonmaker in the next issue, commenting that Munier "seems to feel that a gang of wicked literary cutthroats from back East is trying to side-track the California wine industry, sending it sprawling into the ditch of honest, varietal-geographical names, where it is expected to whither away."[110]

Why did the California old guard respond with such passion to the idea of varietal and geographic labeling? Did they really believe that because perhaps 1 percent of wine bottled in California was varietally labeled, California would lose its right to employ "wine-type" labeling using European place-name appellations? Or were they responding instead to the emerging segmentation of the industry, to a realization that California winemaking was changing, that there was now a spectrum of fine bottled wine produced in California, and that the "one size fits all" formula inherent in "wine-type" labeling did not adequately convey differences in wines?

"Wine-type" labeling was essentially a way of giving a bulk commodity a patina of quality and making producers feel better about themselves and their product. It served a useful purpose because it adequately conveyed the type of product and was not intended to differentiate based upon quality. A heavier dry red wine became "Burgundy," while a lighter dry red was "Claret" or perhaps "Zinfandel." Dry white wine was transformed into "Sauterne," and a white table wine sweetened with Muscat concentrate became "Riesling" or "Moselle." If a winemaker substituted neutral concentrate for the Muscat, the resulting wine might be termed "Haute Sauterne." But all were sold by the gallon, pumped into railcars, and shipped east.

The utility of "wine-type" labeling became questionable when a part of the California industry began to shift from a commodity to a brand focus. The unspoken, and partially unrecognized, problem was what to call higher-quality bottled wines, how to differentiate these "festive" wines from the vin ordinaire? Even the old guard had implicitly recognized the problem of applying "wine-type" labeling to a wide range of quality, especially in bottled wine. In August 1934, H. F. Stoll, publisher of what became *Wines and Vines*, complained that "one of the criticisms today, which the trade and the consumer make, is that no two brands of the same type of wine are similar."[111] Four years later, Harry Caddow of the Wine Institute commented that "the finest wines of California go without purchasers" because "most wine bottles look more or less alike," making it "difficult to induce retailers to stock fine wines."[112] For a while the Wine Institute had considered a "seal of quality," but it abandoned the idea because "there is too wide a range of quality in our wines."[113] The solution supplied by Schoonmaker and Wildman was to break out of the straitjacket of "wine-type" nomenclature and emphasize the inherent differences in wines produced from different grape varieties grown in various regions.

On its face, the system advocated by Schoonmaker and Wildman was simple: name the grape type (or describe the wine as a "dry white" or "dry red"), tell where the grapes were grown, and name the producer. The consumer, the retailer, and the wholesaler would have to be educated as to the characteristics of particular varieties and locales, but that provided an opportunity for a producer to differentiate the brand from those of competitors. Varietal and geographic labeling thus became one mechanism for a handful of high-quality producers to separate themselves and their products from the rest of the industry and ultimately became a symbol of fine wine. There is a mild irony here: in rejecting a demeaned symbol of quality—that is, European place-name appellations as misused in the United States—a new symbol, varietal wine, was substituted. Symbols and content often become confused over time, and the fact that a wine is a "varietal" does not necessarily mean that it is of high quality. Of course, Schoonmaker and Wildman would have insisted that grape variety was just one element out of three that must be considered, and that even then, quality was ultimately found in the glass, not determined by the label. Still, Marvel was essentially correct when he concluded his defense of varietal and geographic labeling in the *Wine Review* by stating: "I feel I am not exaggerating when I say that such a change in nomenclature will mean more to fine American wines than anything that has been done since the vine was first planted in California."[114]

History is more often a continuum of events than it is a collection of disjunctures. It is tempting to the historian to impose order on the continuum by measuring out meaning in decades or ascribing undue influence to key events, such as World War II. Nonetheless, the war clearly did have a profound impact on the California wine industry as a whole, and especially on the quality producers in the Napa Valley. Prior to the entry of the United States into the conflict, it caused eastern wine merchants to take another look at California wines, opening a market for higher-quality wines. A major result of this rediscovery was the introduction of varietal and geographic labeling, which helped differentiate top-end wines from those of the mass producers. On the eve of World War II, varietal labeling was a novelty, but it was slowly to become the major symbol of quality over the next forty years, changing the economics of grape growing and winemaking in the Napa Valley.

Yet the end of the 1930s would have been a natural transition point for the Napa fine wine industry even without the advent of World War II. It is a truism that endings are simply beginnings, and Napa had its share in 1940. In December 1939, Carl Bundschu departed Inglenook, leaving the helm to John Daniel, Jr., who would guide the enterprise for the next twenty-five years. Three months later, in February 1940, Georges de Latour died, aged 83, leaving the operation of Beaulieu to his widow and L. M. Fabbrini, the general manager. Midway through the year, the quality producers of Napa were joined by Louis M. Martini, who had quietly been making wine in their midst since 1934. After he sold his sweet wine operation in Kingsburg in 1940, he released his first offerings of varietally labeled, vintage-dated wines, instantly joining the ranks of California's top producers. And in December 1940, Felix Salmina died, leaving Larkmead to his wife, sons, and daughters.[115]

By December 1941, the Napa fine wine industry was a significantly different and more mature industry than it had been even at the start of the decade. There was a pervasive sense that Napa wine had found its rightful place in the world. Napa winemakers had firmly established themselves as the quality leaders of the California industry. They had withstood the early hectic days following Repeal and had found successful niches, slowly building their branded business until most, if not all, had distribution throughout the United States. The valley's big four, Beaulieu, Inglenook, Larkmead, and Beringer, had been joined by L. M. Martini and Christian Brothers, creating a larger concentration of higher-end producers of bottled wine than anywhere else in California. Ultimately, this critical mass of talent would combine with the nascent but emerging emphasis on varietal and geographic labeling to make Napa the best known and most respected viticultural area in California. None of the Napa quality producers knew what a war economy would mean to them, or to the California industry as a whole. But they faced the future with a definite sense that a new branch of the California wine industry had been born, and that through improved quality and brand development, they would emerge at the end of the war as its leaders.

CHAPTER FIVE

California Wine and World War II

The boom in wine consumption expected after Repeal in 1933 did not arrive until 1942. The result of a managed wartime economy that took whiskey off the shelves and put money in consumers' pockets, the boom permanently changed the structure of wine production and distribution in the United States by breaking the strength of regional bottlers and by creating an economic environment conducive to the introduction of national brands and at-winery bottling. As is characteristic of most boom periods, the five years beginning in 1942 and ending in 1946 saw a massive influx of capital, with resulting fraud, lawsuits, and bankruptcies. Sales and purchases of wineries accounted for at least 40 percent of the production capacity in California. Grape prices tripled, and over 57,000 acres of new vineyards were planted, an increase of over 10 percent from the 1941 acreage.

These structural and organizational changes reached across the entire industry, affecting wineries and growers in Southern California, the Central Valley, the North Coast, and the Napa Valley. The crash of the wine market in 1947, as the industry readjusted to competition, a surplus of output, and the removal of price controls, was felt as deeply in St. Helena as it was in Fresno or San Francisco. Yet, even with the crash and its resulting business failures, the California wine industry emerged from the war years fundamentally different and ultimately stronger.

Prior to World War II, the California industry was, broadly speaking, a collection of commodity processors who produced a bulk, unbranded product and shipped it via rail tank car to independent regional bottlers across the United States. Estimates vary, but probably 80 percent of California wine was shipped out of state in bulk, and much of the remaining 20 percent was bottled in California under contract with out-of-state distributors under their labels.[1] Although such large wineries as Petri, Roma, and Italian Swiss Colony shipped bulk wine to every "wet" state, that was no guarantee that the company brand was known to consumers across the nation. In some instances, wineries owned their own out-of-state bottling facilities and simply shipped bulk wine for convenience. In other cases, independent bottlers operated under "franchises," bottling a California producer's wine and labeling the product with both their own and the producer's names.[2] But the independent bottler usually had its own set of brands and its own distribution sales force in the local market. While such regional bottlers often created on-going relationships with specific producers whose wines and credit terms they liked, the bottlers always knew that the wine they were purchasing was a commodity, one generally in surplus.

Wine was in surplus and often of questionable quality because grapes were abundant and often of the wrong variety. Between 1920 and 1923, owners planted over 300,000 acres of grapes, primarily in the Central Valley, doubling the pre-Prohibition acreage. Of this new grape acreage, over half produced raisin varieties, and fewer than 20 percent of the vines planted were wine varieties.[3] Indeed, by 1940, one raisin variety, Thompson Seedless, covered more acreage than all of the wine grapes in California.[4]

The speculative planting of thicker-skinned raisin and table grape varieties during Prohibition produced a chronic oversupply following Repeal, especially in the wake of four successive large crops in 1937, 1938, 1939, and 1940. For many growers, the fermenter became the last resort for unwanted raisin and table grapes. Ripe raisin grapes such as Thompson and Muscat could be crushed, fermented, and distilled, serving as a source of fortifying brandy for dessert wines. Although these raisin varieties produced poor wines, few growers were concerned about resulting wine quality. Their general attitude was succinctly stated by the manager of the Growers' Grape Products Association: "Any grape may be utilized for wine or brandy."[5] Thus in 1940, although less than 28 percent of California's grape crop consisted of wine grapes, over 54 percent was crushed for wine.[6] The immediate results were easily predicted: low wine prices, poor wine quality, and a buyer's market for out-of-state bottlers. The longer-term outlook was economic disaster.

Had it not been for changes brought about by the war, the California wine industry probably would have faced a decade of decline and consolidation. Instead, by 1942, grape prices had doubled, and wine was in short supply.[7] This dramatic reversal resulted from changes in both supply and demand. The raisin surplus was "solved" in 1942 for the duration of the war when the federal government requisitioned the entire crop for use in the war effort.[8] Compact, high-energy, and relatively non-perishable, raisins were an ideal food for inclusion in K rations. Through the 1945 harvest, the federal government restricted the use of raisin varieties to raisin production.

The effect was immediately evident in the 1942 crush figures: in 1941, California had produced a total of 110 million gallons of wine, but the amount fell to just over 62 million in 1942, the low point for the decade. The loss of raisins was especially felt in dessert wine production, which accounted for roughly 80 percent of all wine sales: production dropped from a 1941 high of 72 million gallons to 37 million gallons in 1942.[9] The 62 million gallons of wine produced in 1942 amounted to slightly less than two-thirds of the wine sold the previous year. With the glut of raisins removed, the wine industry moved abruptly from a state of surplus to one of scarcity in less than a year.

The one-third reduction in supply was combined with an increased consumer demand for wine, since it was the only readily available form of alcohol. Following the outbreak of war, the federal government immediately requisitioned all distilling operations, demanding around-the-clock production of high-proof alcohol for the war effort. By October 1942, whiskey distillation had ended, creating immediate shortages on retail shelves.[10] Although there was ample whiskey in barrels, the distillers chose to hoard their supplies, as they were unsure when they would be allowed to produce whiskey again. Beer, a product of cereal crops used for the war effort, was available but "trade-rationed." Only wine, a beverage produced from a fruit not vital to the war effort, was freely obtainable to a home front whose purchasing power had almost doubled as a result of the war economy. Per capita annual consumption of wine rose from .68 gallons in 1941 to .84 in 1942, reaching a peak of 1.0 gallon in 1946.[11] In all probability, the rise would have been faster and greater had more wine been available to slake America's thirst.

In a free market, increased demand coupled with decreased supply raises prices. But during the war years, the United States was not a free market, and price increases occurred only in the raw product, grapes, and not in wine itself. This was because the government placed price controls on manufactured goods, but not on agricultural raw products. In order to prevent inflation, which had been experienced in World

War I and had already begun to take place in 1941, Congress passed the Emergency Price Control Act in early 1942. It created the Office of Price Administration (OPA), which placed an immediate price freeze on most manufactured goods.[12] However, the act also prohibited price controls on raw agricultural commodities unless the price was at least 110 percent of "parity," a concept more applicable to soybeans, tobacco, and peanuts than to wine grapes. Establishing a parity price was both time-consuming and political. The Department of Agriculture chose not to calculate a parity price for grapes, and the OPA thus never did put price controls on wine grapes. The immediate upshot was that wine prices were more or less frozen for the duration, while grape prices were left free to rise, increasing from an average of $16.50 a ton in 1940 to $100 a ton in 1944.[13]

The predictable effect of government regulation was, therefore, a reduction in wineries' profit margins. This in turn caused an abrupt curtailment of bulk wine shipments from California wineries to out-of-state bottlers. The longer-term consequences were a movement toward bottling at wineries and an invasion of the California industry by out-of-state bottlers and distillers in 1942 and 1943. These repercussions of the wartime disruption of normal supply and demand all followed in a logical, if curious, cascade.

The first effect of price controls was an abrupt decline in the profit on bulk wine, which had accounted for most of California's sales. After initially setting bulk dessert wine prices at 32 cents a gallon, the OPA raised the ceiling to 39 cents, and 21½ cents for "current" table wine, in October.[14] A ton of grapes produces about 170 gallons of new wine, so the ceiling price on table wine in 1942 corresponded to roughly $36.50 a ton, while Central Valley nonvarietal black grapes were selling at slightly over $32 a ton.[15] Assuming, as the federal government did, a cost of 1.7 cents a gallon for base production costs, another $2.90 a ton was incurred for processing, bringing a typical raw product cost of almost $35 a ton by October 1942. Although the OPA continued to raise price ceilings for bulk and bottled wine throughout the war as grape prices increased, the difference between raw material prices and bulk wine ceilings allowed for little, if any, profit.

However, the OPA did permit a significantly higher price for bottled wine. The 1943 price ceilings limited "current" bulk table wine sales to 28 cents a gallon, but allowed the same wine to be bottled and sold at $3.74 a case, roughly $1.55 a gallon.[16] Although wineries incurred the additional expense of packaging, bottled wine sales were thus significantly more profitable than sales of bulk wine. *Wines and Vines* commented, in unusually blunt language, that it was "much better to sell quality wine in cases . . . at prices which may start at around $1.50 a gallon . . . than to sell . . . at tank car prices which provide little or no profit."[17]

The sale of bottled wine was even more profitable for those wineries marketing higher-priced varietal wines, since they could legally sell at prices considerably above the regular ceiling price. Wineries that had only bottled small or special lots, dusted off old labels and diverted more of their production into higher-priced brands. Consequently, price ceilings "had the effect of practically eliminating all the lower-priced brands."[18] This change in turn pushed grape prices higher, since, as *Wines and Vines* commented, "distributors and bottlers" who owned "high priced brands . . . [could] afford to pay more for their grapes than . . . the average winery."[19] The price differential between bulk and bottled wine forced many of California's bulk producers to become bottlers and to develop their own brands. It also created opportunities for outsiders to enter the California industry.

Not surprisingly, the first group to enter the California industry in force were the distillers. After the outbreak of war, the distillers worked continuously to produce alcohol for the war effort and were financially secure, but were left with little or no product for their national sales forces to sell. By becoming wine producers, distillers secured a new product that could be sold in place of whiskey for the war's duration. In 1942, the large distillers entered the California industry, and within a year, four firms, National Distillers, Schenley, Seagram and Sons, and Hiram Walker controlled about 23 percent of California's wine production capacity.[20]

Schenley and National Distillers were the most aggressive in acquiring California wineries. National Distillers had purchased Shewan Jones, a moderately large winery in the Sacramento Delta, in 1939. But National shocked the California industry at the end of 1942 when it bought the two Italian Swiss Colony wineries in Asti and Clovis, effectively increasing National Distillers' production capacity sevenfold.[21] Schenley expanded even more quickly. In January 1941, Schenley bought the Cresta Blanca winery in Livermore, a small, old, higher-quality producer, with a historically higher price ceiling than most wineries. Schenley increased Cresta Blanca's production by purchasing the Colonial Grape Products Winery in Elk Grove in September 1942 and Greystone Cellars in St. Helena from Central Winery in November 1942, operating them all under the name of Cresta Blanca and dramatically expanding the production of the profitable high-priced "Cresta Blanca" wine.[22]

But the transaction that really shook the California industry was the sale of California's largest winery, Roma Wine Company, in November of 1942 to National Distillers.[23] Together, Schenley and National Distillers controlled almost 20 percent of the California wine production at the close of 1942.

The distillers' entrance into the California wine industry was bemoaned by some, feared by many, and ultimately became the subject of a Senate Judiciary Committee hearing.[24] There were charges that the big firms were forcing "tie-in sales," the practice of requiring retailers to purchase five, ten, or sometimes twenty cases of wine in order to buy one case of whiskey. Never proved, tie-in sales undoubtedly occurred and were effective in getting California wine on retailers' shelves. In turn, most retailers engaged in their own subtle form of tie-in sales with customers, encouraging wine purchases before "finding" a bottle of whiskey in the back room for a loyal customer. Such practices flourished in a wartime economy of scarcity and helped introduce California wine to a national audience.

More important, the distillers brought to the wine industry a national system of merchandising and "an influx of new, much desired capital."[25] Schenley nationally advertised both Roma and Cresta Blanca on radio and in print, and National Distillers pursued a similar policy with Italian Swiss Colony. For the first time, because of the distillers' money and sales sophistication, brands of California wine were effectively promoted on a national basis. On the whole, most California wineries adopted a wait-and-see attitude toward the distillers, appreciating their help in building a national market for California wine, but wary of their immense economic strength and political clout.

For the distillers, purchasing a California winery was a matter of seizing an opportunity created by wartime conditions; for out-of-state bottlers, direct involvement in California was a matter of economic survival. The out-of-state bottlers depended upon California wineries for their supply. As long as wine remained abundant, which it had been since Repeal, bottlers had not really needed to assure themselves of a source of supply by becoming actual producers. In some ways, the shipment of bulk wine had worked to the benefit of both groups during the 1930s. The arrangement had let bottlers concentrate scarce capital on creating a local sales and delivery force, acquiring bottling equipment, and building an inventory of bottled goods, while it let California producers focus their funds and energy on production. The war economy threatened the old relationship. Producers could survive without the bottlers, especially under wartime scarcity, but the bottlers could not survive without a secure source of supply. As *Wines and Vines* put it, the problem was "so serious as actually to be a fight for existence." [26]

For the first year of the war, bottlers had attempted to ride out the wine shortage in the hope that it represented a temporary dislocation rather than a sea change in business. Many bottlers initially circumvented the price ceilings on bulk wine by receiving bulk shipments, bottling the wine for the California wineries under contract, and then purchasing the bottled wine from the California producer at close to the higher price ceiling. Such fiction allowed the bottler to pay a higher amount for bulk wine than if the bottler had bought the wine in bulk and bottled it for his own account. Another means used to evade price ceilings was for bottlers to buy their own grapes and to pay wineries to process the grapes. Both methods were effectively ended in early 1943, when the OPA ruled that contract bottling, crushing, and fermentation were essentially services that came under price control. [27] Such price control ended the possibility of producers and bottlers sharing the higher margin allowed on bottled goods, and in most cases it effectively stopped custom crushing operations on a large scale, since the producer could almost always make a higher profit by fermenting and bottling for his own account, rather than for an out-of-state bottler. [28]

The final blow came in the form of an order from the War Production Board to the Office of Defense Transportation on January 5, 1943, that converted the remaining seven hundred tank cars used for wine shipment to "the transportation of essential wartime liquids." [29] This meant that future movement of bulk wine would be in barrels, adding cost and inefficiency to the out-of-state bottlers' operations, even if enough barrels were available. *Wines and Vines* predicted that "once the flow of bulk wine to the East is cut down, some eastern bottling firms will have to shut down," resulting in the sale and movement west of bottling equipment. [30] The handwriting on the wall spelled out "Bottled at the Winery" in rather large letters. As one producer wrote, "It is the cold-blooded truth, and the change is here now." [31]

If 1942 had been the year of the distiller, 1943 became the year of the out-of-state bottler. Bottlers flocked to California to buy wineries and to secure a source of supply for their wholesale operations on the East Coast and in the Midwest. Leading the charge were the larger regional bottlers. Early in the year Renault, an importer and bottler, concluded that "continuation of their national business would be possible only if they acquired property in California." They purchased several wineries, the largest being the St. George Winery in Fresno, with a capacity of over one million gallons.[32] Renault's acquisitions also included Lombardi Wines in Los Angeles and a San Francisco bottler, the Montebello Wine Company, which operated the Fountain Winery in St. Helena. In the spring of 1943, the Gibson Wine Company, a major regional bottler in Ohio, Kentucky, and Indiana, bought the two-million-gallon Acampo Winery near Lodi. Taking advantage of the seller's market, the stockholders of Acampo, led by Cesare Mondavi, had decided to "offer the property to the highest bidder." As *Wines and Vines* noted, the purchase assured Gibson of "a steady supply of well-made and aged dessert and` table wines."[33] Other large-to-medium-sized wineries changed hands prior to harvest: the Eastern Wine Corporation of New York purchased the Burbank Winery in Burbank, and Brookside Distilling of Pennsylvania bought the Alta Winery in Dinuba. Each winery had just under two million gallons of storage, or the equivalent of slightly less than 1 percent of California storage capacity.[34]

The buying frenzy slowed at harvest, as wineries concentrated on processing the vintage, but winery sales picked up again in 1944. In some instances, groups of bottlers banded together to purchase a winery, such as three New Jersey bottlers who purchased the Garden Winery and Distillery in Fowler.[35] New owners and their locations read like a directory of bottlers: Sunwest Wines of Madison; Ignatius Russo of Cleveland; Edward Bragno and Company of Chicago; Midwest Distributing of Milwaukee; R. C. Williams of New York City; Garret and Company of New York City, and John Drumba of New York City.[36] By summer of 1944, new owners held at least 40 percent of the productive capacity of California wineries.

It was not just wineries that changed hands. Sales of vineyards, or land suitable for vineyards, boomed as well. For many wine producers, buying a vineyard was a way both to secure a supply of wine grapes and to lock in raw product prices.[37] With demand for wine high, and raisins off of the market, grapes prices soared up to $100 a ton by the 1944 harvest.[38] Such price inflation dramatically improved vineyard profitability and led in turn to increased plantings from 1944 through 1946. The high point was 1945, with owners planting 22,000 new acres, but in the three-year period, they added just under 50,000 acres of new vineyards.[39]

In 1941, such an expansion would have been considered madness, but by late 1943, perhaps buoyed by the wartime economy, industry leaders predicted a postwar market for 250 to 500 million gallons of wine, almost a fivefold increase over the record 1941 crush. Arguing that "there seems to be little doubt of finding a market to absorb all the wine we can make," *Wines and Vines* urged growers to plant only wine varieties, so as to ensure high-quality wines after the war.[40] Despite this caveat, and the 1944 publication of Amerine and Winkler's *Composition and Quality of Wines and Must of California*, which argued for increased plantings of better-adapted wine grape varieties, not all growers followed such advice. Winkler indicated that of the 35,000 acres planted in 1944 and 1945, only about 19,000 acres, or 55 percent, were in wine grapes. Of these "wine grapes," well over half were varieties that gave heavy yield but low quality, such as Burger, Carignane, Palomino, and Mission.[41] The reason was obvious. Few wineries paid much of a premium for higher-quality grapes, and the vineyard owner, who finally saw his opportunity after almost a decade of low prices, was interested in tonnage, not quality.

Throughout 1944 and 1945, the new owners of California wineries and vineyards continued to invest in new equipment and in brand development and advertising. They bought bottling equipment from defunct regional bottlers and transferred it to California, resulting in increased capacity for at-winery bottling. Roma doubled its bottling capacity, from 10,000 cases to 20,000 cases a day, between 1941 and 1945. Other wineries followed suit. Petri increased output from 4,500 cases to 17,500 cases, the Madera Winery went from 1,500 to 10,000 cases, and the Italian Swiss Colony grew to 3,000 cases a day. Wineries that had bottled by hand mechanized. *Wines and Vines* estimated that by 1945, roughly 60 percent of California wine production could be bottled in California.[42] The growth in bottled wine production was matched by an increase in brand and generic advertising. Harry Caddow judged that in 1945, almost $10 million was spent on brand advertising. A year later, brand and generic advertising was estimated to be close to $15 million, up from barely $500,000 in 1938.[43] By 1945, the California winemakers had irreversibly changed from a group of mainly bulk producers of a commodity in oversupply to producers and marketers of branded commodities in short supply.

The accelerated rate of change in the California wine industry must have been dizzying. Writing in June 1944, Elmer Salmina of Larkmead in St. Helena claimed that "practically everyone with a bonded winery has been approached by buyers" but cautioned that many were "speculators who are gambling in the wine business." He confessed to being "more and more confused when I hear or read of sales of vineyards and wineries at unheard of prices." Unwilling to predict the future, Salmina cautioned that although "this may just be the beginning . . . [but] whenever there is a beginning there is an end."[44] Carl Bundschu echoed Salmina later that year when he warned growers that "the present price of grapes will not last," and that the resulting inflation would eventually "bring ruin to some vintners when business drops to normal." The problem, according to Bundschu, was that high grape prices invariably forced up wine prices, and "no wineman wants to be caught with a large stock of high-priced wine when the crash comes, and it is bound to come."[45] Such predictions fell on deaf ears. Clearly, the prosperity was war-induced, but for those with grapes or wine to sell, it was nonetheless real. The question no one seemed willing to pose was how long the prosperity would last following the war's end.

Throughout 1944, most California wines sold at their maximum ceiling prices, and "mixed black" grapes from the Central Valley reached a high point of $100 a ton during the 1944 harvest. One result was a decline in wine quality, since wineries were forced to turn over inventory quickly if they were to make any profit under price controls, thus leading to the bottling and marketing of young wine as quickly as possible.[46] Still, demand remained high throughout the first months of 1945, and even as the end of the war drew nearer, most producers remained confident that the boom would continue. But as the industry entered the traditionally slow summer months, demand slackened for the first time, exposing producers to the risk predicted by Bundschu.

The reaction was predictable: general price cutting and instances of panic selling. By August, wine sold at below price ceilings, and by fall, prices had fallen on average by 25 percent.[47] Fearing that prices would drop in following months, wholesalers became reluctant to buy wine in any quantity and demanded that producers guarantee proportional credit on purchases should prices continue to decline. The softness of the wine market was exacerbated by the government's decision to purchase only a portion of the raisin crop. Availability of raisin grapes meant the industry could increase its production of dessert wines, which had been curtailed, but also meant an increase in total output, with a potential further decrease in bulk wine prices. As a result, grape prices fell by almost 50 percent, to an average of $57 a ton, and a record 116 million gallons of wine were produced. By late fall 1945, following the crush, dessert wine sold at about 80 cents a gallon, down from $1.10 the previous spring. Prospects seemed strong for a further decline.[48]

The last half of 1945 had demonstrated just how precarious the wine market could be, but pessimists were proven wrong in 1946, when the industry entered another boom period. One result was that for the first time in history, annual U.S. wine consumption passed one gallon per capita. More to the point, the wine sold fetched high prices. Partially as a result of the slackening of wartime price controls, as well as of the scarcity of other forms of alcohol because of the government policy of encouraging grain shipments to war-ravaged Europe, demand and price both increased steadily throughout 1946. Retailers and wholesalers who had purposely kept low inventories while prices were falling in 1945 now rushed to buy as prices rose.

During 1946, almost each month set a new record for wine taken out of winery storage. By February, dessert wine prices had climbed to over $1.00 a gallon; by April, they had reached $1.40.[49] Declaring that "supply of bulk wines for sale is practically non-existent," the editor of *Wines and Vines* commented that price increases were "by five- and ten-cent jumps."[50] Even in the usually slow summer selling season, sales and prices continued to rise, with dessert wine prices escalating to an unheard-of $1.90 a gallon.[51] Wine removals for the first half of 1946 totaled 61 million gallons, 50 percent ahead of comparable sales for 1945, at a time when sales had never topped 100 million gallons for a full year.[52] Herman Wente, the president of the Wine Institute, articulated the prevalent sense of optimism when he declared that "the wine train is set for a long, high-speed run. The track ahead is clear and has no visible ending."[53] *Wines and Vines* shared his view, arguing that there was "little reason to expect a price drop."[54] The industry foresaw continued growth and acted on that belief.

As the California industry entered the summer of 1946, it braced itself for a record crush by increasing fermenting and storage capacity by 45 million gallons.[55] Although availability of raisin grapes assured a large harvest, prices of grapes increased as harvest drew near. Led by distillers, most notably National Distillers' Italian Swiss Colony and Schenley's Cresta Blanca and Roma, wineries competed for uncontracted tonnage, driving prices to between $85 and $90 a ton for Central Valley mixed black grapes.[56] Increased grape tonnage, high grape prices, and expanded fermentation capacity led to a record 1.6 million tons of grapes being crushed in 1946, an increase of almost 50 percent above the previous record the year before, and double the amount crushed two years earlier in 1944.

California wineries ended 1946 with a large and very high-priced inventory. This was not a problem as long as demand and prices increased. Some wineries, believing that wine was still underpriced relative to other forms of alcohol, raised prices, arguing that wine prices should increase with general inflation. Others, remembering the selling panic in the summer of 1945, feared that consumption was likely to drop with any increase in prices and cautioned that "once prices are forced to move down, there is no telling where they will stop."[57] This time the pessimists were right.

Slow sales in January and February, a response to high-priced wine, the new availability of blended whiskeys, and overstocked retailers' storerooms, initiated a round of price cutting by wineries that feared being "stuck . . . with high priced inventories."[58] Industry spokesmen counseled gradual price reductions and argued that the post-holiday decline in sales was a natural "breathing spell" for retailers.[59] But panic sales continued, and by March, *Wines and Vines* reported "cut throat competition at the retailer level" and described ads from regional newspapers that showed wines "being sold at unprofitable figures."[60] In California, the industry attempted to stabilize prices by extending beer "fair-trade" price-posting to wine.[61] Essentially, "fair-trade" required that minimum prices for bottled wine at the wholesale and retail levels be posted with the state each month for every brand. Since prices could be changed only once a month, "fair-trade" slowed price cutting. The price-postings were also public documents, so everyone in the industry could quickly know the price of competing brands.

Although fair-trade helped set a bottom for some brands, it did not stop the slide in bulk wine prices. By June, dessert wine was selling at 40 cents a gallon, roughly 20 percent of its high a year before. Standard table wines fell almost as far, down from $1.30 a gallon to 30 cents.[62] The price drop was huge, and it has been estimated that Schenley and National Distillers, who had been the major bidders for grapes in 1946, lost $11 million and $9 million dollars respectively in the debacle.[63] They were not alone. Only a handful of producers emerged unscathed; most were seriously hurt, and a few were driven to bankruptcy or liquidation.

The crush of 1947 was a dismal affair, more reminiscent of the prewar years than of the past four years of prosperity. Grape prices tumbled to between $30 and $35 dollars a ton, and would have fallen further except for the Department of Agriculture's purchase of 121,000 tons of raisins for shipment to Europe, which diverted roughly 15 percent of the total grape crop.[64] Some growers entered into "share-crushing" agreements with wineries in which the winery agreed to crush the grapes, but the grower's return would be based on the selling price of the wine. Other growers banded together to create new cooperative wineries or to lease existing wineries to crush and ferment their grapes. In either case, growers were gambling on increased wine prices, since wine prices in the fall of 1947 translated to about $30 a ton.[65] The irony was that the 1947 growing season was the best in a decade, with "almost perfect" growing and harvest weather, but with little demand for grapes.[66]

The fall in wine and grape prices in 1947 marked the end of the period of war-induced prosperity and the transition to a new postwar economy in which supply and demand would be driven by the market, rather than by government regulation. The boom from 1943 through 1946 had proved short-lived, but it was nonetheless pivotal to the future of California wine. In four short years, the California industry had changed from production of a bulk commodity to predominantly brand-oriented business. At-winery bottling could not be undone, and producers would more and more also have to become marketers if they were to succeed. The controlled economy of the home front had proved that Americans would drink wine. The task that lay ahead was to increase per capita consumption of California wine in an unregulated economy.

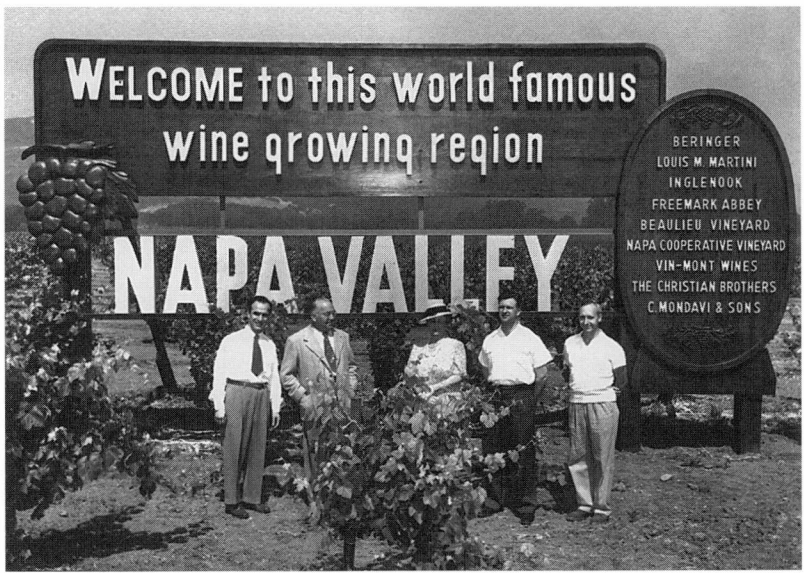

DEDICATION OF SIGN BY THE NAPA VALLEY VINTNERS' ASSOCIATION, JUNE 30, 1950. Original photo from Napa Wine Library. In an act of regional promotion, the NVVA erected this sign in late 1949, the sequence of members' names on it being determined by lot. Winemakers pictured in the dedication are, from left to right, Robert Mondavi (C. Mondavi and Sons/Charles Krug), Charles Forni (Napa Cooperative Vineyard), Madame Fernande de Latour (Beaulieu Vineyard), John Daniel, Jr. (Inglenook), and Al Huntsinger (Vin-Mont was the brand name for the Napa Cooperative Winery, the so-called "Big Co-op").

BEAULIEU VINEYARD

ONE REASON FOR THE EXCELLENCE OF OUR DRY WINES
BURGUNDY — CLARET — RIESLING — SAUTERNES — CHABLIS AND MANY OTHER VARIETIES

OUR 1,250,000 GALLON PLANT AT ST. HELENA, NAPA COUNTY
Insulated and ventilated so that a constant temperature of 50° F is maintained regardless of outside weather conditions. Underground storage facilities are used for aging wines under ideal conditions.

L. M. MARTINI GRAPE PRODUCTS
BRANDIES, SWEET AND DRY WINES
WINERIES: KINGSBURG AND ST. HELENA, CALIF.   MAIN OFFICE: KINGSBURG, CALIF.

BEAULIEU VINEYARD DISPLAY AT 1934 VINTAGE FESTIVAL. *California Grape Grower*, September 1934. Befitting its dominant position in the Napa Valley, Beaulieu arranged for a multitiered display that towered over those of other wineries at the 1934 Vintage Festival.

THE L. M. MARTINI WINERY, ST. HELENA, IN 1935. *Wines and Vines*, June 1935. The Martini winery was the first new winery built in the Napa Valley since the beginning of Prohibition. With insulated walls and a fermenting room cooled by mechanical refrigeration, the winery was reminiscent of a Central Valley processing plant and was the technical leader in the Napa Valley at Repeal.

BERINGER POINT-OF-SALE DISPLAY. *Wine Review*, December 1937. In this 1937 six-color dealer display, Beringer played on the romance of wine, the beauty of the countryside, its long history in the Napa Valley, and its "famous underground caves." Typical of the time, only one of the six bottles displayed was labeled as a varietal wine.

CHARLES KRUG GROUNDBREAKING. Photo: Julie Dickson. During the 1950s, the Charles Krug winery, operated by C. Mondavi and Sons, emerged as the technical leader in the Napa Valley. When increased volume and new technology necessitated a new warehouse and bottling line, the entire winery staff turned out for the 1958 groundbreaking. In the foreground from left to right are Peter Mondavi, Rosa Mondavi, Cesare Mondavi, Robert Mondavi, and an unnamed contractor. Note the head-trained vines in the background.

(Top) GENERIC AD FOR CALIFORNIA WINE. *Wines and Vines*, May 1939. The Wine Advisory Board's mission was to promote California wine. This 1939 advertisement, designed to appear in national magazines and regional newspapers, is an excellent example of the static and generic print-media-oriented promotion later criticized by California's quality producers.

(Bottom) "SERVE IT COLD." *Wines and Vines*, May 1941. This generic Wine Advisory Board advertisement, designed to promote wine sales during the traditionally slow summer months, was the featured cover of *Wines and Vines* in May 1941. Note the use of a European place-name to describe a California product.

LARKMEAD ADVERTISEMENT. 1947. *Wines and Vines*, October 1947. Larkmead was one of the original quality producers following Repeal, but was sold to a midwestern partnership during World War II. This ad from October 1947 appeared just in time to coincide with the crash in wine prices that followed the 1947 harvest and the reappearance of blended whiskey in the marketplace. Two months later, Philip Blum and Co., which owned numerous distilling interests, was bought by National Distillers, owners of Italian Swiss Colony, and Larkmead became a crushing station for Italian Swiss Colony, until shut down in the early 1950s.

CHARLES KRUG BILLBOARD. *Wine and Vines*, April 1946. Following World War II, the Mondavis began active promotion of their top brand, Charles Krug. This 1946 billboard promoted the pairing of quality and region and played on the fact that theirs was the "oldest" winery in the Napa Valley.

BOTTLES AND BINS MASTHEAD. Shields Library. In 1949, in an attempt to build a direct relationship with wine consumers, the Charles Krug winery launched the first winery newsletter in California, soon to be followed by Almaden. Worldly and witty, *Bottles and Bins* helped introduce California wine to postwar America.

NAPA VALLEY VINTNERS' ASSOCIATION CABLE CAR. Napa Valley Wine Library. In October 1949, the NVVA sponsored a San Francisco cable car for a year, giving a bottle of Napa wine each day to a lucky passenger. Member wineries were listed on the front of the car.

White Wines

The Christian Brothers' Rhine Wine

A dry, fruity, white table wine, light and tart, with fine flavor and aroma, resembling the great white wines produced along the Rhine River in Germany.

Beringer Bros. Napa Valley Riesling

A dry wine made from choice Johannisberger Riesling and Franken Riesling grapes. Has a delicate bouquet with the characteristic flavor derived from the two grapes.

Inglenook Riesling 1946

Grown from the Franken Riesling grapes of our own vineyard in a year regarded as outstanding since repeal, this variety combines freshness and softness pleasing to most palates.

Louis Martini Mountain Sylvaner 1948

A delicate, light dry wine made from the Sylvaner grape. The 1948 vintage is soft and extremely pleasant. In character and flavor it recalls the wines of Alsace.

Charles Krug Traminer

One of the aristocrats of California wines. The Traminer grape in Alsace—and in parts of the Napa Valley—yields a fine dry wine of fragrant bouquet and flowery flavor.

Beaulieu Vineyards Beauclair 1947

A wine of fine bouquet and medium body produced solely from Johannisberger (White) Riesling grapes.

Freemark Abbey Sauterne

An aromatic, soft and altogether pleasant wine.

Vin-Mont Sauterne

Napa county has many acres of vineyard which produce pleasant drinking wines like this one which is made in the largest grower owned co-operative winery in the valley.

The Fare

ASSORTED RELISHES

NAPA VALLEY GREEN SALAD

PASTA ASCIUTTA
WITH MUSHROOM SAUCE

·&·

VEAL SAUTE

BARBECUED STEAK

GREEN BEANS AU BEURRE

CAKE   CHEESE   FRUIT

COFFEE

A selection of Napa Valley Dessert Wines will be served with dessert

Red Wines

The Christian Brothers' Claret

A dry, red table wine, of moderate body, smooth but with a pleasant tartness, comparable to the best of the popular Clarets of France.

Vin-Mont Ruby Cabernet

A comparatively new hybrid of the Carignane and Cabernet grapes, the Ruby Cabernet yields a wine lighter than the true Cabernet but partaking of its flavor.

Louis Martini Cabernet Sauvignon 1945

A fine, distinguished red wine made from grapes of the Cabernet Sauvignon variety. The 1945 vintage reveals a finesse and balance, flavor and bouquet comparable to the great Clarets of Bordeaux.

Inglenook Cabernet Sauvignon 1944

Grown in our own vineyards entirely from the variety considered by many to produce the finest of all red wines.

Beaulieu Vineyards Beaumont 1942

A light bodied Burgundy type wine produced solely from Pinot Noir grapes.

Beringer Bros. Barenblut

A medium dry red wine made from our Pinot Noir grapes. Has a very delicate and mellow bouquet.

Charles Krug Gamay 1948

The Gamay grape is found in the Burgundy and Beaujolais wine districts of France; also in a few California vineyards. Charles Krug Gamay is a rich yet delicate wine.

Freemark Abbey Burgundy

A delightful dinner wine. Rich, dark, ruby red color. Full bodied with a distinctive bouquet.

HARVARD CLUB LUNCHEON WINE LIST. Napa Valley Wine Library. In 1949 the Napa Valley Vintners' Association took advantage of the Harvard Club's meeting in San Francisco to introduce members to the charms of Napa wines at a sit-down luncheon held on the Charles Krug winery grounds. The Harvard Club lunch was the first of many mass tastings for upper-class Americans held by the NVVA, and the idea was later imitated on a larger scale by Premium Wine Producers of California in conjunction with the Wine Advisory Board. The twelve-page menu souvenir booklet was prepared by the fine-arts printer Jim Beard. The winemakers presented their best wines, and even in 1949, varietally labeled wines predominated.

NAPA WINEMAKERS AT HARVARD CLUB LUNCHEON, SEPTEMBER 1949. Napa
Valley Wine Library. Members of the Napa Valley Vintners' Association posed
for a group photograph at the Harvard Club luncheon. From left to right:
Brother Timothy of Christian Brothers; Charles Forni of both the Napa Valley
Cooperative Winery and the Napa Cooperative Vineyard; Walter Sullivan and
Aldo Fabbrini of Beaulieu Vineyards; Mike Ahern of Freemark Abbey; Peter and
Robert Mondavi of C. Mondavi and Sons (Charles Krug); John Daniel, Jr., of
Inglenook; Louis M. Martini of the L. M. Martini Winery; Charles Beringer of
Beringer Brothers; Martin Stelling, Jr., of Napa Cooperative Vineyard (Sunny
St. Helena); Fred Abruzzini of Beringer Brothers.

GENERAL ELECTRIC BARBECUE, FEBRUARY 1952. Napa Valley Wine Library. Reaching out to potential higher-income consumers, the Napa Valley Vintners' Association sponsored tastings and luncheons for groups visiting San Francisco. At this western-theme barbecue, the NVVA entertained two thousand General Electric managers at the Napa Valley Fairgrounds.

ZSA ZSA GABOR AND HILLEVI RUBIN ENJOY CALIFORNIA WINES. *Wines and Vines*, November 1956. A public relations campaign was launched in the mid 1950s to persuade affluent postwar Americans that California wine was part of an attractive, successful lifestyle. This 1956 photo of the actress Zsa Zsa Gabor and Miss Universe, Hillevi Rubin, taken at a blind tasting held at the Hollywood Foreign Press Club, was estimated to have reached over forty million Americans.

MASS TASTING IN ST. LOUIS, 1959. *Wines and Vines*, March 1959. By the mid 1950s, California quality producers had demanded that the Wine Advisory Board shift from generic, print-oriented advertisements to a more dynamic form of promotion based on public relations and direct contact with potential consumers. This mass tasting held in St. Louis has obvious parallels with other tastings hosted by the Napa Valley Vintners' Association earlier in the decade, such as that for General Electric. Unlike generic advertisements, mass tastings allowed specific brand promotion by giving consumers a chance to taste hundreds of California wines.

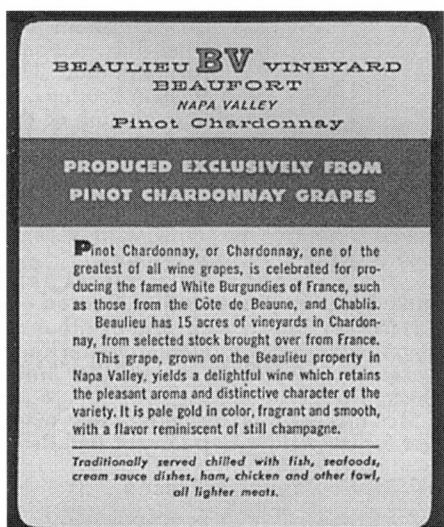

BV BACK LABEL. *Wines and Vines*, June 1956. Beaulieu took a new step in consumer education and brand differentiation in 1956 when it introduced this back label describing "Pinot Chardonnay." Beaulieu had only fifteen acres planted, which might have produced between 3,000 and 4,000 cases.

CHARLES KRUG CHRISTMAS GIFT PACK. *Wines and Vines*, December 1959. The Mondavis built on the success of *Bottles and Bins* to market a special Christmas "volume" of Charles Krug wines to newsletter subscribers, who found the attractive package of six "tenths" a unique upscale gift. The sample was designed by Malette Dean and Jim Beard.

THIS EARTH IS MINE. Napa Valley Wine Library. In 1958, Universal Pictures and Rock Hudson traveled to the Napa Valley to film *This Earth Is Mine,* a loose adaptation of *The Cup and the Sword,* a novel based on the life of Georges de Latour. Napa winemakers were never shy about seizing on a promotional opportunity, and three of them, John Daniel, Jr., Louis M. Martini, and Robert Mondavi, posed with the film's actresses. Louis Gomberg, who had helped create Premium Producers of California, helped secure financing for the film.

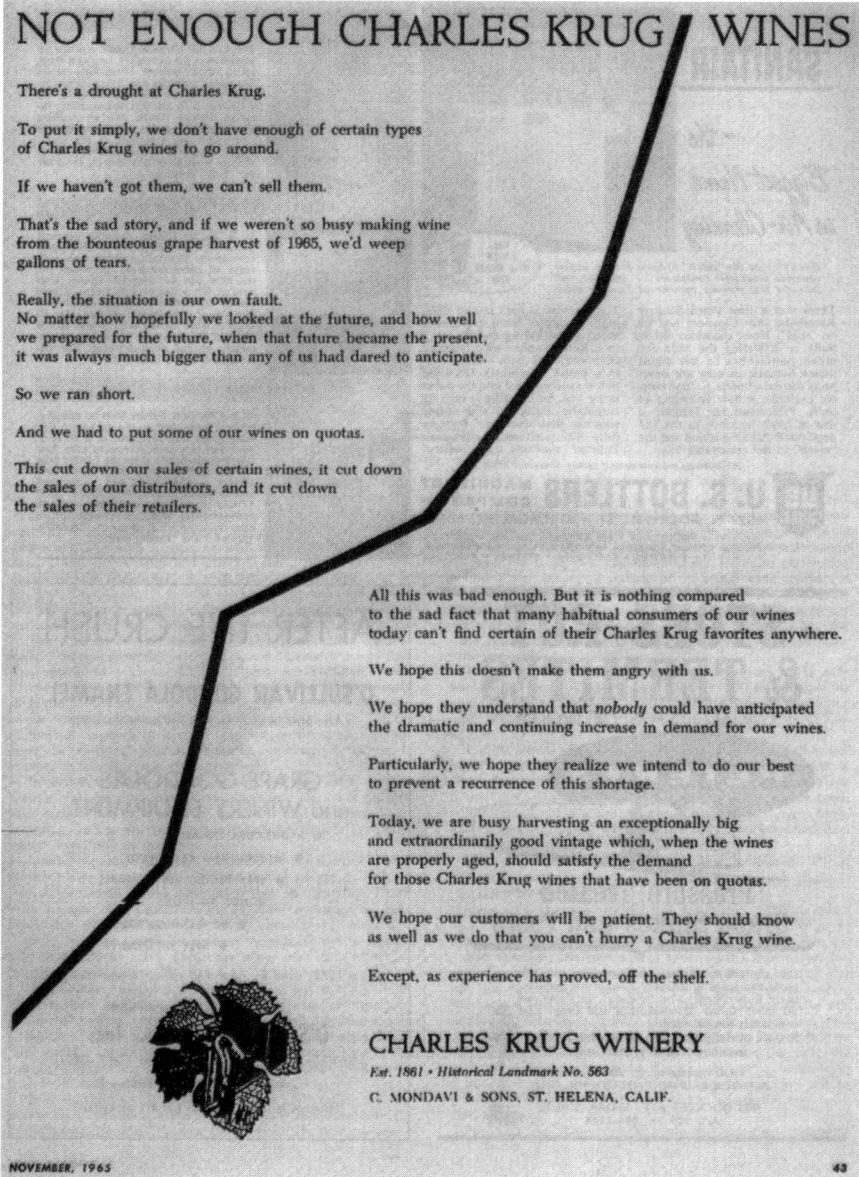

NOT ENOUGH CHARLES KRUG WINES

There's a drought at Charles Krug.

To put it simply, we don't have enough of certain types of Charles Krug wines to go around.

If we haven't got them, we can't sell them.

That's the sad story, and if we weren't so busy making wine from the bounteous grape harvest of 1965, we'd weep gallons of tears.

Really, the situation is our own fault.
No matter how hopefully we looked at the future, and how well we prepared for the future, when that future became the present, it was always much bigger than any of us had dared to anticipate.

So we ran short.

And we had to put some of our wines on quotas.

This cut down our sales of certain wines, it cut down the sales of our distributors, and it cut down the sales of their retailers.

All this was bad enough. But it is nothing compared to the sad fact that many habitual consumers of our wines today can't find certain of their Charles Krug favorites anywhere.

We hope this doesn't make them angry with us.

We hope they understand that *nobody* could have anticipated the dramatic and continuing increase in demand for our wines.

Particularly, we hope they realize we intend to do our best to prevent a recurrence of this shortage.

Today, we are busy harvesting an exceptionally big and extraordinarily good vintage which, when the wines are properly aged, should satisfy the demand for those Charles Krug wines that have been on quotas.

We hope our customers will be patient. They should know as well as we do that you can't hurry a Charles Krug wine.

Except, as experience has proved, off the shelf.

CHARLES KRUG WINERY
Est. 1861 • Historical Landmark No. 563
C. MONDAVI & SONS, ST. HELENA, CALIF.

"NOT ENOUGH CHARLES KRUG WINES." *Wines and Vines*, November 1965. By 1965, the "wine boom" had begun, and supply could not keep up with demand. Other wineries experienced similar problems, but the Charles Krug Winery, in an ad aimed primarily at distributors and retailers, used the shortage to underscore its amazing growth over the past decade.

BEAULIEU WINERY. Photo: Beaulieu Winery Public Relations Department. This photograph of Beaulieu looking east across Highway 29 was taken before 1941 and the erection of the administrative "tower" at the northern end of the building. The rail spur still exists, although it is no longer used.

LARKMEAD. Photo: John Gay. Larkmead was one of the "big four" wineries after Repeal. This photograph from the Salmina family, probably taken during the 1930s, depicts a scene typical even of quality producers: a rail car and barrels ready to be loaded and shipped east to regional bottlers.

MONT LA SALLE / CHRISTIAN BROTHERS. *Wine Review*, December 1939. Following Repeal, Christian Brothers moved from Martinez to the old Gier Winery on
the slopes of Mt. Veeder above the city of Napa, which became known as the
Mont La Salle Winery, after St. Jean-Baptiste de La Salle, founder of the Christian Brothers order. After buying a winery and distillery in the Central Valley,
and later the Greystone facility north of St. Helena, Christian Brothers became
one of the top suppliers of table wine in the 1950s.

CHAPTER SIX

Napa Wine during Wartime

For Napa grape growers and winemakers, the war years were a period of artificial but real prosperity resulting from a war economy that temporarily reversed the supply-and-demand balance prevalent during the 1930s. Like other California regions, Napa witnessed an influx of distilling interests and out-of-state bottlers, the setting out of new vineyards in response to increased demand for grapes, and the onset of a boom mentality, reflected in high land and grape prices, but somewhat tempered by wartime shortages of equipment, bottles, and labor. Although the experience at each Napa winery was unique, the broad pattern mimicked California as a whole.

The distillers' influence entered the valley in 1942 when Schenley bought Greystone Cellars, north of Beringer. The following year old brands changed hands and new brands emerged: Larkmead was sold to a midwestern bottler; a New York marketer leased the old Mt. Eden Winery in Oakville and introduced the Colombo label, proudly proclaiming that it was "bottled in the famous Napa Valley"; and the Mondavis bought Charles Krug to begin their transition from bulk producers to brand owners.[1] Existing quality producers such as Martini, Christian Brothers, Beaulieu, Inglenook, and Beringer used the period to develop strong national marketing relationships and to consolidate their positions in the top tier of California wineries, while bulk producers such as the Napa Valley Cooperative Winery, Lou Stralla's Napa Wine Company, and Louis Bartolucci's revived Oakville Winery, enjoyed the seller's market that existed for bulk wine. Led by an energetic newcomer, Martin Stelling, Jr., Napa grape growers experienced their first truly profitable years since Repeal and responded to winery demand and University of California suggestions by planting almost 1,000 acres of new vines, most of which were varietal.[2] Ultimately, Napa growers and winemakers experienced the same dramatic drop in prices in 1947 that devastated the rest of California's wine industry. But while some wineries went into bankruptcy or closed, the vineyards remained. Their legacy of expanded and improved grape acreage set the stage for an increase in varietal wine production in the 1950s and 1960s.

If Napa's experience during the war years mirrored that of the California wine industry as a whole, it also differed in two fundamental ways. First, although all wine was in demand, fortified "dessert" wine represented at least 70 percent of national sales. Napa, and the North Coast in general, produced dry table wines, and it was during this period that a small, but significant, price differential between "mixed blacks" and varietal grapes emerged. The acknowledgment that Napa's future lay in the production of higher-quality table wines was seen in increased plantings of varietal grapes during the war years, setting the stage for improved wine quality in the 1950s. Second, the quality wine producers of Napa benefited more from government price regulation than did other California producers, since, unlike most California producers, Napa's top wineries had established a track record of at-winery bottling and brand development during the 1930s. Because Napa wines had a history of selling at higher than the average market price, the Office of Price Administration (OPA) granted Napa's quality leaders higher price ceilings during the war years. Although wine produced and sold by these top producers represented only a fraction of Napa's total production, it was by far the most profitable segment. Napa branded producers thus experienced a happy conjunction of increased volume and higher than normal margins, leading to increased profitability. The crash of 1947 affected all wineries, but those with strong brands and deeper cash reserves were in a better position to ride out the market decline. The war years accelerated Napa's top producers' emphasis on quality table wines, a position Napa would dominate in the 1950s and 1960s.

Although the controlled wartime economy eventually produced a seller's market for California wine, the first major ownership change in the valley, the sale of Greystone Cellars in 1940, predated the scarcity economy. Perhaps a year too early, and more a result of the overproduction of the late 1930s than a premonition of increased demand, Central Wineries Inc.'s attempt to launch a national brand ultimately failed, leading to Schenley's purchase of Greystone in late 1942. The product of a quasi-private attempt by the Bank of America to stabilize the California grape market, the Central Winery fiasco illustrates both the dominate role of capital in the wine business and Napa's interconnectedness with the San Joaquin Valley's fortified wine industry.

The Central Winery Association, which later became Central California Wineries Inc., was established in 1939 as a super cooperative of major sweet wine bulk producers for the purposes of underwriting the 1939 grape harvest and marketing excess California wine. Financed by the Bank of America, which both loaned the association $10 million and assigned Burke Critchfield, a Bank of America vice president, as its general manager, the association was hailed by industry leaders as an example of a "new theory of modern banking practice."[3] The notion was that U.S. consumption of wine was increasing, but that the underfinanced California bulk producers could not carry inventory long enough for demand to meet supply, hence distressed selling of bulk wine and a buyer's market for grapes. Bank of America's motivation was not entirely altruistic. Extension of the 1938 prorate to the 1939 harvest had failed, and grape and wine prices were ruinously low. As the major lender to vineyardists and wineries, the bank really only had three options: foreclose on those who could not meet their loan payments, thus gaining title to properties not worth the total indebtedness; make numerous separate loans to individual producers; or group major producers together into a new organization and extend credit to the new company. In establishing and financing Central California Wineries, Bank of America chose the third alternative.

In March 1940, C.C.W. bought the L. M. Martini winery in Kingsburg from Martini and the Greystone Winery in St. Helena from Bisceglia Brothers. The Kingsburg plant was expanded to store and bottle sweet wines produced by member wineries, while the Greystone Winery was refurbished to store, blend, and bottle dry wines. Since most members of C.C.W. were bulk producers with small or no established brands, the company decided to launch its own national brand and hired and financed Louis Golan, formerly vice president of sales and advertising at Schenley, to do the job. Golan saw a definite opportunity, claiming, "With foreign wines virtually cut off from this country, the American wine market belongs to American wines!"[4] Not shy, Golan introduced two lines, both named after himself, GoLan and LaNglo. Bringing "modern American merchandising methods to an ancient industry," Golan initiated advertising in magazines such as *Life*, *Time*, and *Esquire*, produced expensive point-of-sale material, and hired a nationally known model, Kay Aldridge, "a bundle of beauty" whom the showman Billy Rose had called "the most beautiful girl in America," as the "LaNglo Sunshine Girl."[5] The venture may have been undercapitalized, or the timing a year too early, but, for whatever reasons, GoLan wines were not successful. In November 1942, Central California Wineries recouped some of its investment by selling Greystone to Schenley, which incorporated the winery's output into its Cresta Blanca brand.[6] For the remainder of the decade, Greystone was a crushing and fermenting site, with the raw wine shipped elsewhere for finishing and bottling.

Although the GoLan winery was located in St. Helena, it was essentially a marketing ploy by Central Valley bulk producers, and its failure was not representative of marketplace acceptance of Napa wines. Louis Golan had been correct, if premature, in his assessment of the effect of the war on shipments of European wine to the United States. While sales of all types of wine grew simply in response to America's thirst for alcoholic beverages, the curtailment of European imports left a vacuum that California producers, and Napa winemakers in particular, were eager to fill. The question was how to capitalize on the opportunity.

According to *Wines and Vines*, the place to start was with language. In a January 1941 editorial, the magazine applauded the action of the Pennsylvania Liquor Control Board in deciding to classify wines as "United States" and "Foreign" rather than "Domestic" and "Imported." Arguing that the word *domestic* was "unflattering and harmful," suggestive of "the kitchen sink and all that is drab and ordinary," the editors suggested substituting "United States" in its place.[7] In so doing, they played to a growing American nationalism and prejudice against foreign products. "Imported" somehow had a positive cachet, while "foreign" possessed a sinister, un-American, connotation. Although the internal logic of "California Burgundy" and "New York Champagne" was perhaps not consistent, the names were winning combinations when contrasted with the slightly frightening label *foreign*.

Language aside, the curtailment of European shipments left a major void for quality domestic producers. In 1939, Europe had exported almost a million gallons of table wine to the United States. In 1940, this figure dropped to .4 million, and by 1941 and 1942, it fell to .2 million, its low point for the decade.[8] Although at peak, table wine imports amounted to, at most, 5 percent of total U.S. wine consumption, the actual volumes were considerable when placed in the context of the production of a single producer or region. The decline from 1939 to 1941 represented a void of 300,000 cases of wine, at a time when the total bottled production of all Napa quality producers was well under 150,000 cases.[9] The portion of the U.S. market previously controlled by European producers represented a huge opportunity if Napa had enough high-quality wine to meet the potential demand.

The boom period started in 1940 when European exports declined. George Deuer remembered that Inglenook first began shipping outside California "just before the Second World War . . . when the French couldn't ship any wines in here and the Germans couldn't either. . . . Then the market just boomed in New York, Boston and Chicago."[10] André Tchelistcheff echoed Deuer when he observed that Beaulieu's "business started to climb up during the war . . . due to the closed ports," and that their initial contract for 30,000 cases was "expanded to the maximum possibility within our physical operational structure."[11] The demand must have appeared sometime in 1940, since by early 1941, both wineries upgraded their physical plants. In January, Inglenook remodeled its old carriage house, converting it into a "modern bottling, labeling and storage building" in order to "relieve pressure for space at the winery itself."[12] A few months later, Beaulieu initiated a 7,000-square-foot, two-story addition, including "a bottling room and storage space," with the insulated second floor designed to provide space for "1000 additional 50-gallon barrels and 50 180-gallon puncheons."[13]

By the time the United States entered the war, the traditional quality producers of the Napa Valley, joined by Christian Brothers and the Martini Winery, had acquired national distribution and were actively shifting from bulk to bottled wine production. Beaulieu had signed with Park & Tilford in 1937, becoming the first Napa winery with strong national distribution. Besides being a wine importer, Park & Tilford also sold distilled spirits, and the Beaulieu business boomed during the war, when the Park & Tilford sales force engaged in "tie-in" sales tactics, selling ten cases of Beaulieu for every one case of whiskey.[14] Across the highway at Inglenook, John Daniel, Jr., initially sold wine through Frank Schoonmaker, but by 1941 he had selected the importing firm of Bellows and Company to represent Inglenook's limited production nationally. Bellows was led by the dynamic Frederick Wildman, who, along with Schoonmaker, was instrumental in encouraging varietal labeling for California wines.[15] It is unclear why Daniel chose Bellows rather than remaining a part of the Schoonmaker portfolio of California wines. Perhaps Daniel simply did not want to be grouped with another Napa producer. Schoonmaker actively represented Martini and several other California vintners, including Almaden, Korbel, and Wente, from 1940 until he joined the Armed Forces in 1942. At that point, Schoonmaker turned over the "Schoonmaker Selections" to "21 Brands" in New York, which distributed Martini wines east of the Rockies until the mid 1970s.[16]

Not all distribution agreements were as permanent. To the north, Beringer Brothers achieved East Coast distribution in late 1941 when M.C.C. Importing, the U.S. importing arm of Moët & Chandon, the biggest French champagne producer, began representing Beringer on the Atlantic coast. This arrangement did not last, and by early 1944, the American Distilling Company was selling Beringer wines on the East Coast. In late 1946, Beringer again changed distributors, switching to Kobrand Corporation, a large importing firm.[17] Probably the most successful, and certainly the longest-lasting, distribution agreement was that between Christian Brothers and Alfred Fromm.[18] Beginning in 1938 with the importing firm of Picker-Linz, and later with the succeeding company of Fromm & Sichel, Fromm helped build Christian Brothers into the leading volume brand in the Napa Valley by the end of World War II. Partly this was a result of the willingness of Christian Brothers to move beyond dry wines by emphasizing dessert wines and, in 1940, brandy in its product line. Partly it was the result of a policy of moderate pricing, at least vis-à-vis Inglenook and Beaulieu wines, which created a sense of value and helped build volume. But it was clearly also the result of Fromm's hard and thorough work in conjunction with brand advertising, product placement, and innovative use of point of sale. One survey conducted by the *New York Times* in 1942 showed that Christian Brothers had placements in over 90 percent of all liquor stores in New York, 7 percent higher than the second-place, locally bottled "Mission Bell" brand.[19] These placements were then backed up by daily newspaper advertising and, later, during the fall selling season, with a novel window display that mimicked a stained-glass cathedral window. Set under a gothic arch and using seven colors printed on translucent paper to imitate the stained glass, the display employed an electric bulb placed behind it to "pick up the soft colors and the beautiful detail of the stained glass windows." Besides highlighting Christian Brothers wine and brandy, the display met "dimout" regulations, thus providing a retailer with "a unique method of lighting his window within the prescribed regulations."[20] By 1945, the brand had grown to the point where Christian Brothers leased and later bought the Mt. Tivy Winery near Reedly in the San Joaquin Valley.[21] In so doing, it succeeded in combining dry and sweet wine production in one national brand headquarters in the Napa Valley, exactly what Central Wineries and Louis Golan had tried to do four years earlier.

Christian Brothers, Beringer, Martini, Inglenook, and Beaulieu were all established wineries with a history of production and sales. As such, each possessed varying degrees of brand recognition and could relatively easily increase the bottled portion of its business by reducing bulk sales as national opportunities opened up for California wines with the blockade of Europe.[22] But in 1943 and 1944, the Napa quality producers were joined by four "new" entrants to the field, although "new" must be used guardedly, inasmuch as each producer had a history of wine production or sales somewhere. In chronological order, these newcomers were: Napa Valley Grape Products, a New York bottler with ties to California, which bought the Fagiani Winery near Oakville in March 1943; the Mondavis, who bought Charles Krug in March 1943 and began to build their own brand; Bragno and Company, a Chicago regional bottler, headed by Frank Bragno, which bought Larkmead in conjunction with another distributor in June 1943; and Louis Bartolucci, who revived his family's bulk winery in Oakville in 1942 and later formed a partnership with out-of-state interests in 1944 for the purpose of bottling wine. Although the Mondavis' Charles Krug Winery was ultimately the most successful venture, the history of each of the four sheds light on different facets of the wine business during World War II and is worth reviewing.

Of the four, the Mondavi family's revival of the Charles Krug Winery and brand is the best known, primarily because it became one of the leading Napa producers in the 1950s and 1960s. But in March 1943, when Paul Alexander, head of the local Bank of America branch, informed Robert Mondavi that James Moffitt was planning to sell the Charles Krug Winery, few consumers had heard either of the winery or of the family.[23] Cesare Mondavi had built a comfortable life for himself and his family by shipping wine grapes from Lodi to immigrant communities during Prohibition. Following Repeal, he continued growing and shipping grapes, but in 1937 he also acquired a controlling interest in the Sunny St. Helena winery, which produced bulk wine for shipment to regional bottlers. In addition, he assumed the presidency of the two-million-gallon Acampo Winery in Lodi in 1940.[24] A careful businessman, Cesare Mondavi was not given to impetuous decisions.

Robert Mondavi, Cesare's oldest son and manager of Sunny St. Helena, saw the opportunity afforded by the sale of Charles Krug, as well as the necessity of a transition from bulk to bottled wine production. The lack of availability of tank cars for bulk shipment had already caused

Robert to consider installation of a bottling plant at Sunny St. Helena in order to custom bottle wine for the Mondavis' eastern accounts.[25] Bottling was also potentially more profitable for Sunny St. Helena because of the higher price ceilings for bottled wine. Despite the logic of doing so, however, Cesare deferred to his minority partners, who did not wish to expand the business or to incur the additional costs associated with establishing a bottling line.

For Robert Mondavi, the Charles Krug Winery offered the chance to acquire a historic property and to establish a separate, totally family-owned winery that could buy bulk wine from Sunny St. Helena at established prices, bottle it for East Coast customers, and produce its own wine under a new label. In March, Cesare Mondavi visited the Krug winery and vineyards with Robert and his brother Peter, who was on military leave. Covering almost 150 acres, the property was run-down but quite reasonably priced at $75,000. The next day, the Mondavis met Moffitt in San Francisco, and Robert was surprised when his "ultra-conservative" father bought the winery that day. In retrospect, Cesare Mondavi's decision was perhaps not as impetuous as Robert thought. The Acampo Winery in Lodi was in the process of being sold to the Gibson Wine Company, and as its president and a major stockholder, Cesare Mondavi was in a cash-strong position.

Robert Mondavi jumped into the process of rebuilding the Charles Krug Winery and establishing a brand. Persistent visits to federal offices in San Francisco were eventually rewarded with a double-A priority for procuring the rationed building and bottling materials necessary to modernize the winery. Remodeling and construction lasted several years. A June 1945 column in the *Wine Review* reported that walls were being reinforced with concrete, new floors laid, and new tanks and cooperage installed, along with two bottling lines. It concluded that "the firm plans to develop gradually its own complete line of California wines."[26]

From 1943 the new company, C. Mondavi and Sons, made wine at Charles Krug, but augmented its production with bulk wine bought from Sunny St. Helena and bottled at Krug. Most of the wine was packaged in half-gallon and gallon bottles, both as private labels for regional bottlers and under the "C.K." brand, which the Mondavis used for wines of lower quality. The best wines were to be bottled in fifths and branded "Charles Krug" at the suggestion of their New York distributor, R. U. Delaphena, who had told the family, "Mondavi is not a well known name. Krug is a very famous name" (no doubt referring to the well-known French Champagne house, although the Mondavis adopted

Charles Krug's 1861 founding date, as well as the tag "Napa Valley's Oldest Winery").[27] The family began crushing and storing the limited amount of varietal grapes available to them, as well as identifying top lots of their bulk wines for barrel aging, with the idea of releasing the wines later under the Charles Krug label. The total production of wines intended for the Charles Krug label relative to wine destined for the private bottling contracts and the C.K. brand is difficult to determine, but in 1947 the Mondavis entered into a contract with McKesson & Robbins, a major importer, to distribute the entire output of Charles Krug wines nationally, a total of 40,000 cases.[28] Since Sunny St. Helena had sold more than one million gallons in bulk, or the equivalent of over 400,000 cases, in 1942, it is clear that during the war years C. Mondavi and Sons was chiefly engaged in producing wine for the C.K. brand and private labeling for regional bottlers.[29] A 1947 notice in the *St. Helena Star* listing the names under which C. Mondavi and Sons did business included ten brand names in addition to the Charles Krug Winery.[30]

No matter under what label the wine was sold, C. Mondavi and Sons prospered during the 1940s and gradually moved all wine production to the Charles Krug Winery. Three years after buying Charles Krug, in March 1946, the Mondavis sold Sunny St. Helena to a local grape grower, Martin Stelling, and effectively consolidated winemaking operations at Charles Krug.[31] Two months later, Cesare Mondavi, the general manager, announced a reorganization of the firm, appointing Peter Mondavi, who had just returned from war service, as head of production, promoting Robert Mondavi to assistant general manager, and creating a new sales company, Charles Krug Wineries, Inc., to handle all sales of the newly released varietal wines. C. Rossi, who had been the general manager of the competing Napa Valley Grape Products was named general manager of the new sales company.[32]

The Mondavis' appointment of McKesson & Robbins, as national distributor of the newly released Charles Krug wines could not have been made at a worse time. In 1947, the bottom dropped out of the wine market and prices for bulk dry wine plummeted from $1.50 a gallon to under 50 cents. The agreement with McKesson & Robbins was canceled, and the Mondavis vowed to build their own national sales organization, never again to depend upon another sales agency. Unlike several other new wineries, the Mondavis survived the wine crash of 1947, but as Robert Mondavi recalled, "We lost a lot of money in 1947. . . . It took years for that to adjust itself. . . . They were really lean years from '47 on . . . [but] we did hang on."[33]

For the Mondavis, the war economy represented opportunity. For out-of-state bottlers, the dislocation of supply and demand threatened disaster. As California producers like the Mondavis switched from bulk sales to bottled wine, regional bottlers dependent on supplies of inexpensive and plentiful bulk wine from California were faced with increased costs, and in some instances with the specter of no wine at all. The answer, for those with money and guts, was to come to California, buy a winery, and secure a source of supply. This solution was pursued by both Edward Bragno, of the Bragno Wine Company of Chicago, and Ben Migliaccio, of the San Gabriel Wine Company of New York. Although neither company lasted until the end of the war economy, their histories illustrate the complexity of the U.S. wine industry as well as the interactions between California producers and regional bottlers.

In March 1943, Migliaccio and his wife Mary bought the old Fagiani Winery, also known as the Mt. Eden Winery, near the Silverado Trail in Oakville.[34] Although this marked their entry into the Napa Valley as winery owners, Migliaccio had been active in the California wine industry since Repeal as the sales manager and a stockholder of the San Gabriel Wine Company, a New York bottler.[35] Like most bottlers, Migliaccio had shopped around when California wine was plentiful, and he had developed several labels for the use of his company. A BATF investigation of his application for ownership of the Fagiani Winery showed that "some years ago," Migliaccio had visited the San Gabriel Vineyard Company in California, and had returned to New York and "established the San Gabriel Wine Co." there.[36] Migliaccio later apparently contracted with the Cucamonga Pioneer Vineyard Association in Southern California to bottle wine for him in 1941 under the DBAs "B. Migliaccio Winery" and the "Boncore Winery," using the brand names "Colombo" and "Santarpia."[37] In addition to his own brands, Migliaccio also bottled and represented the "Cordova" brand for Colonial Grape Products, a well-established California company owned by the Federspiels, which operated several wineries in the state.[38] In 1943, Roland Federspiel and Migliaccio formed a partnership and took over the Mills Winery, a large dessert-wine-producing facility near Sacramento, to market Cordova wines back east. That same year, he formed a separate partnership, the Mt. Eden Wine Company of New York, to bottle and distribute wine produced at the Fagiani Winery.[39]

By September 1944, Migliaccio had consolidated his holdings into one company, Napa Valley Grape Products, emphasizing the Colombo brand. He and Federspiel had apparently had a falling out and had separated, with Federspiel maintaining control of the vineyard property and the right to the Cordova brand, and Migliaccio retaining the Mills Winery.[40] The two wineries together had a total capacity of over one million gallons, and Migliaccio hired C. J. Rossi, who had previously headed production at Cresta Blanca, as the general manager of winery operations. Sales manager Ralph Santarpia, who had apparently been with Migliaccio long enough to have had a brand named after him, reported that sales staff were being recruited and that "an extensive advertising campaign" was "soon to be launched."[41]

For the remainder of 1944 and 1945, Napa Valley Grape Products continued to grow. A photo of a sales staff meeting in New York shows at least thirty people, and an "ultimate goal" of "full national distribution of Colombo wines" was articulated at a follow-up meeting in May.[42] To that end, the company bought a second winery in Napa, located two miles north of St. Helena on Lodi Lane. The stated purpose was "for a complete finishing plant to handle all wines produced and purchased and the bottling of the Colombo Napa Valley brands."[43] By September, the new winery was ready to bring in the harvest, and combined with the Oakville Winery, it gave Napa Valley Grape Products a capacity of 500,000 gallons, putting it at the same level of production as Beringer. While probably only a small portion of the production was actually bottled as "Colombo" wine, Migliaccio had emerged as a major force in the valley in a few short years.[44]

Whether Napa Valley Grape Products could have survived the downturn of 1947 will never be known. Ben Migliaccio died of osteomyelitis at forty-five in March 1946.[45] His wife, referred to as "M. M." in later press releases, continued the brand, but production seems to have ended by fall 1946. In May, C. J. Rossi was hired by the Mondavis, becoming the head of their sales company. Rossi apparently arranged for the Mondavis to custom produce wine for Napa Valley Grape Products, since an August 1946 announcement in the *St. Helena Star* shows that the Mondavis added Napa Valley Grape Products of California to their list of DBAs, presumably so that they could bottle wine for Napa Valley Grape Products.[46] Thus by 1946, in the space of three short years, the Migliaccios had gone full circle, from brand owners to producers and back to brand owners. The Colombo brand, with its slogan "Discover a New World of Profits" and its picture of a Spanish galleon coupled with the words "Smooth SALE-ing," returned to its roots in New York, but its intensive advertising campaign and its forceful display of the appellation "Napa Valley" on its label and in print advertisements helped build consumer awareness of the Napa Valley as California's premier dry-wine-producing region.

The Bragno Wine Company's foray into California with its purchase of Larkmead in June 1943 was motivated by the same instinct as Migliaccio's involvement with California wine production: survival. Bragno and Company had been established in Chicago by Frank Bragno in 1891 as bulk wholesalers and bottlers. Following Repeal, the company reopened, becoming the Illinois distributor of Italian Swiss Colony bulk wines. In January 1943, the Bragnos' source of supply was completely cut off when National Distillers bought Italian Swiss Colony, switched to at-winery bottling, and initiated its own national distribution network. In the words of the BATF inspector, the Bragnos had to acquire a California winery "in order to assure themselves a supply of wine sufficient to continue their business."[47]

The task of finding a suitable property in California fell to Edward Bragno, one of Frank Bragno's four sons, who served as general manager of Bragno and Company. Two of his brothers were on active service in the military, and his brother James told a BATF inspector, "Father is too old and I can't do it, so it is up to Eddie to keep us in business."[48] In February 1943, Edward Bragno traveled to California, surveyed the situation, and returned to Chicago, where he created a partnership, American Wineries, with his sister, Rose Pendergast. Borrowing funds from Bragno and Company, which included advance payments from area liquor retailers for future wine deliveries, Bragno returned to California and entered into a partnership with Brookside Vineyards and Distillers, another regional bottler located in Scranton, Pennsylvania. Together they bought the Riverbank Wine Company, a dessert wine producer in Riverbank, near Modesto, for $300,000 and then the giant Alta Winery and Distillery in Dinuba, farther south in the San Joaquin Valley, for over $1,300,000. All this was accomplished with a total down payment of $150,000, with "the expectation of borrowing the remainder from eastern banks." Returning to Chicago, Bragno had "time for sober thoughts" and, realizing that "he was acting also for his brothers" and thus "was assuming a large responsibility for them," withdrew from the Alta purchase. American Wineries took the Riverbank Winery, and Brookside, run by Fred Gentile, took over Alta.[49]

With a source of dessert wines secured, Bragno turned north, traveling to the Napa Valley, where he found Larkmead ripe for sale. The smallest of the big four quality producers, Larkmead did not have the fiscal strength of either Inglenook or Beaulieu, or the volume of Beringer. It had won awards, and Schoonmaker had selected one or two Larkmead wines for sale as "Schoonmaker Selections," but in 1942, the winery had limited distribution outside of California, with most of its production sold in bulk. Felix Salmina, Sr., the driving force behind Larkmead, had died in December 1940, leaving the winery to his wife and children, who incorporated as Larkmead Vineyards in April 1941.[50] The next year, the influx of out-of-state bottlers "frantically trying to protect their interests by purchasing wineries" led to a rapid escalation in vineyard and winery prices, which in Elmer Salmina's opinion could not last indefinitely.[51] Concluding that prices could not go much higher, the family agreed to sell the winery and approximately 85 acres of vineyards to Bragno for $320,000 in June 1943, accepting a down payment of $20,000. They apparently experienced a degree of "seller's remorse." The BATF report indicates that Bragno made an additional $1,000 payment to cover any interest on a loan from Bank of America to the Salminas, since he wanted to "forestall any objection on technicalities which might [have carried] the negotiations past the original contract deadline as the seller was showing signs of wanting to do."[52]

The purchase of the Riverbank Winery must have depleted most of the Bragno and Company's cash reserves. In order to complete the Larkmead contract, Edward Bragno incorporated a new company in Illinois, Larkmead Vineyard Sales, Inc., and approached Harry Blum of Philip Blum and Company, Inc., offering half of the stock in the new corporation in exchange for financing the purchase. Philip Blum and Company was a large wholesale liquor dealer, rectifier, and importer of wine and spirits, with a net worth three times that of Bragno and Company. Its diversified holdings included outright ownership of W. P. Squibb Distilling in Indiana, Loretto Distilling of Kentucky, and 25 percent of the James B. Beam distillery of Kentucky.[53] Blum had a massive line of credit with Chicago banks, secured by whiskey warehouse receipts worth over $2 million. He agreed to finance the Larkmead deal, paying his company's 50 percent of the purchase cost and loaning Edward Bragno $100,000, secured by Bragno's stock in the corporation. When the financing was finished, Edward Bragno was president of Larkmead Vineyard Sales, which owned the stock of Larkmead Winery, having put in just $2,500 of his own money. The balance of his $180,000 was derived from a $77,500 loan from Bragno and Company and $100,000 from Blum. It was no wonder that a BATF inspector observed that "although Mr. Bragno appears as one of the large investors, whenever he was asked a question he would look at Mr. Blum and ask him to furnish him with the answers."[54]

The potential for problems between Bragno and Blum was inherent from the onset. Aside from the inequity in investment, they had different goals for the company. Blum had declared to the BATF inspector that although some bulk sales would be made to Philip Blum and Company and to Bragno and Company, "Larkmead Vineyard Sales, Inc. would enter the field as a Wholesale Liquor Dealer selling principally wines under the Larkmead label."[55] Rather than building the Larkmead label, Bragno's primary interest was in supplying wine for and expanding sales of the family's principal brands, Bragno Imperial and Lloyd's Imported.[56] BATF records show that in late 1943 and early 1944, almost 240,000 gallons of wine were shipped in bulk, while only 30,000 gallons were bottled, presumably under the Larkmead label.[57] Bragno's concentration on his family's brands was such that Bragno and Company did not even distribute Larkmead wines in the Midwest, leaving that to Philip Blum and Company.[58] Of course, it is possible that the division of effort and wine was a conscious and agreed-upon choice on the part of both Bragno and Blum, but since the supply of wine produced from the Larkmead vineyard was essentially static, one brand could only grow at the expense of the other.

The original terms of Blum's loan to Bragno were that the $100,000 was to be repaid in a year. Bragno and Company had no doubt been hurt by the mild depression in wine prices in the second half of 1945, and by 1946, Edward Bragno still owed $84,000. In return for extending the loan until June 1947, Blum took an option to purchase Bragno's shares in Larkmead Vineyard Sales Co. He exercised that option in September 1946, and Bragno resigned as president.[59] Wine sales were strong throughout the industry in 1946, and Blum upgraded the winery to emphasize varietal production and initiated a major advertising campaign.[60] Aimed at the wine trade and employing the slogan "Mellow as the Song of the Lark," the full-page advertisements played on Larkmead's history of production and the fact that its winemakers were both "growers and producers," involved in every step, "from nurturing the vine to leisurely aging the wine."[61]

Of course, 1947 was not the best year to begin a national advertising campaign. The slump in wine consumption was in large part a response of the U.S. public to the unfettered availability of distilled spirits. While the decline in wine sales was difficult for wineries, the increase in the consumption of spirits made distilleries quite attractive as an investment. Larkmead was only a minor part of Philip Blum and Company's holdings, most of which were in the distilled spirits sector. In December 1947, Harry Weiss, acting for National Distillers, bought all of the Philip

Blum stock from Harry Blum for $11.8 million, and National Distillers became the effective owner of Larkmead. National Distillers transferred the ownership to its own winery, Italian Swiss Colony, ending Larkmead's operation as a separate winery until the property was bought by Hanns Kornell in the 1950s.[62] It was an odd twist of fate that National Distillers' acquisition of Italian Swiss Colony in 1943 set off a chain of events that resulted in its assuming control of one of Napa's oldest wineries five years later.

The final major "new" winery to appear in the Napa Valley was Louis Bartolucci's Oakville Winery. The Bartoluccis were Napa grape growers and had built a winery in Oakville following Repeal, but they gave up the processing business in 1938. In 1942, Louis Bartolucci decided that the time seemed right to restart the operation. Buying new tanks and a continuous press, he produced 200,000 gallons of wine, which he sold to the Petri Wine Company.[63] In late 1943, he was approached by Andrea Gusmano of San Francisco and Harry Weiner of New York, who convinced him that they could sell all the wine he could make and bottle. They created a partnership the following year, bought out Louis's father, installed a bottling line, doubled the size of the building, and bought a sweet wine plant near Lodi. By 1945, according to Bartolucci, the Oakville Winery was eleventh or twelfth in the state in monthly sales of bottled wine.[64]

Things went well until the price of wine collapsed in 1947. Until then, the partnership was shipping a railcar a day of bottled wine to trade outlets in New York and Ohio. Overnight the market disappeared, wholesalers and retailers went out of business, and Oakville was left with over $300,000 in receivables. By August 1947, operating under the protection of bankruptcy, the winery listed debts of $355,000 and assets of $404,000.[65]

Bartolucci's partners proved unreliable. Harry Weiner, who was also involved in the sale of distilled spirits, was caught making black market sales, arrested, and sentenced to a year in prison. Since felons cannot be holders of alcohol producer permits, Weiner was effectively removed from the partnership. The other partner, Andrea Gusmano, who as a partner would have been personally liable for the winery debt, transferred personal property out of his name. Unhappy bankers forced Gusmano to transfer his "equity" in Oakville to Bartolucci for $500, leaving Bartolucci with sole ownership of the winery and sole responsibility for the final debt of $110,000.[66]

Bartolucci successfully sold his creditors on a reorganization plan of

30 percent down and the balance in two years. He borrowed the first payment from his father, taking his two brothers into the business in return. A short crop in 1949 caused an increase in bulk wine prices, allowing Bartolucci to repay the creditors in full. The winery continued in business as a family operation throughout the 1950s and 1960s, although at a more sedate pace. Bartolucci had learned that rapid expansion in a boom market was generally matched by an equally speedy descent.

Although speculators such as Bartolucci's partners and out-of-state bottlers like Migliaccio and Bragno were attracted to the profits associated with wineries, what they really needed were grapes. Ultimately, wineries were processors, and without access to the raw product, a winery in California was just as useless as a bottling plant in New York or Chicago. It was no coincidence that Mt. Eden, Larkmead, and Charles Krug all had vineyards in addition to a winery. In buying a winery with a vineyard, the purchaser was assured of a base level of production and a controlled level of cost. To expand beyond that base, the winery owner had to buy grapes on the open market, and from 1943 through 1946, Napa grape prices rose dramatically. Although most wineries certainly gained in profitability during the war years, it was the grape growers who benefited most.

During the war years, with raisin grapes diverted to the war effort and an increased demand for wine, grape prices soared statewide, moving from $22 a ton in 1942 to $100 a ton in 1944.[67] Prices rose even higher on the North Coast and in the Napa Valley. Even during the depressed period of the late 1930s, when grapes were in excess statewide and the prorate was in operation, Napa grapes had received perhaps a 10 percent premium over the prices of irrigated grapes from the Central Valley. At prices of $20 to $30 a ton, this premium only amounted to $2 or $3. However, during the four harvests from 1943 through 1946, the differential between Central Valley and North Coast grape prices increased substantially. By 1944, statewide prices averaged $100 a ton, while $135 was asked for "standard black grapes" in Napa, and the scarcer white grapes fetched $150.[68] As a percentage, this differential increased even when grape prices declined somewhat in 1945. That year the statewide average was $57 dollars a ton, whereas $100 a ton was paid for black grapes and $120 a ton for white grapes from the Napa Valley.[69] In 1946, when Schenley and National Distillers bid up the statewide price to $85 a ton, Napa growers received $120 for black and $140 for white grapes, approximately a 50 percent premium over Central Valley grapes.[70]

The difference in price between North Coast and Central Valley grapes was not so much a response to consumer demand as it was regulation-driven. Wineries owning quality brands with a history of higher prices were allowed to charge a higher base price for their wines than standard table wine producers. In the seller's market that operated during the war years, producers emphasized the higher-priced and more profitable brands, creating a demand for higher-quality wine grapes from the North Coast. The competition for grapes was reflected in a series of advertisements taken out each year at harvest by Cresta Blanca, aimed at encouraging local growers to deliver their grapes to Greystone Cellars. Cresta Blanca claimed that it was building a permanent market for higher-quality wines, and that a grower's choice to deliver grapes to Cresta Blanca was an investment in future profitability. One advertisement promised that Cresta Blanca would "crushing the fine varieties of grapes in the Napa Valley, and give them the care they really deserve to build up a lasting market for these particularly fine grape varieties." Another advertisement pointed out that Cresta Blanca was "working constantly to promote better markets — with better products, better packages, better displays and more and better advertising and better selling," concluding "that's only a part of our contribution to the common bond between Grower and Vintner."[71]

The demand for wine grapes and the increased profitability of vineyards led to purchases of existing vineyards and to new plantings in the Napa Valley, as it did throughout California. In the three-year period between 1944 and 1946, over 1,200 acres of new vineyards were set out, expanding Napa's acreage by about 10 percent.[72] In 1943, Louis Martini bought the 250-acre La Loma vineyard in the Carneros area southwest of the city of Napa, John Garetto of Garetto Winery acquired 100 acres of vineyard there too, and Edwin Federspiel of Colonial Grape Products bought the 200-acre Bianchi vineyard in Calistoga.[73] In 1945, Jerome Draper, owner of the 100-acre La Perla vineyard on Spring Mountain, west of St. Helena, bought the historic 1,000-acre Stanley ranch in the Carneros area and declared his intention to "replant many of the old vineyards with fine wine variety grapes."[74] That same year, Charles Forni, director of the Napa Valley Cooperative Winery, set out 40 acres of new vines, Beaulieu planted 55 new acres in Oakville, and a partnership headed by Lou Stralla, owner of the Napa Wine Company, broke ground for 120 acres of vineyard in the adjacent Berryessa Valley.[75]

Most purchases and plantings were by grape growers or winery owners, but one newcomer, Martin Stelling, Jr., played an important role in the expansion and improvement of Napa's vineyards during the war years. Stelling was a San Francisco businessman and socially prominent enough to be a member of the Bohemian Club and to have helped lead the fight to preserve San Francisco's cable cars during the 1940s.[76] In July 1943, the 40-year-old Stelling bought the 500-acre Tokalon estate from the Churchill family and entered the grape-growing business.[77] In March 1944, Stelling acquired an even larger piece of property, the 1,700-acre McGill ranch adjacent to the Churchill holdings. The McGill property included vineyards and the historic, but decrepit, Benson Winery. The two parcels combined gave Stelling "united holdings on the West side of the highway for several miles, reaching far back into the hills."[78]

Stelling quickly made his presence known, arranging for old buildings to be torn down, a creek realigned, and new vineyards planted, including a 400-acre bloc of varietal vines. In André Tchelistcheff's words, Stelling was "an outstanding, energetic man. Unbelievable. It was oxygen to Napa Valley — new oxygen."[79] His energy was contagious. In July 1944, he and Ed Chaix, a local grower and perennial head of the Napa County Grape Growers' Association, bought a 7-acre "vineyard and orchard property" in the Carneros region.[80] Just prior to crushing that vintage, he approached Louis Bartolucci to arrange custom crushing of his and other property owners' grapes.[81] Although that particular deal fell through, Stelling did not give up the idea of making and marketing his own wine. In 1946, he bought the Sunny St. Helena Winery from the Mondavis, forming Napa Cooperative Vineyards with Charles Forni and Ed Chaix.[82] By 1946, he had clearly become an active leader in Napa's grape and wine community, and he served as president of the Napa County Grape Growers' Association in 1947. In May 1950, the 47-year-old Stelling died in a one-car accident north of Yountville as he was returning in the early morning hours from a business meeting in San Francisco.[83] At the time of his death, he was in the process of remodeling the old Benson Winery, apparently with the intention of creating a new premium winery. His legacy to the valley was a major new vineyard of varietal grapes, later used by Beaulieu, and then by Charles Krug, to fuel expansion in the 1950s.[84]

Stelling may have been unusual in the size of his plantings, but his decision to plant varietal grapes was typical of other Napa vineyardists during the war. In 1945, the *Wine Review* reported "a definite move toward improved varieties for dry wine production," listing as examples "Pinot, Semillon and Cabernet." The following year, the Napa agricultural commissioner, W. D. Butler, remarked on "a definite trend to the high class wine grapes, such as Cabernet, Pinot, etc."[85] And in 1947, the

Wine Review listed Lou Stralla as owning 1,200 acres of "varietal wine grapes."[86] There is no way of knowing what percentage of the new plantings in Napa were varietal. But vineyard composition had certainly changed for the better since Repeal, when two-thirds of the valley was planted in Petite Sirah and Alicante, and the leading white variety was Palomino.

We know neither the actual makeup of Napa's vineyards in the war years nor what was really meant by the term *varietal* then. "The vintners of Napa county are asking that growers plant some of the following varieties: Johannisberger [*sic*] Riesling, Pinot noir, Early Burgundy, White pinot, Semillon, white Malvoise, Cabernet, and French Colombar [*sic*]," the Napa farm advisor, Herman Baade, wrote in his weekly column in April 1942. "We are informed that a supply of a number of the more common varieties is adequate," he concluded.[87] The following year, the University of California's Agricultural Experiment Station issued its circular 356, *Grape Varieties for Wine Production*, which essentially summarized Amerine and Winkler's *Composition and Quality of Wines and Musts of California Grapes*, published in early 1944. Both works drew on the experiments in varietal adaptation to climate performed in the late 1930s by Amerine and Winkler, whose recommendations for the St. Helena area included Cabernet Sauvignon, Semillon, Sauvignon blanc, and Chardonnay for production of "high-quality table wines."[88] Napa growers seem to have heeded the university's advice, but not all growers in other areas did so. Two years later, in December 1945, Winkler ruefully wrote: "One cannot help but wonder why large scale plantings of Palomino (Golden Chasselas) continue to be made in the coastal areas."[89]

The planting of a new vineyard, whether in Napa or the Central Valley, was a physical expression of a grape grower's present finances and future expectations. The missionary work of the university during the 1930s had probably convinced most growers that Cabernet and other recommended varietals would produce better wines than Alicante or Palomino. That was not in doubt. What was in question was the grower's economic ability to plant a new vineyard or graft an existing one. Both took cash, and for the first time since Repeal, Napa grape growers earned enough during the war years to be able to forget about mere subsistence and think of the future. Which raised the second question: What variety would return the most money with the least risk over the life of a vineyard? Wineries might prefer fine varietals, but would the varietals give the same yield as Carignane or Zinfandel? If not, would the wineries pay the difference?

Like most economic decisions, the question facing the grower involved two elements that had to be balanced: return and risk.[90] Fine varietal grapes do not bear as heavily as standard varieties, and as the editor of *Wines and Vines* put it in April 1945, "Six tons per acre of Muscats at $125 per ton is a far superior crop to 1½ tons per acre of Pinots, even if the latter can be sold at a premium."[91] That settled the issue of short-term return when grapes were in demand, but what of risk? What would happen when the war ended, price controls were lifted and whiskey and raisins returned? "The years 1937 and 1938, when . . . more grapes were available than anyone knew what to do with, are still well remembered," the same magazine would say a year later.[92] So how was a grower to balance the two elements? *Wines and Vines* counseled that under "normal" market conditions, "vintners would be selective in purchasing grapes for winemaking," that there "would be a glut of grapes on the market," and that "under such conditions it will be the grower of the better variety grapes who will have the strongest financial position."[93]

In deciding what varieties to plant, Napa growers chose quality. This was perhaps a conservative hedge against an uncertain future, but it also reflected a belief that Napa wineries would continue to stand out. An anonymous writer in the *Wine Review* correctly assessed the situation: "The planting of choicer dry wine varieties indicates a strong faith among Napa vineyardists in the future of the dry wine industry."[94] It might have sounded trite, but it was true. Those vineyards, physical expressions of future hopes and expectations, were the basis for expanding production of high-quality wine in the Napa Valley over the next two decades.

The decision of some individual growers to plant shy-bearing varietal grapes was a turning point in Napa's viticultural history. Generally, the lower-yielding varieties, such as Chardonnay and Pinot noir, had been planted by "vintner-growers" who could "take full advantage of the merits of these varieties to produce fine wines."[95] Inglenook's Chardonnay was a case in point. Planted in 1937 on "a small hillside section," the vines were mature enough to produce a representative crop by 1945. Under the title "Yields Good Tonnage," *Wines and Vines* reported that "a harvest of 1½ tons per acre can reasonably be expected in this area from fully grown vines," adding that such tonnage represented a "pleasant surprise" for Inglenook.[96] When compared to a yield of 3 to 4, and in a good year perhaps 6, tons per acre from more standard varieties such as Carignane and Zinfandel, a low-yielding variety would have to command a much higher price, as would the resulting wine. During the 1940s, when the *St. Helena Star* quoted grape prices at harvest, it often referred to "standard black grapes" or "standard white grapes." It is possible to read too much into an omission, but the failure to mention specific varietals seems to imply that little varietal tonnage was on the open market. Yet at the same time, the use of the word *standard* implicitly recognized that other varieties were on the market and did receive different prices.

Even when Napa's independent growers joined the vintner-growers in setting out varietal vines during the war, the time lag from planting to bearing meant that little new varietal tonnage was available to Napa wineries during the 1940s. Although the OPA's regulation of the economy had "made the wineries more aware than ever before of varietal wine types," because of the retail pricing differential, the movement toward varietal wine was still in its infancy.[97] At the urging of F. Wildman, Inglenook had moved "completely to varietal designation" for its wines.[98] The L. M. Martini Winery marketed a full line of varietal wines, but by 1947, Louis P. Martini estimates, varietal wine amounted to less than half of the total bottled production of about 25,000 cases.[99] Beaulieu and, to a lesser extent, Beringer produced varietal wines in limited quantities, amounting to small percentages of their total production, which was dominated by generic wines. The Mondavis at Charles Krug may have wished to emulate Inglenook, but more resembled Beaulieu. "The program was to get into varietals, but it wasn't something you could do overnight," Peter Mondavi recalled.[100]

One winery that had begun to specialize solely in varietal wines was Lee Stewart's tiny Souverain Cellars on Howell Mountain. Perhaps twenty years ahead of his time, Stewart was the first, and for a long time the only, example of a new breed of owner/winemaker who had moved to the Napa Valley and fallen in love with wine. In 1943, Stewart, a Bay Area businessman from Hillsborough, bought a country retreat in the hills above St. Helena from the Starks, who had built a small winery in 1934 in which to vinify their twenty-two acres of Zinfandel and Carignane.[101] Bitten by the winemaking bug, Stewart renewed the vineyards and winery and began producing very small lots of varietal wine. In 1947, his 1945 Zinfandel and Pinot noir both won silver medals at the State Fair, instantly putting him in the same quality category as Martini, Inglenook, and Beaulieu.[102] Although Stewart's operation was barely on a commercial scale, his emphasis on quality varietal wine production was a harbinger of things to come for the valley and placed him among the handful of varietal producers in California.

The small number of varietal producers and small volume of varietal wine are probably best illustrated by a review of the awards given at the State Fair in 1948. The annual State Fair wine judging had ceased "for the duration" of the war, but it recommenced in 1947. The 1948 results are more interesting than the 1947 ones, because they include the number of entrants in each category and the volume of wine produced by each award winner by category. In most instances, the 1948 awards represented white wine from the 1946 vintage and red wine from the 1945 vintage or earlier, so they are illustrative of production during World War II. Generics still predominated. "Burgundy" as a category had thirty-nine entrants, and the total volume produced by the top three medal winners was 62,000 gallons, or about 26,000 cases. Pinot noir, the classic red grape of Burgundy, as a category had just thirteen entrants, and the total volume of the three medal winners was only 3,364 gallons, or just over 1,400 cases. The three Pinot noir awards were all given to Napa producers, and the total volume was somewhat skewed by the Martinis, who received a bronze medal, and whose 2,585 gallons accounted for over 70 percent of the production of the medal winners. Beaulieu had produced 626 gallons and Inglenook only 153 gallons. Similar results could be given for other categories. There were only one entry each in Sauvignon blanc and Folle blanche, three in Chardonnay and Sylvaner, four in "dry Semillon" and Traminer, five in Pinot blanc and White Riesling, and fourteen in Cabernet, probably the best-known dry varietal wine produced in California. The gold medal in Cabernet was taken by Inglenook, with a total production of 3,917 gallons, or a bit over 1,600 cases.[103] From one reference point, varietal wines as a category had made tremendous strides. In 1941, the last prewar wine judging, varietal wines were on "the supplementary wine list," with the exception of Cabernet and Zinfandel, which were afforded generic status.[104] But from the standpoint of volume, varietal wines, no matter how profitable, were only a very small portion of the California wine business at the end of the war years.

Varietal or not, the wines from Napa Valley were clearly the quality leaders of the 1940s. At the 1947 State Fair, which continued to employ the system of single gold, silver, and bronze winners in each category, Napa garnered thirty-one awards, in contrast to second-place Alameda's nineteen and third-place Sonoma's sixteen. Perhaps more important than the total number of awards was that they were spread among ten Napa wineries, indicating that Napa had by far the greatest concentration of fine wine producers in the state.[105] This concentration led during the war to the creation of the Napa Valley Vintners' Association and the

Napa Valley Wine Technical Group, two organizations that were to contribute significantly in the postwar period to improving Napa wines and enhancing public perceptions of them.

The Napa Valley Vintners' Association was proposed by Louis M. Martini in 1944 as a "united front" to handle wartime problems such as labor shortages, allocation of materials, and the pricing of wine by the OPA.[106] The association was officially announced in early 1945, with the stated purpose of advancing "the interest of the industry by bringing to the public's attention the merits of Napa Valley wine."[107] The membership initially consisted of principals from each of the major Napa wineries, including Martini, Beaulieu, Inglenook, the Napa co-op, the Napa Wine Company, Charles Krug, and Larkmead. By the following year Beringer, Freemark Abbey, and Christian Brothers had joined as well.[108] The association met monthly for lunch and informal discussion, and on occasion it hosted dinner meetings with speakers from the University of California or the Wine Institute.[109] Although the purpose of most meetings was primarily social, the association did take positions on issues affecting the wine industry. For instance, in 1945, it urged the federal government to turn over the defunct USDA Oakville Experiment Station to the University of California in order to encourage viticultural research directly relevant to the Napa Valley, and in 1947, it urged approval of city bonds to connect St. Helena to the recently built Conn Valley reservoir, since the wineries were "dependent upon a sure and abundant water source."[110] In the postwar years, the association was to play an important role in building the public image of the Napa Valley as the home of fine wines.

The Napa Valley Vintners' Association represented wineries and was primarily concerned with the business side of wine production and marketing. In contrast, the Napa Valley Wine Technical Group consisted of individual winemakers focused on quality issues and science. Centered on André Tchelistcheff and his Napa Valley Enological Research Laboratory, the members were often younger men with formal training in enology who wished to continue their studies in winemaking and quality improvement. Early members included Louis P. Martini, Peter Mondavi, and Bard Suverkrop, all of whom had graduated from the University of California, as well as more experienced winemakers who lacked technical training, such as Robert Mondavi of Charles Krug, George Deuer of Inglenook, and Al Huntsinger of the Napa co-op.[111] The organization grew out of Tchelistcheff's consulting business and laboratory, which he had initiated in 1945 as a way of circumventing the effects of the wartime salary freeze on his work at Inglenook. Probably the group became a formal society in 1947, although the actual date is not clear.[112]

The Napa Valley Wine Technical Group shared information derived from applied experiments conducted by members at their wineries in areas such as controlling malolactic fermentation, yeast strains, and cold fermentation of white wines. Individuals researched particular issues and then reported to the entire group. Techniques for making different wines, varietal wines, were openly discussed — and, of course, wines were tasted. As Deuer recalled of the tastings, "What could we do better? We were the most critical outfit that ever lived."[113] The Napa Valley Wine Technical Group was part of a growing trend toward professionalization of the industry, which found its fullest expression in 1950 with the establishment of the American Society of Enologists, which became a forum for peer-reviewed academic science. The Napa Valley Wine Technical Group helped translate that science into practice and was a major force in improving Napa wines following the war.

The transition to a postwar economy was not gentle. The prosperity enjoyed by the California industry as a whole and the Napa Valley in particular came to an abrupt end in 1947 with the dramatic decline in wine sales and the resulting fall in wine and grape prices. Grape growers were perhaps the hardest hit, as prices plummeted from well over $100 a ton in 1946 to $35 in 1947, if buyers could be found. In late August 1947, the Napa Valley Grape Growers' Association elected Stelling chairman and directed its officers to "make arrangements for handling the early crop."[114] Working quickly, the directors leased the "huge Alta winery at Healdsburg," which had gone into bankruptcy earlier that year, and arranged to crush 4,000 tons of Napa grapes, which amounted to nearly 60 percent of the uncontracted grapes in the valley.[115]

The 1947 slump had a direct effect on Napa wineries as well. Bartolucci's Oakville Winery declared bankruptcy. Stralla dealt with the impending harvest somewhat differently, selling the Napa Wine Company to John Cella of Cella Vineyards, with whom he had enjoyed a long business relationship.[116] Larkmead was closed when National Distillers acquired it as part of its purchase of the Philip Blum Company. The quality producers tightened their belts and attempted to ride out the slump, although as Robert Mondavi says, it took years to work their way back from the disaster.

Sales slumps are relative, and those producers who had been aggressively expanding production were the worst hit, since they had paid top dollar for grapes in 1946 and thus entered the 1947 decline, not simply with excess inventory, but with high-cost inventory as well. *Wines and Vines* editorialized that the quality wine producers had felt the decline the least, since the "demand for true quality wine, while not tremendous, is still believed to be in excess of production of such wines."[117] The problem was, however, that almost all of the quality producers in the Napa Valley, with the exception of Inglenook and tiny Souverain, were also producing bulk and generic wines. Still, the 1947 sales slump reaffirmed the importance of brand recognition and quality. Sales volumes and prices declined for all producers, but less so for branded producers with known quality standards.

The period from 1941 through 1946 had proved a brief but fortunate period for Napa producers and growers. The war in Europe had opened up East Coast markets previously dominated by French and German producers. Napa producers had acquired national distribution for their brands. The early brand-building attempts and at-winery bottlings of the 1930s paid dividends in the 1940s when OPA regulations allowed most Napa wineries to market their wines at prices higher than those charged by the rest of the industry. The combination of high prices and strong demand practically assured profitability for any winery with access to grapes.

The war years were thus a period of growth and consolidation for Napa's quality producers, as they solidified their valley's claim to being the leading U.S. fine wine region. With ten award-winning wineries in the county, Napa had reached a critical mass where social organization for regional promotion and interchange of technology was assured. The tasks that lay before Napa in the postwar economy were the integration of wine into American culture, continued emphasis on Napa as a region, and the definition of fine wine as varietal wine. World War II had clearly been good to Napa wineries. But the real legacy of the war had been the planting of over 1,000 acres of new, mostly varietal, vineyards, made possible by the temporary profitability of grapes. It was this expansion that would support the slow growth of quality winemaking in the 1950s.

CHAPTER SEVEN

Table Wine Triumphant, 1947-1967

It is difficult to discern why Ed Rossi, president of Italian Swiss Colony, was willing to predict in 1944 what the U.S. wine industry would be like in 1969. A quarter-century projection is a long-range forecast by any standards, and Rossi no doubt took some comfort in the knowledge that by 1969, his audience would have retired, passed on, or grown forgetful. Convinced that the status quo would not prevail, he boldly predicted that "the use of table wines" would "surpass considerably that of dessert wines" by 1969.[1]

There was not much basis then to anticipate this. Since Repeal, table wines had accounted for just over 30 percent of wine drunk, and even in the war year of 1944, when dessert wine production was artificially checked by the wartime diversion of raisins, table wine only claimed 38 percent of a reduced sales base.[2] However, Rossi's optimism proved well founded. By 1967, table wine had grown to 52 percent of the wine market, surpassing dessert wine sales for the first time. Two years later, twenty-five years after Rossi's prediction, table wine had pulled away from dessert wine, continuing a growth trend that had begun in the mid 1950s and persisted into the early 1980s.

The U.S. consumers' shift from dessert to table wine occurred gradually, beginning slowly in the mid 1950s, accelerating in the mid 1960s, and exploding in the 1970s and early 1980s. The change in type of wine consumed was joined with a dramatic increase in the volume of wine sold, as reflected in table 1.

No single cause accounts for the transition and expansion. Rather, they were the consequences of a combination of factors, including the

Table 1 *Sales of Table and Dessert Wines in the United States*

	Table Wine	Dessert Wine
Year	*Gallons*	*Gallons*
1947	23,139,193	70,145,173
1952	37,767,827	93,677,613
1957	45,059,704	94,809,698
1962	59,588,065	82,254,208
1967	87,666,558	78,937,439
1972	170,017,000	71,864,000
1977	261,792,000	60,584,000
1982	397,309,000	40,217,000
1987	338,594,000	32,668,000

SOURCES: *Wines and Vines,* April 1958, p. 42; April 1968, p. 24; May 1976, p. 38; July 1981, p. 34; July 1990, p. 22.

Figures are for total sales from all sources, including imports. They are somewhat inexact, since until the 1970s, vermouth was included under dessert wines, and special (i.e., flavored) natural wines with an alcohol content under 14 percent were included under table wines.

availability of higher-quality wines because of new winemaking technologies and increased tonnage of better grape varieties; the development of new wines, such as low-tannin, slightly sweet rosés, "mellow" red wines with just enough sugar to mask astringency, and "special natural" wines with added fruit flavors, all of which were designed to appeal to new wine consumers; and the emergence of a new form of marketing based on public relations, which effectively cast wine drinking as part of the good life in the postwar era. Most important, these forces operated in the context of an unparalleled period of affluence. The United States was the dominant power in the postwar world and enjoyed ongoing economic expansion.

The shift in consumption created both opportunities and difficulties for the California wine industry. Dessert wine producers, located primarily in the Central Valley, who had long been the industry leaders, saw their influence gradually wane. With raisins returned to the crush pool, Central Valley wineries entered the 1950s burdened by a chronic oversupply of grapes and wine that was exacerbated by a static, and later declining, market. The predictable results were a series of proposals for marketing orders designed to stabilize the industry, the transition by individual producers when possible from dessert wine to table wine, and a sharp decline in the number of operating wineries. In 1950, California boasted 364 bonded wineries; by 1967, the number had fallen by over one-third, to 226.[3] This decrease naturally resulted in increased consolidation. By 1961, the three largest California wineries accounted for over 60 percent of all California wine sold nationally.[4] Led by Gallo and United Vintners, the large volume producers used efficiency of scale and internal integration to lower production costs, reinvesting the savings in market development and building national brands. Ultimately, they became the chief suppliers of table wine in the 1970s.

If the shift from dessert to table wine meant problems for dessert wine producers, it opened opportunities for the table wine producers of the North Coast. Since Repeal, the growers and wineries of the north and central coasts had been the industry's "poor relations." Producing roughly half of California's table wine at a time when table wine generally constituted slightly more than 30 percent of the state's annual production and sales, the coastal table wine producers wielded minimal influence in the industry.[5] During the 1930s and 1940s, grape and wine prices in coastal regions had been tied to the rates paid in the Central Valley, with perhaps a 20 percent premium. Such a premium, although welcome, did not adequately compensate for the lower yields per acre and higher unit costs incurred by growers and wineries.

During the 1950s and 1960s, the pricing relationship between coastal and valley wine grapes gradually came undone. The increased demand for high-quality table wine and the recognition that coastal grapes and wine were superior to those from the Central Valley steadily led to higher prices for "standard" grapes grown on the coast rather than in the San Joaquin Valley. Although a grape surplus clearly existed in the Central Valley, by the early 1960s, there was no excess supply in the coastal counties. This reality was tacitly acknowledged in 1961, when an industry stabilization plan that proposed to increase overall industry profitability by limiting the total tonnage crushed specifically exempted the North Coast vineyards from its program.[6]

The increased profitability and importance of coastal growers and winemakers led to a subtle, but real, change in the politics of the California wine industry. The interests of the North Coast growers and winemakers grew increasingly different from those of Central Valley winemakers, reinforcing a sense of separateness on the part of the table wine producers. The fact that two industries, dessert and table wine, existed was not a change; what was new was a shift in the balance of power. For the first time, table wine producers felt important enough to express their interests and demand that something be done to meet them.

The growth in table wine consumption created its own set of problems for premium wine producers. Wineries are capital-intensive businesses, in which inventories are often cellared for two to three years prior
to sale. Growth meant increased inventory, which had to be funded in
some manner. Growth also required a supply of suitable grapes. Expansion of vineyard acreage meant that land had to be acquired and grapes
planted. Finally, growth required expansion of physical structures and
investment in new technology for wine production. All of this required
capital, from either outside businesses or banks, since internal reinvest-
ment of capital was generally not adequate to sustain high levels of
growth. To be sure, the funding of growth was a problem that the dessert wine producers would have welcomed as they saw their market share
decline. But funding growth was an obstacle that table wineries had to
overcome nonetheless.

Although this short summary of some of the major changes that occurred in the two decades between 1947 and 1967 sets the stage for the
more specific discussion of Napa Valley premium producers that follows,
the danger in distilling twenty years of history into a short synopsis is
that the abruptness of changes is magnified and disjunctures are exagger-
ated. If anything, the reverse is true: the twenty years from 1947 to 1967
were a period of gradual transition, in sharp contrast to the explosion in
table wine consumption that followed. Although the dramatic growth
in table wine consumption did not occur until the 1970s, the year 1967,
when table wine outsold dessert wine, was a watershed.

Few winemakers would have predicted such an outcome in 1947. The
abrupt return from the controlled wartime economy to the harsh realities of supply and demand caught the entire wine industry off guard,
and table wine fell to 24 percent of sales in 1947, the lowest percentage
since Repeal. Wine prices plummeted, grapes went unharvested, and
some wineries were forced out of business. Business failures were one
immediate consequence, but a longer-term effect was the depletion of
the cash reserves of the surviving wineries, creating severe financing
problems, which took many wineries a decade to solve. It was not an
auspicious beginning.

California's quality producers were partly shielded from the 1947
crash in prices for several reasons. The 1947 crash had resulted from a
decline in consumption of ordinary table and dessert wines produced
from overly expensive grapes. It had not been caused by a general economic recession. The U.S. economy was strong, the market for better-
made wines was constant, if minuscule, and no oversupply of quality

wine existed. The small premium market segment was distinct from the markets for dessert and inexpensive table wines. Having spent the previous fifteen years cultivating brand awareness, wineries such as Inglenook and Beaulieu were partially insulated from general market conditions. Furthermore, quality producers such as Martini, Beaulieu, Inglenook, and Beringer were largely estate wineries, growing most, if not all, of the grapes they used.[7] They were therefore not caught with high-priced inventories of ordinary table wines, as were most other producers.

Such shielding was at best incomplete, and it varied from producer to producer. To some degree, all of the Napa producers, with the possible exception of Inglenook, either bought or sold wine in bulk. Not all of their output was high-quality varietal wine. Christian Brothers, for instance, operated the Mt. Tivy winery in the Central Valley near Reedly and sold significantly more dessert wine than table wine.[8] A winery's product mix, and the extent to which it bought or sold wine in bulk, thus partially determined what effect the 1947 slump had on it. Another factor was the degree to which each winery was leveraged. Stable producers such as Beaulieu, Martini, and Inglenook were less affected by the price decline than were rapidly growing wineries such as Christian Brothers and Charles Krug. Finally, all the quality producers relied on distributors and retailers to help sell their wines, and the effects of the 1947 bust reverberated through distribution channels. One telling example was the 1946 Mondavi agreement with McKesson & Robbins, a major national distributor, to distribute Charles Krug wines, beginning in 1947. McKesson & Robbins responded to the 1947 crisis by laying off most of its sales force. The four railcars of Krug wines shipped out by the winery simply sat in inventory, causing the Mondavis to cancel the agreement.[9] There was little any producer could do to force wine through an unsteady distribution system. Still, if the quality producers were not entirely insulated from the effects of the 1947 bust in grape and wine prices, they were much better off than the rest of the industry.

The extent of the separation of California's quality producers from the dessert and bulk table wine industries is readily evident. In 1951, Irving Marcus, the managing editor of *Wines and Vines*, described the U.S. market for premium wines as "the steadiest, surest, most dependable wine market in the trade" since it consisted of "only a small portion of the population," who regarded "quality of greater importance than price."[10] Herman Wente of Wente Brothers echoed this five years later when he told distributors that premium wines "maintained a consistent percentage of profit" because the specialty market was little affected by large or short crops.[11]

During the 1950s, 10 percent at most of California's more than three hundred bonded wineries were quality producers, and they accounted for perhaps 5 percent of the state's dry wine production.[12] Industry members experienced difficulty in defining exactly what quality wine was and determining how much they produced, but estimates for the early 1950s place premium wine production at about 1 million gallons, at a time when California table wine sales averaged 25 million gallons. Marcus put the total volume of premium wine sold at "an even million gallons" for 1953, an increase of "at least" 30 percent over 1947.[13] The industry consultant Lou Gomberg, who had formerly headed the Wine Institute economic statistics division, tracked wine sales by monitoring the state excise tax payments of selected wineries. In a private report, Gomberg tallied the 1952 dry table wine sales of seven premium producers that in his opinion represented "80%–90%" of total premium production at 807,000 gallons.[14] Assuming that these seven producers accounted for 80 percent of premium wine production, Gomberg's estimate fits closely with Marcus's.

By 1950, a small group of premium producers had clearly emerged, along with a new breed of author, the wine writer. During the 1950s, the same wineries constantly appeared in articles about California's best wines. Robert Laurence Balzer started things off in 1949 with the publication of a modestly titled book, *California's Best Wines*, which reviewed thirteen California wineries, five of which were in the Napa Valley. Balzer's lucky thirteen were Almaden, Beaulieu, Concannon, Fountain Grove, Freemark Abbey, Inglenook, Korbel, Charles Krug, Los Amigos, Louis Martini, Novitiate of Los Gatos, Paul Masson, and Wente. The *Wines and Vines* reviewer commented that "there are thousands of potential wine consumers who would buy wines . . . if they could only know that they were getting an excellent wine each time. This is their book."[15]

Other writers during the 1950s listed different combinations of wineries, depending upon individual interpretation of quality and whether the author was limiting his choices to widely distributed brands. Smaller wineries were sometimes mentioned, but a core of eight firms was almost always included in any discussion of California premium wines. This group, with the addition of Charles Krug, was the same collection that Lou Gomberg tracked: Almaden, Beaulieu, Beringer, Martini, Paul Masson, Christian Brothers, and Wente. Gomberg had probably chosen not to include Charles Krug in his list because most Krug wine was sold under the C.K. Mondavi brand and consisted of table wine produced from "standard" grapes such as Petite Sirah, Alicante, and Carignane. Although these were well-made table wines, they were not entirely from the Napa Valley and certainly were not of the same quality as the Mondavi family's top brand, Charles Krug.

Gomberg's records provide an otherwise unavailable statistical base for quantifying the growth of premium wine production in California, and it is worth a slight digression to understand how his figures were derived. Federal and state governments tax alcoholic beverages, but do not insist that taxes be paid when wine is produced, only when it enters commerce. Bulk wine shipped between wineries is generally transported "in bond," and such sales between producers usually do not cause a payment of tax. However, when wine is bottled and shipped to distributors, or sold directly to consumers, a tax must be paid. In California, monthly statements of wine entering commercial channels are tendered to the state government, along with tax payments. Since the early 1950s, Lou Gomberg used these public documents to track the shipments of selected wineries, publishing the information monthly to clients in the private *Gomberg Report*. Such data allow the reader to follow shipments inside and outside California and by tax classification, since wine above 14 percent alcohol is and was taxed at a higher rate than table wine. However, since wine excise taxes are not based on value or quality, tax reports do not tell us what percentage of wine shipped was varietal or generic. Despite this flaw, Gomberg's data provide concrete numbers that allow analysis of the growth in premium wine consumption. Table 2 lists case sales for the dominant premium wine producers.

Three points seem worthy of note. First, in 1952, the premium wine producers were selling comparable volumes of dry table wine.[16] Although Christian Brothers' shipments were twice the average of those of the other producers, all were essentially within the same order of magnitude. Second, while each winery started from about the same base, some grew dramatically, while others expanded much more slowly. Finally, while the rate of growth was high for some producers during the 1950s, primarily because of a low initial base, the major increases in volume occurred during the 1960s as part of a general acceleration of all table wine sales.

Although each producer was unique, with separate goals and circumstances, the premium producers can be divided into two broad categories: estate wineries and volume producers. The estate producers relied primarily on grapes grown in their own vineyards and generally received

Table 2 *Sales of California Dry Wine*
(*thousands of cases*)

	1952	1957	1962	1967
Almaden	49.4	187.3	393.8	1,043.9
Beaulieu	67.1	64.8	85.5	104.2
Beringer	45.9	54.9	47.0	52.9
Christian Bros.	93.6	155.3	277.0	481.9
Martini	55.5	58.9	124.2	200.9
Paul Masson	42.7	106.0	311.3	696.7
Wente	45.4	60.1	79.7	128.3
Krug (est.)	50.0	—	540.0	1,000.0

Data for the first seven wineries have been compiled from the privately printed *Gomberg Report*. The estimate of Krug shipments for 1952 comes from Robert Mondavi, *Creativity in the California Wine Industry* (Berkeley: Regional Oral History Office, Bancroft Library, University of California, 1985), p. 26, and does not include wine bottled under private label contracts. The 1967 figure is an estimate working backward from a 1968 Gomberg report on Charles Krug, the first time Gomberg included the Krug winery in his data.

a higher average price per bottle for their wines. Wineries such as Beaulieu, Martini, Inglenook, and Beringer in the Napa Valley, and Wente in the Livermore Valley, owned or leased established vineyards, which were planted predominantly to varietal grapes, a commodity in short supply in the 1950s.[17] For these producers, expansion entailed either planting or acquiring new vineyards or changing the winery's ratio of premium and generic wine by processing more "standard" North Coast varieties. Either option required cash expenditures in the present balanced against future increased sales. Primarily self-funded, these producers chose slow growth, at least until the late 1950s.

The volume producers owned vineyards, but they supplemented their production with grapes they purchased both from within and outside their regions. Like the estate wineries, they produced high-quality estate wines, but their main volume consisted of more "popularly priced" premium wines, with and without varietal labeling. Each producer had its own technique to differentiate its top quality wines from its generics. The Mondavis reserved the Charles Krug label for their best wines and employed the C.K. Mondavi brand for their more common generic table wines, which they often produced from San Joaquin Valley grapes trucked to St. Helena.[18] Almaden, located in the Santa Clara Valley, bottled all of its wines under the Almaden label, but prefixed its less expensive wines with the word *Mountain*. These "Mountain" varietals and generics proved so popular that by the 1960s, Almaden was buying large quantities of bulk Central Valley wine to blend with wine produced from its own grapes. When questioned about the propriety of calling such blends "mountain wines," Almaden's marketing consultant, Frank Schoonmaker, reportedly pointed toward the coastal foothills that separate Almaden from the San Joaquin Valley and replied that since "the mountain wines came over the mountains," they "obviously were mountain wines."[19] Intent on producing high-quality table wines, but not as constrained by regional or varietal appellations as the estate producers were, Krug, Almaden, Paul Masson, and Christian Brothers opted to expand during the 1950s and 1960s.

Almaden, Paul Masson, and Christian Brothers differed from the other premium producers in another important way that increased their marketing strength. Each winery sold significant quantities of brandy and dessert wine in addition to table wine. Spirits are traditionally a more profitable sector than wine, and Christian Brothers' emergence in the 1950s as maker of the leading brandy established a source of income for funding expansion of its table wine production. To a lesser degree, this was also true of Almaden and Paul Masson, and in each case the distilling operation also served as a source of fortifying spirits for dessert wine production. The importance of dessert wine in the product mix of these three volume producers is demonstrated by comparing their percentage of dessert wine sales with that of the estate producers. In 1967, dessert wine accounted for 36 percent of the collective sales of Almaden, Christian Brothers, and Paul Masson, as opposed to only 11 percent of the aggregate sales of the estate group.[20] After 1957, dessert wine was a declining market, but it still accounted for most wine sales in the United States. The volume producers' ability to compete in the dessert wine market helped secure broader distribution for their premium brands.

Although participation in all market segments was important for the volume producers, the market for wine, let alone fine wine, remained extremely limited relative to that for other beverages. During the 1950s, the Wine Advisory Board surveyed the U.S. public's attitudes to wine and uncovered some disheartening truths. A 1955 consumer survey showed that while roughly two-thirds of the public had tried some alcoholic beverage during the year, only 56 percent of these drank wine. In contrast, 78 percent of this group drank beer, and 70 percent whiskey.[21] Thus, only slightly over one-third of Americans drank any wine at all. Such a base would have been tolerable if it represented regular consumers, but a 1952 poll on frequency of use indicated that only 37 percent of wine drinkers drank wine at least once a week.[22] This was recognized by Alfred Fromm, vice president of Fromm & Sichel, the firm that marketed both Christian Brothers and Paul Masson wines. "Small as our wine consumption is today, it is actually even smaller" since "85 per cent of the wine is consumed by only 15% of the people," Fromm noted in November 1956.[23] To this was added the weight of demographic mortality statistics. The French and Italian immigrants of the 1910s and 1920s, who often consumed twenty-five gallons a year apiece, were growing older, and "death was taking its inevitable toll." And as Irving Marcus pointed out, on the death of one such consumer, the wine industry had to find "34 new individuals to drink the per capita figure of .7 gallons just to hold the established consumption mark."[24]

Such was the limited demand for table wine in general. The premium wine market was even more rarefied. A 1950 consumer survey by the J. Walter Thompson Company, a major advertising firm contracted by the Wine Institute to study U.S. perceptions of wine, found that 45 percent drank sweet table wine, 38 percent consumed port, and 34 percent named sherry. Toward the middle of the list, but behind Sauterne and Muscatel, was "Burgundy," with a frequency rating of just under 15 percent. At the bottom were two varietals, Cabernet and Riesling, at .5 and .4 percent respectively.[25] The 1955 Roper survey postulated that one possible explanation for varietal wines' unpopularity was that "more involved foreign-sounding wine type names" perpetuated the idea that wine drinking was alien, "more foreign than American." In addition, varietal names caused a "hesitancy and a lack of self-confidence in prospective consumers."[26]

Thus, by 1955, California premium wine producers were in an unsure position. They had survived 1947, and table wine sales had grown, but major obstacles remained. If more premium wine were to be drunk, the industry would have to introduce U.S. consumers to wine, show them its uses, and convince them that wine had a place in the new postwar culture. This transcended brand development by individual producers. Public relations and promotion on a large scale by paid professionals were required.

CHAPTER EIGHT

Politics and Promotion

The Napa Valley Vintners' Association
and the Premium Wine Producers of California

Following World War II, the Napa Valley Vintners' Association engaged in various forms of collective action to build awareness of Napa Valley wines, and its early efforts provided a model for larger-scale industry activity later in the decade. In the minds of some quality producers, the Wine Advisory Board's advertisements for "California" wine had backfired, since consumers had "been disappointed with some wines carrying the name 'California,' and had then "erroneously assumed that all California wines are inferior."[1] The goal of the NVVA was to distinguish the Napa Valley from other wine-growing areas by reiteration of the name "Napa Valley" and by promoting interaction with potential wine consumers. To that end, in 1949 the association erected a sign welcoming visitors to "this world famous wine growing region," and sponsored a cable car in San Francisco, which included giving away a bottle of Napa wine each day to "one lucky passenger," a practice that brought "considerable publicity . . . as far away as Fairbanks, Alaska, New Orleans, and Boston."[2]

The association also aggressively sought out influential groups visiting San Francisco and invited them to the Napa Valley. Most notable was its hosting of the Associated Harvard Clubs when they met in San Francisco in fall 1949. The association arranged transportation to the Napa Valley and catered lunch for six hundred Harvard graduates and their guests "at the cost of several thousand dollars." As *Wines and Vines* editorialized, it had done so in the belief that "close contact with the wineries" would "build future demand for the wines made there." The editorial concluded by commenting that eventually with such cooperative action "*where* the wine was made may achieve an equal importance with *who* made it." [3]

The association continued these personal-relationship-building activities throughout the 1950s and 1960s. Francis Gould, the editor of the Charles Krug winery's newsletter, *Bottles and Bins*, referred to the "large assemblages" consisting "of delegates to National and International conventions meeting in San Francisco" hosted by the NVVA, and *Wines and Vines* listed such groups as six hundred members of the American Bar Association and the thousand-strong Building Owners' and Managers' Association as visiting the Napa Valley as guests of the NVVA. [4] Although costly and time-consuming, such promotions helped to build a following for Napa premium wine.

The NVVA's pursuit of public relations extended to the media as well. Writers like Frank Schoonmaker were courted. In the case of Schoonmaker, this paid off when he published an article entitled "California's Vintage Vale" in *Holiday* magazine in 1952. "The Napa Valley is in a class by itself," the article began, and Schoonmaker wondered "why anyone who had ever seen [it] ever lived anyplace else." The piece was one of the first "lifestyle" articles written about Napa, concentrating as much on the gracious living possible there as it did on discussing Napa winemakers. [5]

Other examples of media relations were more prosaic, but helped lodge the name "Napa Valley" in the minds of national audiences. In 1955, the NVVA hosted Leonard Wibberly, author of a popular *Saturday Evening Post* serial set in the mythical European duchy of Grand Fenwick. In one segment, the duchy declared war on the United States over a Napa Valley wine labeled "Pinot Grand Enwick." An exchange of letters to the editor and an invitation to the author kept the appellation "Napa Valley" before the *Post*'s readers as long as possible. [6] Another subtle example of the NVVA's public relations was the sponsorship in 1958 by individual members of the association of *This Earth Is Mine*, a motion picture set in the Napa Valley. Starring Rock Hudson and Jean Simmons, and loosely adapted from Alice Tisdale's *The Cup and the Sword*, a novel based on the life of Georges de Latour, the movie clearly identified the Napa Valley as California's leader in premium wine production. [7]

Such creative uses of public relations represented a new and indirect approach to image-building, in which potential consumers were "surrounded," either physically by visiting the Napa Valley or psychologically through strategically placed articles or pictures calculated to influence perception and behavior. These techniques contrasted with the more static advertisements of the Wine Advisory Board and later became the basis for a public relations campaign sponsored by the premium wineries of California.[8]

By 1955, the need for such a campaign had become obvious to California premium wine producers. It was not that they were dissatisfied with the growth in the production of premium California wines, which between 1949 and 1955 was somewhere between 40 and 50 percent.[9] Rather, they feared that without a specific promotional program, their market would be swamped by imports. By 1955, growing from a base of 1.1 million gallons in 1949, imported European table wines accounted for just under 3.5 million gallons, a net increase of 2.5 million gallons, when California premium producers were selling perhaps 1.5 million gallons.

The makers of California premium wines quite rightly viewed such imports as direct competition. In 1951, according to *Wines and Vines*, imports had "sold at least one bottle of table wine to every bottle sold by U.S. premium wine producers." Four years later, Alfred Fromm estimated that imports "represented about 75 per cent of all table wines sold here in the premium market," or a three-to-one edge.[10] No wonder Inglenook's John Daniel, Jr., spoke of "the serious inroads which imported wines have made in the premium table wine market," and Robert Mondavi warned of the "losses of market outlets" resulting from the "importation of low priced foreign wines."[11] By 1955, it was clear that stemming the import tide would take more than regional action on the part of the Napa Valley Vintners' Association. The *Saturday Evening Post* had missed the real story. Instead of the European duchy of Grand Fenwick going to war over a Napa Valley wine, it would be the California premium wine producers declaring war on European imports in an attempt to end the foreign invasion.

The creation of the Premium Wine Producers of California in 1955 was a historic event in several ways. First, it was the first time that the majority of California premium producers had joined together to form their own trade organization. In the process, they created the first workable definition of premium wine. Second, in its demand for Wine Advisory Board funding, it resulted in the creation of a new subcommittee within the Wine Institute, altering the power structure of the institute and demanding recognition of the importance of premium wines to the entire industry. Third, it marked the introduction of a new type of wine promotion based on public relations rather than on advertising. This new system played to the growing affluence of American society by positioning wine as part of the "good life" to which consumers should aspire. Finally, and most important, it was effective in raising the image of California premium wine in relation to imports.

While the impetus for the creation of the Premium Wine Producers of California was the threat of loss of sales to imported wines, its actual formation was the work of a few individuals, and the idea originated in the Napa Valley. According to Robert Mondavi, he originally approached other members of the Napa Valley Vintners' Association to "raise a small amount of money and appoint a public relations director for the Napa Valley."[12] At an informal meeting at Inglenook held to discuss Mondavi's proposal, Aldo Fabbrini of Beaulieu suggested creation of a statewide group that would then legitimately be able to request funds from the Wine Advisory Board. In the upshot, the Napa winemakers retained the industry consultant Lou Gomberg to contact other makers of fine wine throughout the state to see if they would support the establishment of such an organization.

Sometimes the best route is not always the direct one. Gomberg knew that there had been several previous attempts to unite the makers of California's best wines, but that each attempt had resulted in failure, generally because of disagreements about group goals or definitions of premium wine that effectively eliminated the volume producers.[13] Rather than ask individual producers outright to join the proposed group, Gomberg conducted a study, surveying all potential members to determine what sort of program would be supported. Underwritten by a core group of nine wineries, which probably represented 90 percent of premium production, Gomberg prepared and sent a memorandum reviewing the growth of foreign wine competition, along with a series of questions about possible forms of group response to thirty prestige wine producers.[14]

Essentially a call to action, the memorandum argued for "a dynamic, aggressive program sponsored by the California premium wine producers . . . to offset the natural advantages enjoyed by the foreign product; in short a promotional program aimed to restore the rightful position of California premium wines nationally."[15]

Gomberg then followed up with a series of individual interviews with nineteen premium producers, as well as meetings with members of the Wine Institute, the Wine Advisory Board, and public relations firms. Released in April 1955 as the *California Prestige Wines Study Report*, Gomberg's study summarized the problem, listed possible solutions, laid out a concrete plan of action, complete with cost estimates, and recommended that sufficient funds be secured from the Wine Advisory Board to initiate a public relations program. The report was mailed to prospective members, along with a personal letter from Gomberg urging each producer to attend a meeting in San Francisco on May 5, 1955, to discuss its recommendation that a formal organization be created to oversee the implementation of a public relations program for California premium wines.

The chief operating officers of fifteen premium wineries attended the first meeting and chose Aldo Fabbrini of Beaulieu as chairman, a position he kept for the next two years. As at any first meeting, discussion centered around purpose and financing. Gomberg had estimated that the fine wine producers contributed roughly $60,000 a year in marketing-order assessments to the Wine Advisory Board, a figure that he believed would "provide adequate funds to carry out the prestige wine program for the first year." [16] The unspoken assumption was that the premium producers were not getting their money's worth from the current Wine Advisory Program, which stressed generic advertising of California wines and funded much of the Wine Institute's trade barrier and tariff work. [17] That the group wished to emphasize public relations was made clear when, at Robert Mondavi's urging, they passed the following resolution: "Resolved, that the group stress public relations in any program to be undertaken." [18]

Representatives from the Wine Advisory Board and the Wine Institute were sympathetic to the possibility of reallocating funds to support a public relations campaign in lieu of advertising, but they questioned whether an organization separate from the Wine Institute was really necessary. As they pointed out, the Wine Institute did conduct public relations on behalf of the entire industry and could certainly undertake such activities for the premium producers. After some discussion, a possible compromise was reached: the Premium Wine Producers of California (PWPC) would be formed, but it would also function as an advisory committee to the Wine Advisory Board and the Wine Institute. With that settled, the group created a committee on organization and program to determine the best way to administer and finance a public relations program.

Over the next several months, the PWPC's committee on organization and program, which later became its steering committee, met several times with representatives of the Wine Advisory Board and the Wine Institute to hammer out an agreement. Some members wanted to keep the new organization totally separate from the Wine Institute, fearing that the industry as a whole would have veto power over the public relations program, which might receive minimal attention from Wine Institute staff. The Wine Institute's president, Don McColly, argued that the institute should be given a chance, and, with a thinly veiled threat, commented that the group's chances of getting financial assistance from the Wine Advisory Board would "be greater as a unit of Institute than as a separate organization."[19]

Money talked. The arrangement finally worked out in September called for the Wine Advisory Board to fund a public relations program with $32,000 for the remainder of the fiscal year. The Wine Institute would administer the money, but use it to hire a public relations firm to carry out the program, thus ensuring a degree of separateness as well as coordination. Oversight of the public relations program would be by a Wine Institute standing committee on premium wines and a Wine Advisory Board premium wines policy committee. Membership of these two committees was essentially identical, consisting primarily of members of the PWPC. An additional $6,000 was allocated to the Wine Advisory Board's premium wines policy committee to hire a consultant, Lou Gomberg, who continued as secretary of the PWPC. As with most compromises, no one was entirely happy about the structure and reporting relationships, but in the short run, each group got what it wanted. The Wine Institute retained control over the program, while limiting the activities of a potential splinter group, and the premium producers got funding for a public relations campaign.

With structure and funding secure, the PWPC faced one last organizational hurdle: defining who was a premium wine producer and what constituted premium wine. Was it strictly varietal wine? Must it have won an award at either the State Fair or Los Angeles judgings? Could it be a blend from one or more districts? Did a winery have to grow the grapes and process them? An earlier promotional group, the Association of Château Wine Growers in California, had been formed in late 1950 with the idea of "certifying" members' wines that were at least 85 percent varietal and that passed a sensory test. But the group had disbanded by 1952.[20] Gomberg and the PWPC knew that they needed the broadest possible support, and they cast a wide net, choosing to define quality primarily in terms of price. Producers selling wines that retailed above $1 a fifth were eligible for membership. If they were table wine producers, the wines had to be produced from wine grapes grown in viticultural regions I–IV.[21] For practical purposes that included all principal grape-growing regions except Fresno, Kern, Kings, Madera, and Tulare counties. Aside from a periodic increase in the base price, these remained the membership criteria as long as the PWPC existed. Membership was not intended to be exclusive, and by June 1958, the PWPC had twenty-eight members, representing between 90 and 95 percent of California's premium wine production.[22]

After interviewing thirty-six agencies, the PWPC selected Robinson-Hannigan Associates to orchestrate the envisioned public relations campaign. With offices in New York and Los Angeles, the firm was well situated to cover the East Coast and California, the two areas that respondents to Gomberg's survey had indicated should receive first priority. The basic public relations objectives had also been itemized in the report. First on the list was "heightened public consciousness of the existence and excellence of California prestige wines." Second was "removal of the illusion that because a label says 'imported' or otherwise shows foreign origin, it must be better."[23] With these marching orders, the agency went to work cultivating writers, planting stories, sending out press releases, and generally making news.

In a report to the industry in November 1956, Paul Snell, Robinson-Hannigan's vice president, listed some of the accomplishments of the program's first year. California winemakers or wines were seen or interviewed on nine coast-to-coast television shows, ranging from *Wide Wide World* to *I Love Lucy*, and were mentioned or discussed on over two hundred radio programs. Magazine articles, which took more lead time than television and radio, appeared in *House and Garden* and *House Beautiful*, with favorable pieces scheduled in such journals as *Life, Look, Ladies' Home Journal*, and *Town and Country*.[24] These were all predictable, although useful, forms of public relations. More innovative, and in the long run much more effective, were the comparative tastings.

As the premium producers saw imported wine sales rise in the 1950s, they became more and more convinced that what was really selling was not wine quality, but the imported image. As *Bottles and Bins* put it: "Americans, as a rule, are suckers for any article of foreign origin."[25] Gomberg was slightly more restrained when he commented, "You can't put a dollars-and-cents value on the word 'Imported' but it's beyond argument that it sells many millions of bottles of foreign wine every year."[26] The task was to puncture the panache of imported wines while raising the image of and familiarity with California's premium wines. The answer lay in a simple variant of the Napa Valley Vintners' Association's hospitality: comparative tastings.

Over a hundred comparative tastings were held across the United

States from late 1955 into the early 1960s with a standard format and great success, at least from the California perspective. The basic idea was to invite influential individuals in a community—opinion molders such as restaurant owners, newspaper and magazine editors, radio and television personalities, and members of wine and food societies—to a blind tasting of commercial premium European and California wines. The wines were presented in pairs, and the tasters were asked to mark their preferences on cards, and, if they wished, to try to guess which was the imported wine. At the conclusion of the tasting, the wines were unveiled so that the "judges" could identify what they had been tasting, and the prices were announced.

The results were stunning: the California wines held their own with the European ones. A typical tasting resulted in an almost 50/50 split in preference. In the first twenty tastings, held in New York, Philadelphia, Los Angeles, and San Francisco, 222 tasters sampled 227 wines. On a preference basis, California wines received 404 points as against 403 for the foreign wines.[27] By 1960, the results from ninety-six blind tastings showed California holding a statistically insignificant lead, 31,788 preference points versus 31,265 for foreign wines.[28] In these tastings, where the foreign wines averaged at least a dollar more a bottle, a draw was a clear victory for the Californians.

The intuitive analysis of the numbers was that California wines were the equals of the more expensive, and more prestigious, European wines. California premium wine producers quickly claimed that the tastings conclusively proved that there was no quality difference between premium European and California wines. A more accurate assessment might be, not that the wines were essentially of the same quality, but that the vast majority of Americans did not possess any personal sense of wine quality. Basically unfamiliar with wines, they were not reliable judges. Quite probably, if the same pairs of wines had been offered to the same group of tasters on several successive evenings, the tasters would have discovered that they did not usually prefer the same wine from a given pair; that they could not replicate their initial preference; that, indeed, they had no real preference. The results, when tabulated, would still have shown a 50/50 split, but it would have been owing to the laws of probability, rather than to the essential equality of the wines. Given that this was a preference test, the sad truth may have been that most Americans didn't really enjoy any of the choices presented.

Still, such tastings were news, especially when they involved famous or photogenic individuals. One tasting at the Brown Derby in Los Angeles included Zsa Zsa Gabor and Hillevi Rubin, Miss Universe of 1956, along with members of the Foreign Press Club. California wines came out on top, and the public relations firm distributed pictures and stories to several syndicates, including United Press, all of which picked up the feature. Robinson-Hannigan estimated that by the time attention had died down, the Brown Derby tasting had reached "a minimum of 40,000,000 persons."[29] To the premium winemakers, this was an example of public relations at its best: national exposure of attractive people having fun drinking California wine. When this form of image-building was contrasted to a print advertisement urging Americans to drink California wine, there was simply no comparison.

The comparative tastings were successful on several levels. They clearly created public interest in California wines, while at the same time raising questions about the superiority of European wines. They introduced influential Americans to California premium wines, often for the first time and on a specific brand basis. Although the wines were tasted blind, when the "judging" was over, the actual bottles were brought out and the producers identified. A personal connection between host and consumer was created, which was reinforced the following week when, in a final public relations gesture, "wine-taster" certificates were mailed to all who participated in the blind tastings.[30]

The public relations campaign combined with comparative tastings was successful in increasing consumer awareness of California premium wines. Perhaps too successful. Foreign producers complained that the tastings were designed to harm the wines of other countries, and the Federal Alcohol and Tobacco Tax Division, which had jurisdiction over wine production and marketing, declared that individual producers could no longer advertise the results of such tastings, although the restriction did not apply to "factual news accounts or publicity reporting."[31] More important, larger California wineries also noted the premium producers' success and demanded an expanded public relations effort from the Wine Institute for all California wines.

On March 12, 1957, industry leaders met at the annual public hearing on the Wine Advisory Board and concluded that the "$1 million or so" that was being spent on advertising was "insufficient," and that "a lesser sum used in public relations work" would "achieve more in bettering the consumer attitude toward California wine." The result was that for the first time, the term *public relations* was written into the Wine Marketing Order, and by 1958 some $400,000 was allocated to the publicity program.[32] Robinson-Hannigan, which had been taken over by Hill &

Knowlton, was given the job of promoting all California wines, using the same techniques employed for the premium producers. The major method it chose was a series of "wine festivals" designed to attract media attention, while introducing thousands of Americans to California wine through mass tastings.

The first festival took place in Boston in September 1957, and by March 1959, fourteen festivals had been held in major cities across the United States.[33] Edmund Rossi, the manager of the Wine Advisory Board, compared the festivals to casting stones into "the center of a number of ponds." The rock "creates a considerable splash, which then spreads in concentric ripples to cover the pond's entire surface."[34] The key words in the metaphor were *splash* and *entire*. The public relations aim was to dominate a city's media attention by concentrating a number of events aimed at various audiences into a short period. Generally lasting a week and well publicized in advance, the festivals began with the crowning of a local "wine queen," a media event designed for local television coverage, and the rest of the week included movies, interviews, wine and wine service talks for the general public and the retail trade, a series of tastings and lunches focused on media representatives, wine and food groups, and restaurant owners, and, of course, at least one comparative blind tasting of premium wines. The week would normally end with a mass tasting for the general public of "popular-priced" wines. Such tastings drew between one and two thousand participants.

As Rossi commented, these mass tastings, conducted under "proper and favorable conditions" were intended to influence consumer behavior through the use of "group psychology." Individuals who "might be disappointed" if they sampled "the product by themselves" were instead introduced to wine in "exciting, colorful and unusual surroundings," where they could "witness others, more knowledgeable than they, interested, even enthusiastic about the event." According to Rossi, under such conditions, neophyte tasters would "enter into the spirit and gradually become enthusiasts for wine."[35] Such festivals, operating as part of an overall public relations campaign for California wine, helped build a base for the surge of consumer interest in wine that began in the mid 1960s. But the very success of the general public relations program ultimately spelled the end of a separate program for premium wines.

The word *premium* stuck in the throats of large producers such as Gallo and United Vintners, whose marketing-order assessments contributed most to Wine Advisory Board–sponsored public relations. "Premium" wines implied the existence of "nonpremium" wines, and neither

Ernest Gallo nor Lou Petri was willing to concede that his wines were not premium too. In addition, the volume producers believed that owing to the limited number of premium producers, the special public relations program was effectively a form of brand advertising financed by the entire industry through a marketing order funded by all California wineries. For their part, the premium producers, who had used the "best foot forward" analogy and argued that promoting California's top wines benefited the entire industry by raising the public perception of California wines in general, felt that the new public relations thrust diluted the public relations efforts expended on fine wine. A series of compromises was attempted in late 1958 to heal the emerging rift. The offending word *premium* was stricken from the Wine Institute's lexicon; Hill & Knowlton's services were ended; the Wine Advisory Board assumed management of the festivals; the Philip Lesly Company was retained for 1959 and $120,000 allocated for a public relations program emphasizing, but not solely focused on, premium wine; and Premium Wine Producers of California changed its name to the Academy of Master Winegrowers.[36]

The compromise was essentially unworkable, and it lasted less than a year. In 1960, a new tack was tried: $120,000 was allocated for a "fine wines" public relations program, to be split between the Ty Juras agency on the West Coast and Bell & Stanton on the East Coast, and $300,000 was allocated for "popular" wines public relations, to be administered by Ronald Schiller and Associates. As a consolation prize, the Philip Lesly Company, which had been placed in an untenable situation the previous year, was given the special task of educating the nation's physicians on the health aspects of California wine. One upshot was that for the first time, the Wine Advisory Board spent more money on public relations than on advertising.[37] A second result was that the industry set in motion two competing public relations machines, one promoting all wines from California, the other advancing an elite subset.

This too proved an unworkable solution, although it lasted until 1965. The major producers insisted that "California" was the only appellation that could be used if marketing-order funds were to be spent. This hamstrung the premium producers, who wished to differentiate their products by indicating the role of the growing region on grape and wine quality. As Francis Gould of the Charles Krug winery put it in a letter to the editor of *Wines and Vines*, "California is a very large state. . . . Certain grape varieties do well in some of these areas and not in others. . . . It is therefore helpful to the consumer to know where . . . a wine is made."[38] Stanford Wolf of Cresta Blanca was more succinct when he observed at an Academy of Master Wine Growers' meeting that in the East, "California" was "synonymous with cheapness."[39] Time did not heal the split. In June 1964, in his address to the Wine Institute membership, Robert Mondavi, the retiring board chairman, deplored a public relations attitude that in his opinion "intimated that all California wines were of the same quality."[40] But Mondavi and the other premium producers were the odd men out. At its winter meeting in December, the Wine Advisory Board terminated both the fine wine and popular wine programs in favor of hiring a "top bracket" public relations man to work in-house "to control and coordinate a single, industry-wide, unsegmentized PR program."[41]

Rumor had it that this decision resulted from a "planted" public relations story on California wine in the *Los Angeles Times* that contained a paragraph offensive to industry leaders. The otherwise positive article declared that although many consumers' first introduction to California wine was a Gallo or United Vintners product, "as their taste develops," these consumers would graduate to higher-priced wines from other firms. Ernest Gallo and Louis Petri strongly resented the implications of the story, which had essentially been paid for with Wine Advisory Board funds, and pushed to terminate both contracts.[42] Although the *Los Angeles Times* story may have been the precipitating incident, the decision to end both programs in favor of an internal public relations program had been discussed for at least a year. In a way, it was the logical culmination of a shift in industry thinking away from print advertising to a more active, if less controllable, form of public relations emphasizing direct interaction with people, whether they were potential consumers, wine writers, or restaurant owners. The trail had been blazed by the Napa Valley Vintners' Association, widened and improved by the Premium Wine Producers of California, and had now become a road traveled by the Wine Institute and Wine Advisory Board.

The key idea to the entire public relations program for California wines was positioning table wine as a necessary part of an emerging consumer life style. Philip Lesly, whose company managed the fine wine promotion program in 1959, explained the fundamental changes taking place in the United States to California wine producers and told them how they should react. According to Lesly, Americans were "no longer primarily concerned with making a living" but rather were "searching for self-fulfillment and ways of feeling they have attained high levels of status and taste." He pointed to the postwar booms in "hi-fi, sports, cars, music, travel, outdoor living, photography, art, gourmet foods" and told the winemakers that California wines had "missed out on the stampede" because they had "not been attuned to the psychological forces within people." What was needed was a "multiple-channel approach." The industry had to "surround the public with an atmosphere" suggesting that drinking California wine was "the thing to do," which would in turn "motivate them to adopt California wines to satisfy their hunger for self-esteem."[43]

The potential use of psychology to sell specific products was understood by the more sophisticated members of the industry. Howard Williams, vice president for marketing at the E. & J. Gallo Winery, penned a revealing look at the Gallo strategy in a piece entitled "What Consumers Want." Declaring that "patterns of today . . . are not the patterns of yesterday," Williams argued that Americans were "shopping around for the culture of pleasure," as evidenced by "flood-sale of tickets to Europe, in the enormous sales of cosmetics," and in "the style trends of home architecture."[44] Williams considered wine "a luxury product" that had to deliver "more than a taste or alcohol." Rather, it had to provide "a piece that has been missing in the pattern of life that each person is trying to build." In a rapidly changing world, Williams believed that a product's "strength and longevity" depended upon "the extent to which it serves to express and reinforce a person's opinion of himself."[45]

Such a belief increased the importance of the package, since a successful package "must instantly signal [the consumer] that this product fits into their particular mosaic." Williams concluded that Americans had but one goal, "to live better and better and to exhibit their success." Hence appeals to tradition were misguided. As he put it, "How can we say to these restless consumers, 'Hold still, look back, let us teach you how to drink wine like your grandfather did.' Who wants to live like his grandfather did?"[46]

The message was not lost on the Napa quality producers. Between 1960 and 1962, Christian Brothers, Inglenook, and Charles Krug all changed their packages in some manner, either redesigning front labels, adding back labels, or introducing a new product. A label redesign can be a traumatic experience for a brand owner, since it essentially means a public change in brand image. As wine marketers know all too well, such redesigns also present a classic marketing dilemma. The new label must be more contemporary and attractive than the old one, but it should not be so radically different that brand recognition is sacrificed. As *Bottles and Bins* put it, "When the Mondavis decided that Charles Krug labels should be redesigned, they were skating on thin ice."

Inglenook was the first of the Napa producers to experience a label redesign, introducing a new label for its more expensive "cask" line of varietal wines and changing the classic diamond trademark on its regular bottlings. The cask wines were introduced in early 1960 and sold for almost twice the price of the regular Inglenook wines. Featuring a drawing of a cask as the primary logo, the label retained the familiar "Inglenook" script, emphasized grape variety and the Napa appellation, and was easily recognizable as an Inglenook product.[47] In fall 1960, John Daniel, Jr., introduced the new label for his standard bottlings. It, too, kept the "Inglenook" script name, but the front label featured a vignette, designed by Malette Dean, of the winery building. The famous diamond trademark, in use since the days of Gustav Neibaum, was maintained but moved, becoming the dominant feature of the new back label.[48]

The following year, the Mondavis introduced two changes to their Charles Krug package. First, the front label was subtly redone, eliminating some clutter but still stating, "We are Charles Krug wines."[49] Second was the addition of a back label, something the editor of *Bottles and Bins* had derided in 1948 as "a device to jack up the price to the consumer."[50] By 1961, Francis Gould had changed his position, deciding that if "back labels are informative, their use may be justified."[51] The Krug back label emphasized grape variety, and the label change became the centerpiece of a trade promotion campaign focused around the theme "We have no secrets." Claiming that because of sales growth, it was "simply not possible for us to talk individually with all who merchandise our wine," the winery had decided to add a "back label which in a few words tells the merchandiser or consumer some of the facts about the making of the wine in the very package he is holding."[52]

Of the three wineries, Christian Brothers was probably most in need of a package redesign. The old label had played up the theme of a monastic order by using a gothic arch for the label shape and employing Old English script to identify the brand and wine type. Large, but not particularly legible, the script took up most of the label space. The redesign by Walter Landor maintained and reinforced the arched label by printing an arch-shaped panel where the brand name had formerly been located. Inside the panel was set a picture of the monastery surrounded by vineyards. The effect was as if the viewer were looking out from an arched castle window across acres of vineyards. About an inch below the monastery scene was another sharply bordered box, balancing the top panel, identifying the wine variety in a clear typeface rather than in script. Between the two panels was a reduced-sized brand name, still in script, although a bit less ornate. Actual label color varied according to the wine type, with a light green for white wines, red for reds, and a pink for the rosés. The new look was clearly more modern and designed to appeal to the 1960s consumer, rather than to his or her grandfather.

The redesign of three premium producers' labels in three years was not a coincidence. Rather, it was an attempt by each producer to make wine an easily accessible part of contemporary American culture. The Charles Krug addition of a back label emphasizing and explaining grape variety followed the lead of Inglenook, which had begun use of an informative back label in 1951, and Beaulieu, which introduced a back label describing grape variety, vineyard size, and the resulting wine in 1956.[53] The back label trend pointed to the emerging importance of varietals as an indicator of wine quality and the role of information as a means of differentiating fine wines from the generic California product. Gallo's Williams had been entirely correct in his assessment that wine was a luxury that had to deliver more than taste and alcohol. Cecil Kahmann, who in 1964 surveyed newspaper and magazine editors about their readers' perceptions of wine, said, "Editors see that the expanding leisure has made urgent the need for the cultural. Wine, infinitely complex, capable of a lifetime of study, is a true cultural medium."[54] The back labels helped make the "infinitely complex" world of wine accessible to Americans seeking ways to differentiate themselves. "Capable of a lifetime of study," wine could provide intellectual and cultural satisfaction in addition to sensual enjoyment.

Would the wine boom that began in the late 1960s have taken place without the public relations groundwork that was begun in 1955? No definite answer is possible, but certainly the campaigns for premium and "popular" wines were effective in introducing Americans to a new product, both through actual tastings and through various forms of the communication media. By 1965, when the premium wine promotion campaign effectively ended, premium wine sales had broken above five million cases, representing a 245 percent growth rate over 1955, when the campaign had begun. To be sure, imports had also grown during the same period, but at the slower rate of 159 percent.[55] Much of the growth in imports was, moreover, in the less expensive wines, which were more competitors for California's "popular" wines than for California's best. Overall, the premium wine public relations program had proved successful in blunting the tide of imports.

CHAPTER NINE

The Transformation

Enology and Viticulture in the Napa Valley

If premium wine became a product that was "consumed" intellectually and socially in the late 1950s, it was nevertheless still consumed physically as well. In order to sell a second bottle, wineries had to produce wines that tasted good. There is, after all, a limit to what U.S. consumers will accept in their quest for status. During the 1950s, the quality of California wine in general, and of premium wine in particular, rose dramatically. In 1956, Frank Schoonmaker, whose *The Complete Wine Book* had so angered the California industry when published in 1934, went on record as saying, "The finer wines of California today have ABSOLUTELY NO RESEMBLANCE to those produced between 1934 and 1937," and Cecil Kahmann reported that magazine editors in 1964 were convinced that the "quality of California wines . . . has sharply improved."[1] Schoonmaker and the magazine editors were undoubtedly correct in their assessment, and the reasons for the improvement are easily identified: more advanced science and technology in the production process and increased availability and use of varietal wine grapes.

Beginning in the late 1940s and extending through the 1950s, advances in enological science and winemaking technology dramatically increased California wineries' ability to produce wine of consistently higher quality. Winery owners rapidly adopted new technology, including cold fermentation; inert storage containers of glass or stainless steel; blanketing of wines with carbon dioxide or nitrogen; the use of bentonite to ensure protein stability; and early bottling employing sterile filtration and new low-oxygen-pickup bottling systems. Such new technology completely redefined the possibilities for white wine production, allowing winemakers to emphasize inherent varietal flavors in such varieties as Gewürztraminer, Riesling, and Chenin blanc, and in Napa Gamay for making rosé, with the result that they were able to introduce U.S. wine drinkers to a new type of white wine with distinct fruit aromas.

In red wines, understanding of malolactic fermentation and the isolation of reliable malolactic strains led to improved stability and quality, while the introduction of new oak barrels produced a striking change in the style of some red wines. All wines benefited from improved grape-processing equipment, such as bladder presses, and from the introduction of pure yeast cultures in an easily available, compressed form. This industrywide blossoming of technology and enological science made winemaking a profession, a change that found concrete expression in the formation of the American Society of Enologists in 1950.[2] Although the University of California helped develop ideas, which the society in turn disseminated, the early experiments and applications almost invariably occurred in the Napa Valley.

Napa's leadership role in quality improvement resulted from a unique combination of trained individuals, wineries dedicated to improving quality, and geographical proximity to one another, which made cooperation relatively easy. Nowhere else in the state was there a similar constellation of winemakers ready to try new ideas to improve quality. The existence of the Napa Valley Wine Technical Society offered a neutral meeting ground where Napa winemakers could gather and share ideas as individuals. Such transfer of technical information was allowed, and in most cases encouraged, by winery owners, who themselves were working together cooperatively as members of the Napa Valley Vintners' Association to build the reputation of their region. The result was that new ideas were tried earlier, experimental results were disseminated faster, and improved technology was adopted sooner by the Napa Valley wineries than elsewhere in the state.

Perhaps the most important set of technological changes were in the making of white wine. Prior to the 1950s, most white wine was produced from inferior varieties such as Palomino, which were processed with excessive skin contact and fermented at warm temperatures. The resulting coarse wine was stored for several years in redwood tanks prior to bottling, producing an oxidized, unaromatic, and often astringent white wine that did not sell well. During the late 1940s and early 1950s, the Mondavis at Charles Krug and André Tchelistcheff at Beaulieu developed a new way of producing white wine that resulted in a delicate, fruity product.[3]

Central to the process was cold fermentation of the juice, which produced a notably fruitier white wine. Peter Mondavi had seen firsthand the difference that temperature could make to white wine when he participated in enology short courses at Berkeley prior to World War II. "The colder we fermented the whites, the fruitier and better was the quality," he concluded.[4] During the war years, as the Mondavis rebuilt the Charles Krug winery, they made significant investments in refrigeration and replanted the Krug vineyards extensively to white varietal wine grapes. In 1945, the Mondavis sponsored a research project with André Tchelistcheff to compare commercial-scale fermentations at various temperatures. Tchelistcheff specifically noted the "freshness and fruitiness" of the cold fermented wines, which were also extremely low in volatile acidity, a measure of acetic acid formation and wine spoilage in general. In contrast, the wines fermented between 78° and 88° F exhibited "a complete absence of freshness . . . [with] pronounced oxidation" and a "garlic or mash flavor of aldehydes."[5]

The efficacy of cold fermentation was confirmed when the Mondavis won gold medals at the 1948 State Fair competition for their Riesling, Traminer, and Rhine wines, quickly becoming known for their white wines.[6] That same year, Tchelistcheff convinced Mrs. de Latour of the importance of cold fermentation, and Beaulieu built a special fermentation room and invested in a fifty-horsepower refrigeration system using both ammonia and freon. By 1949, *Wines and Vines* reported that cold fermentation was "almost universal among the leading wineries of the Napa Valley."[7]

Cold fermentation was perhaps the most important single variable, but it was only one aspect of ensuring white wine quality. Also important were the processing equipment, early bottling, and, for sweet wines, sterile filtration. Crushing and pressing of unfermented grapes was a problem for premium producers in the early 1950s. Two types of presses were commonly available, the standard 56-inch-diameter vertical basket press, holding about four tons of grapes, which were compressed with a hydraulic ram, and the continuous screw press, which was essentially a helix that rotated within a screened cylinder, from which the juice drained. In the case of the continuous press, the helix was reduced into a cone at the exit end, causing greater compression, but more grinding, of the grapes. The advantage of the continuous press was that it eliminated batch operations and could process large volumes of grapes. The disadvantage was that it produced low-quality juice. Al Huntsinger, who in the late 1940s managed the Napa Valley Cooperative Winery, which processed about 25 percent of all grapes grown in the valley, and who in 1954 became the winemaker at Almaden, believed continuous press juice was only fit for distilling material.[8] For those making premium wine in smaller quantities in the early 1950s, the only choice was the vertical basket press.

Labor-intensive and unsanitary, basket presses were not satisfactory. In the early 1950s, the standard processing of dry white wine involved crushing and destemming grapes into a tank fitted with a screen, allowing the free-run juice to drain for eight to twelve hours, and then shoveling the remaining wet pomace out of the tank into a basket mounted on a moveable press cart.[9] This method prolonged skin contact, increased oxidation, and meant that the skins were shoveled twice, once from the tank to the press and then again from the press to the pomace pile. In an attempt to find a better method, the Charles Krug and Martini wineries experimented with moveable hoppers that could be fitted on top of baskets to increase initial volume.[10] Grapes could then be crushed directly into the basket press and allowed to settle, while the free-run juice drained prior to pressing. This method reduced grape handling but produced only a modest increase in wine quality.

The real quality breakthrough in presses occurred in the mid 1950s when new types of European presses were exported to America. From Italy came the Garolla press, a modified continuous screw press with two sumps, which reduced the grinding associated with earlier continuous screws and allowed the operator to recover different press fractions of juice. Christian Brothers experimented with a Garolla in 1955 and 1956, and in 1957 purchased a Garolla capable of pressing thirty to fifty tons an hour.[11] The Almaden and Charles Krug wineries continued with batch presses but chose the newly available Wilmes bladder press from Germany, which was essentially a horizontal cylindrical cage with an internal rubber bladder extending the length of the center axis. As the bladder was expanded by compressed air, grape skins were pressed against the interior surface of the cage. Because of its low operating pressures, the bladder press produced very high-quality juice, and at eight tons of grapes every hour and three quarters, the press cycle was a bit faster than basket presses, although it was not nearly as productive as the Garolla.

In 1955, Almaden became the first California winery to use a Wilmes, and Charles Krug winery purchased its first Wilmes in 1957.[12] In the late 1950s, the Martini winery bought a Garolla, which it used for a few years, before switching to a Wilmes in 1961.[13] Both types of presses allowed for immediate processing of fresh grapes, eliminating the need to hold and drain crushed white grapes in a tank, thus reducing the amount of skin contact and possible bitterness in the wines. Of the two, the Wilmes clearly produced the higher-quality juice.[14]

In 1955, Julius Fessler of the Berkeley Yeast Lab noted "a trend toward smoother and fruitier wines" in his column in *Wines and Vines* and cautioned that "aging usually causes loss of fruitiness."[15] This was especially true in the case of white wines, which, prior to the 1950s, were generally stored in wooden cooperage for one or two years prior to bottling. Having worked hard to emphasize fruitiness through the use of cold fermentation and better presses, Napa wineries experimented with earlier bottling of white wines.

At Charles Krug, Peter Mondavi concluded that the wines were best after about three months in wood. However, since it was impossible to bottle all the white wine at once, the Mondavis invested in inert storage containers. In 1957, the Krug winery purchased seventeen glass-lined steel tanks with a total capacity of 125,000 gallons.[16] To minimize oxidation of wine stored in partially filled tanks, the Mondavis developed a system in which the head space in the tank was filled with nitrogen gas, the first such recorded use in the industry. Storing the white wines in inert containers under a positive nitrogen atmosphere maintained the varietal character and fruitiness of the wines, and, as Peter Mondavi told industry members at a technical conference, such storage had the benefit of "cutting down case goods inventory to two months' supply against nine months' supply previously required," since it was no longer necessary to bottle the wines immediately to preserve quality.[17]

One result of the earlier bottlings of white wines was the occasional development of cloudiness in the bottle because of the tendency of proteins in wine to become denatured and coagulate when warmed, creating a thin haze. White wines may be filtered and appear brilliantly clear at cellar temperature, but nonetheless throw a protein haze after bottling and being moved to a warmer storehouse or retail shelf. Protein instability had not been much of a problem for white wine produced prior to the 1950s because of the style of production. As a result of excessive skin contact earlier wines generally had more tannin, which bound with the proteins. In addition, the wine was stored for one or two years, allowing some protein to precipitate naturally during storage. The wines were often also fined with bentonite as a clarifying agent, which helped remove protein, although winemakers in the 1940s did not realize it was doing so.[18] Finally, many wines were pasteurized prior to bottling, which effectively denatured the protein. The new style of white wine production developed by Charles Krug and emulated by other quality producers increased the chances that a wine would not be protein-stable.

In the mid 1950s, Tchelistcheff and Joe Heitz tackled protein instability in white wines at Beaulieu. Tchelistcheff first tried to solve the problem by heating the wines to 140°F in combination with large doses of sulfur dioxide to minimize oxidization. The wines became "very brownish — clear, but brownish, fatigued, not corresponding to the quality at all."[19] He then began examining stability on a wine-by-wine, variety-by-variety basis and discovered tremendous variation between wines. Ultimately, he and Heitz hit on bentonite and developed a method to test wines for potential heat-stability problems and determine the amount of bentonite required, thus creating a solution tied to the unique needs of each wine, rather than attempting a generic solution, such as heating. With the protein-instability problem solved, the last obstacle to the production of high-quality white wines was eliminated.[20]

Having produced a fine wine, a winery had to bottle it in confidence that it would remain of high quality. Wines with residual sugar always posed the threat of refermentation in the bottle, and delicate white wines could be marred by oxygen pickup at bottling. The addition of high levels of sulfur dioxide helped reduce the risk of either occurrence, but such levels had a negative effect on wine quality. During the 1950s, two technologies were introduced, sterile filtration and low-oxygen-pickup bottling, and Napa wineries were in the forefront of their adoption.

Cold sterile bottling following a sterile filtration was a significant quality improvement, since it eliminated the need for pasteurization, which adversely affected wine quality. Following World War II, sterile pad filtration developed by the pharmaceutical industry in West Germany was extended to the German wine industry, and by the late 1940s pad filters of 1 micron or less in porosity were available to U.S. winemakers. Julius Fessler of the Berkeley Yeast Lab worked with several quality producers to develop a protocol that would ensure, not just sterile filtration, but sterile bottling of the filtered wine. One of the earliest adopters of the new technology was Christian Brothers, which began sterile bottling of all its table wines in 1949.[21] Its success encouraged Peter Mondavi to sterile bottle a slightly sweet Chenin blanc in 1954, creating a new style of white wine that was "so well accepted it sold itself."[22]

Christian Brothers was again the industry leader in 1955 when it added a new filler to its bottling line. The Biner Ellison bottom-filler was a new piece of machinery designed to reduce oxygen pickup by filling the bottles from the bottom.[23] Once again, the technology spread rapidly. The following year, Beaulieu Vineyards added an automatic bottling line, including the Biner-Ellison bottom filler.[24] The Martini winery automated its bottling line in 1958, choosing to use a Horix filler but filling the bottles with carbon dioxide prior to filling them with wine, thus minimizing oxygen pickup. The Martini bottling line also introduced a new piece of equipment to the Napa Valley, a corker that pulled a vacuum on the bottle prior to inserting the cork.[25] In the same year, the Charles Krug winery added its bottling line, choosing a bottom filler and pushing the white wine to the bottling line with nitrogen gas, rather than using a pump. In 1959, Krug upgraded the line by adding a vacuum corker supplied by I. F. Schnier.[26] Thus, in the four years from 1955 to 1958, four Napa producers made the transition from manual to state-of-the-art automatic bottling lines, a rapid adoption of new technology that was typical of Napa's quality wineries.

In red wine production, the most important discovery clearly was the understanding and eventual control of malolactic fermentation, in which André Tchelistcheff played a key role. Malic acid and tartaric acid are the two major acids found in grapes and are primarily responsible for a wine's acidity. Under certain conditions, a group of bacteria now known as malolactic bacteria can consume one of the acid groups in malic acid, producing lactic acid and carbon dioxide. The result is a general lowering of acidity in the wine and, in some cases, depending upon the bacterial agent, a "definite flavor and aroma reminiscent of fermenting cabbages."[27] The loss of acidity might or might not be desirable, depending upon the wine's initial acidity, but the cabbage flavor was universally considered a defect. The malolactic fermentation had been described in European wines in the early twentieth century, but had not been recognized in California wines until after Repeal, and it was generally considered to be the effect of an unwanted spoilage organism.

Tchelistcheff had begun his study of malolactic fermentation at his Napa Valley Enological Research Laboratory during World War II, and he presented his findings in 1949 at a meeting of the American Chemical Society in San Francisco. Tchelistcheff identified different bacteria that could produce a malolactic fermentation, explained factors that seemed to affect such fermentations, and discussed possible forms of control, concluding that it was perhaps desirable to encourage malolactic fermentations at the winery to ensure that wines remained stable after bottling.[28] His seminal work, done in cooperation with Charles Krug,

Inglenook, Martini, Souverain, and Beaulieu, gave California vintners a basic level of understanding and set the stage for work by other researchers during the 1950s, which resulted in the successful inoculation of wine with a pure bacteria culture in 1959 by Brad Webb and John Ingraham.[29] By the mid 1960s, the malolactic fermentation was generally understood by California winemakers, pure cultures that did not produce off odors were available for inoculation, and paper chromatography for relatively easy monitoring of a wine's status was being used by progressive winemakers throughout the state.

The practical solution of malolactic fermentations in the early 1960s was concurrent with another microbiological advance, the development and introduction of commercially available compressed yeast cultures. More a commercialization of technology used in the baking industry than a true technological or intellectual advance, compressed yeast was an important step for improved wine quality, since it meant that pure yeast became widely available in an easily used form. Most winemakers in the 1950s understood the desirability of using pure yeast cultures to conduct fermentations, but their use meant either purchasing an active culture from a laboratory or building a starter culture from a culture purchased from a laboratory, a tedious process at best. Such a starter culture was then carefully maintained during the fermentation season and used to inoculate tanks. The system was surer than relying on wild or endemic yeasts, as had often been done in the 1930s, but it had two main drawbacks. First, it was difficult to maintain the starter culture's purity. Second, since keeping a large active volume was sometimes a problem, inoculations were often made at a concentration of yeast cells that was lower than optimum.

During the 1950s, John Castor, a microbiologist in the Department of Viticulture at Davis, advanced the idea of developing compressed cakes of wine yeast similar to those used by commercial bakeries.[30] Castor was unable to persuade commercial yeast manufacturers of the potential market, and it was not until 1960, when Gallo began working with the Red Star Yeast Company, that Castor's idea was tried. Gallo experimented with small lots of compressed wine yeast in 1961, and in 1962, the "new method of fermentation was used exclusively with much success" in its commercial production.[31] One benefit of the compressed-yeast method was that larger initial concentrations of yeast could be employed, allowing less sulfur dioxide to be added, since the pure yeast culture rapidly crowded out any spoilage yeast present. In 1963, compressed pure yeast became commercially available from Red Star, and California winemakers were given another tool for making fine wine.[32]

The period from the early 1950s through the mid 1960s was thus a time of rapid advance in the science of winemaking. New understanding of biological processes was coupled with new technology, giving winemakers more control over the winemaking process. In turn, the quality of red wines was improved, and fruitier, more attractive new white wines were produced. Essentially, winemaking had changed from a craft into a science, and much of that transformation was centered in the Napa Valley.

The extent of the change is seen in a revealing 1949 article in which the wine broker Charles Schilling noted that there were "somewhere between ten and twenty wineries in California" that specialized in "the preparation of the finest quality wines for sale under their own label." These wineries always produced extra wine, which often would be sold on the open market. Schilling explained that such excess wine represented "insurance," since "in spite of their use of only the finest grape varieties, together with the greatest care in fermentation, finishing and aging, there is always the possibility that something may go wrong."[33] In other words, the fine wine producers accepted some degree of spoilage as an inevitable cost of doing business. The fine wine industry that Schilling described in 1949 was an artisan affair, with little intellectual understanding of critical control points, no real means to measure quality or spoilage, and primitive technology. Were Schilling to have visited the Napa Valley in 1965, he would have been amazed, not just at the general increase in wine quality, but at the overall sophistication of an industry that no longer accepted spoilage as a cost of doing business.[34] It is likely that what little wine he might have found available would have been quite expensive.[35]

The contributions of technology and science represented one set of factors in the quality equation. Equally important to improved wine quality were grapes. In the twenty years from 1947 to 1967, the North Coast, led by the Napa Valley, began a transition from "standard" to varietal vineyards. During the 1950s, the relatively low profitability of vineyards planted to standard varieties led to a decline in North Coast and Napa acreage, but by the early 1960s, a growing consumer demand for varietal wine fueled renewed interest in vineyards and spurred the beginning of a major replanting of the Napa Valley to varietal grapevines. Management techniques developed by researchers in the 1950s and the availability of virus-free vine selections from the University of California would make these new vineyards more productive, increasing the yields per acre, the availability of varietal grapes, and the general profitability of business. The growing importance of varietal grapevines received concrete expression in the Napa County agricultural commissioner's report in 1966, when grape acreage was listed by varieties for the first time, "because of so many inquiries on the subject." [36]

The movement toward varietal wine production began slowly, and even by 1967, it represented only a small portion of the total table wine production. A Gomberg private study published in 1981 estimated that in 1971, varietally labeled wines accounted for just over 30 percent of the total production of twenty-six premium producers, which in turn represented slightly over 10 percent of all California table wine sold that year. [37] Although there is no way of knowing how much varietally labeled wine was sold in the 1950s, it was probably about 1 percent of total table wine production. We know that the premium wineries accounted for less than 5 percent of all table wine produced, and it is safe to assume that the sales mix in 1971 reported by Gomberg did not represent a decrease in the importance of varietal wine.

Another indication of the limited volume of varietal wine is the number of entries and gallonage of entries in the State Fair wine judging. For instance, in 1950, Chardonnay had only eight entries, and the four medal-winning wines totaled only 2,916 gallons. Cabernet Sauvignon, more widely planted throughout the state, had wines submitted from seventeen wineries. The six medal winners totaled 6,767 gallons. [38] The Beaulieu entry, the Georges de Latour Private Reserve, amounted to 218 gallons, less than 100 cases. Certainly, the State Fair entries represented neither all varietal producers nor all of the production of those who chose to enter, but the volumes attest to the limited availability of varietal wines at the start of the decade.

The story of the relationship between varietal wine sales and varietal grape supply is a modern version of the riddle of the chicken and the egg. Clearly, varietal wine could not be made without varietal grapes, but additional acreage of shy-bearing varietal grapes would not be planted without increased demand. For the most part, it seems that in the 1950s, the premium wineries were self-sufficient in grapes for premium wine production, and that they acquired or replanted vineyards as needed to match their own sales growth. A rough estimate of Napa acreage controlled or owned by the county's premium producers in 1952 totals about 2,300 acres, or roughly 23 percent of Napa's 10,351 bearing acres that year. [39] By 1962, total county acreage had dropped to 9,800 acres, but winery-controlled or -owned vineyards had risen to about 3,200 acres, no doubt in response to increased premium wine sales (see table 3).

During the 1950s, Beringer's dry wine sales were static, averaging be-

Table 3 *Winery-Owned or -Controlled Napa County Acreage (estimated)*

Producer	1952	1962
Beringer	580	280
Beaulieu	600	720
Christian Brothers	500	1,000
Inglenook	170	225
Charles Krug	100	600
Martini	350	400
Total	2,300	3,225

The above figures are estimates derived from various sources and deserve review.

tween 50,000 and 60,000 cases each year, and its acreage was more than adequate to meet its cased goods sales.[40] The *Wine Review* estimated that in 1945, Beringer controlled about 450 acres, but 300 of these consisted of the leased Fawver property, just north of Napa, a lease that ended in 1956.[41] In 1951, Beringer bought the old Garetto Winery in the Carneros area, which included about 130 acres of vineyards, bringing Beringer's acreage to a high of 580, most of which was planted to standard varieties.[42] Following the termination of the Fawver lease, and until Beringer began planting new acreage in Knight's Valley, north of Calistoga, in 1962, Beringer-owned vineyards fell to a low of about 250 acres.

In 1952, Beaulieu had 600 acres of grapes spread over four vineyards in the Rutherford area, giving it probably the largest supply of higher-quality varietal grapes in the Napa Valley.[43] In addition, during the mid and late 1950s, Beaulieu enjoyed an advantageous long-term grape contract with Ivan Schoch, who had bought some 450 acres of the old Stelling vineyard from Italian Swiss Colony.[44] According to Tchelistcheff, Beaulieu sales had grown in the late 1950s to the point where the home vineyards were insufficient, and the Schoch vineyard contract allowed it to expand production without the expense of planting new acreage. Tchelistcheff's memory corresponds with Gomberg's tracking of sales of cased wine, which showed Beaulieu sales of dry wine as essentially level at around 65,000 cases until 1959, when sales increased, reaching 85,000 cases by 1962. When Schoch sold the vineyard to Charles Krug in 1962, Beaulieu was forced to plant additional acreage, and bought 160 acres in the Carneros region, west of the city of Napa, a cooler region than Rutherford and well suited to Burgundian varieties. Tchelistcheff put in Chardonnay and Pinot noir grapes there.[45]

Christian Brothers was the largest premium producer in the Napa Valley, selling over 100,000 cases of dry wine in 1952 and reaching 277,000 cases by 1962. One of the three high-volume producers of popularly priced premium wine, Christian Brothers was not self-sufficient in grapes, although its purchase of 520 acres of producing varietal vineyard from Charles Forni and Sons in 1956 brought its total acreage to somewhat more than 1,000 acres.[46] Throughout the 1950s and into the 1960s, Christian Brothers did not emphasize varietally labeled wines. After the vineyard acquisition, it probably produced about half the grapes needed for dry wine production, making it one of the largest grape buyers in the Napa Valley. More concerned with grape maturity, as expressed by sugar-acid balance, than with varietal labels, Christian Brothers was an industry leader in setting quality standards for growers, and it paid bonuses for grapes that met its desired maturity standards.[47]

The smallest of the estate producers, Inglenook, probably owned about 170 acres of producing vineyards in the early 1950s, then expanded acreage slowly, until by 1964 it totaled 225 acres of premium varietals.[48] A true estate winery, Inglenook produced Cabernet Sauvignon, Pinot noir, Gamay, Charbono, Riesling, Traminer, Semillon, Pinot blanc, Gamay rosé, and a small volume of Chardonnay from the vineyard surrounding the winery and the small Napanook vineyard near Yountville.[49] By 1964, according to the *Gomberg Report*, Inglenook was selling 26,000 cases of wine, which at two tons to the acre would account for almost all of Inglenook's grape production.

The Martini Winery owned vineyards in Napa and Sonoma counties and was largely self-sufficient in grapes. Louis M. Martini lived at the home ranch, which he had bought in 1935, and which included 100 acres of vineyard. In 1937, Martini also bought the old 580-acre Monte Rosso vineyard in the hills overlooking Sonoma, which bore less than a ton an acre and was gradually replanted. At the start of World War II, Martini acquired the 250-acre La Loma vineyard on Stanley Lane in the Carneros region west of the city of Napa. This brought his Napa acreage to 350 acres. In 1958, the winery added an additional 40 acres to La Loma. Four years later, Martini bought both the Las Amigas vineyard, a separate 60-acre parcel adjacent to the property recently acquired by Beaulieu, and a 200-acre vineyard in the Russian River Valley near Healdsburg in Sonoma County. Finally, in 1964, the winery bought a 900-acre ranch in Chiles Valley to the east, and planted 200 acres of grapes there.[50] The winery more than doubled its output, from 55,000 cases in 1952 to 142,000 in 1962, and with 1,070 acres of producing vine yards in Napa and Sonoma, it must have been almost completely self-sufficient.

Such self-sufficiency contrasts sharply with the case of Charles Krug, which until 1962 owned only some 100 acres of vineyard surrounding the winery. When the Mondavis acquired the property in 1943, most of the vineyard was planted to standard varieties, and they slowly replanted it during the 1940s and 1950s, choosing such varieties as Cabernet Sauvignon, Pinot noir, Riesling, Traminer, Chenin blanc, Muscat Canelli, and Gewürztraminer. Peter Mondavi recalled that they deliberately chose varieties not readily available, and decided not to plant Zinfandel or Gamay because local growers had adequate supplies.[51] Prior to the purchase of Charles Krug, the Mondavis had not owned any vineyards in the Napa Valley and had bought grapes from growers in Napa and San Joaquin counties for crushing at the Sunny St. Helena Winery. This continued after the move to Charles Krug, although during the 1950s, some of the San Joaquin County grapes were crushed for the Mondavis by wineries in the Lodi area.[52]

In 1957, the Mondavis formed a new cooperative with twenty-eight local growers, the Sunny St. Helena Cooperative. The co-op served two basic purposes. First, it allowed the Mondavis to concentrate production of much of the C. K. Mondavi brand nonvarietal wine at the leased Sunny St. Helena Winery south of town. Second, it helped them finance grape purchases, since payments to members were not made until after the wine was purchased by the Krug Winery. In the late 1950s, the co-op crushed slightly less than 3,000 tons of member grapes each year, which should have provided enough wine for about 200,000 cases.[53]

Starting in the 1960s, the Mondavis acquired their own vineyard properties. First was the Tokalon vineyard, purchased from Schoch in 1962. Covering 500 acres and established by Martin Stelling during World War II, the vineyard was "one of the best premium wine growing locations in California" and included over 100 acres of Cabernet, with significant acreage in Sylvaner, Riesling, Pinot noir, Sauvignon blanc, Chenin blanc, Semillon, and Gamay. The Mondavis estimated that the new vineyard would provide an additional quarter million gallons of varietal wine.[54] In 1966, they bought a 100-acre vineyard near St. Helena, and followed that with an additional 57 acres in 1968 and 105 acres in 1969. In 1968, they acquired property in the Carneros area for the first time, buying the 174-acre Brown ranch. Two years later, they purchased the 196-acre Cabral ranch, adjoining the Beaulieu and Martini properties.[55] Thus by 1970, the Mondavis owned well over 1,000 acres of

Napa County vineyards, although they remained a major purchaser of Napa grapes, since Gomberg estimated C. Mondavi's 1968 sales at over one million cases, and the Mondavi vineyards could only have supplied a quarter of such production at best.

The pattern that emerges is that the premium producers added vineyard land sufficient to meet their varietal needs as sales expanded in the late 1950s and early 1960s. The attempt by premium producers to secure sources of supply meant that varietal vineyards changed hands from independent growers to wineries, such as Christian Brothers' purchase of the 520-acre Forni vineyard in 1956 and the Mondavis' purchase of the 500-acre Tokalon vineyard in 1962, and that new vineyards were planted in new areas, such as the expansions of Beaulieu and Martini into the Carneros area in 1962 and Beringer's planting of vineyards in Knight's Valley. For large producers, there was also a need to assure a supply of high-quality Napa Valley standard varieties, as evidenced by the establishment of the Sunny St. Helena Cooperative by the Mondavis in 1957 and Christian Brothers' attempts to define and reward high grape quality.

For Krug and Christian Brothers, access to Napa Valley standard red grapes had been a problem ever since Gallo had contracted with the Napa co-op and the St. Helena co-op in 1952 and 1954 to buy all the wine produced from their members' grapes. Throughout the 1950s and into the 1960s, the majority of Napa's vineyards were planted to standard mixed black grapes such as Carignane, Petite Sirah, Zinfandel, Alicante, and other black varieties not normally considered varietal. Even by 1966, after several years of replanting in the valley, such standard black varieties accounted for 36 percent of Napa's 11,381 acres and over half of the total red wine acreage.[56] During the 1950s and early 1960s, probably slightly more than half of all the standard mixed black varieties were crushed and fermented by either the Napa (or "big") co-op, south of St. Helena, or by the St. Helena (or "little") co-op, located north of St. Helena. A comparison of the Napa co-op's crush records with county tonnage figures provided in the county agricultural commissioner's annual report shows that on average the big co-op processed 27 percent of all Napa County grapes from 1952 through 1965. A similar record is not available for the little co-op, but a *Wines and Vines* article in 1959 indicates that in 1958, it had crushed 5,503 tons, as opposed to the 11,937 tons processed by the Napa co-op that year.[57] Thus in 1958, the two cooperatives combined to process 17,440 tons out of Napa County's total production of 39,959 tons, or 43 percent of all the grapes grown in the county. Since varietal vineyards controlled by the premium wineries accounted for at least 3,000 acres, and thus a minimum of 6,000 tons, it is clear that the two co-ops combined to crush at least half of the standard varieties produced in the county. After 1954, all of this wine went to Gallo.

The founding premise of both co-ops had been to liberate the grower from the forced sale at harvest of a perishable crop by processing the grapes and then marketing the relatively nonperishable wine. The premise was sound, if the wine could be sold. The Napa co-op had been a member of the Fruit Industries marketing cooperative, but had withdrawn from it during World War II, believing itself able to sell its bulk wine without Fruit Industries' aid. In 1945, the St. Helena co-op had joined Wine Growers' Guild, the other major cooperative marketing organization, and it apparently was still a member of the guild in the early 1950s.[58]

Most California wine cooperatives felt the pinch for a few years following the collapse of the wine market in 1947. From 1947 through 1950, the Napa co-op pursued bulk sales, hired and fired brokers, and even invested in a bottling line in order to sell bottled wine under its own brand, Vin Mont, and to private label customers such as Safeway. Nothing had helped until Gallo approached the co-op to discuss a long-term agreement to buy all of its production.

Gallo saw a future in table wine and realized that wine made from standard North Coast grapes could be blended with Central Valley wine to raise the overall quality of Gallo table wines. During World War II, Gallo had bought specific lots of wine from the numerous co-ops and small wineries on the North Coast, and it now wanted to secure a source of supply. Gallo offered to buy all the co-op members' grapes at an average North Coast price, and to pay the co-op a flat fee per ton for processing. The main disadvantage was that the co-op was essentially abandoning its original plan, which had been to market wine as a winery and to profit when wine prices were high. It would also be putting all of its eggs in one basket, since it would have to terminate its own sales program, which might prove difficult to revive if the proposed arrangement with Gallo did not work out. On the other hand, the immediate advantages were obvious. All sales risks were eliminated, and the members would receive payment for their grapes within a year, rather than over a period of years as the wine was sold by the co-op.

In 1951, the co-op eased into the arrangement, selling roughly half its production to Gallo. The following year, the members signed a renewable five-year contract to crush and sell all of their production to Gallo.[59]

The St. Helena co-op had watched the negotiations, and in 1953, it began its own discussion with the Gallos. The result was that in 1954, the little co-op closed out all of its old pools and paid off members, reorganized to admit new members, and signed a ten-year contract with Gallo.[60] Thus, by the 1954 crush, Gallo had essentially acquired 40 percent of the Napa Valley's grape tonnage, including well over half of its output of standard grape varieties.

The Gallo contracts came at a time when North Coast acreage was declining but table wine consumption was beginning to rise. In a review of the table wine outlook for 1953, Robert Mondavi pointed out that grape acreage had fallen by 25 percent in the North Coast counties, from almost 63,000 acres in 1936 to just under 48,000 acres in 1951, and that much of the acreage was "already definitely committed" to specific producers.[61] The trend was not as dramatic in Napa, but acreage did decline in the 1950s, falling from a high of 10,514 acres in 1953 to a low of 9,623 acres in 1960, a decline of almost 10 percent.

North Coast acreage of standard varieties decreased in the 1950s for the simple reason that growing them was not a very profitable endeavor. A Cooperative Extension cost survey for Sonoma County reviewed seven vineyard operations in 1953 and 1954. Only two of the seven had made money in 1954, and the overall group averaged a profit of just $4.21 an acre, an improvement over an average loss of $32.34 a year before.[62] The following year, Herman Wente of Wente Brothers in the Livermore Valley and Eugene Seghesio of Seghesio Winery in Sonoma County presented papers on grape growing in their respective areas at the annual meeting of the American Society of Enologists. Both concluded that grape growing was a marginal occupation under current conditions. Wente cautioned that it required a heavy capital outlay by the viticulturist, for a "net return less than if he were employed in industry."[63] Pointing to the aging vineyards, declining yields, generally low prices, industry instability, and high overhead, Seghesio was even less sanguine. Sonoma County might "cease to be a grape and wine producing area," he concluded.[64] In 1956, Dr. Sherwood Shear, agricultural economist with the University of California's Giannini Foundation, apparently confirmed their opinions in a study comparing the profitability of twenty-four fruit and nut crops for the period 1949–53. Wine grapes came in dead last, grossing $153.60 per acre.[65]

The North Coast grower confronted two major problems: price and productivity. Although there was an increasing demand for North Coast grapes at a time of slowly declining supply, grape prices did not increase, but instead remained fairly constant during the 1950s. The probable cause was the continued oversupply of grapes in the northern San Joaquin Valley. Most wineries that produced lower-priced "generic" Burgundies recognized the superiority of North Coast grapes, but they blended wine made from them with wine made from Central Valley grapes. The availability of standard wine grapes in the Central Valley thus acted as an indirect check on the prices received for North Coast grapes. Throughout the 1950s, standard black grapes from the North Coast fetched $50 a ton, while the same varieties grown near Lodi in San Joaquin County averaged around $40 a ton.[66] It was not until 1959, when standard North Coast grapes brought $85 a ton, with San Joaquin County grapes getting $45, that the old price relationship broke down.[67]

During the 1950s, yields averaged slightly over three tons per acre on the North Coast. This figure represented the break-even point, and the 1954 Cooperative Extension study concluded that "yields below three tons per acre will not cover costs at current levels."[68] There was little that could be done to increase yields from existing vineyards. Most were forty to fifty years old and coming to the end of their economic lives. Virus diseases were endemic, and the Napa farm advisor, Jim Lider, believed that if mosaic and fan leaf could be controlled in some way, yields might double.[69] But in the 1950s, no practical means to control viruses existed.

In 1951, in response to the virus problem and the need for improved varietal selections, the University of California initiated a program to select and import healthy, high-yielding clones of important wine grape varieties, to heat-treat these selections to eliminate viruses, and to propagate and provide certified cuttings to commercial nurseries, which in turn would increase the number of cuttings in "mother blocks" for commercial sale to California vineyardists.[70] In 1952, the California Grape Certification Association was formed, and in 1951 and again in 1953, Dr. Harold Olmo, the university's grape breeder, traveled to Europe to select cuttings of wine grape varieties for inclusion in the new certification program.[71] These importations were included in Olmo's clonal evaluation trials for Cabernet Sauvignon and his new trial of Chardonnay clones, which began in 1955 at Martini's La Loma vineyard.[72] The virus-free certified stocks finally became available to the industry in 1959 and provided the basis for the vineyard expansion that took place in the 1960s.[73]

Concurrent with grape certification and clonal evaluation were other university research efforts intended to increase yield and grape quality.

New rootstock trials were conducted to find phylloxera- and nematode-resistant rootstocks to replace the old industry standby, Rupestris St. George, which suckered badly and tended "to make shy bearing varieties bear less."[74] These studies resulted in the university's recommendation in the 1960s to replace St. George with AXR (Aramon X Rupestris), a rootstock that had grown well in trials conducted in soils with moderate phylloxera populations and that consistently gave increased yields.[75] The effectiveness of nitrogen fertilization was studied at the Oakville Experimental Vineyard, and petiole analysis was introduced, allowing growers to monitor the nitrogen status of their own vineyards and control levels of fertilizer application based on actual need.[76] Vineyard spacing and trellising were examined, and researchers concluded that less densely planted vineyards ripened grapes earlier and more evenly, maintained or increased yields, allowed increased mechanization, and ultimately lowered management costs.[77] While nutritional analysis and respacing of dense vineyards were management decisions that could be implemented in existing North Coast vineyards, much of the university's research was not applied until the 1960s, when the North Coast began replanting.

In 1963, John Daniel of Inglenook observed that growers would "plant better grapes when it's made worth their while to do so."[78] By 1964, that had already occurred, as is evident in the listing of prices per ton for standard and varietal grapes (see table 4).

Napa vineyard acreage ended its decline in 1960, at 9,623 bearing acres, and by 1967 had expanded to 11,449 bearing acres, almost 1,000 acres more than in 1953, when acreage had begun to decrease. The new plantings represented almost a 20 percent increase over 1960 acreage, and they were only the beginning.

Not surprisingly, the majority of the new vineyards were planted to varietal grapes. The vineyard-management techniques developed in the 1950s combined with newly available heat-treated varietal selections to ensure that fine varietal grapes would be almost as prolific as standard varieties, but at a much higher return per ton. A 1964 university cost study estimated that a head-pruned variety with a yield of four tons an acre, which was quite a reasonable output, would cost just under $80 a ton to grow, including depreciation and interest. In 1964, varietal grapes were selling at a minimum of $200 a ton, depending upon variety, and standard black grapes sold for between $115 and $130. There was a significant return on investment in both cases, but the logic of planting varietal wine grapes was clear.

Table 4 *Napa Grape Prices*

	Standard	Varietal
1951	$55–$65	—
1954	$50	—
1959	$85	$110–$120
1961	$120	$200–$240
1963	$90–$95	—
1964	$115–$130	$200+
1965	$130–$135	$145–$300
1967	$140	$275

Wines and Vines, reports of harvest prices in September and October issues, various years.

In 1960, there were enough Napa growers interested in replanting their vineyards for the farm advisor to hold a series of five evening meetings to examine the issues involved in replanting. By 1964, he reported that "planting of grapes continue[s] to increase," with a "definite trend towards the planting of fine wine types" including Johannisberg Riesling, Pinot noir, Gamay Beaujolais, Cabernet Sauvignon, Chenin blanc (White Pinot), Gray (*sic*) Riesling, and Gewürztraminer.[79] The following year, he estimated that "there would be approximately 1,000 acres of premium grapes planted per year for the next five years," of which the "principal interest centers on Cabernet Sauvignon and Pinot Chardonnay."[80]

The varietal boom was not confined to Napa County. Professor Emeritus Winkler conducted a survey of varietal acreage and plantings in the coastal counties in 1963 and concluded, "It is heartening to note how the plantings of Cabernet Sauvignon, Chardonnay, Pinot noir, and White Riesling are being extended in this area."[81] According to Winkler's survey, the variety with the most nonbearing acreage, and thus new plantings, was French Colombard, with 597 acres. But right behind Colombard were Cabernet Sauvignon with 538 new acres, Pinot noir with 438, and Chardonnay with 406. The Napa agricultural commissioner was thus bowing to a trend when he gave an acreage breakdown by variety in his annual report in 1966, rather than lumping all grapes into two categories, black and white.

By 1967, the year table wine passed dessert wine in sales, the grape world was no longer "black and white." The scientific and technological changes of the 1950s had made possible many intermediate shades. A public relations campaign had introduced U.S. consumers to California wine, educating them in the differences between regions and varietals. Consumer demand for fine varietal wines led to higher grape prices, which in turn spurred vineyard replanting to varietals. For both vineyard owners and wineries, the mid 1960s were a point of departure, a threshold. No one knew what lay on the other side, except that it seemed prosperous and different from the 1950s. Few had any idea just how different it would be.

CHAPTER TEN

The Cost of Growth

By the late 1950s, increased consumption of table wine in general and premium wine in particular created a basic challenge for producers: how to react to and fund growth. Some wineries aggressively pursued growth, plowing profits back into the company and funding additional growth with loans or capital infusions. Other wineries seemed content to expand slowly, if at all. These were individual decisions, responses to the opportunity for brand development inherent in an expanding economy. Although the old saw, "A rising tide lifts all ships," may be true, in the 1950s some of the craft that sailed on the sea of wine rose more than others.

Between 1955 and 1967, California table wine sales almost tripled, moving from 23.1 million gallons to just under 62 million gallons. The growth in consumption began in the late 1950s, and each year brought a new record. Partly this was owing to an expanding population base, but primarily it came from increased per capita consumption of wine, perhaps caused by the industry's public relations campaign to represent wine as part of "the good life"; perhaps simply as a result of increased affluence. The acceleration in table wine sales was vividly shown in a table in *Wines and Vines* in March 1968 that displayed increases in three-year increments:

1955–58	3.4 million gallons gained
1958–61	7.5 million gallons gained
1961–64	10.0 million gallons gained
1964–67	12.9 million gallons gained[1]

In 1962, the "impossible" happened when table wine outsold dessert wine in California for the first time since Repeal, and by 1967, table wine was in a virtual dead heat with dessert wine in national sales.

As impressive as the growth of table wine was, premium wine sales expanded even more dramatically. In 1952, Christian Brothers, Almaden, and Paul Masson, the three wineries that were to become the leaders in popularly priced premium wine, marketed 190,000 cases of dry wine. Fifteen years later, their combined sales totaled 2,221,000 cases. They were the leaders, but estate wineries also posted impressive gains. Martini's sales almost quadrupled, growing from 55,000 cases to 200,000, while Wente's sales in the Livermore Valley nearly tripled, from 45,000 cases to 128,000.[2] Still, not every premium winery grew. Beringer and Inglenook each remained essentially static, their later expansion coming only after a change of ownership.

Why did some wineries seize the opportunity to expand aggressively while others seemed content to grow slowly, if at all? There is no single answer, other than that each winery had a unique entrepreneurial response. Unique or not, each winery faced the same fiscal reality that in order to grow, it had to reinvest profits or infuse external capital, either borrowed from banks or taken from other sources. An owner's willingness to fund growth came not just from his or her estimation of the future of California premium wine; it also was a function of the owner's perception of why the winery existed, and of how much the owner was willing to sacrifice for growth. The different paths taken by Beaulieu and Charles Krug show just how different those perceptions could be.

Following World War II, Beaulieu was the leading U.S. premium winery. In some circles, Inglenook may have commanded a higher reputation for consistent quality or for its devotion to varietal labeling, but at almost 100,000 cases of total wine sales, including dessert and sparkling wines, Beaulieu was four times larger and enjoyed national distribution. With no debt, 600 acres of producing varietal vineyards, a technological innovator in the person of André Tchelistcheff, and an experienced management team, Beaulieu was the logical candidate for growth. Instead, in 1969, de Latour's daughter, the marquise de Pins, sold Beaulieu to the Heublein Corporation, and the family retired from the wine business.

The sale was the logical outcome of a mindset that saw Beaulieu as a finished piece of work, which existed to produce income for the family. The expansion of the winery, the acquisition of vineyards, and the building of the brand had all been the work of the founder, Georges de Latour. After his death in 1940, the push for change and expansion no longer came from the owners, but rather from hired managers such as Tchelistcheff and, later, Legh Knowles, who joined Beaulieu in 1962 as national sales manager.[3] This does not mean that Beaulieu did not change with the times and expand production during the 1950s and 1960s, but that such change came grudgingly, only after the managers had convinced the family that the change was necessary to protect the status quo. By 1951, when she took over the winery at the death of her mother, Hélène de Pins did not have a vision of what Beaulieu could become; she only knew what it was — a machine for producing income for the family. As Tchelistcheff explained to his successor, Dr. Richard Peterson, who was shocked at how technologically backward Beaulieu was in 1968, "After you know Madame DePins [*sic*] a little better [you will] understand that she does not, of her own free will, put money into the winery. . . . She's trying to take money out of the winery, not put it in."[4]

Hélène de Pins had grown up with the winery, but had never been an integral part of it. Her early life was spent in San Francisco and at Beaulieu, but in her teens she was sent to France for schooling, where she met her future husband, the marquis Henri de Pins, a French nobleman with an ancestral home in Gascony. The marriage in 1924 set a pattern for the future. The marquis and Hélène alternated between France and California, never really creating a permanent life in either place. Skeptical of American business, the marquis accepted a position with Beaulieu that supported the couple, but remained aloof, never aspiring to or desiring an intimate relationship with Beaulieu. When Georges de Latour died in 1940, it was his wife, Fernande, who became president of the board of directors, not the marquis.[5] For Hélène de Pins, who succeeded her mother in 1951, the winery had always been in existence, had always supported the family, and had always enjoyed a high reputation. From her perspective, there was little reason to make changes in a successful enterprise.

Such an attitude tended to preclude expansion or adoption of new technology, making it difficult for Beaulieu to remain competitive in quality. The 1950s were a period of technological innovation, and as Tchelistcheff put it when he spoke of Beaulieu's attempt to "follow the curve of technological process" after World War II, "Wineries are known as the sharks . . . continuously asking for more and more fish to be fed."[6] Technological advances such as stainless steel equipment to receive and process grapes, refrigeration to cool fermentations, and new automatic bottling lines improved wine quality, but they also increased the cost of doing business. The same was true in viticulture. Newly available heat-treated, certified selections were planted in fumigated fields, strung along wires spread on new trellis systems, improving grape production, but requiring increased initial cash outlay. Not adopting new systems and technology was not a viable option for quality producers; doing so was simply a necessity if they were to remain leaders in producing premium wine. It was part of the price of success. But at Beaulieu success was measured primarily in dollars paid to family members, not in increased sales.

Beaulieu had changed, if not grown, during World War II. Like other California wineries, it had emphasized the sale of bottled wine (distributed nationally by Park & Tilford) rather than bulk wine production and had benefited from the controlled war economy. Although Beaulieu had increased its sales of bottled wine, however, it had not really grown in size. Indeed, following her husband's death in 1940, Fernande de Latour turned down an opportunity to purchase the Tokalon vineyard from the Churchill estate, which was then bought by Martin Stelling.[7] Fernande de Latour had presided over the shift from bulk wine production to sale of cased wine, and by 1952, Beaulieu sold just under 100,000 cases of table, dessert, and sparkling wine.

During the 1950s, Beaulieu's sales were essentially static, averaging slightly over 100,000 cases each year and ranging from a low of 97,121 cases in 1957 to a high of 109,411 two years later. Such sales differences were more a result of a natural variation in harvest each year than they were the consequence of a sales strategy by Beaulieu's general manager, Aldo Fabbrini. Fabbrini had been the winery's New York sales manager during the war years and became the general manager in 1946, when his predecessor and brother died.[8] Described by his successor, Legh Knowles, as "a real Florentine gentleman," who believed "it was not dignified to ask for an order," Fabbrini essentially managed a static system, selling the available wine each year and maintaining the product mix of 65 percent table wine, 32 percent dessert wine, and a little carbonated Burgundy.[9] Given Beaulieu's existing brand recognition and the growing market for varietal wines, his job was not a difficult one.

By the late 1950s, the changing nature of the premium wine market must have been becoming obvious to Hélène de Pins and her board of directors. The future lay in varietal table wines at a time when roughly a third of Beaulieu's production was dessert wine and the table wine it made most of was Sauterne. Nor did Beaulieu possess an adequate supply of varietal grapes, since a good deal of its better varietal grapes came from the Tokalon vineyard, owned by Ivan Schoch.[10] Although Beaulieu had a long-term contract with Schoch to buy the vineyard's output, the arrangement had become strained because the Tokalon vineyard was producing more grapes than Beaulieu could use, but Beaulieu insisted that Schoch split the difference between the Beaulieu-contracted price and the open market price on any grapes he sold to other wineries with Beaulieu. The solution to an unsure supply of grapes lay in planting a new vineyard. Rather than reduce compensation to family members, in 1960, Beaulieu borrowed $250,000 from the Bank of America and purchased 160 acres in the Carneros area. The winery began planting in 1962, the year that Schoch escaped from his onerous contract by selling the Tokalon vineyard to Charles Krug.[11]

In 1962, too, Madame de Pins hired a brash ex-trumpet player, Legh Knowles, away from Gallo to become her sales manager. Knowles, who ultimately replaced Fabbrini in 1964, was a streetwise salesman who had worked for Taylor in New York, for the Wine Advisory Board, and for Gallo. Unlike Fabbrini, he did not find it undignified to ask for an order. It was a good thing he felt that way, because by 1962, Park & Tilford was no longer doing an adequate job of representing Beaulieu. In 1954, Schenley Distillers had acquired 70 percent of Park & Tilford, but decided to continue the company as a separate operation until 1958, by which time it owned more than 95 percent of Park & Tilford. Schenley also owned Cresta Blanca, a rival premium California winery, and after absorbing Park & Tilford, Schenley gave less and less attention to Beaulieu.[12] Knowles went to work securing a network of regional salesmen and devising a marketing plan for Beaulieu.

When he was hired, Knowles had asked, "Madame de Pins, what is the job?" He claimed she replied, "Bring in the money, but for God's sake, don't use up the wine."[13] Whether apocryphal or not, the admonishment summarized Knowles's strategy. He narrowed the product mix, emphasized higher-priced table wines, and spread the wines thinly across many markets, creating a system of allocation that assured full prices for Beaulieu wines. He did this by personally selling the wines in locations where they had never been sold before, places like "Keene, New Hampshire, or Sheboygan, Wisconsin." In the past, high-volume retail accounts had often required some sort of promotional discounts from the winery. Knowles ended such discounts and told retailers and restaurant owners that they had better sell all they could, because in the future, the wine was going to be allocated based on previous sales. Ultimately, the allocation system became his best sales tool, creating a sense of scarcity. He later claimed, "We allocated every bottle and I knew where every bottle was in all the United States."[14]

Knowles's strategy was effective. Between 1963 and 1969, Beaulieu's sales grew a modest 16 percent, but the more profitable table wine portion expanded 40 percent, from 82,000 cases in 1963 to 115,000 in 1969.[15] During a time of increased interest in premium wine, Knowles extended Beaulieu's market faster than Beaulieu could increase production, allowing Knowles to maintain a system of allocation and enforced scarcity. In a sense, Knowles had made a virtue of necessity and succeeded in placing a positive interpretation on the fruits of Beaulieu's owners' past inaction.

The message that scarcity equated with quality was articulated in print in November 1966, when Beaulieu placed a large display advertisement in the *Wall Street Journal* and previewed it with commentary in such trade journals as *Wines and Vines*. Entitled "Have you noticed Beaulieu Vineyard wines are harder to find?" the advertisement explained the "three inescapable limits" to Beaulieu's "production of fine wines." First was "Beaulieu's family heritage," which represented a "great devotion to quality," still "upheld by the second and third generations of [Georges de Latour's] family." Second was "Vintage Bottling," which led to "subtle nuances of flavor that are a joy to discover." Third was "Estate Bottling," meaning that "*every* step of the winemaking process is painstakingly guided by our winemaker." The advertisement concluded that although the family were "sorry there is no way safely to increase our capacity," they were sure the consumer would "be rewarded for the extra search and slight extra cost."[16]

It was not just scarcity that was equated with quality; so was price. Knowles had been instructed "to bring in the money" but not "to use up the wine." When told more money was needed, Knowles would raise the price on the wine he thought "could bear the traffic," perhaps the Cabernet or Burgundy. As Knowles recalled, he "didn't raise the price until we needed the money for some special reason and we had good cause."[17] Since it was these price increases that funded Beaulieu's modest growth, he was called upon to raise prices quite often during the mid 1960s. Replanting of old vineyards, planting of new vineyards, purchase of new cooperage, and the construction of a new warehouse were all funded out of cash flow, while maintaining high salaries for family members. It was a hard stretch, but somehow Knowles managed it in the short run. In the long run, it proved impossible.

In 1968, Dr. Richard Peterson, a Berkeley-trained chemist, left Gallo to become Tchelistcheff's hand-picked replacement. He was shocked at how primitive Beaulieu was, that the winery was fermenting and storing white wines in redwood tanks instead of stainless steel. He realized that Beaulieu had managed to fund some capital items by forgoing technological improvements, by not feeding more fish to Tchelistcheff's insatiable shark. Only now Beaulieu had fallen so far behind the technological learning curve that the white wines were suffering in quality. What had been good enough in 1958 was not nearly good enough in 1968.

In 1969, Peterson delivered a report to the board of directors requesting $500,000 in capital improvements over the next three years. He recalled that he presented the case "pretty strongly," telling them that they "must put this in if you intend to remain competitive with the rest of the industry."[18] At roughly the same time, Knowles had told Madame de Pins that competition was increasing, and that the winery would have to hire a national marketing company if it were to compete with Seagrams and National Distillers.[19] Clearly, the family would either have to reduce its salaries or borrow money. But Madame de Pins chose a third alternative.

As the market for premium table wine expanded in the 1960s, the California wine industry attracted the attention of corporate America. Inglenook had sold to United Vintners in 1964. In 1966, Brown-Foreman, owners of Jack Daniels, became the national distributors of Korbel Champagne. National Distillers purchased Almaden in 1967. Seagrams controlled both Paul Masson and Fromm & Sichel, the marketers for Christian Brothers. And in late 1968, Heublein acquired majority control of United Vintners, thus gaining Inglenook as well. In a feature article on the California wine business, *Forbes* noted that the only remaining independent premium wineries were "smaller outfits like Louis Martini, Wente Bros., Beaulieu, Beringer, C. Mondavi and perhaps a half dozen others." *Forbes* went on to speculate that "with the costs of surviving and expanding in the wine business increasing year by year, the pressure on some of these companies to give up their independence may become too powerful to resist."[20]

On June 5, 1969, Madame de Pins sold Beaulieu, "the beautiful place," to Heublein for a bit over $8 million. The family retained the original estate and the surrounding one hundred and ten acres of vineyard.[21] They had apparently decided that the money, if invested wisely, would create a steadier, more secure source of income for family members, which after all, had been the purpose of Beaulieu as Madame de Pins saw it. One cannot argue with her position regarding the purpose of the winery. One can, in hindsight, fault the family's business sense. In the coming wine boom, money borrowed in 1969 to maintain Beaulieu's competitiveness would have paid extraordinary dividends. Had the winery been sold a decade later, it quite possibly would have brought from $40 to $60 million. But that would have meant wanting to stay in the wine business as well as the family business, something for which neither Madame de Pins nor her daughter and son-in-law were willing to sacrifice.

The Charles Krug Winery and the Mondavi family stand in such sharp contrast to Beaulieu on so many points as to be almost its polar opposite. In 1950, Beaulieu was probably the best-known premium winery in the United States, while Charles Krug was essentially unknown. Beaulieu was slow to adopt technology to improve its wines, Charles Krug pioneered new technology and experimentation. Beaulieu essentially remained static, growing perhaps 40 percent from 1950 to 1969. Charles Krug expanded at an annual rate of between 5 and 10 percent, passing one million cases in sales in 1968.[22] Beaulieu relied on a national distributor to market its wines during the 1950s, while the Mondavis developed an innovative form of public relations to build a loyal following for their wines. The de Latours and de Pins remained owners, separate from the day-to-day management of Beaulieu. The Mondavis were the management of Charles Krug, with Peter Mondavi overseeing wine production and Robert Mondavi building sales and acting as winery manager. Perhaps most important, the Mondavis sacrificed returns to achieve an essentially nonfinancial goal, making Charles Krug the state's leading premium wine producer, both in quality and quantity. That the goal was not quite met, and that the strain of growth ultimately divided the family, in no way detracts from their achievement: in two decades, the Mondavis built Charles Krug into a nationally recognized premium brand and a position of leadership in the Napa Valley.

Tracing the growth in volume of Charles Krug wines is difficult for several reasons, although it is obvious that the winery grew dynamically in the 1950s and 1960s. First, the Mondavis promoted three brands: Charles Krug, Napa Vista, and C. K. Mondavi. Thus, when a contemporary article speaks of "Charles Krug" wines, is it referring to the Charles Krug brand in particular, or the wines made by C. Mondavi and Sons at the Charles Krug Winery? Second, Louis Gomberg did not track the Mondavi shipments until 1968, when he listed C. Mondavi and Sons as selling just over a million cases of wine. Thus, the internally consistent figures that Gomberg provided for other premium wineries of the period are not available for Charles Krug and must be deduced from other, probably less reliable, sources. Third, while the 1968 figure provides a reliable ending point, a final obstacle in charting the winery's growth is determining a starting point and volumes for the brands.

The Mondavis purchased Charles Krug in 1943 with the idea of bottling much of Sunny St. Helena's bulk wine, which in 1942 had amounted to over one million gallons in sales, including bulk wine purchased and resold.[23] If their production remained constant during the war years, and if they reduced their bulk sales by half, then they would have bottled perhaps 200,000 cases a year.[24] Such volume should not be confused with wine produced for their own brands, since probably most of C. Mondavi and Sons' volume consisted of private labeled wine for former bulk wine clients. By 1944, the familiar "Charles Krug" typeface appeared in *Wines and Vines*, and a 1946 advertisement displayed a bottle of "Charles Krug Burgundy" along with the selling message "for those who put quality above price."[25] That same year, a press release describing the creation of the Mondavi's new sales company, Charles Krug Wineries, Inc., announced that the new company would "promote the sale of the famous Charles Krug wines, which have returned to the markets after a long absence."[26] Although sales of Krug wines may have begun during the war years, the volume must have been quite small, and the Charles Krug brand was not really introduced until 1947, just in time for the postwar crash in table wines.

In 1947, the Mondavis signed a ten-year contract that called for the national distributors and importers McKesson & Robbins to market Krug's "entire output." According to Robert Mondavi, that amounted to 40,000 cases, which would grow to 100,000 cases by 1949 and then stabilize at that level.[27] Although the sales crash of 1947 effectively terminated the contract before it had really begun, the failed agreement provides a rough estimate of the volume of bottled premium wine that the Mondavis planned to produce. Since the 1947 crash slowed sales and forced the Mondavis to build their own sales organization at a time of poor growth for table wines, they probably did not achieve the total volume originally projected for 1949. A reasonable estimate of Charles Krug and Napa Vista brand wine sales in the early 1950s is probably somewhere between 50,000 and 60,000 cases, which would put the Mondavis in the same league as Beringer, Martini, Almaden, and Paul Masson. No doubt this represented a small portion of C. Mondavi and Sons' output, since they were building the C. K. Mondavi brand and were still engaged in bulk wine sales and private-label bottling for out-of-state distributors, but total production volumes are not available.[28]

In the absence of a total volume figure as a starting point, it is impossible to estimate the rate of growth for all of the Mondavi brands, but Peter Mondavi recalled that in the late 1960s, the Krug and Napa Vista wines accounted for about 25 percent of C. Mondavi and Sons' total sales.[29] Factoring this percentage into Gomberg's figure of just over a million cases gives an estimated sales volume for Charles Krug wines in 1968 of about 250,000 cases, which corresponds to a yearly growth rate of 10 percent for the Mondavi's premium wines. Such an internal growth rate is impressive, but the growth of the C. K. brand to 750,000 cases is equally notable.

Gomberg knew that the vast majority of the Mondavi sales consisted of lower-priced and nonvarietal C. K. Mondavi wine, generally sold in gallons and half-gallons. While this perhaps explains why Gomberg did not include C. Mondavi and Sons among his premium producers earlier than 1968, the Mondavis' exclusion is perhaps misleading. Multiple quality levels, if not brands, existed at other wineries, yet their total volumes were considered to represent premium wine. Almaden's growth was fueled by sales of half-gallon and gallon bottles of "Mountain Burgundy" and "Mountain Chablis," and much of Beaulieu's and Christian Brothers' production consisted of generic "Sauterne" and "Chablis."[30] Given that fact, a cautious comparison of total sales volumes of premium producers can be made. By 1968, if all of its brands are combined, C. Mondavi and Sons was probably the second-largest producer and marketer of premium dry wines in California, behind Almaden but ahead of Christian Brothers and Paul Masson.[31]

The success of C. Mondavi and Sons and its flagship brand, Charles Krug, resulted from innovative marketing that relied on a novel form of public relations to build brand loyalty among consumers, from development and adoption of technology that made Krug wines recognized quality leaders, and from a management system based on family involvement that fostered expansion and growth and allowed family members to excel in their own areas of expertise and responsibility. Headed by the father, Cesare Mondavi, C. Mondavi and Sons was a partnership, with the parents, Cesare and Rosa Mondavi, holding 40 percent; the brothers, Robert and Peter, 20 percent each; and the two married sisters, Mary and Helen, 10 percent each.[32]

Management duties were divided between Robert and Peter, with each assuming responsibilities for separate spheres of action. Robert oversaw sales and acted as the general manager, representing the winery at industry meetings and generally serving as its "front man" at public gatherings. Peter was responsible for production, experimenting with new technology and ways to improve varietal wines while supervising the fermenting, blending, and bottling of the generic wines that were C. Mondavi and Sons' bread and butter. Both reported to "The Chief," Cesare Mondavi, who reviewed policy and acted more as chairman of the board than as chief executive officer.[33] With ultimate authority lying with the patriarch, the management system nonetheless gave each brother latitude for action and served C. Mondavi and Sons well during the 1950s.

Although the reasons for the Mondavis' success were interrelated, the high quality of Charles Krug wines was a major component. From the 1940s through the 1960s, the Mondavis were leaders in experimentation and technological development. During the late 1940s, they hired André Tchelistcheff as a consultant and pioneered cold fermentation of white varietal wines. In the 1950s, Peter Mondavi experimented with various fermentation regimes for different grape varieties, adopted new pressing and filtration systems, and introduced inert storage containers, nitrogen topping of tanks, and early bottling of white wines. And in the 1960s, the Mondavis became the first large winery to import French oak barrels for red wine maturation.[34]

Although costly in time and money, the experimentation and technology paid off in wine quality, as was reflected in wine awards at the State Fair. From 1948 through 1956, C. Mondavi and Sons was either the top, or among the top, medal winners. In 1956, for instance, the winery took five golds, eight silvers, eight bronzes, and three honorable mentions.[35] The Mondavis' technological edge was most evident in white wines, and all thirteen of their gold and silver medals in the 1956 judging were awarded to white wines. Probably the best example of the fruits of technological innovation was the Charles Krug Chenin blanc. Bottling the wine with a bit of residual sugar, Peter Mondavi combined cold fermentation and sterile bottling technologies to create a new style of varietal white wine, richly fruity but slightly sweet. The Chenin blanc became a best-seller for Krug for the next decade and clearly marked a new style of white wine. At the State Fair in 1955, the year of its introduction, it was entered in the "Miscellaneous White Table Wines" category and won a gold medal.[36]

New wines needed to be marketed in new ways. Following the collapse of the McKesson & Robbins contract in 1947, the Mondavis decided to build their own sales force, direct from the winery as much as possible. They really had no other choice. None of the San Francisco wholesalers approached by Robert Mondavi were interested in the wines or in helping to build an unknown brand.[37] If the Mondavis could not "push" the wine through the system, as McKesson & Robbins might have done with its marketing clout and established relationships, then they had to "pull" the wine through by creating a demand for it at the consumer and restaurant level, so that distributors would receive requests for it and want to carry the brand.

In 1949, the Mondavis focused on California in general and the San Francisco Bay Area in particular. At first they tried a traditional "heavy advertising campaign" but saw little results and, like the Napa Valley Vintners' Association and later the Premium Wine Producers, decided to take a different approach by creating direct relationships whenever possible through tastings and visits to the winery.[38] Winery employees such as their cellar foreman, Joe Maganini, and friends such as Francis Gould, who composed the Krug newsletter, *Bottles and Bins*, called on restaurant owners and key retailers to introduce them personally to Charles Krug wines and to invite them to visit and taste at the winery. The first summer they held six or seven tastings, out on the lawn under the oaks, with 250 to 300 people invited to each event. The personal approach worked. Restaurant owners and retailers recognized the quality, appreciated the connection and ordered the wine, creating the "pull" needed to gain attention from wholesalers in the Bay Area. Within a year, Charles Krug wines were being distributed there by wholesalers who had originally declined to carry them.[39]

Hospitality and establishing direct connections, what the Mondavis referred to as "personalizing," and what was later termed "public relations," were quickly extended to the general public interested in wine.[40] In 1949, a "Visitors Welcome" sign went up on Highway 29, and Francis Gould or other staff members gave guided tours to the general public at the newly opened Visitors' Room, educating visitors about wines in general and Charles Krug wines in particular.[41] Such treatment, now taken for granted, was novel. Beringer had long had a tasting room, and most wineries accommodated VIP groups by appointment, but the idea of a tour, of providing education about wine, was something new.[42] It was also typical of much of the Mondavi interaction with the public in that it combined information, fun, and brand development in a low-key atmosphere.

Another Mondavi public relations "first" occurred the same year with the publication of the Charles Krug newsletter, *Bottles and Bins*.[43] Written by Francis "Paco" Gould, a former East Coast wine importer, bon vivant, and man of letters who had retired to the Napa Valley; printed by James Beard, a St. Helena native and fine-arts printer; and illustrated by the noted West Coast artist Malette Dean, who had designed the Krug label, *Bottles and Bins* possessed a unique look and feel, combining the sophisticated tone of the *New Yorker*'s "Talk of the Town" with the informality and fun of a country picnic with friends.[44] Published quarterly, it unabashedly promoted the Charles Krug wines and winery, but it equally promoted the culture and romance of wine. As Gould editorialized on the occasion of the newsletter's fourth birthday, "Wine, and everything pertaining to wine, is irresistible enchantment."[45] *Bottles and Bins* extended a personal connection from the Mondavis to postwar Americans who were just beginning to learn about wine and who were wondering how it might fit into their lives. The newsletter was the next best thing to a visit to the winery, or for cementing a relationship that had begun there, and within four years, the mailing list grew to over 7,000 names.[46]

The articles in *Bottles and Bins* varied, ranging from cooking with wine and readers' recipes (using Krug wines, of course!) to bits of trivia on wine lore, but generally included somewhere in each issue was an invitation to attend what the Mondavis called "amateur tastings" at the winery.[47] An outgrowth of their production tastings with Tchelistcheff in the late 1940s, which had been expanded to include restaurant owners and retailers, the amateur tastings began in the early 1950s. Gould spoke of the "back log of requests for invitations" and attempted to convey "the charm and good fellowship that pervade the tastings held on the broad lawns of the Krug Ranch, 'neath the ancient and majestic oaks."[48] To attend, wine lovers simply contacted the winery and were sent an invitation for their group. In 1960, when the program was operating at peak capacity, *Bottles and Bins* reported that "the traditional Lawn Wine Tastings lured 1734 guests," most of whom probably returned home with a new interest in wine and Charles Krug firmly embedded in their minds.[49]

The tastings were part of an overall program of public relations designed to create personal connections and to keep Charles Krug in the public eye. Portions of groups hosted by the Napa Valley Vintners' Association, such as the Harvard Club, always toured and tasted at Charles Krug, and often the group dinner would be held at Krug on the spacious lawns. In 1959, a barbecue area was added, "where clubs, organizations and other groups may foregather for an al fresco meal, preceded by a tour of the winery and a tasting of Charles Krug wines."[50] The use was such that a system of reservations had to be developed to accommodate requests. By 1960, the tastings, hosted group dinners, and picnic facilities combined to bring almost ten thousand people to Charles Krug.[51] No doubt, most left with at least one bottle of their favorite wine.

The combination of high-quality wine and public relations worked well for the Mondavis, and sales of all their brands expanded each year. Starting with sales in the San Francisco Bay Area, they moved south to Los Angeles, and then into other western states. Building on family contacts from their Sunny St. Helena days as bulk wine providers, the Mondavis also sold on the East Coast, going so far as to create their own sales agency in New York in 1956; but the majority of their sales in the 1950s were on the West Coast.[52] *Bottles and Bins* acknowledged and apologized to Krug devotees outside of California, claiming that "there was no deliberate intention to ignore markets in the rest of the country" and that the absence was owing to a "lack of inventory and nationally trained salesmen."[53] By 1965, the winery was running a full-page advertisement entitled "Not Enough Charles Krug Wines." The two columns of text were bisected by a growth trend line, which moved sharply upward from the bottom left of the page to the top right. "No matter how hopefully we looked at the future and how well we prepared for the future, when the future became the present, it was always much bigger than any of us had dared to anticipate. So we ran short," the Mondavis explained.[54]

The year 1965 was a pivotal one for Charles Krug and the Mondavi family. Since the early 1950s, C. Mondavi and Sons had grown at a rate of between 5 and 10 percent each year.[55] The physical signs of growth were readily evident: the 1958 building addition, with its new glass-lined tanks and bottling line; the 1962 acquisition of the Tokalon vineyard from Schoch; the increased volume of bottled wine and the new equipment. Less easily seen were the personal costs of such growth.

Wineries are among the most capital-intensive businesses in the world. For almost two decades, the family had invested and reinvested profits and energy into Charles Krug and the premium wine industry. Unlike Beaulieu, the Mondavis had fed Tchelistcheff's shark all the fish it could eat, but the price had been slim rations for the family. The crash of 1947 had almost ruined them, and as Robert Mondavi recalled, "It took years for that to adjust itself. . . . We were living but we weren't getting much money from the business. All of us worked very, very hard and it was a strain. . . . They were really very lean years from '47 on, up until '66."[56] The joint management system and the emphasis on growth had functioned well while Cesare Mondavi was alive, but with the death of "The

Chief" in late 1959, the family lost the patriarch who had defined goals and created consensus. As Robert Mondavi put it, following his father's death, "things became a little bit more difficult because there were misunderstandings."[57]

According to Robert Mondavi, the central misunderstanding was over the need to maintain growth. His goal was to have the winery grow large enough so as to be able to include the third generation. Each year he pushed to increase the volume of C. K. Mondavi wine in order to reach an economic size that would cover what he termed the "overhead nut." Continued growth meant diverting resources away from the family at a time when Krug was finally becoming profitable. In an attempt to find a solution, the family brought in management consultants to review the business and make suggestions. One of their recommendations to Rosa Mondavi was that one person should be named to be clearly in charge of all operations. Rosa Mondavi chose Peter, and Robert, who had essentially been the general manager at Sunny St. Helena since 1939, was no longer in charge of Charles Krug.[58]

No doubt there were personal differences between the brothers, as became clear in the proceedings of a court battle a decade later over Robert Mondavi's stock and the management of Charles Krug. But the differences were exacerbated by the stress of growing the brands so rapidly, and the split between the brothers may indeed ultimately have been the real price the family paid for the success of Charles Krug. The beneficiaries of the rise of Charles Krug were perhaps not the family members, but the newcomers who moved to the Napa Valley in the following decade, intent on starting their own wineries. They gained from the technology and public relations pioneered by the Mondavis, which helped produce and define premium wine and make it part of American culture. The irony was that many of the newcomers were successful business owners who had turned to winemaking and to the Napa Valley to escape the stress of American business. Perhaps they should have spoken with Madame de Pins or the Mondavis prior to their move.

CHAPTER ELEVEN

Harvest

Following 1967, when table wine first surpassed dessert wine in gallons sold, the California wine industry entered a boom period reminiscent of the years immediately after Repeal, when hundreds of new wineries opened, or during World War II, when industry profitability caused a scramble of out-of-state bottlers intent on acquiring a secure source of supply. Both of those booms had been short-lived. The proliferation of new wineries following Repeal had been based on individual entrepreneurs' expectation of a large national demand for commercial wine, a demand that did not materialize. The prosperity of the war years, although real, had proved temporary, the result of artificial scarcity imposed by a controlled economy.

The wine boom of the late 1960s and the 1970s differed in that it was fueled by a dramatic increase in the national per capita consumption of wine as a growing number of Americans tried and then integrated wine into their diets. During the 1970s, table wine became an accepted beverage for many Americans, not one reserved for skid-row "winos," first-generation immigrants, or upper-class connoisseurs. By early 1981, when the boom slowed and the Napa Valley became the first officially defined viticultural appellation area in California, premium wine had won a place on the tables of Americans who had grown up in families for whom wine was an alien, immigrant beverage. In the minds of these new consumers, the best-known area for premium wines was the Napa Valley.

The change in American attitudes toward and use of wine was so dramatic that some writers, such as wine publicist Leon Adams, referred to it as "the Wine Revolution."[1] The driving economic force was increased per capita consumption of table wine, which doubled in ten years, surging from 1.2 gallons in 1971 to 2.4 gallons in 1980.[2] Since per capita consumption factored in population growth, for California growers and vintners, the increase in gallonage was even greater, and gross volume expanded from 109 million gallons in 1971 to 248 million gallons in 1980.[3] Other measures reveal a similar tale of growth. During the five years from 1970 to 1974, California vineyardists set out almost 200,000 acres of wine grapes, resulting in a bearing acreage of over 290,000 acres by 1980.[4] The number of wineries kept pace as well. In 1967, California counted 227 bonded wineries, but by 1980 the figure had swelled to 470.[5] By any gauge, the wine boom was real. But unlike previous booms, this one was based on actual growth in consumer demand, rather than on entrepreneurial expectations or artificial scarcity.

If the scope of the wine revolution is easily described, a single cause is not. That a cultural shift occurred during the second half of the 1960s is clear, and the U.S. public's discovery of wine was epitomized in a 1972 *Time* cover story entitled "American Wine: There's Gold in Them Thar Grapes." The magazine cover featured a half-gallon bottle with the pictures of Ernest and Julio Gallo on the label, and the five-page article pointed to "wine clubs and college wine courses . . . multiplying as fast as yeast," "wine tastings" that were "taking their place alongside cocktail parties," the popularity of home winemaking, and fifty new wine books "flowing from the press" annually as evidence that the United States had embraced wine.[6] Yet the only explanation offered was that somehow the United States had matured, or, as the editor of *Vintage* magazine put it when interviewed by the *Time* writers, "was coming of age."[7]

American society changed dramatically during the late 1960s and early 1970s as the combined forces of technology, the peaking of affluence and the onset of inflation, and the social upheaval engendered by the Vietnam War met squarely with the emergence of the post–World War II "Baby Boomers" as young adults. The advent of wine as a popular beverage is perhaps best understood as one facet of a massive cultural change that had begun in the 1960s and extended into the 1970s, a shift that included eating and drinking habits in addition to tonsorial and sartorial fashion.

During the 1960s, middle-class America became more cosmopolitan and affluent, family structure altered as more women entered the workforce, and a set of inner-directed values centered around personal experience emerged. Table wine, gourmet cooking, and "foreign" foods benefited from these changes. First, and perhaps most basic, was the rise in affluence. Between 1950 and 1970, median family income tripled, creating discretionary income that allowed indulgence in personal gratification, whether in the form of travel or clothes, cars or homes.[8] Such affluence coupled with the new technology of the commercial jet plane opened up new worlds and experiences to Americans. Foreign travel tripled in the decade of the 1960s, and middle- and upper-class Americans were exposed to "new foods, tastes, eating and living patterns," including wine.[9] One result was that by the end of the 1960s, two-thirds of U.S. households reported serving some "foreign" food at least once a week.[10] The old patterns were breaking down, new styles were emerging, and wine was finding a place on the table.

The rise in disposable income was in part owing to increased participation by middle-class women in the workforce, which in turn affected eating habits. Poorer women had always worked — they had no choice — but almost 60 percent of the women who entered the workforce between 1960 and 1977 were married to men with above-average incomes.[11] Not surprisingly, coincident with this shift was a rise in the use of convenience foods, visits to restaurants, and gourmet cooking. One food-industry analyst speculated that working women might experience "a guilt complex about not being on the job at home," which could partially be assuaged by serving better food.[12] Wine was a minor part of this movement, but the California Wine Advisory Board was not shy in pointing out in its own cookbooks that wine could "be the element to arouse . . . flavor magic when it is added to a dish," and thus reminded busy women of "one simple rule of thumb that will uplift the merely plebeian flavor to something really special: when water is called for in the preparation of a convenience food, use some California wine."[13] The management firm of Arthur D. Little echoed this point in its 1972 three-volume study *Wine/America*, when it noted that although public perception of wine as "something special" might act as a barrier to its use, it was also an advantage, since "when wine is served, it helps to make the occasion 'special'."[14]

This attribute fitted in well with an emerging lifestyle that emphasized diversity, variety, and hedonic experience. Although it contained alcohol, advocates claimed that wine was primarily consumed because it produced pleasure, not drunkenness; that it possessed subtle and not-so-subtle flavor differences, depending upon variety, region, and winemaker. When the Coca-Cola Company of Atlanta entered the wine business in 1977, its director for corporate business development commented that wine "was an art form" that appealed to the "higher aesthetics of the human experience," and as such was part of a "lifestyle some observers call 'voluntary simplicity,'" which emphasized "qualities as opposed to quantities."[15] The Arthur D. Little Company had made essentially the same point, although not quite so poetically, five years earlier, in its study of U.S. wine, when it commented that "wines fit much better with the slower more intimate party–discussion types of occasions" as compared "with the more raucous 'cocktail party.'"[16] For a growing number of inner-directed Americans, choosing wine rather than spirits was a clear rejection of the "gray flannel suit" values of 1950s corporate America and an affirmation of individual experience and choice.

Expensive wine has always been a status symbol, and the growth of connoisseurship allowed Americans to indulge in an aesthetic personal experience while simultaneously affirming social status. Already the second-largest market for high-quality "fine" wines retailing above $3 a bottle by 1972, and with U.S. consumption of such wines increasing by from 20 to 30 percent annually in the first years of the 1970s, the United States seemed destined to surpass France in this respect by the end of the decade.[17] During the 1970s, production of varietally labeled California wine grew 400 percent, from a base of 5 million gallons in 1971 to over 25 million gallons by 1980.[18]

Varietally labeled wine was more expensive, but according to one observer, most consumers recognized and appreciated the difference in quality. In 1974, R. R. Cant, a consultant to the Australian Wine Board, paid a two-month visit to the western United States to assess the opportunities for Australian wines. He found "a discerning market in which the difference between vintage varietal wines and good quality generic wines" was "really understood." He concluded that better Australian wines might find room in the U.S. marketplace, but only if "varietal, regional, and brand identities" were stressed, particularly in the context of a national guarantee of quality similar to the European system of appellation control.[19] In some ways, the West Coast, with its more relaxed lifestyle, proximity to wineries, and a per capita consumption of wine twice that of the rest of the nation, was atypical. But according to the Arthur D. Little study, the far west represented the future, and the study predicted that upon increased exposure to wine "the rest of the country" would "develop consumption patterns more . . . like those of the West."[20]

Another reason for the increased per capita consumption of wine during the 1970s was that it appealed to young adults just as the first members of the Baby Boom came of legal drinking age. The Arthur D. Little study in 1972 commented that over half the increase in numbers of wine consumers was concentrated in the under-thirty age bracket. If the consumption patterns of the 1950s had continued, this group would have numbered about eleven million wine drinkers. Instead, by 1972, over twenty-seven million Americans under thirty drank wine at least once a month.[21] To some degree, what these young Americans were consuming was not "wine" in the traditional sense. A whole beverage category of artificially flavored wines such as Ripple and Boone's Farm appeared in the late 1960s. Sweet, fruity, and low in alcohol, these so-called "pop" or "mod" wines appealed to first-time drinkers searching for a new alcoholic beverage that differed from the mixed drinks of their parents' generation. But although youth disproportionately consumed such products, the Arthur D. Little study noted that young Americans also consumed and enjoyed traditional wines, the major barrier to increased consumption being price. As young Americans matured and gained in earning power, the study predicted, they would move to more traditional table wines.

Both young adults and middle-aged Americans turned to wine because they discovered that it tasted good. That wine fitted into new social patterns of behavior and provided a means of defining social identity and status perhaps explains why increasing numbers of Americans tried wine during the wine boom. But these Americans continued to drink wine because they liked the taste. Wine as a beverage had improved dramatically in the early 1960s, thanks primarily to the introduction of stainless steel, cold fermentation, and the use of better grape varieties. Such technology, pioneered in the Napa Valley and adopted by Central Valley producers, created fruity, slightly sweet white and rosé wines that could be enjoyed chilled. By the end of the 1970s, these wines accounted for roughly 80 percent of the table wine market.[22] The technological transformation of *vin ordinaire* into a beverage readily enjoyable to Americans was a key in helping wine maintain a place at the U.S. table.

A final factor that encouraged wine consumption and kept wine in the limelight was the heavy brand promotion of table wines by the large national and international corporations that entered the California wine industry during the boom. National brand promotion on the same scale as other food commodities was new to the California industry. In the late 1950s and early 1960s, Gallo had been the only major wine advertiser. But as the wine boom progressed, corporate giants such as Heublein, Nestlé, Pillsbury, Coca-Cola, and Seagram entered the wine industry and launched new brands or revitalized old ones. They brought dollars and marketing savvy that had been largely absent from the California wine industry. Even such controversial television advertisements as Coke's promotion of Taylor California Cellars, which compared Taylor wines with brand leaders through the use of testimonials from wine writers and results from head-to-head consumer tastings, ultimately benefited the entire industry by keeping wine interesting, provocative, and in the consumer's mind.[23] By the mid 1970s, table wine had become big business and had secured a place on America's table or, in the case of the white and rosé wines, in the refrigerator.

Although no one cause explains the increased acceptance of table wine in the United States, the reality of increased per capita consumption unleashed a boom in new wineries and vineyards that reverberated statewide in California, from as far north as Ukiah to as far south as Cucamonga, and across the state from Monterey to the Sierra foothills. During the late 1960s and early 1970s, sales of premium and fine wines grew at between 15 and 20 percent each year on average, and well-marketed brands could expect to do much better. Revitalized by cash infusions from its new Swiss owner, Nestlé S.A., and expanding from a small base, Beringer tripled its sales in 1971. Peter Jurgens, who had been hired away from Almaden by Nestlé, predicted that Beringer would settle down to a 20 to 25 percent annual growth rate during the 1970s and end the decade with sales of over 1.5 million cases, having started at barely over 100,000.[24]

Such estimates seemed reasonable given increasing per capita consumption of wine. When compared to Italian and French per capita levels of almost 40 gallons, U.S. consumption of 2.5 gallons per adult appeared minuscule. The real problem facing the industry seemed not how to increase consumption but how to produce enough wine. In 1971, Larry Solari, the head of United Vintners and chairman of the Wine Institute, thought it "unlikely we [the California wine industry] can meet this demand" and believed a consumption rate of 5 gallons per capita might be expected by the mid 1980s.[25] The two major California banks, Bank of America and Wells Fargo, agreed with Solari's assessment. In 1972, Wells Fargo released a study calling the outlook for the state's wine grape industry "the brightest of any agricultural enterprise in the state" and predicting that per capita consumption of all wine would increase from 2.5 gallons in 1971 to about 3.4 gallons by the end of the decade, which in turn would require 490 million gallons of wine.[26] Not to be outdone, Bank of America, the major agricultural lender in California, forecast a market for 400 million gallons in 1974, and 650 million gallons by the end of the decade.[27]

Such projections and expectations sparked the interest of a diverse group of Americans and fueled investment in vineyards and wineries throughout California. Giant food and beverage companies such as Nestlé, Pillsbury, Coca-Cola, Schlitz Brewing, and R. J. French Co. all entered the industry, purchasing existing brands or building new ones. At the other extreme, individual investors, lured by projected rates of return, favorable tax write-offs, and the cachet of owning part of a vineyard or winery, subscribed to real estate syndicates or limited partnerships.[28] In between were the new wineries and vineyards managed and run by the main investor, who often turned out to be an émigré from corporate America in search of a lifestyle that combined diversity of tasks, business acumen, family involvement, and aesthetics, all in a rural setting. Lou Gomberg described these newcomers as "a new breed" that brought new energy and an outlook derived from such nonvinous occupations as "medicine, law, physics," and business. He hailed their entrance into California wine as "one of the greatest developments this industry has experienced in 200 plus years." Lauding their "sense of dedication, devotion and commitment," their "determination to excel," and their "financial staying power," Gomberg was convinced that this new wave of winery owners would propel California wine to "future greatness."[29]

Although the "new breed" established wineries and vineyards throughout California, Napa was the address of first choice, a combination of Shangri-la and Eden. Between 1967 and 1980, eighty-eight new wineries were established in Napa County, well over a third of all the new wineries in the state.[30] Drawn by Napa's reputation for excellence as well as its scenic beauty, the newcomers brought money, energy, and a cosmopolitan style to what had been a slow-paced rural community. The influx of wineries and vineyards, coupled with rising wine and grape prices, permanently altered the local economy, inflating land values and creating an economy based almost entirely upon grapes and wine production. According to the *Annual Report* of the Napa County agricultural commissioner, in 1967, slightly over a quarter of all agricultural income had been derived from grapes. By 1980, the gross value of Napa grapes had increased eightfold, grapes accounted for 75 percent of all agricultural receipts, and vineyard acreage had essentially doubled, growing from just over 11,000 bearing acres in 1967 to 22,000 by 1980.[31] Yet the change was mostly in scale and style, not in basic direction. The newcomers had traveled to Napa to pursue excellence in winemaking, and the ranks of the Napa Valley Wine Technical Group and the Napa Valley Vintners' Association were soon swelled by new voices eager to promote Napa Valley wines.

Gomberg's phrase "new breed" invokes images of disjuncture, of novel ways of doing things, and, although useful, it perhaps misses an underlying thread of continuity that existed in the industry in general and in Napa in particular. For one thing, although the wineries were new to the valley, often the individuals were not. Freemark Abbey (1967), Caymus (1971), Raymond Vineyards (1974), Rutherford Hill (1976), Rutherford Vintners (1977), Cassayre-Forni (1977), and Mont St. John (1978) were all started by longtime valley residents, and in other cases, such as Silver Oak (1972) and Grgich-Hills Cellars (1977), Napa winemakers with at least a decade of history in the valley joined with financial partners from outside the valley to create new wineries. Nor did the newcomers' goals differ from those of earlier Napa winemakers. The ambition to be an artisan vintner personally involved with the growing of a crop and the production of distinct and flavorful wine had certainly also been that of Lee Stewart of Souverain (who sold out in 1970, his winery ultimately becoming Burgess Cellars), of the Taylors of Mayacamas (who in 1969 sold to a group led by Bob Travers, formerly employed at Heitz Cellars), and of Fred McCrea of Stony Hill. The influx of new wineries was thus not so much a turning point as the logical progression in a search for excellence. This same thread of continuity is readily identified in what was, on the surface, another disjuncture: the Paris tasting of 1976.

In 1976, Steven Spurrier, an English master of wine who owned a wine shop in Paris, organized a modest wine tasting to celebrate the bicentennial of the United States of America: a comparison of the best California wines with their French first-growth counterparts. The nine French judges were all influential and experienced professionals, and when they were done, they discovered, much to their chagrin, that the wines they had rated as best were from the New World — Napa to be exact. Much was made in the press of how the French judges had verbally denigrated wines that they took to be Californian during the judging: "Ah, back to France!" exclaimed one as he sipped a 1972 California Chardonnay; "This is definitely California. It has no nose," declared another as he tasted a Bâtard-Montrachet (one of Burgundy's top whites).[32] The story played well, calling up images of chauvinistic Frenchmen hoisted by their own petard, and the popular press took the judging to mean the

Californians had "defeated" the French on their own ground. From a public relations perspective, perhaps California had bested France, but a statistical analysis indicated that all of the wines were of high quality, with no significant difference between the wines. What the tasting really showed was that the best California wines were on a par with the most expensive French wines.

The two California "champions" were a 1973 Stag's Leap Wine Cellars Napa Valley Cabernet Sauvignon and a 1973 Château Montelena Chardonnay. Neither winery had existed a decade prior to the tasting. Château Montelena, the older of the two, had been dormant since Chapin Tubbs's death until it was purchased and refurbished in 1969. Stag's Leap had been established in 1972. How could two young wineries, members of the "new breed," have achieved excellence so early in their histories?

The answer is that the victory was the Napa Valley's, that Château Montelena and Stag's Leap were the representatives and beneficiaries of forty years of experimentation and technological advancement by Napa winemakers. Château Montelena's winemaker was Miljenko "Mike" Grgich, a Yugoslav who had migrated to the Napa Valley in 1958. The owner and winemaker at Stag's Leap was Warren Winiarski, a Midwesterner who had fallen in love with wine in Italy, and who left an academic position with the University of Chicago in 1964 to make wine in California. Although they were from diverse backgrounds, their histories are remarkably similar.

For each, his first job in California was at Lee Stewart's Souverain winery, the prototype of the California boutique winery. Grgich moved on to Christian Brothers and then to Beaulieu, where he worked with André Tchelistcheff for nine years. Both Grgich and Winiarski joined Robert Mondavi soon after he founded his own winery in 1966. Both left in 1972, Winiarski to found his own winery, Grgich to become winemaker at Château Montelena. Although each was and remains an extraordinary winemaker, both were the recipients of decades of hard-won but freely shared technical information, which by 1970 had become part of the assumed base of quality winemaking in the Napa Valley. The movement toward planting varietal grapevines begun by growers such as Martin Stelling during the war years, Tchelistcheff's work with malo-lactic fermentation in the late 1940s, the Charles Krug Winery's leadership of cold fermentation of white wines in the 1950s, and the use of French oak barrels at Krug and later at the Robert Mondavi Winery in the 1960s were all essential elements of the backdrop when the two Napa wines briefly assumed center stage in Paris. A public relations coup and

a milestone of sorts, the Paris tasting solidified the Napa Valley's reputation as the top quality area in the United States, the equivalent of a
Burgundy and Bordeaux rolled into one.

If the roots of the Paris tasting triumph trace back to the Napa Valley's historic leadership in technological innovation and adoption, the
1980 appellation hearings, which resulted in Napa becoming the first
approved viticultural area in California, showcased the collective promotional action that had characterized Napa winemakers since the war
years. The belief in the importance of viticultural place in wine quality
was a European notion, but was also implicit in the Napa Valley Vintners' Association's regional promotion following World War II. That
Napa growers and winemakers enthusiastically supported proposed federal action to define and limit the use of viticultural appellations is not
surprising. Indeed, the Napa Valley Grape Growers' Association and the
Napa Valley Vintners' Association presented the first notice of intent to
the Bureau of Alcohol, Tobacco and Firearms to request the establishment of the Napa Valley as an official viticultural area.[33] Ironically, the
result was that because the name "Napa Valley" had become so well
known and so valuable, the concept of appellation was stretched to include diverse climatic areas, and "Napa Valley" for all intents and purposes became synonymous with "Napa County."

The issue of appellation of origin was raised in the mid 1970s by the
BATF as part of a proposed series of regulatory changes to define and
upgrade premium wine. On November 13, 1976, at an industry meeting
at the University of California at Davis, Rex Davis, director of the BATF,
unveiled what he termed "a new framework" that would allow U.S.
wines to "attain a higher plateau," and that would "influence consumer
acceptance of American wines well into the 21st century."[34] The rationale
for the new system was that the regulations then current did not "adequately advise consumers on a wine's origin" or varietal composition.[35]
Davis's assertion was no doubt correct, but the fact that regulations that
had stood for over forty years now needed to be changed was tacit testimony to the rise of varietal labeling, the increasing prevalence of vineyard and regional designations, and the integration of wine drinking
into American life.

The BATF proposed to maintain the current regulations for most
wines, but to create a special category of "seal" wines that would meet
more stringent requirements with regard to production, varietal composition, and region of origin. Davis proposed that a varietal "seal" wine
derive at least 85 percent from the named variety, a major increase from

the 51 percent then required; that the label of a seal wine bear a statement of origin in an approved viticultural area; and that 95 percent of the seal wine be derived from grapes grown in the area named. Finally, as part of the new framework, he proposed that the BATF "formally define the term 'viticultural area'" and "set up procedures . . . for delineating such areas." [36]

The proposal was sweeping, far-reaching, and ill-received. The industry feared that the seal category, although voluntary, would implicitly become a symbol of quality, an endorsement from the federal government. As the usually outspoken August Sebastiani put it, "It would give people with a seal an edge without any assurance the seal means a damn thing." [37] At hearings in February 1977, Louis Martini, the Wine Institute's chairman, presented the Wine Institute's counterproposal, which eliminated seals and called for all varietally labeled wine to derive at least 75 percent from the named grape, and the entire 75 percent to be from the viticultural area named on the label. [38] The counterproposal set off a year and a half of hearings, informal discussions, and drafts, until in August 1978, the industry and the government reached a consensus and the BATF issued its new regulations, having dropped the voluntary category of "seal" wines. [39]

The new regulations allowed the continued use of geopolitical boundaries as functional appellations of origin, such as county or state lines, but they also spelled out a process to create and define viticultural appellations, which, once approved, could appear on a label. Early in 1979, the Napa Valley Grape Growers' Association and the Napa Valley Vintners' Association filed a joint petition requesting a hearing to establish the Napa Valley as a viticultural area. As *Wines and Vines* noted, the request was "likely to be controversial," since it proposed to define the area as the watershed of the Napa River, thus making "outcasts of growers" in the eastern portions of Napa County. [40] The disagreement was not just about a name, it was about money. At the original 1977 hearings, Burton Blackwell, a grower in the eastern portion of Napa County, had commented that his family had "a half-million dollar investment," and that if grapes from his vineyard were not considered to be part of the Napa Valley appellation, "we will have lost our market." [41]

On April 28 and 29, 1980, in the Oakville-Rutherford Rooms of the Holiday Inn in Napa, the BATF heard testimony from over thirty individuals on the issue of just what the boundaries of the Napa Valley were. Winery owners and vineyardists, consultants, professors, and consumers all had their say. It was a thorny issue, which raised difficult questions.

Was a valley simply a watershed, or did elevation play a role? Could grapes grown on a mountainside be termed "Napa Valley" simply because water from the vineyard drained to the Napa River? Was the notion of a watershed as a defining feature germane if it could be shown that historically wine made from grapes grown in other valleys had been considered as much "Napa Valley wine" as wine made from grapes grown in Oakville, Rutherford, or Calistoga? What was the purpose of appellation in the United States, if it did not define or encompass a particular set of qualities inherent in grapes grown in the named region? If grapes in the cool Carneros region made significantly different wine than grapes grown in the much warmer Calistoga area at the northern end of the valley (and they did), then did the term "Napa Valley" have any true meaning to the consumer? Was the term "Napa Valley" primarily an indicator of quality, essentially a state of mind, perhaps unrelated to the provenance of the grapes?

The practical question before the BATF was whether to follow a strict definition of *valley* as meaning a watershed, and thus exclude 2,000 of Napa County's 24,000 acres of vineyards, or to take a broader view of the Napa Valley and perhaps risk setting the precedent that in the United States appellation was not simply a matter of geographic boundaries, soil types, or climatic records. The presenters, a "Who's Who" of the Napa Valley, hardly clarified any of these questions for their BATF listeners.

The economic significance of the sobriquet Napa Valley was starkly brought home in a short letter from Jean Pierre Labruyere, owner of Wine World, a firm that distributed Beringer wines. "For us in France," he wrote, "Napa Valley wines have been the standard of excellence for U.S. wines. . . . If Beringer had not been located in the Napa Valley we would not have invested in the business."[42] John Gay, a wine retailer and son-in-law of Elmer Salmina, whose family had started and sold Larkmead, explained that for his customers the name Napa Valley served as a "badge," as a "testimony to the quality of the wine."[43] An eastern Napa grape grower commented that the Napa Valley appellation was "a well-recognized trademark of long standing" and was thus "very valuable property." Who was the owner of this common trademark? It was, he said, "held jointly by all the growers and all of the vintners who have created this appellation . . . who have built it into the valuable property that it is today."[44]

The proponents of the watershed definition, when questioned, often expressed a desire to include their eastern neighbors. Both Robert Mondavi and Louis Martini spoke of a basic character inherent in Napa Valley grapes, as opposed to those from Sonoma or Santa Clara counties. In describing the Napa character, Mondavi claimed that "the grapes from Calistoga, from St. Helena, from the . . . Carneros, each have their own characteristics, but there is an underlying character . . . typical of the Napa Valley." When questioned about the character of grapes grown in the Wooden Valley, which would be excluded under the proposed definition, Mondavi replied, "They are different, but there is a relationship that is unique that you will pick up as being Napa Valley."[45] The following day, Mondavi gave additional and succinct testimony, declaring that the eastern portions of Napa County should be included in the proposed appellation because the areas produced grapes with the same distinctive characteristics as those grown within the Napa Valley proper, because historically they had been used for Napa Valley wines, and because excluding them would reduce grape supply and raise prices to consumers.

At the end of the second day, after all scheduled speakers had testified, Dick Maher, president of Beringer and the individual responsible for coordinating presentations in favor of the joint appellation petition, came forward to make his concluding remarks. He pointed out that in past hearings, the winemakers had attempted to include eastern portions of the county through a "grandfather" clause, that they saw their petition as a *minimum* definition of the Napa Valley, and that neither the Napa Valley Vintners' Association nor the grape growers objected to the inclusion of the eastern vineyards. Following Maher, BATF Deputy Director Steven Higgins thanked everyone for their patience and concluded the hearing by saying:

> I remember the story about the little boy who was drawing a picture and the man asked him what he was drawing a picture of. And he said, "I'm drawing a picture of God." He said, "That's impossible. Nobody knows what He looks like." And the boy says, "Wait 'til I'm done and you'll know."
> I hope that when we are done you will know what the Napa Valley is.[46]

In January 1981, the BATF defined the Napa Valley. It accepted the basic petition and broadened it to include the eastern growers, commenting that "ATF has not attempted to delimit the geological formation known as the 'Napa Valley,' but has identified a grape-growing region which takes its name from a recognizable geographic feature in the grape-growing area."[47] It was a Solomonesque decision, affirming the essential unity of Napa County as a geographic community producing quality wine and deferring to another day the question of the specific importance of location to wine quality.

From the historical view, it was a correct decision. Napa Valley had been the locus for all viticultural activity within Napa County. The fact that it was the one major valley in the county had encouraged the cooperation and interaction of such individualists as Georges de Latour, John Daniel, the Salminas, the Martinis, and the Mondavis in the joint promotion of their area, of their "appellation," long before the BATF had entertained the idea of appellations. The concept of the Napa Valley as an area devoted to the pursuit of quality wine transcended the weight of gravity or the determination of where water flowed. To be sure, Napa winemakers relied upon the characteristics of the grapes, but they relied as much or more on a notion of and devotion to excellence, on an overriding desire to achieve "bottled poetry."

It had been just a century before, in 1880, that Robert Louis Stevenson had visited the valley on his honeymoon and had paused to taste the wine. His estimation was that the wine was "merely good wine" but he foresaw its promise. He wrote in terms that today's winemakers would understand, if they were to read him, saying, "Wine in California is still in the experimental stage," and that "bit by bit" California winemakers searched for "their Clos Vougeot and Lafite" for "those lodes and pockets of earth, more precious than precious ores, that yield inimitable fragrance and soft fire." He concluded that such locations lay "still undiscovered" but predicted that they awaited "their Columbus," and he assured his reader, "The smack of California earth shall linger on the palate of your grandson."[48]

Stevenson could scarcely have predicted the barbarous intervention of Prohibition in the progress of California and Napa wine. And yet his sense of timing was prophetic. It had taken about three generations for Napa winemakers to produce "world class" wines that "lingered on the palate." If skeptics existed, one might point to the new joint venture between Robert Mondavi and Baron Philippe Rothschild as evidence that Rothschild, too, was searching for his own Lafite in the New World, in the company of at least another hundred "prospectors."[49] Some pockets had been found and mined, if yet unnamed by the BATF, and others lay to be discovered. "And the wine is bottled poetry" had become reality, rather than a promotional slogan on a sign.

Postscript

Reflections on a Historic Wine Tasting

The rewards of the study of history are generally intellectual, but they sometimes take more tangible forms. This thought crossed my mind on a beautiful June morning in 1994 as I pulled off Highway 29 north of St. Helena and turned up the hill to Stony Hill Vineyard to attend a historic tasting of Napa wines from the 1940s through the 1980s. Several weeks earlier, I had completed my dissertation, submitted the manuscript to the Graduate Division at U.C. Davis, and phoned a few friends in the industry to inform them that I was now "Dr. Jim." Word traveled quickly. Mike Martini called to tell me that he was pulling together a tasting of wines from Beaulieu, Inglenook, Beringer, Charles Krug, and Martini as part of the annual Napa Valley Wine Auction and invited me to be the "recording" historian. Writing history is one thing; drinking it another. I of course accepted.

Bottled Poetry was never intended as a comprehensive, up-to-the-minute history of the Napa Valley. First, there is the philosophical problem: the moment the historian stops writing, the present begins to recede into the past. More practically, the amazing growth in the numbers of wineries in the Napa Valley from 1970 to the present is simply too complex and deserves its own history or collective sociological study. Various metaphors for history abound, and one I at times favor is that of the tree, with its trunk, main limbs, branches and twigs, leaves, and fruit. The book you have just finished was a study of the major limbs and branches of the tree called "Napa Wine." (I would employ the metaphor of the grapevine, but since the fruit only appears on new wood, the vine is pruned every year, reducing the branching and complexity of the grapevine and its utility as a metaphor.) Can we really deal with the luxurious emergence of new growth on the perimeter — the literally hundreds of branchings that occurred in the 1970s and 1980s — within a context that examines the main structure of the tree? Perhaps not, but the tasting at Stony Hill does afford an opportunity to discuss the tension between the old and the new in the Napa Valley and to trace briefly to the present, however fleeting it may be, the fortunes of the handful of Napa wineries that were responsible for Napa's emergence as the premier wine region of the United States.

Napa wine is expensive wine. In one sense, Napa vintners are victims of their own success: having made their finite valley synonymous with excellence, they have also created a demand for vineyards and grapes, causing prices for land and labor to increase dramatically. The resulting grapes are expensive, as must be the wine. Yet people who enjoy $20 wines are not simply drinking a beverage — they are also consuming an image as seen in the bottle, the label, the uniqueness of the wine, and its place in the market, articulated by such arbiters of "quality" as Robert Parker or the *Wine Spectator*. Collective marketing programs can increase the value of the Napa appellation, but the problem of individual brand differentiation still remains. For the older wineries of the Napa Valley, the Napa Wine Auction is a classic case of opportunity and problem, and the historic tasting at Stony Hill, with its elements of new and old, can be seen as a very rational response by the older Napa wineries to set themselves apart from the myriad "newcomers."

If I were writing a current history of the Napa Valley, the Napa Valley Wine Auction would certainly be the focal point for a chapter on the collective marketing of the Napa Valley. Napa winemakers have always attempted to draw parallels with the fine wine regions of Europe and to gain media attention for their valley. What better way than to emulate Burgundy's auction for the Hospice de Beaune? Such an event would capture the attention of U.S. wine writers while raising large sums for Napa's Queen of the Valley hospital. In addition, items sold at auction for a charitable purpose generally draw inflated prices, which helps to raise the collective image of the value of Napa wines. Beginning in 1981, the auction has been a tremendous success. For the past several years, it has raised over a million dollars for community health care at each auction, while focusing the attention of leading American wine consumers on the Napa Valley. For the almost two hundred Napa wineries that participate, the auction allows personal interaction with the top tastemakers in the United States. Newer wineries can generally attract attention — most Americans seek out new experiences — but what of the older wineries? How can they benefit from the auction? How can they draw attention to themselves?

One point of difference for the established wineries is history. They can offer wines from the 1940s, 1950s, and 1960s — wines produced before the owners of today's new wineries were of legal drinking age, or even born. Thus in 1994, Mike Martini conceived the idea of holding an exclusive tasting for high bidders from past auctions. He invited the current and past winemaker (or representative) from Beaulieu, Beringer, Charles Krug, Inglenook, and (of course) Martini to pour wines from five decades at the Stony Hill winery, in the Mayacamas mountain range, overlooking the Napa Valley. Had Mike Martini been able to include representatives from Christian Brothers and Larkmead, the historic septet would have been complete. Still, the venue of Stony Hill, one of the first of the small artisan producers, was historic, beautiful, and indicative of the tension between new and old. So, with that as an introduction, let us continue to trace the main limbs, remarking on new branches, which are at the same time typical and unique, while trying to keep the whole tree in view.

I am not sure why Mike Martini chose Stony Hill Vineyard to hold his tasting, aside from the fact that it is exclusive and thus represented a treat for the high bidders he wanted to entertain. As a historian, I would say his choice was excellent, since Stony Hill is a defining example of the exclusive small producers that have helped further Napa's reputation in the 1970s and 1980s. Founded by the advertising executive Fred McCrea and his wife Eleanor in 1953, Stony Hill followed a new, indistinct path blazed by Lee Stewart of Souverain, to the west across the valley, and Jack and Mary Taylor of Mayacamas Vineyards, twenty miles to the south. The McCreas planted their vineyard in 1947 to Riesling and Gewürztraminer, wines for which Charles Krug had already shown a market existed, and a little known Burgundian variety called "Pinot Chardonnay." Stony Hill Vineyard wines, most especially the Chardonnay, which in the 1950s was not widely planted, gained a following among wine enthusiasts. Certainly, the quality of the wine was important, but so was the notion that it was a finite, scarce commodity. Connoisseurs who enjoyed a bottle or two of Stony Hill Chardonnay over dinner not only savored the wine, and the fact that the variety was rare in the United States, but the knowledge that they had just drunk one or two of perhaps 20,000 bottles. Stony Hill was one of the first wineries to achieve "cult" status for its wines, selling out almost all of its production directly to consumers (at retail prices!) by mail order each year, with limited quantities reserved for a handful of top retail accounts and restaurants. Stony Hill became a model for other Napa artisan vintners who desired to create a distinctive, limited-volume, unique product. Stony Hill was a pioneer, and as such it suffered the reversals and problems associated with being first or second in a new niche—but in the process it staked out the high ground. For the hundreds of newcomers that followed Stony Hill in the 1970s and 1980s, both in the Napa Valley and throughout California, establishing points of distinctiveness, balancing the need to maintain scarcity but also to spread costs across increased volume, and gaining consumer attention in an increasingly crowded marketplace became key problems. Some artisan wineries, such as Dunn and Forman became well-known and sought after, others quietly folded, with the principals moving on to other endeavors.

The twenty years from 1965 on were a period of tremendous expansion for California's premium wine industry—literally over four hundred wineries were begun throughout California. Many were patterned on such artisan producers as Stony Hill. Others were larger, financed by private wealth or corporate money, offering a full line of wines. The growing interest of U.S. consumers in wine fueled the boom, creating a market for distinct wines and an opportunity for growth. But with opportunity came competition, and some of the older Napa producers discovered to their chagrin that their own brands—so distinct in the 1950s and early 1960s—were now lost in a sea of new labels. The growing consumer focus on varietal labeling, a trend initiated by Napa producers, led retailers to reorganize their shelves. The "brand set," in which all the wines from one producer were grouped together, dominating space and forcing brand recognition, gave way to the "varietal set," in which wines from various producers were set out by varietal content. Gone were the Charles Krug, Martini, and Beringer shelf allocations. In their place were groupings of Chardonnay and Cabernet Sauvignon, in which the wines of the old Napa producers were simply a few among many offerings. The problem of competition and shelf space was compounded, not just by the sheer number of new entrants, but by the types of wines being produced. The artisan wineries, with their distinctive handmade products, created new competition at the top for the older Napa wineries' reserve wines, while larger producers introduced new lines of less expensive varietal wines produced from new coastal plantings outside the Napa Valley, effectively applying pressure from below. It was a period of growth, but not necessarily a time of continuity, and most of Napa's old guard underwent changes during the 1960s.

The first of Napa's quality leaders to falter was Inglenook, which John Daniel, Jr., sold to United Vintners in 1964. Inglenook's fortunes over the next thirty years are illustrative of many facets of winemaking in the valley — from demonstrating the reach of the Central Valley, through the corporate invasion of the 1970s, to the quest for quality demonstrated by individuals. It is perhaps the most tangled branch of our tree.

Although the story of the sale of Inglenook must revolve around Daniel, part may be traced back to the Central Valley in 1951, when Lou Petri created a new cooperative, Allied Grape Growers, to help finance wine production for his new company, United Vintners. In 1953, the Petris and United Vintners bought Italian Swiss Colony from National Distillers (which had previously tried to interest the Gallos in the property), creating the largest wine-production and -marketing company in California. The grape-pricing formula between the cooperative, Allied Grape Growers, and the marketing/production company, United Vintners, became too complex, relying as it did on determination of United Vintners' profits, and in an attempt to simplify the relationship in 1959, Allied Grape Growers bought United Vintners from the Petris. Allied Grape Growers, a cooperative of over 1,000 growers spread across California, now owned the largest wine-producing and -marketing organization in the United States, with such brands as Italian Swiss Colony, Petri, Mission Bell, and Lejon. United Vintners continued to grow, acquiring new members and wineries. In 1961, it made its first major foray into the Napa Valley when the Cellas, who were already members of Allied, contracted the grapes from Cella Vineyards to Allied and sold their wineries to United Vintners, including the Napa Wine Company in Oakville which the Cellas had bought from Lou Stralla in 1947.

No one will ever know why Daniel sold Inglenook. The winery had been a labor of love, rather than a business, and in the early 1960s, he had no family members with whom to share that love. His wife, a Mormon, had little interest in the winery. His two daughters were in their early twenties and seemed uninterested in the wine business at the time too. So Daniel sold to United Vintners, which promised him it would treasure Inglenook and maintain its reputation. He retained the family home, some surrounding vineyards, and the Napanook vineyard near Yountville, which he had bought with Stralla in 1947.

United Vintners did not honor its promise to Daniel. It moved wine production south and across Highway 29 to the old Napa Wine Company, increased production, lowered quality, and quickly devalued the Inglenook name. Matters were not helped in 1968 when Allied Growers, seeking cash for its growers and marketing savvy, sold 80 percent of

United Vintners to Heublein, a Connecticut-based spirits corporation, whose main cash cow, Smirnoff, was the leading vodka in the United States. Following the bankruptcy of the Oakville Vineyards, which had been leasing Bartolucci's winery adjoining the old Napa Wine Company's facility at the Oakville Cross Road, Heublein bought the Bartolucci winery, turning the two wineries into one large production facility for producing "Inglenook" wines. Inglenook was not forgotten. The old château was used for entertaining tourists and for bottling the blends made across the highway. To add insult to injury, Heublein erected a warehouse in the Inglenook vineyard, effectively blocking the view of Niebaum's historic winery. Small volumes of high-quality wines were still produced, but they were eclipsed by mass bottlings of generic and varietal "plonk," and Inglenook fell from the pantheon of estate producers.

The Inglenook tale does have several endings — all interesting, some happy. Robin Lail, John Daniel's daughter, was never able to reclaim Inglenook, but did gain possession of the Napanook vineyard and established a joint venture with Christian Moiux of Château Petrus, creating a new wine, Dominus. So at least one of Niebaum's heirs remains in the wine business. In 1976, the noted film director Francis Ford Coppola acquired the old Niebaum/Daniel home and the surrounding vineyard, where he raised his own family and, true to his heritage, made wine. In 1978, as with so many less famous individuals, home winemaking led Coppola to establish his own commercial winery, Niebaum Coppola, which sells a distinctive Cabernet-based wine, Rubicon. In the fall of 1995, Coppola accomplished a rare feat when he bought the Inglenook château and vineyards from Heublein, effectively recreating the Niebaum estate, although without the use of the name Inglenook. And Heublein? Small fish get eaten, but so do bigger ones. Heublein is still an active company, but it was acquired by R. J. Reynolds, which later sold it to the British conglomerate Grand Metropolitan. In 1994, restructuring its California portfolio, which had grown to include numerous other properties, Heublein/Grand Met. sold the Inglenook brand to the Canandaigua Wine Company, a New York–based winery whose California acquisitions have moved it into second place in total production behind Gallo. The Inglenook label remains in the marketplace, but a generation of wine drinkers associate it with inexpensive, lower-quality table wine.

In 1965, it was Charles Krug's turn to experience change, when Robert Mondavi, relieved of leadership by his mother, took a leave of absence from the winery. Rather than return to Charles Krug in a subordinate role, Robert Mondavi pulled together a small group of local investors, used the years of goodwill he had built up with industry vendors to purchase equipment and supplies on credit, and started the Robert Mondavi Winery in 1966. The original investment did not go very far, and all of Mondavi's personal wealth was tied up in his shares of the Charles Krug Winery, so he sought a major investor that would allow him to remain in control. In 1968, he found the investor in Rainier Brewing, a cash-rich, family-owned company interested in the wine industry but content to let Mondavi guide the winery.

The Robert Mondavi Winery was the first major new winery to begin in the valley since Repeal, and its importance should not be underestimated. Mondavi aspired to combine the quality goals of the emerging artisan producers with the volume goals of a Beaulieu, Martini, and Charles Krug. Always ahead of the curve, the winery became a leader in experimentation and marketing, and in the process became a training ground for winemakers. Warren Winiarski and Mike Grgich, whose wines surprised the French in the Paris tasting of 1978, had both worked at the Robert Mondavi Winery. So, too, did Zelma Long, who has become nationally known at Simi Winery in Healdsburg, and Ric Forman, who helped start Sterling in Calistoga before beginning his own artisan brand. The list could go on—more recently, Kendall-Jackson lured Charles Thomas away from Robert Mondavi—but Mondavi's importance to the wine boom of the 1970s clearly transcends the development of his own brand.

While Robert Mondavi was working to establish his own brand, Charles Krug was well positioned to enjoy the economic opportunities associated with the U.S. public's growing interest in wine in the late 1960s. One of the major differences between Robert and Peter Mondavi had been whether to continue to reinvest profits into expanding Charles Krug, as opposed to distributing the gains to family members. Under Peter Mondavi's leadership, Charles Krug did continue to grow in the late 1960s and early 1970s, but family members, as employees of Charles Krug, were well rewarded—essentially paid back for the lean times of the 1950s. In 1973, after resigning as a director of Charles Krug, Robert Mondavi filed suit against the old family partnership, C. Mondavi and Sons, claiming that the family had engaged in practices designed to reduce the value of his holdings in Charles Krug and to deny him shareholder profits, since income was distributed to family employees to reduce total profits. The trial was messy and public. In 1976, the judge found in favor of Robert Mondavi and valued the Charles Krug Winery at $47 million.

Speculation in the valley following the verdict was that the Charles Krug Winery would have to be sold in order to raise the cash needed to buy out Robert Mondavi's interest in it. However, the final arrangement, which included transfer of assets in lieu of cash, allowed the Peter Mondavi family to retain Charles Krug. The stripping of assets and cash did result in the winery being less adoptive of technological trends, a reduced ability to compete for the highest-quality grapes, and diminished market presence for Charles Krug in the 1980s, as scores of other brands competed for scarce retail space. The one positive result for Peter Mondavi was that he and his family ended up in sole control of the winery. Today, he and his two sons, Peter, Jr., and Marc, manage the winery.

For Robert Mondavi, the judgment and eventual settlement allowed him to regain control of the Robert Mondavi winery by buying out Rainier. Part of the settlement involved real property as well as dollars. Mondavi acquired the Tokalon vineyard, thus increasing his holdings in the Napa Valley, and gained possession of bulk wine at the leased Krug facility in Woodbridge, enabling him to expand production of the Robert Mondavi White and Red Table wines (now varietal), which had been introduced a few years prior to the settlement. The settlement thus fueled the growth of the Robert Mondavi Winery and allowed Robert Mondavi to gain full ownership of it. Since then, the Robert Mondavi family has expanded on many fronts: it has bought vineyards in Santa Barbara County and introduced a distinct line of wines from there; the Robert Mondavi Woodbridge brand has grown from generic "Bob Red" and "Bob White" to over several million cases of varietally labeled wine; it has bought other wineries, such as Byron in Santa Barbara County and Vichon in the Napa Valley; and it has established historic joint ventures, the first being Opus with Baron Phillipe de Rothschild of France, and the most recent being a partnership with the Marchesi de' Frescobaldi family of Italy. Expansion takes cash, and in 1993, the Mondavis broke new ground by being the first Napa Valley winery to go public, offering shares in the winery. Through the use of a system of common and preferred stock, Robert and his two sons, Michael and Tim, remain in firm control of the business. The Mondavis clearly remain in the forefront of California wine industry, both in pursuit of quality and in business acumen. The tree may have branched, but both new limbs remain strong.

Four years following Robert Mondavi's departure from Charles Krug, the valley again reverberated — this time with the news that Beaulieu had been sold to Heublein. The details of the 1969 sale have been discussed previously, but a brief review of the history under Heublein is warranted. To its credit, Heublein has maintained the Beaulieu reputation, treating it quite differently from Inglenook (acquired the previous year when Heublein bought United Vintners). Under Heublein, the necessary investments in new technology — put off by Hélène de Pins — were made, and new vineyards were planted. The tension inherent between a winery staff in the Napa Valley, focused on Beaulieu and its needs, and a corporate hierarchy in Connecticut for which Beaulieu is but one small part of many holdings, has gradually decreased as corporate management has slowly learned about the realities of producing and marketing fine wine. The early years were the roughest — both André Tchelistcheff and his chosen successor, Dick Peterson, left. Later managers have been victims of corporate politics, but the winemaking staff has generally remained constant, as have the vineyards and the resulting wines. The Georges de Latour Reserve Cabernets continue to be stunning examples of excellence, exhibiting both the difference inherent in each vintage along with a continuity of style and sense of place. If Beaulieu is not one of the few shining stars in the firmament of Napa wine, it is not because it has fallen, but because it has been joined by so many other stellar wineries, all vying for attention. Corporate ownership has not been unkind to Beaulieu.

In Beringer's case, Nestlé's purchase of the winery in early 1971 has resulted in a definite improvement. Beringer had certainly been one of the big four, but by the start of the 1960s, it had lagged behind leaders such as Inglenook and Beaulieu and had been passed by "newcomers" such as Martini and Charles Krug. By the late 1950s, control of the family winery had passed to Otto Beringer, Jr., and his brother-in-law, Roy Raymond, both of whom represented the third generation, and who saw the need for change. Following the loss of the Fawver property in Napa, which eventually became the location for Trefethern, the Beringers realized that they would need a new source of grapes, preferably varietal, and they began setting out vineyards in Knight's Valley, to the north of the Napa Valley. By 1969, when Otto Beringer's mother, Ethel, died at eighty-one, he and Roy Raymond were confronted with two problems, both involving money. The first was the realization that the premium wine industry was growing in volume and in competitiveness, and that for Beringer to remain competitive, major investments in equipment would have to be made. This was not a new problem for Napa's old guard—it had confronted Beaulieu and perhaps figured in John Daniel's decision to sell Inglenook. The second problem was more specific to Beringer: estate taxes. With the death of Ethel Beringer, the second generation of owners had departed, and the government wanted its share of the increased value of the estate before the third generation could become owners. The reluctant decision of the third generation was to sell.

Like most food and beverage corporations, Nestlé had been watching the wine boom in the United States and had considered various investments, including the Robert Mondavi Winery several years earlier. For Nestlé, Beringer represented an excellent opportunity: a well-known brand, a historic and scenic property, new vineyards, and a straightforward purchase agreement. Nestlé established a holding company for its wine interests, Wine World Estates, and over the next twenty years introduced a multibrand strategy that centered around Beringer but included the development of other brands and regions. Wine World Estates bought and planted more vineyards, including, like the Mondavis, large holdings on California's south central coast. With grape sources secure, it introduced several new brands. First came Napa Ridge, Wine World's entry in the "fighting varietal" category. In the mid 1980s, it bought Château Souverain in Sonoma County, giving it a brand centered in that growing appellation. In the late 1980s, Wine World bought the Meridian Winery, from a group led by Chuck Ortman, which had acquired and renamed the Estrella Winery in Paso Robles. The acquisition of Meridian in San Luis Obispo County gave Wine World a processing facility for the fruit from the over 3,000 acres it controlled on the south central coast and, through the brand, a new place on retailers' shelves for a newly emerging price and appellation segment. Through all this acquisition, Beringer has remained the primary focus for Wine World, accounting for roughly half of its total sales of approximately 4 million cases. The Beringer Reserve Cabernet and Chardonnay effectively compete with wines produced by Napa's artisan producers, while its regular line of varietals are respected as quality leaders in their respective price categories.

Wine World Estates's growth from roughly 100,000 cases in 1971 to over 4 million in 1995, while raising the quality image of Beringer wines, is an impressive success story. Apparently for Nestlé, the general wine category, with its low volume relative to other food and beverage segments and its high capital cost, has not proved as attractive an investment as originally expected. In late 1995, the Napa Valley was shocked to hear that Nestlé was selling Wine World Estates. The shock turned to relief when the managing partners for the Texas oil concern that Nestlé sold to were announced: Silverado Partners, a partnership of local Napa residents led by the financier David Freed, former Wine World Estates President Michael Moone, Richard Lemon, a partner in the Napa legal firm of Dickenson, Peatman & Fogarty, and George Vare, president of Luna Vineyards, an industry veteran. The new group announced there would be no changes in the management of Wine World Estates, and this historic limb remains strong and healthy.

The Beringer story would not be complete without brief mention of one branch added to the tree of Napa wine: the Raymond Winery. Roy Raymond, who had come to St. Helena during the Great Depression to work in the cellar, married into the Beringer family, and risen to general manager, was not content simply to leave the wine industry. With his two sons, Walt and Roy, Jr., Roy used his share of the proceeds from the sale of Beringer to plant vineyards south of St. Helena and to establish the Raymond Vineyard and Cellar in 1974. During the 1980s, foreign firms were actively searching for investment opportunities in the Napa Valley, and in 1989, the Raymonds sold major equity in the winery to Kirin Brewery of Japan, remaining as managing partners and minority owners. Thus a fourth generation of Jacob Beringer's descendants remains active in Napa winemaking.

The straightest branch of the Napa tree is undoubtedly that of the L. M. Martini winery, which has remained family-run and operated from its inception in St. Helena in 1933 to the present day. Part of the continuity is owing to the structure of the business: in 1947, Louis Michael Martini, the autocratic founder, changed the company from a sole ownership to a corporation, giving the winery its own legal standing and freeing the company from the threat of estate taxes, which forced the sale of Beringer. Organizational structure can provide opportunities, but ultimately there must be a will to continue, to participate in, and to maintain a family business. The second and third generations have exhibited such a desire.

Louis Peter Martini, the current "Louis," was raised with the family business in Kingsburg, trained at the University of California in wine production, and then joined the armed forces during World War II. He admits that he considered making the military a career, rather than work for his strong-willed father, but after the war, he decided to return to the family business, initially taking over winemaking responsibilities and slowly assuming management duties from his father, who died in 1974.

Louis Peter's four children grew up with the winery, but he never pushed them to participate. Ultimately, two of them, Carolyn and Michael, joined the family corporation. Carolyn returned in 1975, assuming managerial responsibilities and becoming president in 1985. Michael decided to pursue a career in wine production and, after graduate study at U.C. Davis, joined the winery in 1977, working in production and becoming winemaker in 1979.

The Martini Winery has taken a cautious approach to growth, which has meant that it did not benefit from the wine boom of the 1970s as much as some other brands. The sale of the Kingsburg facility in 1939 to the Bank of America–backed Central Wineries allowed L. M. Martini to operate primarily from cash flow, rather than from bank loans. Under Louis Peter Martini, the winery expanded slowly, acquiring vineyards and equipment as possible from operating profits, and keeping bank loans to a minimum. Carolyn and Michael Martini, after experiencing firsthand how bank loans can undermine autonomy, have seen the wisdom of their father's position, and the winery is currently financed from cash flow. To some degree, being self-financed with little debt insulated the Martinis from the marketplace. During the 1970s and 1980s, the winery delivered sound, probably underpriced wines to an expanding but increasingly competitive market. The old retail shelf sets by brand were being replaced by varietal sets, and sometimes the Martinis were informed that their brand was perceived as excellent value, but unexciting, and that some of their wines would not be included in the new shelf sets. For many consumers, wine is not simply a beverage but an experience, and even value must be marketed. In the past five years, the third generation has reenergized the brand. Prices have been raised, investments made in new stainless steel fermenters and French oak barrels, Michael Martini has been sent out to sell his wines, and the wines have attracted favorable review from the critics. Exhibiting vigorous new growth, this mature limb remains strong and healthy.

Our update would not be complete without a brief review of two other wineries not present at the 1994 tasting: Christian Brothers and Larkmead. Both are essentially pruned branches, and any new growth will be directed elsewhere. Christian Brothers' history is the most straightforward. During the 1950s and 1960s, Christian Brothers, actively marketed by Fromm & Sichel, Inc., expanded production by purchasing facilities in both the Napa Valley and the Central Valley. In 1950, it acquired the historic Greystone Cellars, north of St. Helena, from Schenley, which like National Distillers, was trying to divest itself of its wartime acquisitions. In 1964, it bought the Bisceglia Brothers Winery in Fresno, effectively increasing production capacity in dessert wines, and erected a new processing and aging facility south of St. Helena. Eventually, all the Napa winemaking of Christian Brothers was consolidated there. As the wine industry changed in the 1970s and 1980s, Christian Brothers found itself more and more in competition with the volume table wine producers, such as Almaden, Paul Masson, and Gallo. The business had been created to underwrite the Christian Brothers' educational activities, and increased competition meant decreased profit margins. In 1985, with Napa production centered on the south St. Helena facility, Christian Brothers leased its historic winery in the hills west of Napa to Donald Hess, a Swiss businessman and art collector, who had started the Hess Collection Winery two years earlier. In 1989, the religious order sold Christian Brothers to Heublein, which, according to insiders, was primarily interested in the brand's brandy business. Heublein's later actions show such speculation was probably correct. Heublein, through United Vintners, owned major brands in the Napa Valley, and the purchase of Christian Brothers created redundant processing facilities. Greystone was sold at a much reduced price — "given" might be a better choice of words — to the Culinary Institute of America, which was seeking a West Coast adjunct to its main campus in Hyde Park, New York. The St. Helena facility was sold to Sutter Home, which had outgrown its original site across Highway 29. The Château La Salle brand was sold to Canandaigua, which also acquired the Inglenook brand. Heublein still owns the Christian Brothers brand for wine, since the name is important for brandy sales, but since Heublein also acquired the Glen Ellen brand, the continued future of Christian Brothers wines is unsure.

The Larkmead story is also complex, involving several winemaking and marketing families, and once again involves United Vintners and Allied Growers. In 1948, B. C. "Larry" Solari, manager of the Wine Growers Guild marketing cooperative, bought the Larkmead Winery and surrounding vineyards from Italian Swiss Colony, which had acquired the property when National Distillers, owner of Italian Swiss Colony, acquired the Philip Blum Company, a distilling company that also owned Larkmead. Solari announced that he would produce varietal wines and revitalize the Larkmead label, but instead went to work for Italian Swiss Colony as vice president for sales. Solari established a small cooperative at the Larkmead Winery, crushing his and his neighbors' grapes and selling the new wine to Italian Swiss Colony. In 1952, Solari left Italian Swiss Colony, becoming sales manager for the California Wine Association — the successor organization of Fruit Industries, a marketing cooperative for wine produced from cooperative wineries across the state — in 1953. Following the Petri / United Vintners purchase of Italian Swiss Colony in 1953, the Larkmead Cooperative continued to produce wine for Italian Swiss Colony. In 1957, Solari rejoined Italian Swiss Colony as vice president for sales, and the Larkmead Cooperative joined Allied Grape Growers. Solari later became president of United Vintners, presiding over the purchase of Inglenook and the sale of 80 percent of United Vintners to Heublein.

In 1957, Allied sold the Larkmead facility, although not the brand name, which was still owned by Solari, to an immigrant, Hanns Kornell. Kornell was a German-trained winemaker who fled Germany in the late 1930s, becoming production manager for the American Wine Company out of St. Louis, where he supervised the production of the company's sparkling wines — most notably Cook's Champagne. In the 1950s, neither the U.S. public nor the U.S. wine industry was terribly fastidious about the word *champagne*. To the average consumer, champagne was wine with bubbles. It did not particularly matter what grapes the wine was made from or where it was produced — indeed, Cook's was produced in the Midwest, and New York was the national leader in sparkling wine production. Kornell moved to California in 1952, bought the Sonoma Wine Company in Sonoma, and began production on his own. In 1957, he purchased the Larkmead facility and moved to the Napa Valley. True to his Germanic heritage, Kornell preferred Riesling as the base wine for his "Champagne." Perhaps it was just as well — there was little Chardonnay or Pinot noir available in the 1950s and 1960s. Producing a distinctive wine using classic champagne techniques, if not the traditional grapes, Kornell prospered, and by 1965, he was signing his letters "Hanns J. Kornell, Champagne Master to America."

Kornell may have been correct, if somewhat immodest, in his assessment. Prior to the wine boom of the late 1960s and 1970s, Kornell essentially had no competition in his role as artisan producer. Large companies produced quantities of mediocre wine with bubbles, and one or two other producers, such as the Heck family's F. Korbel & Brothers in Sonoma County did ferment their wine in the bottle, but no other producer concentrated solely on in-bottle-fermented sparkling wine made in limited quantities. This changed during the wine boom. In 1965, Jack and Jamie Davies revitalized Schramsberg, in the hills northwest of Larkmead Lane, and began to produce small amounts of *méthode champenoise* sparkling wine made from the classic varieties used in Champagne. Schramsberg represented the artisan producer. Competition in volume came in the mid 1970s, when the French Champagne and brandy producer Moët-Hennessy, invested in vineyards in the Napa Valley and established its own production facility in Yountville, releasing the first sparkling wines from Domaine Chandon in late 1976. Other European producers followed Moët-Hennessy to Napa: Mumm Napa Valley in 1984, owned by Seagram, which also owned the French Champagne house; Domaine Carneros in 1988, owned by the Taittingers, and Codorníu Napa in 1991, financed by the Raventos, owners of Codorníu in Barcelona. A small niche market, operating to some degree on the cachet of "Champagne," had become flooded with high-quality wines more similar to the real French product than Kornell's. The Kornells tried to compete, taking out loans, purchasing Chardonnay and Pinot noir base wines for their cuvées, redesigning the label, and investing in marketing. It was too late. In 1992, Kornell was forced out of business by its lender, and the historic facility was bought by Koerner Rombauer, owner of Rombauer Vineyards on the Silverado Trail north of St. Helena. Yet the tree lives and new branches begin: the Larkmead name lives on, continued by Solari's daughter and son-in-law, the Bakers, who have had limited volumes of wine made from the Larkmead vineyard and bottled under the Larkmead label, and Paula Kornell, Hanns and Marylouise Kornell's daughter, is employed in Napa's fine wine industry as general manager of Vichon, owned by the Mondavis.

Our historical review is complete, brought up to date as of this writing on New Year's Day, 1996. By the time this book is released, there will no doubt have been other changes that should be included. Yet the basic outline of the tree remains clear, despite new growth and dead limbs, and the twin roots of Napa's success, the pursuit of quality and the promotion of that pursuit, secure the tree's health.

But what of the wines at the Stony Hill tasting? What were they like? I am reminded of Professor Emeritus Vernon Singleton's remark when a woman at a U.C. Davis Extension class kept pushing him to criticize an old, tired wine, one well over twenty years of age: "Madame," he replied, "wines of this age are like grandmothers—we only say nice things about them." Tasting is a personal and subjective experience, based on past history with the types of wine and perhaps emotional attachment as well. I found the wines tasted at Stony Hill to be surprisingly good, even those from the 1940s—and would the reader, having come this far, really be surprised if I described them all as "bottled poetry?"

Notes

In the notes that follow, the abbreviation "BL" refers to the Regional Oral History Office, Bancroft Library, University of California, Berkeley. "BATF records" refers to Bureau of Alcohol, Tobacco and Firearms records held by the Department of Special Collections, Shields Library, University of California, Davis. The Napa Valley Wine Library Association's *History of Napa Valley: Interviews and Reminiscences of Long-Time Residents* is abbreviated to *HNV*.

Introduction

1. Raymond interview, *HNV*, 1:246.

2. Robert Rossi, "Post-Repeal Wine Consumption," *Wines and Vines* 16, 1 (January 1935): 3–4.

3. "Wine Men Gather," *St. Helena Star*, April 10, 1936, p. 1.

4. "Buyers for Wine," *St. Helena Star*, February 16, 1934, p. 8.

5. The legacy of this grafting is discussed later in chapter 3. The Alicante Bouschet, a hybrid developed by Henri Bouschet as a *teinture*, or coloring variety, for Southern France, had remarkable coloring properties. During Prohibition, Alicante skins could be mixed with sugar and water and refermented to produce a "second" wine. Reports indicate that 500–600 gallons of such "wine" could be produced from a ton of Alicante Bouschet. See Maynard A. Amerine and Vernon L. Singleton, *Wine: An Introduction*, 2d ed. (Berkeley: University of California Press, 1972), p. 288.

6. Jessie S. Blout, *A Brief Economic History of the California Wine-Growing Industry* (San Francisco: Bureau of Markets, California Department of Agriculture, 1943), p. 5.

7. Maynard Amerine, letter to George Alcorn, quoted in James Lapsley, "Note: Popular Courses in Wine Appreciation," in *The University of California / Sotheby Book of California Wine*, ed. Doris Muscatine, M. A. Amerine, and Bob

Thompson (Berkeley: University of California Press; London: Sotheby Publications, 1984), p. 454.

1. The Quality Producers, 1934–1940

1. Frederic Bioletti, "Winemaking on a Small Scale" (reprint of a University of California pamphlet), *Wines and Vines* 16, 8 (August 1935): 5.

2. The *Wine Review* counted sixty-eight operating wineries in 1936, while *Wines and Vines* only tallied sixty-six. See "Grape Crop Summary," *Wine Review*, March 1936, p. 11; "Grape Districts of the Coast Region," *Wines and Vines* 17, 9 (September 1936): 8.

3. Tchelistcheff interview, *HNV*, 2 : 15; Robert Mondavi, *Creativity in the California Wine Industry* (BL), p. 11.

4. For much of this biographical material on Georges de Latour, see Ruth Teiser and Catherine Harroun's interview with André Tchelistcheff, *Grapes, Wine and Ecology* (BL), pp. 43–44, and Richard G. Peterson's interviews with Tchelistcheff, cited in n. 3 above. There is also a section on de Latour in William F. Heintz, *Wine Country: A History of Napa Valley: The Early Years, 1838–1920* (Santa Barbara: Capra Press, 1990), pp. 289–93.

5. Heintz, *Wine Country*, pp. 291–92; Tchelistcheff interview, *HNV*, 2 : 37–38.

6. Archbishop of San Francisco, letter to Georges de Latour, March 25, 1920, in Beaulieu file, box 47, BATF records.

7. "Memorandum to the Administrator," December 21, 1925; letter to federal Prohibition administrator, December 18, 1925, Beaulieu Files, BATF records.

8. Ernest A. Wente, *Wine Making in the Livermore Valley* (BL), pp. 65–66.

9. The Beaulieu distribution system is well described in a letter from de Latour to the Prohibition commissioner dated July 7, 1921, in Beaulieu file, box 47, BATF records.

10. Georges de Latour, letter to federal Prohibition commissioner, August 15, 1922, in Beaulieu file, box 47, BATF records.

11. Tchelistcheff, *Grapes, Wine and Ecology*, pp. 47, 49. No sales figures are available from Beaulieu, and it should be remembered that Tchelistcheff did not arrive at Beaulieu until 1938. Still, his estimates seem to be in keeping with the sales of other wineries in the first years after Repeal.

12. Tchelistcheff interview, *HNV*, 2 : 13.

13. "Wine Juries Select California Blue Ribbon Wines for 1939," *Wines and Vines* 20, 10 (October 1939): 14–15. Unlike in current competitions, the judgings of the 1930s generally awarded just one gold, silver, and bronze in each category, no matter how many wines were entered.

14. Tchelistcheff interview, *HNV*, 2 : 5; Louis M. Martini and Louis P. Martini, *Wine Making in the Napa Valley* (BL), p. 54.

15. Tchelistcheff describes his first meal at Beaulieu in 1938, a multicourse affair starting with crayfish, running through trout and pheasant, and ending with fruit, all grown on the estate. See *Grapes, Wine and Ecology*, pp. 36–37.

16. In his interviews in *HNV*, Tchelistcheff says he first met de Latour in 1933, but he must be mistaken. In the Bancroft oral history, *Grapes, Wine and Ecology*, in which he describes the problems associated with acquiring a work permit to emigrate to the United States during the depression, he correctly gives the date as 1937. He arrived at Beaulieu in September 1938, in time for the harvest.

17. There are many reviews of Tchelistcheff's early history, both in his oral histories and in books. These particular facts are taken from John Hutchison, "Man of the Year—André Tchelistcheff," *Wines and Vines*, March 1990, pp. 24–29.

18. Tchelistcheff, *Grapes, Wine and Ecology*, p. 68.

19. Interviewed by Bernard Skoda, in *HNV*, 2:110–11, George Deuer, the winemaker at Inglenook from 1935 to 1965, commented that not all of the Inglenook vineyards had been planted to premium grapes at Repeal, and that until better varieties such as Pinot noir and Cabernet had replaced them, the wine made from lesser varieties was sold in bulk. However, this wine was not sold as Inglenook wine.

20. This sketch of Niebaum's life is based on several sources: "Niebaum of Inglenook," *Wine Review*, November 1939, pp. 11–13, 18, 22; Tom Parker, *Inglenook Vineyards: 100 Years of Fine Winemaking* (Rutherford, Calif.: Inglenook Vineyards, 1979); and Heintz, *Wine Country*, pp. 166–74.

21. "A Pillar of the Industry," *California Wine Review*, December 1935, p. 20.

22. Parker, *Inglenook Vineyards*, pp. 73–74.

23. "Niebaum Winery at Rutherford to Be Operated by Carl E. Bundschu," *St. Helena Star*, August 18, 1933, p. 1.

24. *Wine Review*, January 1934, p. 9.

25. Parker, *Inglenook Vineyards*, p. 76.

26. "State Fair Awards," *St. Helena Star*, September 1934, p. 1.

27. Deuer interview, *HNV*, 2:110.

28. Heintz, *Wine Country*, pp. 150–52.

29. Raymond interview, *HNV*, 1:246.

30. "All Ready for Eastern Trip," *St. Helena Star*, November 25, 1932, p. 1.

31. Raymond interview, *HNV*, 1:247–48.

32. *California Grape Grower* 15, 10 (October 1934): 16.

33. Raymond interview, *HNV*, 1:252–53.

34. This early history is the work of Heintz, *Wine Country*, pp. 247–49, 293.

35. "F. Salmina & Co.," *California Grape Grower* 5, 12 (December 1933): 21.

36. Wilson Wade, "Report by Treasury Department Technical Division," July 21, 1932, Larkmead file, box 58, BATF records. As will be discussed later, high volatile acidity was to be expected in wines stored for twelve years. Treasury records from inspections at other wineries yield similar indications of spoilage. All of Chapin Tubbs's wines were spoiled, and the Fawver vineyard north of Napa held over 300,000 gallons of wine of high volatile acidity, which was distilled by Beringer in 1935.

37. Information is derived from "summary of operations" sheets submitted by government inspectors as part of their annual inspections. Unfortunately, the files are incomplete, but reports exist for 1935, 1937, 1939, and 1940 and can be found in the Larkmead file, box 55, BATF records. I have assumed that wine

marked "removed tax paid" was probably bottled wine, since the vast majority of bulk wine was removed in bond to other wineries or wholesalers.

38. "Wine Awards at the State Fair," *Wines and Vines* 18, 10 (October 1937): 12–13.

39. "Diplome D'Honneur Award confirmed," *Wines and Vines* 19, 9 (September 1938): 21. The three non-Napa wineries to win the awards were Cresta Blanca and Wente Brothers from the Livermore Valley, and Italian Swiss Colony from Sonoma. "Editorial," *St. Helena Star,* August 12, 1938, p. 2.

40. Marilouise Kornell, "Presentation for the St. Helena Friends of the Library," October 3, 1980, in *HNV*, 3 : 324.

41. "Summary of Operations July 1, 1935 to December 31, 1935" and "Declaration of Domestic Vintage Wine Stocks," November 16, 1939, in Larkmead file, box 55, BATF records.

42. "Association for Prohibition Reform Meets and Elects New Officers," *St. Helena Star*, April 7, 1933, p. 1; "F. W. Salmina Elected Member of Western Wine Code Committee," ibid., May 18, 1934, p. 1; "Personnel of Vintage Festival Committees Is Made Public," ibid., June 15, 1934, p. 1; "Raise Quality Is the Aim," ibid., July 12, 1935, p. 6; "Dry Wine Situation," ibid., August 23, 1935, p. 1; "Wine Institute Meeting," ibid., April 24, 1936, p. 5; and "Local Items of Interest," ibid., April 2, 1937, p. 1.

43. Information for this introductory paragraph is gleaned from three sources. Brother Timothy's oral history *The Christian Brothers as Winemakers* (BL), pp. 10–23; "Mont La Salle and the Fine Wines of the Christian Brothers," *Wine Review*, December 1939, pp. 13–14; and Leon Adams, *The Wines of America* (Boston: Houghton Mifflin, 1973), pp. 209–11.

44. Brother Timothy, *Christian Brothers as Winemakers*, p. 40.

45. "Mt. La Salle Vineyards," *California Grape Grower* 15, 10 (October 1934): 16; "Mont La Salle's Production," *California Wine Review*, November 1934, p. 38.

46. "Mt. LaSalle Vineyard," *Wines and Vines* 17, 10 (October 1936): 7; "Mt. La Salle Vineyard," ibid. 18, 10 (October 1937): 5.

47. Alfred Fromm, *Marketing California Wine and Brandy* (BL), pp. 6–10.

48. "Mont La Salle and the Fine Wines of the Christian Brothers," *Wine Review*, December 1939, p. 14.

49. "[Martini] Purchases Tract of Land," *St. Helena Star*, March 24, 1933, p. 3.

50. This brief summary of Louis M. Martini's early life comes primarily from Martini and Martini, *Winemaking*; see p. 15 on the enemies of wine. There is a brief biography of Martini in Adams, *Wines of America*, p. 222.

51. The reference to kosher wine is found in Louis P. Martini's oral history, *A Family Winery and the California Wine Industry* (BL), p. 8; Louis M. Martini is quoted from id. and Louis P. Martini, *Winemaking*, p. 28.

52. Martini and Martini, *Winemaking*, p. 31.

53. Ibid., p. 30; "[Martini] Will Crush Grapes," *St. Helena Star*, August 19, 1932, p. 1.

54. "Work on Winery Begun," *St. Helena Star*, June 9, 1933, p. 5; L. H. Pedlar and J. H. Heintz, "Report on Application," Treasury Department, September 26, 1933, Martini file, BATF records.

55. Martini and Martini, *Winemaking*, p. 32.

56. Louis P. Martini, *Family Winery*, p. 52.

57. Treasury Department, "Summary of Operations," 1934–40; L. M. Martini, letter to Treasury Department, December 13, 1935, Martini file, BATF records.

58. Robert Peffer, "Report of Inspection," August 15, 1936, Martini file, BATF records.

59. "[Martini] Purchases Fine Property," *St. Helena Star*, March 9, 1934, p. 4. This later became the Flora Springs Winery.

60. "C.C.W. Absorbs Martini," *Wine Review*, March 1940, p. 42.

61. Louis P. Martini, *Family Winery*, p. 4.

62. Adams, *Wines of America*, p. 223.

63. Martini and Martini, *Winemaking*, pp. 46–47.

64. Robert Peffer, "Report of Inspection," August 15, 1936, Treasury Department, Martini file, BATF records.

65. Actually, the idea of a "White Zinfandel" goes back to the nineteenth century. George Husmann mentions that Zinfandel grown on the valley floor tended to be too productive, producing a weak-flavored red wine, but very suitable for production of a white (Husmann, *Grape Culture and Wine-Making in California: A Practical Manual for the Grape-Grower and Wine-Maker* (San Francisco: Payot, Upham, 1888). The list of varieties in the Martinis' tanks is worth preserving. In alphabetical order, they included: Barbera, Barberone, Beclan, Burger, Cabernet, Charbono, Chasselas (Palomino), Franken Riesling, Folle blanche, Gütedel, Mataro, Mondeuse, Muscat (variety not specified), Pinot noir, Petite Sirah, Riesling, Johannisberg Riesling, Red Pinot (Pinot St. George?), Salvador, Semillion, Sylvaner, Tannat, Traminer, Valdepeñas, White Pinot (perhaps Pinot blanc or Chenin blanc), White Zinfandel, and Zinfandel. "Report of Wine Inventory," August 21, 1941, Martini file, BATF records.

66. W. J. I. McCallan, "Memorandum on Labeling of Wine," January 31, 1944, Treasury Department, Martini file, BATF records.

67. Napa County agricultural commissioner, *Annual Report*, 1934–40.

2. Bulk Producers and Failures, 1934–1940

1. "Grape Grower Meeting," *St. Helena Star*, November 25, 1932, p. 8.

2. *St. Helena Star*, December 2, 1932, p. 1; "Of Organization and Consolidation," *California Wine Review*, February 1934, p. 7.

3. "Shortage of Cooperage," *St. Helena Star*, July 27, 1934, p. 1.

4. "Napa Valley Wine Men Form Co-operative At Meeting Yesterday," *St. Helena Star*, August 3, 1934, p. 1; "New Building Completed," *California Wine Review*, October 1934, p. 34.

5. "Napa Valley Cooperative Winery May Locate Second Unit Near St. Helena," *St. Helena Star*, February 15, 1935, p. 1.

6. A. Setrakian as quoted in "Towards the Stabilization of the Grape Industry," *Wine Review*, August 1940, p. 12.

7. "Grape Growers Organize," *St. Helena Star*, October 7, 1938, p. 4.

8. "Little Explaining Done," *St. Helena Star*, September 2, 1938, p. 1.

9. "Cooperative Buys Navone Winery, *St. Helena Star*, August 25, 1939, p. 1. The Markham Winery currently occupies the former home of the "little co-op."

10. "History of Napa Valley Co-operative Winery," *St. Helena Star*, April 30, 1937, p. 8.

11. Stralla interview, *HNV*, 2 : 325. This interview is a classic description of the bulk wine producer's point of view and is extremely entertaining reading.

12. Ibid., p. 318.

13. Ibid., p. 319.

14. Ibid.

15. Ibid., p. 324.

16. "New Method of Marketing Wine at Krug Winery Is Meeting with Success," *St. Helena Star*, September 14, 1934, p. 1.

17. Stralla interview, *HNV*, 2 : 359.

18. Ibid., p. 332.

19. Ibid., p. 344.

20. "Jack Riorda Is Summoned," *St. Helena Star*, November 6, 1939, p. 1.

21. "Building Large Winery," *St. Helena Star*, June 8, 1934, p. 4. Later occupants would claim that Sunny St. Helena was the first winery built in the Napa Valley following Repeal, and technically they were correct, since the L. M. Martini Winery further south was constructed during Prohibition.

22. "Summary of Operations," December 31, 1935, Treasury Department, and February 28, 1937, Sunny St. Helena file, BATF records.

23. "Affidavit and Certificate of Secretary," September 15, 1937, Sunny St. Helena file, BATF records.

24. Robert Mondavi, *Creativity in the California Wine Industry* (BL), p. 3.

25. Ibid., p. 8.

26. Ibid., p. 9.

27. "Winery Has Good Year," *St. Helena Star*, August 18, 1939, p. 3.

28. "Minutes of Regular Monthly Meeting of the Board of Directors of Sunny St. Helena Wine Company, A Corporation, Held Wednesday, October 4, 1939," in Sunny St. Helena file, BATF records.

29. Robert Mondavi, "Letter to Treasury Department," October 25, 1939; "Affidavit of Information in Support of Application for Wine Producer's and Blender's Basic Permit," August 20, 1941, both in Sunny St. Helena file, BATF records.

30. "Grape Harvest In Full Swing," *St. Helena Star*, September 13, 1940, p. 1; "Crushing to Start Next Week," ibid., August 29, 1941, p. 1.

31. Crabb was even better known as a vineyardist, collecting over two hundred varieties of *Vitis vinifera* and introducing "Crabb's Black Burgundy," later identified as Refrosco, to the region. A 20-acre portion of the vineyard was deeded to the U.S. Department of Agriculture in 1902 for an experiment station, later passing to the University of California and becoming the Oakville Field Station. For information on the Crabb vineyard and Tokalon, see William F. Heintz, *Wine Country: A History of Napa Valley: The Early Years, 1838–1920* (Santa Barbara: Capra Press, 1990), pp. 155–56, 175, 271, 318.

32. Lyle Pedlar, "Special Instructions Report," November 16, 1931, Tokalon file, BATF records.

33. "To Kalon Winery to Increase Capacity," *California Wine and Spirits Review*, February 1934, p. 30.

34. Mary Churchill, "Letter to Bureau of Industrial Alcohol, March 9, 1934; E. C. Mosby, "Tokalon Vineyard Floor Tax Report," April 16, 1935, both in Tokalon Vineyard file, BATF records.

35. Production and bulk removal data derived from "Annual Report of Inspection," for 1935 and 1937, Tokalon Vineyard file, BATF records.

36. "Lombarda Winery Sold," *St. Helena Star*, March 24, 1933, p. 5.

37. "Suit over Wine Filed," *St. Helena Star*, February 23, 1934, p. 5.

38. "Will Buy Many Grapes," *St. Helena Star*, August 31, 1934, p. 8.

39. "Litigation Now Ended," *St. Helena Star*, August 30, 1935, p. 6.

40. "Suit against Wine Company," *St. Helena Star*, August 6, 1937, p. 1.

41. Freemark Abbey is now operated by Charles Carpy, who in partnership revived the name and location in 1967.

42. Heintz, *Wine Country*, pp. 294–95.

43. "Lombarda Winery Sold," *St. Helena Star*, March 24, 1933, p. 5; "Incorporation Papers," February 20, 1934, Lombarda file, BATF records.

44. Deuer interview, *HNV*, 2:119.

45. C. Warrington, "Report on Operation and Re-Establishment of B/W 3820," September 23, 1941, Lombarda file, BATF records.

46. "Letter to Alcohol Tax Unit," May 10, 1935, Lombarda file, BATF records.

47. Charles O'Conner, "Letter to Federal Alcohol Administration," November 10, 1936, Lombarda file, BATF records.

48. "Winery Firm Is Sued," *Wine Review*, June 1937, p. 25.

49. T. C. Johnson, "Report on Application," September 17, 1941, Lombarda file, BATF records.

50. Martini was still bitten by the wine bug. A short notice in the *St. Helena Star* on May 16, 1941, indicates that Martini did incorporate a new winery, "Monte Dorado Cellar, Inc.," but that is the only mention of it.

51. "Distillery Opens," *California Wine Review*, May 1934, p. 31.

52. *American Wine Review*, June 1934, p. 31.

53. *California Wine Review*, October, 1934, p. 34.

54. Leonard Rhodes, "Letter to Supervisor, Bureau of Industrial Alcohol," June 9, 1932, Tubbs file, BATF records.

55. Chapin Tubbs, "Letter to Supervisor of Permits," September 11, 1933, and November 1, 1933, Tubbs file, BATF records.

56. P. T. Carre, "Napa — Valley of the Vine," *California Wine Review*, January 1934, p. 9; H. S. Ogden, "The Work of a Winery Chemist," *California Wine Review*, May 1934, pp. 14–15.

57. "Montelena Wineries," *California Wine Review*, July 1934, p. 36.

58. Chapin Tubbs, "Letter to District Supervisor, Bureau Internal Revenue," September 13, 1934, Tubbs file, BATF records.

59. Chapin Tubbs, "Letter, District Supervisor, Alcohol Tax Unit," June 15, 1936, Tubbs file, BATF records.

60. J. F. Corridan, "Letter to Collector of Internal Revenue," November 6, 1945, Tubbs file, BATF records.

61. *Wines and Vines Yearbook of the Wine Industry*, 1941–42, pp. 31–49.

62. Most of these figures are derived from "Grape Harvest in Full Swing," *St. Helena Star*, September 13, 1940. Estimates are derived from typical production figures. The Central California Winery was Greystone Cellars, north of Beringer, previously owned by Bisceglia Brothers. Greystone was part of a statewide cooperative and acted as a storage and bottling location for wines produced in Mendocino and Sonoma counties. See "Changes Hands," *St. Helena Star*, April 19, 1940, p. 1.

3. Grape Growing and Winemaking in the Napa Valley

1. André Tchelistcheff, *Grapes, Wine and Ecology* (BL), p. 62.

2. Ibid., p. 50. Tchelistcheff took advantage of the 1938 prorate to substitute much of the older, spoiled wine for wine from the 1938 vintage.

3. "Wine Juries Select California Blue Ribbon Wines for 1939," *Wines and Vines*, October 1939, p. 14; Charles B. Rubinstein, "Beaulieu's Proud Heritage," *Wines and Spirits*, February 1991, p. 16. It is somewhat telling that the Beaulieu Cabernet that won the grand prize for red wine was entered in the "Burgundy" category at the Golden Gate International Exposition.

4. Frank Schoonmaker and Tom Marvel, *The Complete Wine Book* (New York: Duell, Sloan & Pearce, 1934), p. 37.

5. Titus Cronise, *The Natural Wealth of California*, as quoted in William F. Heintz, *Wine Country: An History of Napa Valley: The Early Years: 1838–1920* (Santa Barbara: Capra Press, 1990), p. 114. Much of this brief summary of viticulture in the Napa Valley up to 1920 is based on Heintz's exhaustive work.

6. Heintz, *Wine Country*, p. 155.

7. Ibid., p. 159.

8. "Varieties of Grapes Planted in Napa County," *Annual Report of the Board of State Viticultural Commissioners*, 1887, as reproduced in Heintz, *Wine Country*, p. 190.

9. Heintz, *Wine Country*, p. 283.

10. A. J. Winkler, "Grape Varieties for Dry Wines," *Wine Review*, May 1936, p. 6.

11. H. H. Marquis, "The Valley of the Crushed Grape," *California Wine Review*, August 1934, p. 10.

12. Ibid.

13. Tchelistcheff interview, *HNV*, 2:37–38; Brother Timothy, *The Christian Brothers as Winemakers* (BL), p. 10; Deuer interview, *HNV*, 2:106, 109–10; Emil Schmidt interview, *HNV*, 3:109–10; see also Amerine interview, *HNV*, 4:146–47.

14. "Bearing and Non-Bearing Acreage of Principal Wine Grape Varieties in California," *Wine Review*, March 1938, pp. 18–19.

15. Harry Caddow, "The New Wine Labeling," *Wines and Vines*, December 1936, p. 18. One wonders just how much "Cabernet" really was included in varietally labeled wine prior to the 1936 ruling. The impact of labeling in general, and of varietal labeling in particular, is discussed more fully in chapter 4, which examines the marketing of California wine and the great debate over varietal versus generic labeling and the misappropriation of European place-names.

16. "Vineyard, Orchard and Farm," *St. Helena Star*, June 23, 1933, p. 10.

17. Prices are gleaned from the *St. Helena Star* and include the following citations: "Local Items of Interest" and "Price of Grapes," September 14, 1934, p. 1; "Increase in Crop Values," January 17, 1936, p. 1; "Wine Institute Sets Minimum Prices for Grapes at San Francisco Meeting," August 23, 1935, p. 1; "Good Prices for Grapes," September 17, 1937, p. 1; "Vintage Begins," September 16, 1938, p. 1; "Vintage in Progress," September 15, 1939, p. 1; "Grape Harvest Now in Full Swing," September 13, 1940, p. 1; "Tentative Grape Prices Set," September 5, 1941, p. 1.

18. "Facts on Dry Wine Industry," *St. Helena Star*, September 17, 1937, p. 1.

19. "Vineyard, Orchard and Farm," *St. Helena Star*, April 11, 1941, p. 9.

20. Felix Salmina (quoted in source cited in n. 18 above) estimated that dryland vineyards in Napa produced 2.5 tons per acre. The Napa County agricultural commissioner published annual reports of tons produced, but the actual number of bearing acres of vineyards was not included in them. Estimating an average of 11,000 acres of bearing vines, Napa produced a low of 1.9 tons per acre in the scorching summer of 1935 through 3.5 tons per acre in the prorate year of 1938. From 1934 through 1941, Napa averaged just over 30,000 tons of grapes a year, or 2.75 tons per acre.

21. William C. Ockey, "The Cost of Producing Wine Grapes," *Wine Review*, March 1935, pp. 22–25; L. W. Fluharty, *Standard Grape Costs* (Berkeley: University of California Extension Service, 1939).

22. Amerine interview, *HNV*, 4:147.

23. Roy Raymond, Sr., interview, *HNV*, 1:256.

24. Tchelistcheff, *Grapes, Wine and Ecology*, p. 63.

25. "Vineyard, Orchard, and Farm," *St. Helena Star*, April 9, 1937, p. 9.

26. Amerine interview, *HNV*, 4:145.

27. Ibid., p. 144. Quotation from A. J. Winkler, *Viticultural Research at University of California, Davis, 1921–1971* (BL), p. 16.

28. Winkler, *Viticultural Research*, p. 16.

29. Ibid., p. 37.

30. *Wine Review* articles either written or co-authored by Winkler included: "Grape Varieties for Dry Wines, Part I" (May 1936); "Grape Varieties for Dry Wines, Part II" (June 1936); "What Climate Does, Part I" (June 1937); "What Climate Does, Part II" (July 1937); "Factors Determining Wine Quality" (September 1937); and "The Effect of Climatic Regions" (June 1938). This last piece was initially presented at the statewide Dry Wine Conference held at St. Helena on April 30, 1938.

31. Amerine interview, *HNV*, 4:157. Amerine's first program participation was in 1937, but programs on winemaking and grape-growing featuring university speakers were popular from 1934 on and were often mentioned in the *St. Helena Star*. These "schools" are discussed later in this chapter in the section on winemaking.

32. Herman Baade, "Vineyard, Orchard, and Farm," *St. Helena Star*, February 26, 1937, p. 7.

33. Amerine interview, *HNV*, 4:157.

34. A. J. Winkler, "Grape Varieties for Dry Wines, Part I," *Wine Review*, May 1936, p. 6.

35. Ibid., p. 7.

36. Ibid.

37. A. J. Winkler, "The Effect of Climatic Regions," *Wine Review*, June 1938, p. 14.

38. Ibid., p. 16.

39. Ibid., p. 32.

40. A. J. Winkler, "Grape Varieties for Dry Wines, Part II," *Wine Review*, June 1936, p. 8.

41. Ibid., p. 9.

42. Ibid., p. 8.

43. M. A. Amerine and A. J. Winkler, *Composition and Quality of Musts and Wines of California Grapes* (Berkeley: University of California, 1944), 563.

44. "Bearing and Non-Bearing Acreage" (cited in n. 14 above), pp. 18–19; "Crop Report," *St. Helena Star*, January 13, 1933, p. 8.

45. The figures for 1934 are derived from H. H. Marquis, "Valley of the Crushed Grape," p. 10, and the 1936 numbers from "Bearing and Non-Bearing Acreage" (cited in n. 14 above), pp. 18–19.

46. Tchelistcheff interview, *HNV*, 2 : 38; Deuer interview, *HNV*, 2 : 112; Raymond interview, *HNV*, 1 : 249.

47. Amerine interview, *HNV*, 4 : 152.

48. "Vineyard, Orchard and Farm," *St. Helena Star*, May 31, 1940, p. 7.

49. W. V. Cruess, "Knowing the Condition of Your Wine," *Wines and Vines*, May 1937, p. 12 (originally a paper presented at the Napa County Wine Institute in 1937).

50. H. A. Caddow, "Marketing California Dry Wines since Repeal," *Wines and Vines*, May 1937, p. 14.

51. Tchelistcheff interview, *HNV*, 2 : 18.

52. Frederic T. Bioletti, *The Principles of Wine-Making* (Berkeley: University of California Agricultural Experiment Station, 1911), p. 395.

53. Rudolf Jordan, Jr., *Quality in Dry Wines.* . . . (San Francisco: Pernau Publishing, 1911), p. 6.

54. Bioletti, *Principles of Wine-Making*, p. 430.

55. Ibid., p. 433; Jordan, *Quality in Dry Wines.* . . . , p. 143.

56. It is worth noting in passing that these steps are the basis for most commercial wine production today. The major difference is that with stainless steel and refrigeration on a scale that Bioletti and Jordan could only have dreamed of, today's winemakers have dramatically reduced the levels of sulfur dioxide added at crush.

57. References to Larkmead, Beringer, and Tubbs can be found in chapter 2. Beaulieu's spoiled wines are mentioned by Tchelistcheff in both of his oral histories.

58. "Vinegar Industry Is Now Important, Big Plant Operating Near St. Helena," *St. Helena Star*, August 22, 1932, p. 1.

59. Amerine interview, *HNV*, 4 : 156.

60. Léon Bonnet quoted in "Dry Wine Situation," *St. Helena Star*, August 23, 1935, p. 1.

61. Tchelistcheff, *Grapes, Wine and Ecology*, p. 52.

62. "The Wine Analysis Conference," *California Grape Grower*, May 1934, p. 19. Cruess's gender choice tells us that the wine industry was a man's world in the 1930s. It remained so for many decades. It was not until 1965 that the Department of Viticulture and Enology at Davis graduated a woman enologist, Mary Ann Graff.

63. Tchelistcheff interview, *HNV*, 2:10.

64. Brother Timothy, *Christian Brothers as Winemakers*, p. 36.

65. Raymond interview, *HNV*, 1:248–49.

66. Deuer interview, *HNV*, 2:123.

67. "Specialists Give Instruction in Use of Pure Culture Yeast," *St. Helena Star*, September 14, 1934, p. 1; "Vineyard, Orchard and Farm," ibid., September 7, 1934, p. 8.

68. "Receive Yeast Culture," *St. Helena Star*, October 14, 1935, p. 6.

69. Brother Timothy, *Christian Brothers as Winemakers*, p. 36.

70. See such articles as W. V. Cruess, "Results of the Use of Pure Yeast and SO2," *California Grape Grower*, March 1934, pp. 6–7; id. and L. Quaccia, "Results of Use of Cooling and Metabisulfite," *Wine and Vines*, May 1935, pp. 14–15; and Leon Brendel, "Bisulfites, Metabisulfites, and Liquid Sulphurous Acid in Vinification," *Wines and Vines*, September 1935, pp. 5, 21.

71. Tchelistcheff, *Grapes, Wine and Ecology*, p. 66.

72. "The Wine Analysis Conference," *California Grape Grower*, May 1934, p. 19.

73. "Vineyard, Orchard, and Farm," *St. Helena Star*, October 5, 1934, p. 8.

74. W. V. Cruess, "Knowing the Condition of Your Wine," *Wines and Vines*, May 1937, p. 12.

75. Louis P. Martini, *A Family Winery and the California Wine Industry* (BL), p. 52; Tchelistcheff interview, *HNV*, 2:18.

76. Martini, *Family Winery* , p. 52.

77. "Cooling Coils Installed," *St. Helena Star*, January 10, 1936, p. 1.

78. Tchelistcheff interview, *HNV*, 2:17; Deuer interview, *HNV*, 2:121.

79. Deuer interview, *HNV*, 2:122.

80. Raymond interview, *HNV*, 1:272; Deuer interview, *HNV*, 2:121.

81. Raymond interview, *HNV*, 1:270.

82. Deuer interview, *HNV*, 2:129–130.

83. For production statistics, see "The Production of California Wines," *Wine Review*, March 1939, pp. 10–11; "Statistics — Consumption," ibid., March 1940, p. 20; and "Statistical Section — Production," ibid., March 1941, p. 12.

84. This is according to Peter Mondavi who studied with Cruess in 1937. See Peter Mondavi, *Advances in Technology and Production at Charles Krug Winery, 1946–1988* (BL), pp. 10–11.

85. Tchelistcheff interview, *HNV*, 2:18.

86. For years, because of lack of tanks and refrigeration, the Louis M. Martini winery fermented juice direct from the press, rather than settling the juice prior to fermentation. Louis P. Martini, interviewed by the author, March 3, 1991.

87. Raymond interview, *HNV*, 1:270–71.

88. "Books on Winemaking," *St. Helena Star*, March 9, 1934, p. 4.

89. "Vineyard, Orchard and Farm," *St. Helena Star*, September 28, 1934, p. 8.

90. "Wine Courses," *California Spirits and Wine Review*, February 1934, p. 35. This magazine went through several name changes before finally settling on *The Wine Review*.

91. "The Wine Analysis Conference," *California Grape Grower*, May 1934, p. 19.

92. "Vineyard, Orchard and Farm," *St. Helena Star*, August 24, 1934, p. 9.

93. "Vineyard, Orchard and Farm," *St. Helena Star*, August 3, 1934, p. 8.

94. "An Important Meeting Held," *St. Helena Star*, April 5, 1935, p. 1.

95. "Wine Men Gather," *St. Helena Star*, April 10, 1936, p. 1.

96. "Wine Men to Be Here," *St. Helena Star*, April 9, 1937 p. 1; "Many Attend Wine Institute," ibid., April 16, 1937, p. 1; "Wine Men Here Tomorrow," ibid., April 29, 1938, p. 1.

97. H. F. Stoll, "Second Wine Conference at Berkeley," *Wines and Vines*, January 1935, p. 21.

98. "Many Attend Wine Institute," *St. Helena Star*, April 16, 1937, p. 1.

99. W. V. Cruess, "Non-Bacterial Spoiling of Wine," *Wines and Vines*, January 1938, p. 20.

100. Tchelistcheff, *Grapes, Wine and Ecology*, p. 83.

101. E. M. Mrak, "Metals for Wine Contacts," *Wine Review*, January 1938, p. 11.

102. Tchelistcheff, *Grapes, Wine and Ecology*, p. 83.

103. George Marsh, "Chillproofing of Wines, *Wines and Vines*, May 1938, p. 5.

104. Ibid., pp. 5, 24.

106. Cruess, "Some Observations on Tannin," *Wines and Vines*, January 1935, pp. 5–7. The university experiments showed that additions of 18 pounds per 1,000 gallons were necessary before any antimicrobial effect became evident. In Cruess's words, this was a "massive dose."

107. L. G. Saywell, "The Clarification of Wine," *California Wine Review*, May 1934, pp. 16–17; id., "The Bentonite Process for Clarifying Wine," *California Wine Review*, January 1935, pp. 14–15; id., "Large Scale Clarification of Wines," *Wines and Vines*, April 1935, pp. 10–11.

108. Saywell, "Large Scale Clarification of Wine," p. 10.

109. Saywell, "Bentonite Process for Clarifying Wine," p. 14.

110. Louis P. Martini, interviewed by the author, March 4, 1991; Tchelistcheff, *Grapes, Wine and Ecology*, p. 129. Martini studied at Berkeley with Saywell and recalls first using bentonite following World War II to stabilize some returned bottled wine. Tchelistcheff claims to have "introduced this method of protein stabilization," but in light of Saywell's published articles in the 1930s, "reintroduced" might be more accurate.

111. See Raymond interview, *HNV*, 1:243.

112. Tchelistcheff interview, *HNV*, 2:19.

113. Martini, *Family Winery*, p. 58.

114. Tchelistcheff interview, *HNV*, 2:19–20. Most wineries used tin or wooden plates on which to spread label glue, but Beaulieu, in keeping with its status, used marble.

115. M. A. Joslyn and W. V. Cruess, "Bottling of Wine — A Few Observations," *Wines and Vines*, November 1935, p. 6.

4. Building a Market for Napa Wines

1. "All Ready for Eastern Trip," *St. Helena Star*, November 25, 1932, p. 1.

2. Napa wines had consistently taken more than their share of medals at most judgings at World's Fairs, which seem to have been held often during the 1890s. See William F. Heintz, *Wine Country: A History of Napa Valley: The Early Years, 1838–1920* (Santa Barbara: Capra Press, 1990), pp. 259–61, for results of judgings during the 1890s, pp. 306–8 for judgings in the 1900s, and pp. 320–21 for results from the Panama-Pacific Exposition of 1915.

3. Robert Rossi, "Post-Repeal Wine Consumption," *Wines and Vines*, January 1935, p. 3.

4. A. R. Morrow, "Improving Quality of California Dry Wines," *Wines and Vines*, May 1938, p. 6.

5. "High Gear" (editorial), *St. Helena Star*, September 8, 1939, p. 2.

6. Numbers of festival attendees are derived from the following sources: "St. Helena Vintage Festival Great Success," *St. Helena Star*, September 7, 1934, p. 1; "40,000 Attend Festival," *California Wine Review*, September 1935, p. 36.

7. For more information on the early festivals, see Heintz, *Wine Country*, p. 303.

8. "May Revive Vintage Festival," *St. Helena Star*, November 3, 1933, p. 1.

9. "Vintage Festival Plans Progressing and Committee Chairman Named," *St. Helena Star*, June 1, 1934, p. 1.

10. A. G. Haskell, "The St. Helena Vintage Festival," *California Grape Grower*, August 1934, p. 16.

11. "Personnel of Vintage Festival Committees Is Made Public," *St. Helena Star*, June 15, 1934, p. 1; "Cast for Vintage Play Being Selected," ibid., July 27, 1934, p. 1.

12. Haskell, "St. Helena Vintage Festival."

13. "Festival Plans Progressing," *St. Helena Star*, July 20, 1934, p. 1.

14. "Cast for Vintage Play Selected," *St. Helena Star*, July 27, 1934, p. 1.

15. Pictures of several of the displays, including the Beaulieu tower, can be found in *California Grape Grower*, September 1934, p. 2. The description of the model of the Golden Gate Bridge, which was then still under construction, is found in "St. Helena Vintage Festival Great Success," *St. Helena Star*, September 7, 1934, p. 1.

16. H. F. Stoll, "The St. Helena Vintage Festival," *Wines and Vines*, September 1935, p. 8.

17. *California Wine Review*, October 1934, p. 34.

18. "Chamber of Commerce Makes Plan for This Year's Vintage Festival," *St. Helena Star*, June 14, 1935, p. 1; "Plans for the Festival," ibid., August 16, 1934, p. 1.

19. "40,000 Attend Festival," *California Wine Review*, September 1935, p. 36.

20. "Vintage Festival Next Year," *St. Helena Star*, September 13, 1935, p. 4.

21. Editorial, *St. Helena Star*, September 20, 1935, p. 2.

22. "No Vintage Festival, Chamber of Commerce Directors Decide," *St. Helena Star*, March 6, 1936, p. 1.

23. "Wineries to Sponsor Festival?" (editorial), *St. Helena Star*, March 10, 1936, p. 2.

24. "No St. Helena Vintage Festival" (editorial), *Wines and Vines*, April 1936, p. 18.

25. "Vintage Fete Is Discussed," *St. Helena Star*, October 9, 1936, p. 1.

26. "In Our Own Yard" (editorial), *St. Helena Star*, March 12, 1937, p. 2.

27. Discussion of Gordon's proposal can be found in the following *St. Helena Star* issues: "We Should Have Some Also" (editorial), March 5, 1937, p. 2; "Common Sense" (editorial), March 19, 1937, p. 2; "Ways and Means of Financing Vintage Festival Are Talked Over," March 26, 1937, p. 1.

28. "No Vintage Festival," *St. Helena Star*, May 14, 1937, p. 1.

29. Editorial, *St. Helena Star*, May 6, 1938, p. 2.

30. "Businessmen Tour Wineries," *California Wine Review*, June 1934, p. 30; "Will Advertise Napa County," *St. Helena Star*, October 6, 1933, p. 4; "Photograph Wineries," ibid., July 9, 1937, p. 7.

31. "Bundschu Creates Winner," *California Wine Review*, June 1934, p. 30; "Float in Bridge Event," ibid., November 1936, p. 28 (photograph in December 1936 issue, p. 24). The float for the Bay Bridge was designed by Salmina of Larkmead, Bundschu of Inglenook, Abruzzini of Beringer, Riorda of Sunny St. Helena, and Bonnet of Beaulieu.

32. "Wine Directors Meet," *St. Helena Star*, January 17, 1936, p. 1; "Wine in Air Mail," *California Wine Review*, June 1938, p. 33.

33. A. R. Morrow, "Judging the California Wines at the 1936 State Fair," *Wines and Vines*, October 1936, p. 8.

34. Lists of California State Fair wine judging results can be found in the following: "Wine Awards at the State Fair," *Wines and Vines*, October 1935, p. 5; "Judging the California Wines at the 1936 State Fair," ibid., October 1936, pp. 8–9; W. V. Cruess, "Wines at the State Fair," ibid., October 1937, pp. 12–13; "Wine Awards at the 1938 California State Fair," ibid., October 1938, p. 10; "State Fair Awards," *Wine Review*, September 1939, p. 12.

35. Cruess, "Wines at the State Fair," p. 12.

36. "Los Angeles Wine and Food Society," *Wines and Vines*, October 1936, p. 6. See also "Rutherford Items," *St. Helena Star*, September 18, 1936, p. 3.

37. "Wine Tasting Successful," *California Wine Review*, November 1936, p. 26. See also "A Novel Wine Tasting Event," *Wines and Vines*, November 1936, p. 15.

38. "Napa Wine Growers Stage San Francisco Exhibit," *California Wine Review*, November 1937, p. 26. See also "Napa Valley Wine Display," *St. Helena Star*, October 29, 1937, p. 1.

39. Ernest A. Wente, *Winemaking in the Livermore Valley* (BL), p. 69.

40. André Tchelistcheff, *Grapes, Wine and Ecology* (BL), p. 40.

41. "Leon Bonnet," *Wines and Vines*, October 1941, p. 26.

42. "Beaulieu Vineyard Wines," *California Grape Grower*, February 1934, p. 21.

43. *California Wine Review*, December 1935, p. 34.

44. "Leon Munier Goes with Beaulieu," *Wines and Vines*, December 1936, p. 13. See also "Munier Joins Beaulieu," *Wine Review*, December 1936, p. 24. Information on Stanton can be found in *Wine Review*, April 1936, p. 21, and *St. Helena Star*, February 21, 1936, p. 1, which reported Stanton's talk before the 20–30 club of St. Helena.

45. "Beaulieu Vineyard Wines," *Wines and Vines*, March 1937, p. 14.

46. Ibid.

47. "L. M. Fabbrini," *Wines and Vines*, April 1938, p. 18. See also "Charles Fay Dies — Fabbrini Appointed," *Wine Review*, January 1938, p. 26, and "Beaulieu's New Manager," *Wines and Vines*, February 1938, p. 13.

48. "Beaulieu Wines in Chicago," *Wines and Vines*, April 1938, p. 22.

49. Tchelistcheff interview, *HNV*, 2:9.

50. According to George Deuer, who eventually succeeded John Gross as winemaker, Gross had originally received training at Gundlach-Bundschu in Sonoma. He had also worked for Sam Sebastiani prior to Prohibition. See Deuer interview, *HNV*, 2:9–10; "Inglenook Bottling," *California Wine Review*, April 1934, p. 29; and "Niebaum of Inglenook," *Wine Review*, November 1939, p. 13.

51. A brief description of Carl Bundschu can be found in chapter 1.

52. For information on varietal dating, see "Niebaum of Inglenook," *Wine Review*, November 1939, p. 13. "We called the wine by the name of the grape," George Deuer claimed (interview in *HNV*, 2:12). Certainly, the advertisements for Inglenook wines listed varietal as well as generic names. Vintage dating was somewhat unusual at this time, requiring 100 percent of the stated vintage (current regulations allow 95 percent) and an inspection of records by the California Department of Health.

53. It is unclear whether there was a falling out between John Daniel and Carl Bundschu. In his interview in *HNV*, Deuer indicates that Bundschu's departure was abrupt: "He was gone." Daniel was young, energetic, and identified with Inglenook. It may be that Inglenook was simply too small for two active individuals. Following Inglenook, Bundschu briefly worked as a San Francisco representative to F. Schoonmaker and Co., but apparently left the company when Schoonmaker advocated that the California industry stop using generic names such as "Burgundy" and "Sauterne."

54. Raymond interview, *HNV*, 1:7–8.

55. A cursory examination of the results of the California State Fair wine competition bears this out. From 1935 through 1939, in the dry red wine categories (Claret, Burgundy, Cabernet, and Zinfandel), Beaulieu took nine awards, Larkmead eight, Inglenook seven, and Beringer one, a bronze.

56. Both Roy Raymond's and Fred Abruzzini's interviews for the Napa Valley Wine Library Association imply that Abruzzini was definitely in charge at Beringer. Charles Beringer lived in San Francisco, where he managed a laundry supply company, the John P. Lynch Co., from the office of which Beringer sales were made. This was confirmed to me in a phone conversation on December 28, 1992, by Roy Raymond, who worked for a year in the Lynch Co.'s office.

57. Abruzzini interview, *HNV*, 3:87.

58. Raymond interview, *HNV*, 1:252. Raymond's estimate correlates well

with production figures released to *Wines and Vines*, in the October 1937 issue of which, Beringer announced that it planned to produce 70,000 gallons of dry wine and 150,000 gallons of sweet wine (p. 5).

59. In fairness to Beringer, it should be noted that almost all of the Napa producers sold fortified wine, either purchased from Central Valley producers or made at the winery through the addition of high-proof alcohol. The major difference between Beringer and other Napa Valley wineries was the degree to which fortified sweet wine dominated Beringer's total production mix.

60. Abruzzini interview, *HNV*, 3 : 87.

61. "Beringer Bros. Wines," *Wines and Vines*, March 1937, p. 16.

62. Abruzzini interview, *HNV*, 3 : 52. Abruzzini's map was later adopted by the St. Helena Chamber of Commerce and turned into a generic advertising piece for Napa wineries.

63. The estimate of percentage of sales comes from Abruzzini interview, *HNV*, 3 : 87; the estimate of total bottled wine sales comes from Raymond interview, *HNV*, 1 : 253. Beringer was clearly the first Napa winery to encourage informal visits, but it is not known whether visitors were allowed to taste the wines.

64. "Film Stars Get Beringer Wines," *St. Helena Star*, July 26, 1940, p. 6; "St. Helena Wines Displayed at Premiere," ibid., November 11, 1940, p. 4.

65. "Beringer's New Sales Builder," *Wines and Vines*, December 1937, p. 9. For a photograph of the display see *Wine Review*, December 1937, p. 33.

66. Many California producers considered Riesling to be a wine type, rather than a grape variety. See the editorial "F.A.A. Wine Regulation Hearing," *Wines and Vines*, December 1935, p. 1.

67. Harry Caddow, "A Wine Temple for the 1939 Exposition," *Wines and Vines*, October, 1937, p. 1. See also C. E. Bundschu, "California Wines on Parade," ibid., July 1937, p. 12.

68. "California Wine Display at the 1939 Golden Gate International Exposition," *Wines and Vines*, February 1938, p. 16.

69. The figure of 38 wineries is from Harry Caddow, "California Wines at the 1939 Exposition," *Wines and Vines*, December 1938, p. 1. The estimate of the number of bonded wineries in California comes from J. V. Bare, "Advertising Program Nears Success," ibid., July 1938, p. 21.

70. "Ready for Fair Opening," *St. Helena Star*, February 17, 1939, p. 1. The big four also joined together later in June, on the occasion of the Wine Temple dedication, to sponsor a homing pigeon race from Treasure Island to St. Helena. Onlookers were invited to pick which birds would win the race, with the best four handicappers receiving a case of wine from each producer. See "St. Helena Homing Pigeons to Feature Wine Temple Dedication at Fair," *St. Helena Star*, June 2, 1939, p. 1.

71. For a complete list of winery participants, see "The California Wine Temple: A Dramatic Tribute to the Industry," *Wine Review*, March 1939, pp. 40–41.

72. Louis Gomberg, *Analytical Perspectives on the California Wine Industry, 1935–1990* (BL), p. 42. Most states did not allow bulk sale of wines directly to consumers but required that wine be bottled in one-gallon or smaller containers.

73. J. V. Bare, "Advertising Program Nears Success," *Wines and Vines*, July 1938, p. 21.

74. H. A. Caddow, "Advertising California Wines," *Wines and Vines*, November 1938, p. 1.

75. "Wine Advertising," *St. Helena Star*, September 1, 1939, p. 2.

76. "California Wine Advertising Campaign Is Launched," *Wines and Vines*, May 1939, p. 5.

77. "Vintners Hear Success of Wine Advertising Campaign," *St. Helena Star*, May 17, 1940, p. 1.

78. Gomberg, "Analytical Perspectives," p. 23.

79. Harry Caddow, "Major Wine Industry Problems in 1937," *Wines and Vines*, January 1937, p. 10.

80. Ibid.

81. H. A. Caddow, "Wine Industry's Advertising Program," *Wines and Vines*, January 1939, p. 14.

82. Gomberg, "Analytical Perspectives," p. 23.

83. No reliable figures are extant; 5 percent is only an estimate. Two tables in Amerine and Joslyn's *Table Wines: The Technology of Their Production in California* (Berkeley: University of California Press, 1951), compiled by S. W. Shear, an agricultural economist for the Giannini Foundation of Agricultural Economics, list "Apparent Consumption of Still Wine in the United States" (table 26, p. 334) and "United States Wine Imports for Consumption by Kinds" (table 27, p. 335). A comparison of estimated consumption by year of commercial table wine under 14 percent alcohol with imports for the same type and year indicates that imports accounted for 4 percent of still wine consumption from 1934 to 1939.

84. E. M. Sheehan, "The Wine Situation in California," *Wines and Vines*, January 1938, p. 1.

85. Marion DeVries, "Why Import Duties Must Not Be Reduced," *Wines and Vine*, April 1935, p. 4. Other examples of this sort of thinking can be seen "Drink American Wines," *California Grape Grower*, December 1933, p. 1; "American Wines Belittled," *Wines and Vines*, April 1936, p. 1; and "Choice California Wines," ibid., May 1935, p. 1.

86. The United States has still not signed the Madrid treaty, and all of the above terms may legally be used in this country today (1995). However, U.S. wines so labeled cannot be exported to countries that are treaty signatories, most notably the members of the European Economic Community. The Quady Winery, which is well known for its dessert wines, recently introduced a version of its "Port" called "Starboard" for export to Europe.

87. "Names of California Wine Types," *California Grape Grower*, December 1933, p. 1.

88. Marion DeVries, "Congress Reduces Wine Taxes," *Wines and Vines*, July 1936, p. 5.

89. "Wine Names Approved," *Wines and Vines*, May 1936, p. 28. New York producers would similarly, of course, use the adjective "New York" to describe a "Burgundy" produced there. This was not a major change for California producers, most of which had historically included "California" when using a European place-name for a wine, although the adjective was not always emphasized or placed in direct conjunction with the European appellation.

90. See H. H. Marquis, "New Rules — New Labels," *Wine Review*, February 1936, p. 13, for the phrase "veritable revolution" and Harry Caddow's com-

ment about "definite, nationally enforceable nomenclature." The estimate of 60,000 labels needing approval is from "Label Regulations Effective Soon," ibid., November 1936, p. 17. See also Caddow's "Permanent Wine Labeling Regulations," *Wines and Vines*, February 1936, p. 10, which provides an excellent review of previous labeling laws, and his article "The New Wine Labeling," ibid., December 1936, p. 18, which covers the Wine Institute's response to the new laws.

91. F. W. Salmina, letter to W. F. Alexander, April 7, 1936, and R. W. Janney, senior label examiner, letter to F. W. Salmina and Co., April 28, 1936, in Larkmead file, box 55, BATF records.

92. Harry Caddow, "The New Wine Labeling," *Wines and Vines*, December 1936, p. 18.

93. Current regulations (1995) require that 75 percent of varietally labeled wines come from the stated variety; require only 95 percent of the wine to come from the stated vintage (thus allowing for evaporative loss during storage); and require that 75 percent of the grapes come from a named political subunit of a state.

94. Editorial, *St. Helena Star*, January 22, 1937, p. 2.

95. "Distributes Fine Wines," *Wine Review*, September 1937, p. 24. In selecting wine in cask to be bottled for its own account, Wildman and Co. was following in the tradition of the English wine trade. Wildman later joined Bellows and Co., a national importing firm.

96. "Park & Tilford Will Handle Beaulieu Wines," *Wines and Vines*, August, 1938, p. 6. The first wines actually shipped were, as we have seen, a disaster.

97. W. N. McDonald, "California Wine . . . on Eastern Seaboard Merchandising Front," *Wine Review*, June 1940, p. 10.

98. Schoonmaker was actually a friend of good wine with an excellent palate and forthright opinions. His book included an honest assessment of California wine at Repeal and was fairly gentle in its comments.

99. McDonald, "California Wine . . . on Eastern Seaboard Merchandising Front," p. 11.

100. "Importer Now Sells California Wines," *Wines and Vines*, December 1939, p. 8. At the time, Inglenook and Larkmead were the only quality Napa producers available to Schoonmaker. Beaulieu was represented by Park & Tilford, and Christian Brothers by Alfred Fromm; L. M. Martini had not released his Napa wines yet, and Beringer was of slightly lesser quality.

101. "Schoonmaker to Handle Wente and Korbel Wines," *Wine Review*, November 1940, p. 24. See also "C.C.W. Absorbs Martini," *Wine Review*, March 1940, pp. 42, 43, 48.

102. Frank Schoonmaker & Co. spring bulletin, 1940, as quoted in McDonald, "California Wine . . . on Eastern Seaboard Merchandising Front," p. 10.

103. McDonald, "California Wine . . . on Eastern Seaboard Merchandising Front," p. 10.

104. "Schoonmaker to Handle Wente and Korbel Wines," *Wine Review*, November 1940, p. 24.

105. Hal Marquis, "War and Wine," *Wine Review*, December 1940, pp. 6–7.

106. "Chamber of Commerce Plans to Advertise Valley Wines," *St. Helena Star*, September 13, 1940, p. 1.

107. "Defense Program for U.S. Wines: An Editorial," *Wine Review*, July 1941, p. 7.

108. Ibid.

109. Leon Munier, "Wine Men Are Warned," *Wine Review*, January 1942, p. 34.

110. Tom Marvel, "California Wines under California Names," *Wine Review*, February 1942, p. 10.

111. H. F. Stoll, "Advertising California Wines," *California Grape Grower*, August 1934, p. 1.

112. Harry Caddow, "The Consumer's Wine Quality Problem," *Wines and Vines*, January 1938, p. 16.

113. Ibid.

114. Marvel, "California Wines under California Names," p. 11.

115. "Carl Bundschu Joins Frank Schoonmaker and Co.," *Wines and Vines*, December 1939, p. 32; "George De Latour Passes Away," *St. Helena Star*, March 1, 1940, p. 1; Felix Salmina's death is mentioned in a partnership statement dated April 13, 1943, Larkmead file, box 55, BATF records.

5. California Wine and World War II

1. See "Bulk Shipments to Increase," *Wines and Vines*, November 1945, p. 15.

2. See Jack Conrad's article "Building Prestige in the New Wine Market with the Winery Name," *Wines and Vines*, February 1942, pp. 12–13. Conrad was manager of Conrad's Inc., a franchise bottler in St. Louis, and he differentiated his "Hourglass" brand by adding the producer's name, in this case, Italian Swiss Colony, to the label.

3. H. E. Jacob and A. J. Winkler, "Limit Grape Plantings to Good Wine Grape Varieties," *Wines and Vines*, January 1945, pp. 14–15.

4. J. A. Hunter, "Summary of 1942 Grape Season," *Wines and Vines*, August 1943, p. 18.

5. E. L. Markell, "Grapes in the Land of Sunshine," *Wines and Vines*, August 1941, p. 11.

6. "Grape Council Meets: Growers and Vintners Discuss Joint Grape Problems," *Wines and Vines*, March 1941, p. 24.

7. Average statewide grape prices in 1940 were about $14–15 a ton, but by 1942 they had increased to $32 for standard black varieties. See "Grape Council Meets," *Wines and Vines*, March 1941, p. 23, and Hunter, "Summary of 1942 Grape Season," p. 18.

8. The government requisitioned all nongirdled Thompsons, Muscats, and Sultanas on August 24, 1942. See Hunter, "Summary of 1942 Grape Season," pp. 18–19.

9. Figures are based on Wine Institute figures in "Statistical Review of 1947," *Wines and Vines*, April 1948, pp. 21–36.

10. "Magazine Reviews Situation in Wine Field," *Wines and Vines*, February 1944, p. 22.

11. "Statistical Review of 1947," p. 29.

12. See the following articles: "Need for Price Adjustment," *Wines and Vines*,

February 1942, p. 7; "Expected Grape Price Increase Complicates Price Freeze Order," ibid., May 1942, p. 27; and "Price Ceiling for Wine," ibid., September 1942, pp. 6–7.

13. These were for standard quality Central Valley grapes. Napa and other North Coast grapes rose even more. Grape prices are gleaned from several sources. See J. A. Hunter, "1943 Grape Season Summary," *Wines and Vines*, September 1944, pp. 22–23, and Irving Marcus, "Gold Strike in California!" ibid., October 1944, pp. 15, 33.

14. See "Expected Grape Price Increase Complicates Price Freezing Order," *Wines and Vines*, May 1942, and "New Wine Price Formula," ibid., October 1942, p. 7.

15. Hunter, "Summary of 1942 Grape Season."

16. "New Wine Ceiling Regulation," *Wines and Vines*, October 1943, pp. 10–11.

17. "Opportunity Unlimited," *Wines and Vines*, August 1942, p. 8.

18. Richard N. Haight, "Price Ceiling Headaches," *Wines and Vines*, February 1943, p. 9.

19. "Commenting on the News," *Wines and Vines*, August 1944, p. 11. See also "Wine Price Ceiling Yet to Come," *Wines and Vines*, September 1943, p. 11.

20. E. B. Wienand, "The Big Four and the Facts," *Wines and Vines*, February 1944, pp. 10–14.

21. For more information on the purchase of Italian Swiss Colony, see "Interview with MacNamara," *Wines and Vines*, June 1944, pp. 21, 32–33.

22. Both Tchelistcheff and Amerine indicate that Schenley pursued an active policy of diverting lower-quality wine into the higher-priced Cresta Blanca brand. Amerine indicates that Schenley "was reputed to have made their purchase price back in the first year." See M. A. Amerine, *The University of California and the State's Wine Industry* (BL), p. 21. See also André Tchelistcheff, *Grapes, Wine and Ecology* (BL), pp. 112–15.

23. See "Schenley Buys Cresta Blanca," *Wine Review*, January 1941, p. 20; "Schenley Extends Wine Holdings," *Wines and Vines*, October 1942, p. 30; Harvey Martin, "Schenley Buys Roma and CWI," ibid., November 1942, p. 9; and "Greystone Winery Changes Hands," *St. Helena Star*, November 20, 1942, p. 1.

24. "Committee Cries Wolf," *Wines and Vines*, February 1944, p. 9.

25. "Commenting on the News," *Wines and Vines*, November 1942, p. 5.

26. "Fight for Life," *Wines and Vines*, December 1942, p. 7.

27. Richard N. Haight, "Price Ceiling Headaches," *Wines and Vines*, February 1943, p. 9.

28. *Wines and Vines* noted that "the number of wineries willing to do contract grape purchasing and crushing for bottlers and distributors is becoming less due to the lowness of the price ceiling placed by OPA on such 'processes.'" See "Distribution Undergoes Change," *Wines and Vines*, May 1944, p. 15.

29. Harvey W. Martin, "The Tank Car Emergency," *Wines and Vines*, January 1943, p. 8. See also "Tank Cars" in the "Commenting on the News" section of *Wines and Vines*, January 1943, p. 7. Ironically, the "essential wartime liquids" were in part industrial alcohol produced by the large distillers.

30. Martin, "Tank Car Emergency," p. 9.

31. W. J. Massoni, "Progress in Reverse," *Wines and Vines*, February 1943, p. 27.

32. "Renault Buys Wineries," *Wines and Vines*, February 1943, p. 19.

33. "Gibson Buys Acampo," *Wines and Vines*, April 1943, p. 13.

34. See "Winery Ownership Changes," *Wines and Vines*, April 1943, pp. 16–17. *Wines and Vines* estimated total California storage capacity at slightly over 200 million gallons for (Wienand, "The Big Four and the Facts," pp. 10–14).

35. "Garden Vineyard Purchased," *Wines and Vines*, June 1943, p. 28.

36. See "Changes in Winery Ownership," *Wines and Vines*, July 1944, pp. 20–22.

37. "Boom in Vineyards" in "Commenting on the News," *Wines and Vines*, November 1943, p. 9.

38. Irving Marcus, "Gold Strike in California!" *Wines and Vines*, October 1944, p. 15.

39. For plantings in 1943–44 and 1944–45, see A. J. Winkler, "Grape Plantings during 1945," *Wines and Vines*, December 1945, pp. 26–27.

40. Irving Marcus, "The Industry Looks Ahead," *Wines and Vines*, September 1943, p. 15.

41. Winkler, "Grape Plantings during 1945," p. 27.

42. "Bulk Shipments to Increase," *Wines and Vines*, November 1945, p. 15.

43. H. A. Caddow, "The Industry Shows Its Confidence," *Wines and Vines*, October 1945, p. 25; H. C. Bernsten, "The Complex American Wine Market," ibid., November 1946, pp. 25–26.

44. Elmer Salmina, *Wines and Vines*, June 1944, p. 16.

45. "Bundschu Attacks Grape Prices," *Wines and Vines*, November 1944, p. 37.

46. See Elmer Salmina, "1944 Outlook," *Wine Review*, January 1944, p. 11, and Arthur Tempe, "Lowering Quality in Winery Bottling Endangers Your Future," *Wines and Vines*, March 1945, p. 11.

47. See "Prices" in "Commenting on the News," *Wines and Vines*, August 1945, p. 11, and Irving Marcus, "Wine Price Bugaboo," ibid., November 1945, p. 11.

48. "Processor Prices Strong," *Wines and Vines*, February 1946, p. 13.

49. See "Processor Prices Strong," *Wines and Vines*, February 1946, p. 13, and "Bulk Dessert Wine Prices Zoom," ibid., April 1946, p. 21.

50. "The Editor Comments on the News," *Wines and Vines*, April 1946, p. 21.

51. "Bulk Dessert Wine," *Wines and Vines*, September 1946, p. 19.

52. "Half-Year Consumption Mark," *Wines and Vines*, September 1946, p. 9.

53. Herman Wente, "Wine Goes Full Speed Ahead," *Wines and Vines*, February 1946, p. 29.

54. "Bulk Dessert Wine," *Wines and Vines*, September 1946, p. 19.

55. See Irving Marcus, "Record Crush Still Looms as Good Possibility," *Wines and Vines*, July 1946, p. 11, and "Construction At Record Level," ibid., January 1947, pp. 16–17.

56. Italian Swiss Colony and Roma had both raised their prices in early summer of 1946; see "Case Goods Prices Rising," *Wines and Vines*, June, 1946, p. 9. For information on the distillers' attempt to purchase surplus grapes, see "High

Grape Prices Loom," *Wines and Vines*, May 1946, p. 9, and John Cella, *The Cella Family in the California Wine Industry* (BL), p. 36. For grape prices during the 1946 crush, see "Grape Prices Firm as Crush Hits Peak," *Wines and Vines*, October 1946, p. 13.

57. "Market Forecasts — A Business Essential" and "Reasons Pro and Con on Wine Prices," *Wines and Vines*, December 1946, p. 13.

58. "Holding the Price Line," *Wines and Vines*, February 1947, p. 13.

59. John Margolis, "Confidence in the Wine Industry," *Wines and Vines*, February 1947, p. 16.

60. "Wine Price Headache Continues," *Wines and Vines*, March 1947, p. 13.

61. "Price-Posting, Fair Trade in California," *Wines and Vines*, March 1947, p. 48. Price-posting and fair-trade laws had been in effect for beer since the late 1930s, and the extension to wine and spirits was intended to stabilize the industry. See also John Anderson, "The Fair Trade Principle," *Wines and Vines*, October 1946, p. 22.

62. For dessert wine prices, see "Bulk Market Turns Strong," *Wines and Vines*, July 1947, p. 9. Table wine prices are referred to in Cella's oral history, *Cella Family*, p. 36.

63. See Louis A. Petri, *The Petri Family in the Wine Industry* (BL), p. 22.

64. For prices, see "The Shape of the 1947 Crush," *Wines and Vines*, December 1947, p. 16. For the USDA raisin purchase, see "Raisin Group Proved Right," ibid., November 1947, p. 9.

65. Irving Marcus, "Grape Prices Uncertain as Crush Begins," *Wines and Vines*, September 1947, p. 9; "New Cooperative Interest Evident," ibid., October 1947, p. 11.

66. "The Shape of the 1947 Crush," *Wines and Vines*, December 1947.

6. Napa Wine during Wartime

1. See advertisement in *Wines and Vines*, May 1947, p. 35.

2. Approximately 600 acres were planted in 1945 and an additional 300 in 1946. See "More Dry Wine Grapes in Napa County," *Wine Review*, June 1945, p. 32, and "Wines and Vines Previews 1946 Plantings," *Wines and Vines*, August 1946, p. 19. University of California recommendations were made in M. A. Amerine and A. J. Winkler, *Composition and Quality of Musts and Wines of California Grapes* (Berkeley: University of California, 1944), and a year earlier in Agricultural Experiment Station Circular 356, *Grape Varieties for Wine Production*.

3. "C.C.W. Absorbs Martini," *Wine Review*, March 1940, pp. 42, 43, 48.

4. "New Sales Organization Established by C.C.W. Members," *Wines and Vines*, May 1941, p. 11.

5. "GoLan Wines, Inc., Begins Operations at St. Helena," *Wines and Vines*, September 1941, pp. 12–14. See also "The GoLan Bottling Plant at St. Helena," ibid., October 1941, p. 19.

6. See Harvey Martin, "Schenley Buys Roma and CWI," *Wines and Vines*,

November 1942, p. 9; "Greystone Winery Changes Hands," *St. Helena Star*, November 20, 1942, p. 1. See also an advertisement for Cresta Blanca wines in *Wines and Vines*, July 1946, p. 4, which describes the other Cresta Blanca locations. A brief discussion of Schenley's expansion of Cresta Blanca is found in chapter 5. Schenley later sold Greystone to Christian Brothers in 1950.

7. "Exit Domestic" (editorial), *Wines and Vines*, January 1941, p. 4.

8. Figures are from Amerine and Joslyn, *Table Wines: The Technology of Their Production in California* (1951), tables 26 and 27, pp. 334–35.

9. This total is an estimate, inasmuch as no actual figures for bottled wine are available. In 1940, after its initial bottling disaster with Park & Tilford, Beaulieu was selling perhaps 30,000 cases of branded wine; Inglenook was certainly selling under 20,000 cases; Beringer, with its active at-winery sales program, had perhaps expanded to 30,000 cases, and Larkmead was probably producing around 10,000 cases of wine under its own label. Estimates for Christian Brothers are not available, and Louis Martini indicates that the Martini Winery, which had only just released its first wines in 1940, did not reach 30,000 cases until after World War II.

10. Deuer interview, *HNV*, 2:15.

11. André Tchelistcheff, *Grapes, Wine and Ecology* (BL), pp. 73, 119.

12. "Remodeling and Expansion at Inglenook Vineyards," *Wine Review*, January 1941, p. 31. See also "Remodeling at Inglenook," *St. Helena Star*. January 3, 1941, p. 1.

13. "Addition to Beaulieu Winery," *St. Helena Star*, March 21, 1941, p. 1; "Beaulieu Undertakes Major Improvement Program at Winery," *Wine Review*, April 1941, p. 23; and "Ageing Facilities Will Be Increased by Beaulieu Vineyard," ibid., June 1941, p. 32.

14. Tchelistcheff, *Grapes, Wine and Ecology*, p. 73.

15. John Daniel, Jr., "Notes on the History of Napa County Viticulture and Winemaking," in *HNV*, 1:235–36.

16. See "New Schoonmaker Distributor," *Wines and Vines*, September 1941, p. 28, and "Growers Retain Schoonmaker," ibid., February 1946, p. 48. "21 Brands," the exclusive U.S. distributor of Ballantine Scotch, was affiliated with the 21 Club in New York.

17. "Beringer Brothers Appoint East Coast Distributors," *Wine Review*, December 1941, p. 27; E. B. Wienand, "The Big Four and the Facts," *Wines and Vines*, February 1944, p. 13; "Beringer Bros. Agencies Set," ibid., October 1946, p. 38.

18. The genesis of this relationship is covered in chapter 1.

19. Dave H. Boley, "Some Reasons for Our Success," *Wines and Vines*, March 1942, p. 28.

20. "Unique Display," *Wines and Vines*, December 1942, p. 27.

21. "Christian Brothers Take Over Mount Tivy," *Wines and Vines*, July 1945, p. 9.

22. It is true that Martini had not sold wine under the Martini label prior to 1940, but he had done so out of his Kingsburg plant, which had been sold to Central Wineries for $1,000,000.

23. Much of this synopsis is derived from two interviews by Ruth Teiser:

Robert Mondavi's *Creativity in the California Wine Industry* and Peter Mondavi's *Advances in Technology and Production at Charles Krug Winery, 1946–1988* (both BL). See also the discussion of the Mondavi family and their Sunny St. Helena Winery in chapter 2.

24. "Gibson Buys Acampo," *Wines and Vines*, April 1943, p. 13.

25. "Wine Industry Faces Problems," *St. Helena Star*, January 12, 1943, p. 8. See also Robert Mondavi, *Creativity*, pp. 12–13.

26. "Charles Krug Winery Undergoes Improvement," *Wine Review*, June 1945, p. 34.

27. Robert Mondavi, *Creativity*, pp. 19, 21, 16; Charles Krug advertisement, *Wines and Vines*, December 1944, p. 32. See also "Moffitt Sells Krug Ranch," *St. Helena Star*, March 5, 1943, and "Wineries Change Hands," *Wines and Vines*, March 1943, p. 41.

28. Robert Mondavi, *Creativity*, p. 26.

29. "Successful Year Reported at Winery Directors' Meet," *St. Helena Star*, August 20, 1943, p. 1.

30. "Wine Firm Files Certificate, *St. Helena Star*, July 25, 1947, p. 6.

31. See the following: "St. Helena Winery Sold," *St. Helena Star*, February, 26, 1946, p. 1; "Sunny St. Helena Sold to Stelling Jr.," *Wine Review*, April 1946, p. 90; "Sunny St. Helena Winery Sold," *Wines and Vines*, April 1946, p. 94; and BATF correspondence from District Supervisor J. H. Maloney dated March 15, 1946, included in the Sunny St. Helena file, BATF Archives, Shield Library. Stelling later entered into a partnership with Charles Forni, and after Stelling's death, Forni ended up with ownership of the winery. In 1957, he leased the winery to C. Mondavi and Sons, who subleased the winery to a group of growers who formed a cooperative operation to crush nonvarietal grapes for sale to Charles Krug. See Arthur H. Schmidt, "Sunny St. Helena Winery," September 7, 1975, in *HNV*, vol. 2.

32. "C. Mondavi and Sons Announce Expansion," *St. Helena Star*, May 3, 1946, p. 1; "Mondavi Reorganizes Firm," *Wine Review*, May 1946, p. 19; "Mondavi Sales Program," *Wines and Vines*, May 1946, p. 46.

33. Robert Mondavi, *Creativity*, p. 22.

34. "Third County Winery Sold," *St. Helena Star*, March 26, 1943, p. 1.

35. "Report on Application," July 29, 1944, in Napa Valley Grape Products file, BATF records.

36. Report from F. E. Rilling to J. H. Maloney regarding San Gabriel Wine Co., September 2, 1944, in Napa Grape Products file, BATF records.

37. Ibid.

38. See advertisement in *Wines and Vines*, June 1941, p. 24, listing the San Gabriel Wine Co. of Long Island as distributing "Cordova," a "delicious, far-famed quality wine from grapes of the famous Cordova Vineyard."

39. "New Winery Formed," *Wines and Vines*, September 1943, p. 27.

40. "Colombo Wines Now Property of Napa Valley Grape Products," *Wines and Vines*, October 1944, p. 31; "Colombo Wines Distributed by Napa Grape Products," *Wine Review*, October 1944, p. 32. See also Roland Federspiel's "Announcement" in *Wines and Vines*, January 1945, p. 23.

41. "Colombo Wines Now Property of Napa Valley Grape Products," *Wines and Vines*, October 1944.

42. "Colombo Wine Salesmen Meet," *Wines and Vines*, February, 1945, p. 42; "Colombo Sales Staff Meets," ibid., May 1945, p. 30.

43. "Winery Expansion in Napa County," *Wine Review*, June 1945, p. 34; see also "New Winery to Be Operated in St. Helena," *St. Helena Star*, June 8, 1945, p. 1.

44. "Napa Valley Winery Now Completed," *Wine Review*, September 1945, p. 26. All Colombo advertisements mentioned that Colombo wine was "also available in bulk." The press announcements pointed out that the two wineries together had a total storage capacity of 500,000 gallons, but did not mention the Mills Winery in Sacramento, which Migliaccio had perhaps sold to help finance the St. Helena operation.

45. "Migliaccio Will Filed," *St. Helena Star*, April 26, 1946, p. 10; "B. Migliaccio Passes Away," *Wines and Vines*, April 1946, p. 90.

46. Legal announcement, *St. Helena Star*, August 30, 1946, p. 7. A later legal listing of DBAs included the "Bon-Core Wine Company," a variation on the DBA filed for Migliaccio by the Cucamonga Pioneer Vineyard in 1941. See "Wine Firm Files Certificate," *St. Helena Star*, July 25, 1947, p. 6.

47. Quotation and information on history of Bragno and Co. from Bruce McCubbin's July 17, 1943, report to J. H. Maloney on sources of funds for winery purchase, Larkmead file, BATF records.

48. L. G. Welch, inspection report, August 6, 1943, p. 5, quoting James C. Bragno, Larkmead file, BATF records.

49. Ibid., pp. 3–4. Joseph Gentile's name surfaces again in 1947. He had expanded Brookside and purchased a large winery in Healdsburg in order to secure dry wine. Ultimately, the Alta Winery went bankrupt, and during the 1947 price slump, Gentile leased the Healdsburg plant to a group of Napa growers who had formed an informal cooperative. Riverbank was later transferred from American Wineries to Bragno and Co.

50. Statement of Ownership, April 13, 1943, in Larkmead file, BATF records; "Larkmead Vineyards Files Articles of Incorporation," *Wine Review*, April 1941, p. 29.

51. Elmer Salmina, *Wine Review*, June 1944, p. 16.

52. See L. G. Welch, inspection report, August 6, 1943, in Larkmead file, BATF records, p. 1; "Famous Larkmead Winery, Owned by Salmina Family, Changes Hands," *St. Helena Star*, June 25, 1943, p. 1. The sale actually involved two properties: Larkmead Vineyards, Inc., which owned the winery, and Salmina Lands, Inc., which owned the surrounding vineyards.

53. Blum was also already involved in the California wine industry. He was a minority shareholder in the Colton Winery, managed by Louis Golan of LaNglo fame. See "Wineries Change Hands," *Wines and Vines*, March 1943, p. 41.

54. Bruce McCubbin, report to J. Maloney, July 17, 1943. For details of the financing, see Welch's report of August 6, 1943. The organization of Philip Blum and Co. is laid out in a "Chart of Organization," dated January 28, 1948. All are located in the Larkmead file, BATF records.

55. Welch report, August 6, 1943, p. 1, Larkmead file, BATF records.

56. "Bragno Wines," *Wine Review*, November 1944, p. 26.

57. "Summary of Operations during Period July 26, 1943 to January 26, 1944," Larkmead file, BATF records.

58. See typical trade advertisements for Larkmead in *Wines and Vines*, April 1945, p. 62, and *Wine Review*, August 1945, p. 129.

59. Inspector C. G. Dudley, report, December 5, 1946, Larkmead file, BATF records.

60. "Fermenting Room Versatility at Larkmead Vineyards," *Wines and Vines*, January 1947, p. 31.

61. Larkmead advertisement, *Wine Review*, April 1947, p. 37. See also an advertisement in *Wines and Vines*, October 1947, p. 5.

62. "Harry Blum Sells Larkmead," *Wines and Vines*, January 1948, p. 39; "Larkmead Sold to National Distillers," *St. Helena Star*, January 2, 1948, p. 1.

63. Bartolucci interview, *HNV*, 3 : 6.

64. Ibid., p. 8.

65. "Oakville Winery Seeks Time Extension in Bankruptcy," *St. Helena Star*, August 29, 1947, p. 1.

66. Bartolucci interview, *HNV*, 3 : 10–11.

67. See the discussion of grape prices in chapter 5 for more details.

68. "Grape Prices Discussed," *St. Helena Star*, September 15, 1944, p. 8.

69. "Napa County Growers Set Basic Grape Price, $100 Black, $120 White," *St. Helena Star*, September 21, 1945, p. 1.

70. "Prices of Black Grapes Set at $123, White $141," *St. Helena Star*, September 20, 1946, p. 1.

71. Cresta Blanca advertisements, *St. Helena Star*, November 15, 1943, p. 5, and ibid., July 28, 1944, p. 8.

72. "More Dry Wine Grapes in Napa County," *Wine Review*, June 1945, p. 32, indicates that over 600 acres were planted in 1945 and that 300 had been planted previously. In 1946, an additional 200 acres were set out. See "*Wines and Vines* Previews 1946 Plantings," *Wines and Vines*, August 1946, p. 19. Total vineyard acreage in the Napa Valley was about 11,700 in 1945.

73. Louis M. Martini and Louis P. Martini, *Wine Making in the Napa Valley* (BL), p. 35; "Garetto Winery Buys Vineyard," *Wines and Vines*, November 1943, p. 36; "Federspiel Buys Vineyard," ibid., June 1943, p. 28.

74. "Stanley Ranch Changes Ownership," *Wine Review*, March 1945, p. 26. See also "St. Helenans Buy Stanley Ranch at Napa," *St. Helena Star*, February 16, 1945, p. 1.

75. "More Dry Wine Grapes in Napa County," *Wine Review*, June 1945.

76. See "Martin Stelling Dies in Crash," *Napa Register*, May 7, 1950, p. 1, on his membership in the Bohemian Club. His participation in the campaign to save the cable cars is mentioned in Gunther Detert, "Historical Materials on Far Niente," in *HNV*, 4 : 96.

77. "To-Kalon Changes Hands," *St. Helena Star*, July 23, 1943, p. 1; "To-Kalon Vineyards Sold," *Wines and Vines*, August 1943, p. 29. The *Wines and Vines* article mistakenly dropped a zero, placing the total acreage at 50 acres. They did correctly mention that Stelling in turn sold a portion of the property to Beaulieu Vineyards. Tchelistcheff reports that the Churchills had first offered the property to Mrs. de Latour, but that she thought the asking price of $200 an acre too high. According to Tchelistcheff, Mrs. de Latour later paid Stelling $450 an acre. See Tchelistcheff, *Grapes, Wine and Ecology*, p. 73.

78. "Martin Stelling Buys McGill Ranch," *St. Helena Star*, March 31, 1944, p. 1. The reported sale price was $350,000.

79. Detert, "Historical Materials," pp. 51–52; Tchelistcheff, *Grapes, Wine and Ecology*, p. 73.

80. "Purchase Vineyard Property," *St. Helena Star*, July 28, 1944, p. 1.

81. Bartolucci interview, *HNV*, 3 : 6–7.

82. "St. Helena Winery Sold," *St. Helena Star*, February 22, 1946, p. 1. The actual relationship between Stelling, Chaix, and Forni is confused. Tchelistcheff asserts that Forni put the group together for the purpose of processing their grapes and selling bulk wine and claims that they were producing "good quality wines" (Tchelistcheff, *Grapes, Wine and Ecology*, p. 100). Since Chaix and Forni were both members of the Napa co-op, one wonders why they would have sought another arrangement. It may be that they went into business with Stelling to produce varietal bulk wines, although, if so, no records are extant. Certainly, Forni was involved. Following Stelling's death, Forni ended up with ownership of Sunny St. Helena. The winery was later operated from 1956 through 1970 as a cooperative of local growers for crushing nonvarietal grapes. The resulting wine was then sold to C. Mondavi and Sons. See Arthur Schmidt, "Sunny St. Helena Winery," in *History of Napa Valley*, 2 : 2.

83. "County Growers Refuse $35 Ton; Form Pool to Crush Own Grapes," *St. Helena Star*, September 12, 1947, p. 1; "Martin Stelling, Prominent Valley Agriculturist, Killed in Accident," *St. Helena Star*, May 11, 1950, p. 1.

84. The Benson Winery later became Far Niente. See Detert, "Historical Materials," p. 52. The property was purchased by Italian Swiss Colony, and then later sold to the former vineyard manager, Ivan Schock, who provided grapes for Beaulieu. After a dispute with Beaulieu, Schock sold the vineyard to Charles Krug, greatly increasing its supply of varietal grapes. See Tchelistcheff, *Grapes, Wine and Ecology*, pp. 74–75.

85. "More Dry Wine Grapes in Napa County," *Wine Review*, June 1945, p. 32; "*Wines and Vines* Previews 1946 Plantings," *Wines and Vines*, August 1946, p. 19.

86. "Cella Buys Napa Winery," *Wine Review*, September 1947, p. 26.

87. H. J. Baade, "Vineyard, Orchard and Farm," *St. Helena Star*, April 3, 1942, p. 7.

88. "Practical Guide for State Wine Growers," *St. Helena Star*, December 24, 1943, p. 3. See also Irving Marcus, "Which Grapes in Which Districts for Which Wines: An Introduction to One of the Most Important Writings on Grapes That Has Ever Been Placed in the Hands of Our Winemen," *Wines and Vines*, December 1943, p. 11.

89. A. J. Winkler, "Grape Plantings during 1945," *Wines and Vines*, December 1945, p. 26.

90. Some financial analysts refer to return and risk as "greed" and "fear." They may be correct.

91. "Commenting on the News—Plantings," *Wines and Vines*, April 1945, p. 17.

92. Walter S. Richert, "What Grapes to Plant," *Wines and Vines*, December 1946, p. 36.

93. "Commenting on the News — Grapes," *Wines and Vines*, January 1945, p. 9.

94. "More Dry Wine Grapes in Napa County," *Wine Review*, June 1945, p. 32.

95. H. E. Jacob and A. J. Winkler, "Limit Grape Plantings to Good Wine Grape Varieties," *Wines and Vines*, January 1945, p. 28.

96. Martin Gould, "Inglenook Pinot Chardonnay Yields Good Tonnage," *Wines and Vines*, April 1945, p. 31. This is the first instance I have found of Chardonnay being grown in Napa Valley after Repeal.

97. Irving H. Marcus, "Give the Devil His Due," *Wines and Vines*, December 1946, p. 17. This one-page article on the end of OPA regulations is probably the single best summary of the effect that OPA regulations had on the California wine industry.

98. John Daniel, Jr., "Notes," in *History of Napa Valley*, 1:236.

99. Louis P. Martini, interview with the author, March 14, 1991; Martini and Martini, *Wine Making*, p. 45.

100. Peter Mondavi, "Advances in Technology and Production," p. 19.

101. "New Winery in Month," *California Wine Review*, July 1934, p. 34; "Sell Fine Mountain Ranch," *St. Helena Star*, October 1, 1943, p. 1.

102. "The Rough Road to Quality," *Wines and Vines*, August 1948, p. 19.

103. "State Fair Awards," *Wines and Vines*, September 1948, p. 13.

104. "Wine Awards at the California State Fair," *Wines and Vines*, September 1941, p. 17.

105. "Napa County Wines Take State Fair Honors," *St. Helena Star*, September 12, 1947, p. 1; "Awards in Wine Competition," *Wines and Vines*, September 1947, p. 12. The ten award-winning Napa wineries were: Beringer, Beaulieu, Mont La Salle (Christian Brothers), Inglenook, Martini, Pocai & Sons, Garetto, Larkmead, Charles Krug, and Souverain. In historical fairness, it should be noted that Wente Brothers of Alameda County was the clear individual winner. Wente took over half the awards given to Alameda County, including seven gold medals. See also *Time* magazine's coverage of the State Fair, which antagonized the California industry by pointing out that "for 14 different varieties out of the 45 judged, the entries were so poor that no gold medals were awarded" ("Judgment Day," *Time*, September 22, 1947, p. 86). *Time*'s use of the word *varieties* is incorrect, however; it should have been *categories*.

106. Martini and Martini, *Wine Making*, p. 42.

107. "Napa Valley Vintners in New Organization," *St. Helena Star*, January 26, 1945, p. 1. See also "Napa Valley Vintners from New Association," *Wine Review*, February 1945, p. 16, and "New Winery Association Formed," *Wines and Vines*, February 1945, p. 42.

108. "Wine Week Observed," *St. Helena Star*, November 18, 1946, p. 1.

109. "Napa Valley Vintners Host to Technical Committee," *Wine Review*, July 1945, p. 20; "St. Helena Featured Wine Week Banquet," *Wine Review*, November 1945, p. 32; "Banquet Honors California Wines," *Wines and Vines*, November 1946, p. 62; and "Problems of Wine Growers Discussed," *St. Helena Star*, February 13, 1948, p. 5, are all representative of the Vintner's Association's activities.

110. "Seek Experiment Station for U.C.," *St. Helena Star*, March 16, 1945, p. 1; "Vintners in Favor of Conn Water Bonds," *St. Helena Star*, July 25, 1947, p. 6. The USDA site was not turned over to the university until after the war, but Martin Stelling did sell twenty acres of McGill ranch land to the university in 1947. This became the "south" vineyard of the Oakville Experiment Station. See "U.C. Buys Valley Land for Grape Experiments," *St. Helena Star*, May 2, 1947, p. 1.

111. This collection of early members is derived from several different sources. See Tchelistcheff, *Grapes, Wine and Ecology*, p. 91; Martini and Martini, *Wine Making*, p. 43; Deuer interview, *HNV*, 2:132; and Robert Mondavi, *Creativity*, p. 28.

112. Deuer maintains that the Napa Valley Wine Technical Group was started "before the war," but he is almost certainly mistaken. Louis P. Martini puts the date at 1947, and Tchelistcheff maintains that the group grew out of a series of classes he taught for returning veterans.

113. Deuer interview, *HNV*, 2:37.

114. "Martin Stelling Heads Grape Growers Group," *St. Helena Star*, August 29, 1947, p. 1.

115. "County Growers Refuse $35 Ton; Form Pool to Crush Own Grapes," *St. Helena Star*, September 12, 1947, p. 1. See also "Napa County Association Leases Alta's Healdsburg Wine Plant," *Wine Review*, October 1947, p. 26.

116. "Cella Vineyards Buy Napa Wine Co.," *St. Helena Star*, August 22, 1947, p. 1.

117. "Producers Least Affected by Slump," *Wines and Vines*, September 1947, p. 6.

7. Table Wine Triumphant, 1947–1967

1. Edmund A. Rossi, "The Coming Expansion of the Table Wine Market," *Wines and Vines*, December 1944, p. 29.

2. In 1944, sales of sweet wine totaled 57.7 million gallons, as compared to 36.1 million gallons of table wine. See "Statistical Review 1947," *Wines and Vines*, April 1948, p. 30.

3. "Active California Bonded Wine and Brandy Production and Storage Premises," *Wines and Vines*, April 1951, p. 41; "California Bonded Wine and Brandy Premises," *Wines and Vines*, April 1967, p. 32. The low point was reached in 1967, inasmuch as "boutique" wineries joined the industry in subsequent years.

4. Fred S. Orth, "A Banker Takes the Measure of the California Wine Industry," *Wines and Vines*, April 1963, pp. 27–28, 30, 32. Orth does not name the wineries, but they must have been Gallo, United Vintners/Allied Growers, and Guild/Roma, in that order.

5. Between 1934 and 1947, table wines had averaged 31 percent of total sales. In 1952, the north and central coasts produced 18 million of the state's total 37.3 million gallons of table wine, roughly 48 percent. That percentage held in 1957, when the coastal counties combined to deliver 16.3 million gallons out of a total

of 34 million. By 1962, as increased acreage came into bearing in the northern San Joaquin Valley, the figure dropped to 38 percent. See the April "statistical issue" of *Wines and Vines* for each year.

6. See "Stabilization Order Proposed," *Wines and Vines*, March 1961, p. 15. The 1961 Grapes for Crushing Marketing Order is also discussed in Orth, "Banker Takes the Measure of the California Wine Industry," p. 28.

7. The actual grape acreage controlled by these quality producers is covered later in this chapter.

8. The industry consultant Lou Gomberg's figures for 1952, derived from California excise tax payments, indicate that Christian Brothers sold five times as much dessert as table wine in that year: 93,600 cases of table wine and 508,000 cases of dessert wine.

9. Robert Mondavi, *Creativity in the California Wine Industry* (BL), p. 26.

10. Irving Marcus, "The U.S. Market for Premium Wines," *Wines and Vines*, November 1951, p. 20.

11. Herman Wente, "Special Problems in Merchandising Premium Wines," *Wines and Vines*, May 1956, p. 21.

12. This estimate is derived from membership in the Premium Wine Producers of California (PWPC), established in 1955, which accounted for virtually all of the premium wine produced in California. Between 1955 and 1959, the PWPC's membership generally hovered around 25, and there were in all 315 bonded California wineries in 1955. The PWPC is discussed in chapter 8, along with the problem of defining premium wine.

13. Irving Marcus, "The Seven Fat Years of Table Wine Sales in California," *Wines and Vines*, October 1954, p. 22.

14. Louis Gomberg, "Comparative Growth Rates of Table Wines in the U.S., According to Origin," Appendix 1 of Report #61 to Academy of Master Wine Growers, August 8, 1966 (mimeo).

15. "The Book Shelf," *Wines and Vines*, January 1949, p. 20.

16. This should not be taken to mean that the wineries were the same size. In 1952, Christian Brothers' total sales were significantly greater than those of other premium producers because Christian Brothers sold over 500,000 cases of dessert wine in addition to its dry wine sales.

17. Grape acreage and expansion are covered in greater detail in chapter 9. Of the five, Beringer probably had the fewest varietal grapes, with most of its vineyards planted in "standard" black varieties such as Petite Sirah, Zinfandel, and Carignane.

18. Robert Mondavi, "Creativity in the California Wine Industry," p. 30.

19. Frank Schoonmaker as quoted by William Dieppe in *Almaden Is My Life* (BL), p. 21.

20. Data from the *Gomberg Report*. There were significant differences *between* the volume producers as well. Christian Brothers was by far the dominant dessert wine producer in the group. In 1967, roughly 55 percent of all of its sales were of dessert wines, while dessert wine accounted for only about 20 percent of Almaden's sales mix, for example. More important than percentage, however, is volume. In 1967, Almaden sold more dessert wine than the largest member of the estate group sold table wine.

21. "What the U.S. Public Thinks about Wine," *Wines and Vines*, October 1955, p. 20.

22. "1952 Consumer's Survey Traces Pattern of Current Wine Buying," *Wines and Vines*, August 1952, p. 10.

23. Alfred Fromm, "The Bright Road to the Future," *Wines and Vines*, November 1956, p. 35.

24. Irving Marcus, "The Seven Fat Years of Table Wine Sales in California," *Wines and Vines*, October 1954, p. 22.

25. "1952 Consumer's Survey Traces Pattern of Current Wine Buying," *Wines and Vines*, August 1952.

26. "What the U.S. Public Thinks about Wine," p. 22.

8. Politics and Promotion

1. Walter S. Richert, "Regional Promotion of Wines," *Wines and Vines*, August 1949, p. 14.

2. "See-Through Poster Welcomes Napa Valley Visitors," *Wines and Vines*, October 1950, p. 32; "Vintners Sponsor Cable Car," ibid., November 1949, p. 32; "Give-Away Too Good," ibid., April 1950, p. 86. The title of the last article derives from the fact that the cable car company curtailed the practice, fearing that it would make it a "freight carrier" in the eyes of the Public Utility Commission.

3. "Cooperative Promotion" (editorial), *Wines and Vines*, October 1949, pp. 3–4. Italics in original.

4. Francis Gould, "Napa Valley Vintners," *Bottles and Bins*, October, 1962, p. 2; "Lawyers Guests of Calif. Vintners," *Wines and Vines*, August 1962, p. 7; and "Napa Valley Vintners Play Host," ibid., June 1962, p. 14.

5. Frank Schoonmaker, "California's Vintage Vale," *Holiday*, August 1952, pp. 103–7. Quotations are from p. 103.

6. See "Wise and Otherwise," *Wines and Vines*, February 1955, p. 16, and "Napa Vintners Honor Author," ibid., April 1955, p. 9. The duchy earned wider notoriety in the 1959 Peter Sellers comedy *The Mouse That Roared*, but in the movie war was declared, not to defend national honor, but to win U.S. aid as a vanquished foe.

7. "Vintners, Movie Stars Meet," *Wines and Vines*, October 1958, p. 9, and "Wine Movie Opens to Considerable Fanfare," ibid., July 1959, p. 7.

8. Philip Lesly of the Philip Lesly Company, which was hired to promote premium California wines in 1959, spoke of the need to "surround the public with an atmosphere favorable to the idea we want to get across." See Lesly, "The Way We Plan to Do It," *Wines and Vines*, October 1959, p. 21.

9. Because the definition of "premium wine" was so imprecise, estimates of volume varied. Using a weighted average, Louis Gomberg compared the years 1948–50 with 1955–57 and estimated a 50 percent increase (see Gomberg, "What's Up, What's Down in Wine Consumption," *Wines and Vines*, August 1958, p. 40). Ed Wooton, representing the Wine Institute at federal hearings on wine tariffs,

defined premium wine as wine costing more than $1.00 a bottle. According to his figures, 1955 projected sales represented a 39 percent increase over 1949 figures. See "Why U.S. Vintners Fight Lower Import Duties," *Wines and Vines*, April 1956, pp. 28–29.

10. "The Impact of Imports," *Wines and Vines*, May 1952, p. 11; Alfred Fromm, "It's the Truth!" ibid., April 1955, p. 29.

11. John Daniel, Jr., ". . . And We Quote," *Wines and Vines*, December 1953, p. 11; Robert Mondavi, "Table Wine Prospects for 1953," ibid., February 1953, p. 20.

12. Robert Mondavi, *Creativity in the California Wine Industry* (BL), p. 31.

13. Two groups, the North Coast Table Wine Producers and the Association of Chateau Wine Growers, had been created in 1950 to further the interests of table wine and premium wines. Neither was successful, although the Chateau group was active through 1952.

14. The nine core wineries were Almaden, Ambassador District Wines, Asti Vineyards, Beaulieu, Beringer, Buena Vista, Christian Brothers, Cresta Blanca, Hallcrest Vineyards, Inglenook, Korbel, Charles Krug, Paul Masson, Signature Vintners, Weibel Champagne Vineyards, and Wente Brothers. See Louis Gomberg, *California Prestige Wines Study Report* (San Francisco: Producers of California Prestige Wines, 1955), p. 1.

15. Louis Gomberg, "Memorandum: Co-operative Action by California Wine Producers to Combat Foreign Competition" (n.d.; included in the minutes of the California Academy of Master Winegrowers), p. 4.

16. Gomberg, *California Prestige Wines Study Report*, p. 23.

17. Edmund Rossi, manager of the Wine Advisory Board, indicated that the $2,000,000 taken in each year by the marketing order was spent in the following way: $1,000,000 for advertising, $450,000 to the Wine Institute for legislative work, and the remaining $550,00 for field men to "merchandise the advertising" by working with retailers. Minutes, Premium Wine Producers of California, May 5, 1955, p. 2.

18. Ibid., p. 4.

19. Don McColly as quoted in minutes, Working Committee Meeting, Premium Wine Producers of California, June 23, 1955, p. 1.

20. See "Chateau Wine Growers Assn. Formed," *Wines and Vines*, December 1950, p. 30; "Chateau Group Outlines Program," ibid., January 1951, p. 6; "Chateau Group Okays Special Label," ibid., February 1952, p. 34. For a more general discussion of industry attempts to define quality, see "How Much Quality Wine?" ibid., April 1952, pp. 6, 8; and Edgar Millhauser, "Quality Wine — Why Not Specific Categories?" ibid., May 1952, p. 6.

21. These viticultural regions were conceived of and defined by Amerine and Winkler of the University of California during the late 1930s.

22. Minutes, Third Annual Membership Meeting, Premium Wine Producers of California, June 25, 1958, p. 1.

23. Gomberg, *California Prestige Wines Study Report*, p. 24.

24. Paul Snell, "Public Relations and the California Wine Industry," *Wines and Vines*, November 1956, pp. 24–26.

25. "French Wine Blues," *Bottles and Bins*, July 1950, p. 2.

26. Gomberg, *California Prestige Wines Study Report*, p. 10.

27. "Results of First 20 Tastings," Minutes, Premium Wine Producers of California, September 28, 1956, p. 1.

28. As reported by H. Peter Jurgens, "We Have Only Begun to Fight on the PR Front," *Wines and Vines*, January 1960, p. 21. The difference amounted to less than .05 percent.

29. Snell, "Public Relations and the California Wine Industry," p. 25.

30. Edmund Rossi, "What We Are Getting from Our Wine Festivals," *Wines and Vines*, March 1959, pp. 16–18.

31. "Can't Advertise Tasting Results," *Wines and Vines*, June 1956, p. 6. The Alcohol and Tobacco Tax Division (ATTD) was later upgraded and became the present-day Bureau of Alcohol, Tobacco and Firearms (BATF).

32. "Marketing Order Hearing," *Wines and Vines*, March 1957, p. 15. The $400,000 figure comes from "What Happened in St. Louis," ibid., February 1958, pp. 22–23.

33. See Rossi, "What We Are Getting from Our Wine Festivals," pp. 16–18.

34. Ibid.

35. Ibid.

36. This is derived from minutes of the standing committee of the Premium Wine Producers of California (later Academy of Master Wine Growers) for October 2, 1958; April 15, 1959; July 15, 1959; and December 28, 1959. See also "Public Relations for California Wine: The Record of Its Changing Pattern from 1934 to 1965," *Wines and Vines*, March 1965, pp. 14–15.

37. See "How the Industry PR Program Is Doing," *Wines and Vines*, November 1960, pp. 22–23, and "Public Relations for California Wine," ibid.

38. Francis Gould, *Wines and Vines*, June 1961. See also Louis Gomberg, "California—Plus or Minus for a Wine?" ibid., September 1961, p. 22.

39. Stanford Wolf, as quoted in minutes of the standing committee, Academy of Master Wine Growers, April 15, 1959, p. 5.

40. Robert Mondavi as quoted in "Major Talks Highlight 30th Annual Wine Institute Meeting," *Wines and Vines*, June 1964, p. 21.

41. "Action on Palm Springs Front," *Wines and Vines*, December 1964, p. 15.

42. Ibid.

43. Philip Lesly, "The Way We Plan to Do It," *Wines and Vines*, October 1959, p. 21.

44. Howard Williams, "What Consumers Want," *Wines and Vines*, November 1962, p. 26.

45. Ibid., p. 27.

46. Ibid.

47. "New 'Cask' Label for Inglenook," *Wines and Vines*, July 1960, p. 11. The regular Inglenook Cabernet Sauvignon retailed for $1.65 a bottle, while the "Cask" wine sold at $3.25.

48. "Inglenook Label Change," *Wines and Vines*, November 1960. Inglenook had undergone a minor label change in 1951 when it repositioned the diamond logo and added a back label describing the winery and grape variety. See "Packaging Page," ibid., August 1951, p. 11. There is a bit of irony here. When Heublein decided to "reposition" Inglenook as a high-quality producer once again in 1987,

it decided to return to the original diamond logo. The redesign by Colonna & Farrell won an award.

49. "The New Labels," *Bottles and Bins*, October 1961, p. 1. Actually, this was the second modification of the basic Charles Krug label, which had undergone changes in 1952 as well. See "New Label," ibid., July 1953, p. 1.

50. Francis Gould, "Room for Improvement," *Wines and Vines*, August 1948, p. 17.

51. [Francis Gould], "The New Labels," *Bottles and Bins*, October 1961, p. 2.

52. "We Have No Secrets" (Charles Krug advertisement), *Wines and Vines*, November 1962, p. 14.

53. For Inglenook, see "Packaging Page," *Wines and Vines*, August 1951, p. 11; for Beaulieu see "New Beaulieu Back Label," ibid., June 1956, p. 5, and "Beaulieu Brochure Emphasizes Informative Back Labels," ibid., December 1961, p. 11.

54. Cecil Kahmann, "Has America Discovered Wine?" *Wines and Vines*, October 1964, pp. 16–17; quotation on p. 16. A thoughtful article on newspaper and magazine editors' perceptions of California wine.

55. Gomberg data in Appendix 1 of Report #61 to Academy of Master Wine Growers, August 8, 1966 (mimeo).

9. The Transformation

1. Frank Schoonmaker, "California vs. Imported — An Impartial Appraisal," *Wines and Vines*, December 1956, p. 24. (The capitals are in the original, and the entire sentence was printed in italics in order to underscore the point. However, it is worth noting that Schoonmaker had become a paid marketing consultant for Almaden, and that this article originally appeared in the Almaden newsletter, *News from the Wine Country*.) Cecil Kahmann, "Has America Discovered Wine?" *Wines and Vines*, October 1964, pp. 16–17.

2. See "Winemakers' Professional Group Formed," *Wines and Vines*, January 1950, p. 26, and "Enologists' Group Activated," ibid., February 1950, p. 26.

3. The Louis Martini winery had cold-fermented its Muscat since its establishment in 1934. However, it was primarily known for red wines and did not sponsor research into quality differences resulting from fermentation temperature.

4. Peter Mondavi, *Advances in Technology and Production at Charles Krug Winery, 1946–1988* (BL), p. 10.

5. André Tchelistcheff, "Researches on Cool Fermentation," *Wines and Vines*, September 1948, pp. 23, 24.

6. "Wine Judging Box Score," *Wines and Vines*, September 1949, p. 14.

7. "Full Scale Cold Fermentation," *Wines and Vines*, February 1949, p. 22. See also "A Year of Progress," ibid., December 1948, p. 21, which commented that "the principal center for these researches" was in the Napa Valley, "where a number of wineries carry on all of their fermentation of quality wines at reduced temperatures, from about 50 to 60 degrees."

8. Al Huntsinger, "Back to the Basket Press," *Wines and Vines*, March 1949, p. 17. Charles Krug had three basket presses and one continuous screw press. "It

didn't take long to learn that a continuous screw press was only good to get maximum recovery of press wine for distillation purposes," Peter Mondavi noted ("Wilmes Press vs. Basket Press," ibid., April 1965, p. 68).

9. Louis P. Martini, "Basket Press Hopper," *Wines and Vines*, February 1953, p. 29.

10. Ibid.; Mondavi, "Wilmes Press vs. Basket Press," p. 68.

11. "Garolla Press at Work," *Wines and Vines*, May 1956, p. 29; John Hoffman, "The Garolla Press," ibid., April 1965, p. 70.

12. Al Huntsinger, "The Wilmes Press at Almaden," *Wines and Vines*, November 1956, p. 51; Mondavi, "Wilmes Press vs. Basket Press," p. 68.

13. Louis P. Martini, personal communication to the author, December 20, 1993.

14. The French Vaslin press, essentially a two-headed horizontal basket press, was also introduced into the United States in the late 1950s. See "French Horizontal Press Tested Here," *Wines and Vines*, January 1958, pp. 29–30.

15. Julius Fessler, "Winemaker's Notebook," *Wines and Vines*, May 1955, p. 30.

16. Peter Mondavi, *Advances in Technology and Production*, p. 22.

17. Peter Mondavi, "Bottling Techniques under Nitrogen Pressure," *Wines and Vines*, June 1960, p. 12. See also William Bonetti, "Problems Encountered in Storage of Wine under Nitrogen," ibid., June 1966, p. 62, and R. R. Cant, "The Effect of Nitrogen and Carbon Dioxide Treatment of Wines on Dissolved Oxygen Levels," *American Journal of Enology* 11, 4 (1960): 164–69. Bonetti and Cant both worked at Charles Krug.

18. In conversations with me, Louis P. Martini and Peter Mondavi both claim that they used bentonite to achieve protein stability in the 1940s. While they undoubtedly did use bentonite to *clarify* their wines, I doubt whether they did so to *protein stabilize* their wines. Bentonite clay was widely used to clarify wine, and M. A. Amerine and M. A. Joslyn note in *Table Wines: The Technology of Their Production in California* (Berkeley: University of California Press, 1951) that "about ½ to 1 pound is used per 100 gallons," and that if bentonite is used with "hot wine, 1 to 2 pounds per 1,000 gallons is sufficient" (p. 107). Later Amerine and Joslyn comment that "protein cloudiness is poorly understood," and that "many white wines throw down a voluminous precipitate when heated to 150 F." (p. 234). Clearly, the bentonite reaction with positively charged proteins was not understood.

19. André Tchelistcheff, *Grapes, Wine and Ecology* (BL), p. 138.

20. Tchelistcheff should be given credit for working on protein instability, but other researchers contributed too. In 1951, R. O'Neal and William Cruess of the University of California noted that "bentonite fining gave greater stability" when they were comparing wines heated to 120° F that had been fined with various fining agents. But they did not explain a probable mechanism of action. See R. O'Neal and W. V. Cruess, "Comparative Effects of Casein, Gelatin and Bentonite Fining," *Wines and Vines*, January 1951, pp. 17–18.

21. John Hoffman, "Sterile Filtration: Present and Future," *Wines and Vines*, April 1955, pp. 63–64. Christian Brothers was certainly one of the first wineries to adopt sterile filtration and bottling, but it was not the first. Morrie Turbov-

sky of Grape Gold Vineyards, which later became Madrone Winery, wrote in June 1949 that they had used sterile filtration for "a period of seven months," and that it had "proven quite successful" ("Practical Value of Sterile Filtration," ibid., June 1949, p. 22). Ernest Gallo indicates that the first commercial use of sterile filtration was at Wente Brothers ("Outlook for a Mature Industry," ibid., June 1958, p. 30).

22. Peter Mondavi, *Advances in Technology and Production*, p. 7.

23. "TAC Holds Full-Day Meet in Napa," *Wines and Vines*, June 1955, p. 32.

24. "TAC Holds Full-Day Meeting in Napa Valley," *Wines and Vines*, June 1956, p. 31.

25. Louis P. Martini, *A Family Winery and the California Wine Industry* (BL), pp. 58–59, and personal communication to the author, December 20, 1993.

26. "Krug Plans New Bottling Line," *Wines and Vines*, March 1957, p. 7; "Start New Krug Bottling-Cellar," ibid., June 1958, p. 9; "Wise and Otherwise," ibid., May 1959, p. 14.

27. Reese Vaugh and André Tchelistcheff, "Studies on the Malic Acid Fermentation of California Table Wines, I: An Introduction to the Problem," *American Journal of Enology* 8, 2 (1957): 75.

28. Bard Suverkrop and André Tchelistcheff, "Malo-lactic Fermentation in California Wines," *Wines and Vines*, July 1949, pp. 19–23.

29. Brad Webb was the winemaker at Hanzell in Sonoma County and later at Freemark Abbey in St. Helena. John Ingraham was a microbiologist in the Department of Viticulture and Enology at U.C. Davis. See R. B. Webb and John I. Ingraham, "Induced Malo-lactic Fermentations," *American Journal of Enology and Viticulture* 11, 2 (1960): 59–63.

30. John Castor, "Experimental Development of Compressed Wine Yeast as Fermentation Starters," *Wines and Vines*, August 1953, pp. 27–29, and ibid., September 1953, pp. 33–34.

31. George Thoukis and R. J. Bouthilet, "The Use of Pressed Yeast Cake in Winery Fermentation," *Wines and Vines*, January 1963, p. 25.

32. "Red Star Yeast Appoints Zacher," *Wines and Vines*, April 1963, p. 19.

33. Charles Schilling as quoted in "Fine Wines, Private Labels," *Wines and Vines*, September 1949, p. 16.

34. Amerine estimates that prior to the technological and scientific changes in the industry, North Coast producers accepted anywhere between 5 and 25 percent spoilage, partially because grapes were inexpensive. See Amerine interview, *HNV*, 4:174.

35. A decrease in grape acreage during the 1950s combined with a short crop in 1964 led to high bulk wine prices in 1965. See "Short Supply, Big Demand Boost Varietal Grape Prices," *Wines and Vines*, February 1965, p. 22.

36. Aldo Delfino, Napa County Agricultural Commissioner, *Annual Report*, 1966, p. 1.

37. Aggregate data from Louis Gomberg, *Special Report*, July 22, 1981.

38. "Wine Awards at the 1950 California State Fair," *Wines and Vines*, September 1950, pp. 25–26.

39. Total grape acreage is from *Napa County Agricultural Commissioner's Report* for 1951. Estimates for acreage owned or controlled by premium wineries are derived from several sources.

40. Gomberg excise tax data.

41. Charlotte Siegel, "Beringer's: A Winery with an Open Door Policy," *Wine Review*, July 1945, p. 12. On the Fawver property, see Raymond interview, *HNV*, 1:246, 255. Raymond estimated that after the lease ended in 1956, Beringer had "around 275 acres."

42. "Beringer Buys Garetto Winery," *Wines and Vines*, July 1951, p. 24.

43. Charlotte Siegel, "Beaulieu Vineyard," *Wine Review*, November 1944, p. 13.

44. "Italian Swiss Buys Napa Vineyards," *Wines and Vines*, February 1951, p. 28. Italian Swiss Colony had bought the vineyard from the Stelling estate in 1951. For a discussion of the arrangement between Beaulieu and Ivan Schoch, see Tchelistcheff, *Grapes, Wine and Ecology*, pp. 74–75.

45. Tchelistcheff, *Grapes, Wine and Ecology*, p. 121.

46. "Christian Brothers Buy Vineyards," *Wines and Vines*, May 1956, p. 5.

47. "Growers Receive Quality Bonus," *Wines and Vines*, January 1958, p. 12.

48. The 225 acres is mentioned in "United Vintners Negotiating to Buy Inglenook Vineyards," *Wines and Vines*, April 1964, p. 13. Charlotte Siegel, "Inglenook Vineyard Company," *Wine Review*, September 1945, p. 12, lists 155 acres of bearing vineyard.

49. The list is derived from "State Fair Wine Awards," *Wines and Vines*, September 1948, pp. 13–14; and from a Bellows and Co. advertisement for Inglenook wines that appeared in ibid., September 1949, p. 54.

50. The chronology can be reconstructed from Louis M. Martini and Louis P. Martini, *Wine Making in the Napa Valley* (BL), pp. 35–36, 86–87.

51. See Robert Mondavi, *Creativity in the California Wine Industry* (BL), p. 18, and Peter Mondavi's oral history, *Advances in Technology and Production*, pp. 17–18. The Krug winery property covered about 140 acres, and Robert Mondavi recalled that about 25 acres were not planted to vineyard.

52. Peter Mondavi, personal communication to the author, December 21, 1993.

53. "New Co-op Formed," *Wines and Vines*, June 1957, p. 7; see also Arthur Schmidt, "History of Sunny St. Helena Winery," in *HNV*, vol. 2, and Robert Mondavi, *Creativity*, p. 22.

54. "Charles Krug Buys 500 Acre Napa Valley Vineyard," *Wines and Vines*, February 1962, p. 7; "The New Vineyard," *Bottles and Bins*, April 1962, p. 1.

55. Peter Mondavi, *Advances in Technology and Production*, p. 36 and appendix 1.

56. "Wine Grapes Grown in Napa County, 1966: Black Wine Grapes," in Napa County Agricultural Commissioner, *Annual Report*, 1966.

57. Napa County annual tonnage figures are derived from the annual reports of the agricultural commissioner; tonnage figures for the Napa co-op from 1947 through 1965 were supplied by the Napa co-op, which is still in business; the tonnage for the St. Helena co-op is derived from "St. Helena Co-op Mortgage Burning," *Wines and Vines*, October 1959, p. 7.

58. "St. Helena Cellars Acquired by Wine Guild," *St. Helena Star*, November 9, 1945, p. 10. The St. Helena co-op was still a guild member at the end of 1947, when several members visited the guild bottling cellar in Lodi. See "Inspect Blending, Bottling Cellars at Lodi," ibid., December 26, 1947, p. 5.

59. See Napa Valley Cooperative Winery, "Minutes of Quarterly Membership Meeting," July 13, 1951, and "Minutes of Special Membership Meeting," June 2, 1952.

60. "Wise and Otherwise," *Wines and Vines*, October 1954, p. 14.

61. Robert Mondavi, "Table Wine Prospects for 1953," *Wines and Vines*, February 1953, p. 19.

62. R. L. Sisson, *Sonoma County Wine Grape Management Study* (Santa Rosa: Cooperative Extension Office, 1954).

63. Herman Wente, "Grape Growing in the Livermore Valley, Past and Present," *American Journal of Enology* 7, 1 (1956): 70.

64. Eugene Seghesio, "Grape Growing in Sonoma County," *American Journal of Enology* 7, 1 (1956): 77.

65. "How the Grape Grower Fares," *Wines and Vines*, September 1956, p. 23.

66. Grape prices are derived from the September and October issues of *Wines and Vines* during the 1950s. Each month the magazine provided a brief, one- or two-page review of industry news. During harvest, this review usually included grape prices.

67. See "Vintage Hits Peak," *Wines and Vines*, October 1959, p. 19, and "What California Vintners Paid for Grapes, By Varieties," ibid., March 1960, p. 16. The latter article mentions that short crop conditions on the North Coast were responsible for the "wide price range" between the San Joaquin Valley and the North Coast. This may be so, but it seems to have set a precedent for the 1960s.

68. Sisson, *Sonoma County Wine Grape Management Study*, p. 5.

69. "Double Napa Grape Yield Held Possible," *Wines and Vines*, February 1954, p. 6.

70. See "Industry Meets Researchers — and Vice Versa," *Wines and Vines*, January 1951, p. 15; H. P. Olmo, "A Proposed Program for the Introduction, Improvement, and Certification of Healthy Grape Varieties," ibid., July 1951, pp. 7–9; and "Industry Group Gives Consideration to Controlled Cuttings Program," ibid., August 1951, pp. 9–10.

71. "Grape Certification Association Formed," *Wines and Vines*, September 1952, p. 16; "Olmo Collecting Cuttings in Europe," ibid., October 1951, p. 32; "Olmo on European Tour," ibid., August 1953, p. 11. As usual, Napa vintners took a lead in the new Grape Certification Association. Of three industry directors or officers, two were from the Napa Valley: Robert Mondavi served as vice president, and Al Huntsinger, of the Napa co-op, was a director.

72. See the following for discussion of work begun in the 1950s: Harold Olmo, "Improvements in Grape Varieties," *Wines and Vines*, February 1964, pp. 23, 25; Cornelius Ough and C. J. Alley, "An Evaluation of Some Cabernet Varieties," ibid., May 1966, pp. 23–25; and Harold Olmo, "Clonal Selection in the Vinifera Grape 'Chardonnay,'" ibid., July 1968, p. 30.

73. C. J. Alley, "Certified Grape Stocks Available," *Wines and Vines*, February 1959, p. 30.

74. Lloyd Lider, "A Grape Rootstock Trial in the Napa Valley: A Nine-Year Progress Report of Three Stocks on Bale Loam Soil," *American Journal of Enology* 8, 3 (1957): 121. See also id., "Phylloxera-Resistant Rootstock Trials in the Coastal

Valleys of California," ibid. 8, 2 (1957): 58–67; and id., "Selecting Proper Root-stocks for California Vineyards," *Wines and Vines*, February 1959, pp. 19–20.

75. AXR ultimately proved not to be phylloxera-resistant, collapsing in the mid 1980s and causing a major replanting of North Coast vineyards in the 1990s. In fairness to Dr. Lider, it should be pointed out that he never claimed that AXR was totally resistant to phylloxera. Previous trials by other researchers before Prohibition and after Repeal had shown AXR to prosper in soils that contained phylloxera.

76. James Cook and Thomas Kishaba, "Nitrogen Fertilization of Unirrigated Vineyards in the North Coastal Areas of California," *American Journal of Enology* 8, 3 (1957): 105–12; "New Vineyard Fertilization Check," *Wines and Vines*, February 1955, p. 7.

77. Robert Sisson, "Yield and Quality Response of Some Respaced North Coast Vineyards," *American Journal of Enology* 10, 1 (1959): 44–47. Yield per vine increased primarily as a result of increased berry size. Today, many vineyardists are experimenting with more densely planted vineyards in order to reduce berry size and increase wine quality.

78. John Daniel as quoted in Academy of Master Wine Growers, "Minutes of Standing Committee Meeting," June 26, 1963, in *Report No. 49*, July 3, 1963, p. 3.

79. "Meetings on Vineyard Replanting," *Wines and Vines*, January 1960, p. 9; James Lyder, "Napa County," ibid., March 1964, p. 34.

80. John Fiske, "Napa County," *Wines and Vines*, February 1965, p. 31.

81. A. J. Winkler, "Varietal Wine Grapes in the Central Coast Counties of California," *American Journal of Enology* 15, 4 (1964): 205.

10. The Cost of Growth

1. Irving H. Marcus, "The Coming 100,000,000 Gallon U.S. Market for Table Wine," *Wines and Vines*, March 1968, p. 15.

2. All of the above figures are derived from Gomberg's tracking of tax-paid wine removals.

3. This is perhaps an overstatement. Beaulieu's case sales did grow during the controlled economy of World War II, but this was more a transition from bulk production to cased-goods sales and did not involve expansion of vineyards or the winery.

4. Tchelistcheff as quoted in Richard G. Peterson, self-interview, in *HNV*, 2: 175.

5. This brief family history is based on James Conaway's *Napa* (Boston: Houghton Mifflin, 1990), pp. 106–7, 111–16. Conaway's book is not a standard history, lacks notes, and is based primarily on interviews. However, it is generally accurate, if melodramatic.

6. André Tchelistcheff, *Grapes, Wine and Ecology* (BL), p. 120.

7. Ibid., pp. 72–73. She did, however, buy a portion of the vineyard from Stelling in 1942, which became "B.V. #4."

8. "L. M. Fabbrini Dies," *Wines and Vines*, September 1946, p. 46; "A. J. Fabbrini Succeeds Brother," ibid., October 1946, p. 42.

9. Legh Knowles, *Beaulieu Vineyards from Family to Corporate Ownership* (BL), p. 31; sales percentages are derived from the *Gomberg Report*.

10. I have not come across any listing of the varietal composition of Beaulieu's vineyards in the 1950s. A 1956 back label stated that Beaulieu had fifteen acres of Chardonnay. See "New Beaulieu Back Label," *Wines and Vines*, June 1956, p. 5.

11. The above is derived from Tchelistcheff, *Grapes, Wine and Ecology* pp. 74–75, regarding the Schoch vineyard, and pp. 120–21, regarding the move to Carneros.

12. "Schenley Absorbs Park & Tilford," *Wines and Vines*, April 1958, p. 9; Knowles, "Beaulieu Vineyards," p. 31.

13. Knowles, "Beaulieu Vineyards," p. 32.

14. Ibid.

15. *Gomberg Report* data.

16. Beaulieu *Wall Street Journal* advertisement as reprinted in *Wines and Vines*, November 1966, p. 30. Italics in original. Actually, as we shall see, the Beaulieu advertisement was not terribly original—Charles Krug had used the idea in a 1965 advertisement that began, "Not Enough Charles Krug Wines."

17. Knowles, "Beaulieu Vineyards," p. 61.

18. Peterson, self-interview, in *HNV*, 2:178.

19. Knowles, "Beaulieu Vineyards," p. 44.

20. "California Wine: Everybody Wants In," *Forbes*, December 1, 1968, p. 77.

21. Tchelistcheff, *Grapes, Wine and Ecology*, p. 122.

22. Estimated growth is from Robert Mondavi, *Creativity in the California Wine Industry* (BL), p. 30; case-sales figures for 1968 are from the *Gomberg Report*.

23. "Successful Year Reported at Winery Directors' Meet," *St. Helena Star*, August 20, 1943, p. 1.

24. Such a scenario would fit the industry average, which saw bulk wine shipments out of California fall by at least 50 percent, but in the case of Krug, it is, of course, pure conjecture.

25. See full-page advertisement, "One of the Great Names in Table Wine," *Wines and Vines*, December 1944, p. 32, and "For Those Who Put Quality above Price," ibid., April 1946, p. 95.

26. "C. Mondavi and Sons Announce Expansion," *St. Helena Star*, May 3, 1946, p. 1. Similar articles appeared in the May 1946 editions of *Wine Review*, under the heading "Mondavi Reorganizes Firm," and *Wines and Vines*, under the title "Mondavi Sales Program."

27. Robert Mondavi, *Creativity*, p. 26. In his oral history, Robert Mondavi says that the McKesson & Robbins contract was signed in 1946. This may be correct, but the contract was not announced to the industry until July 1947, so Mondavi may be incorrect in his dates. See "McKesson to Distribute Krug Wines," *Wines and Vines*, July 1947, p. 40, and "Krug Distributor Named," *Wine Review*, July 1947, p. 26. The latter article comments that the announcement was made "at a general sales meeting and picnic luncheon held late in June at the Krug winery estates."

28. The Napa co-op's minutes show that it had sold 120,000 gallons of wine to the Mondavis in 1948 on a consignment basis in which the co-op's price depended upon the sale price. Apparently, most of the wine was sold in bulk. See minute books, September 10, 1948, p. 29; April 6, 1949, p. 71; and August 12, 1949, p. 95.

29. The 75 percent estimate comes from Peter Mondavi.

30. See "California Wine: Everybody Wants In," *Forbes*, December 7, 1968, p. 73, for information on Almaden, and Knowles, "Beaulieu Vineyards," p. 53 for more on Beaulieu.

31. Using the Gomberg data for *dry* wine only, the 1968 sales of the four wineries were: Almaden, 1.2 million cases; C. Mondavi and Sons, 1 million cases; Paul Masson, .86 million cases; and Christian Brothers, .56 million cases. Almaden, with cash infused by its new owners, National Distillers, quickly pulled away from the others in the 1970s.

32. Robert Mondavi, *Creativity*, p. 19.

33. See "Who's Who at the Winery," *Bottles and Bins*, January 1950, p. 3, and Robert Mondavi, *Creativity*, p. 36.

34. Details on technological development in the 1940s and 1950s are covered in chapter 9. The tiny Hanzell winery in Sonoma is generally credited with the first use of French oak in the late 1950s (Irving Marcus, "The Ambassador's Winery," *Wines and Vines*, January 1960, pp. 16–18). In his interview with Ruth Teiser, *Advances in Technology and Production at Charles Krug Winery, 1946–1988* (BL), p. 20, Peter Mondavi recalled importing French barrels in 1963, after having tasted the Hanzell wines, while Robert Mondavi claimed the impetus came from his trip to France in 1962 (Robert Mondavi, *Creativity*, pp. 23–25). "Things Are Moving at Charles Krug," *Wines and Vines*, October 1966, p. 16, noted that the winery had recently imported 540 French oak barrels.

35. See "A Trademark Dedicated to High Quality Wine" (advertisement), *Wines and Vines*, November 1956, p. 28. The Mondavis joined other premium producers in boycotting the judging at the State Fair, and 1956 was the last year they entered the competition. See "Wine Judging," *Bottles and Bins*, October 1957, p. 1, and "Till Arguments Do Us Part" (editorial), *Wines and Vines*, March 1958, p. 4.

36. "Something New," *Bottles and Bins*, January 1956, p. 4.

37. Robert Mondavis recalled going "out to wholesalers in San Francisco, trying to get them to handle our wine. Nobody wanted it because it was an unknown entity." Robert Mondavi, *Creativity*, p. 27.

38. Peter Mondavi, *Advances in Technology and Production*, p. 26. See also "Years of Progress," *Bottles and Bins*, January 1960, p. 3.

39. See Robert Mondavi, *Creativity*, p. 27.

40. "We felt that wine was a living thing and we had to personalize it," Robert Mondavi said (ibid., p. 26).

41. "Visitors Welcome," *Bottles and Bins*, July 1950, p. 1. See also Gould's historical review, "Years of Progress," ibid., January 1960.

42. There is the classic philosophical problem of disproving a negative. I cannot "prove" that other wineries in the Napa Valley did not provide regular tours earlier than did Krug. However, the Krug program of tours was the first of its kind to my knowledge.

43. To my knowledge, *Bottles and Bins* was the first. Almaden followed it with *News from the Vineyard*, written by Frank Schoonmaker, sometime in the 1950s.

44. I had the pleasure of knowing the printer James Beard, and of his love for the *New Yorker*. The walls in the lavatory off of his print room were papered in old *New Yorker* covers. His use of a typeface and layout similar to that of the *New Yorker* was, I'm sure, deliberate and yet another example of his deep understanding of the power of design. It was Beard who arranged for Malette Dean to design the Krug label and the *Bottles and Bins* logo.

45. [Francis Gould], "Going on Four," *Bottles and Bins*, July 1952, p. 1.

46. Ibid.

47. By the second year, Gould had begun a quarterly recipe contest, with winning recipes printed in *Bottles and Bins*. In 1965, the Mondavis collected the recipes and published them, selling 2,000 copies of the resulting book before publication. See "Book Review," *Wines and Vines*, July 1965, p. 10.

48. "Tastings," *Bottles and Bins*, April 1954, p. 1.

49. *Bottles and Bins*, January 1961, p. 4.

50. *Bottles and Bins*, April 1959, p. 4.

51. "Around Home Plate," *Bottles and Bins*, April 1961, p. 1.

52. See "Establish Wine Firm," *Wines and Vines*, March 1956, p. 11.

53. "Years of Progress," *Bottles and Bins*, January 1960, p. 3.

54. "Not Enough Charles Krug Wines," *Wines and Vines*, November 1965, p. 43. This ran a full year before the Beaulieu advertisement discussed above.

55. This is Robert Mondavi's estimate and seems consistent with existing sales data; indeed, it is perhaps conservative. See Robert Mondavi, *Creativity*, p. 30.

56. Ibid., p. 22.

57. Ibid.

58. The above paragraph is based on Robert Mondavi's oral history, *Creativity*, pp. 36–37. See also "Changes in Mondavi Set-Up," *Wines and Vines*, April 1966, p. 9.

11. Harvest

1. Leon Adams, "Who Caused the Wine Revolution?" *Wines and Vines*, February 1979, p. 38.

2. "Adult per Capita Consumption of Specified Beverages in the United States, 1971–1980," *Wines and Vines*, July 1981, p. 42. Tracing per capita consumption is confusing, since different sources used different definitions of wine. The figures are for all "wine" under 14 percent alcohol, thereby excluding dessert wine. Louis Gomberg generally then tried to determine what percentage of this was accounted for by the new "special natural" wines such as Ripple and Boone's Farm. The figures cited include such wines.

3. "The Major Continued Trend: Market Expansion," *Wines and Vines*, July 1981, p. 34.

4. In "A Possible Solution to Supply-Demand Imbalance," *Wines and Vines*,

January 1975, p. 34, Louis Gomberg estimated that 212,361 acres were planted to wine grapes in California in 1970–74. Kirby Moulton, the University of California's grape and wine economist, tracked plantings each year, and his total comes to a bit below 200,000 acres. The increase in bearing acreage is not really in doubt, but involves subtraction as well as addition, since old acreage was pulled out. By 1980, California had just over 290,000 acres of bearing wine grapes, a major increase from the 125,000 acres in 1967. See *Wines and Vines*, May 1976, p. 46, and ibid., July 1981, p. 55.

5. For 1967 figures, see *Wines and Vines*, April 1968, p. 22. The 1980 figures can be found in ibid., July 1981, p. 44.

6. "American Wine Comes of Age," *Time*, November 27, 1972, p. 76.

7. Ibid.

8. The tripling of income is cited in Harvey Levenstein's *Paradox of Plenty: A Social History of Eating in Modern America* (New York: Oxford University Press, 1993), p. 218. It might be argued that part of the increase was owing to inflation, which began in 1965 when Lyndon Johnson attempted to give the United States both guns and butter without raising taxes, but since inflation is estimated to have tripled prices between 1965 and 1982 (see Sidney Ratner, James Soltow, and Richard Sylla, *The Evolution of the American Economy* [New York: Macmillan, 1993], p. 538), it cannot have been the primary cause of the major increase in discretionary income between 1950 and 1970.

9. Leon Ullensvang, "Food Consumption Patterns in the Seventies: The Dimensions of Change," *Vital Speeches of the Day*, February 1, 1970, p. 241.

10. Ibid., p. 243.

11. Maxine Margolis, *Mothers and Such: Views of American Women and Why They Changed* (Berkeley: University of California Press, 1984), p. 225, as cited in Levenstein *Paradox of Plenty*, p. 225.

12. Ullensvang, "Food Consumption Patterns in the Seventies," p. 241.

13. California Wine Advisory Board, *Adventures in Wine Cookery* (San Francisco: California Wine Advisory Board, 1965), pp. 4, 118.

14. Arthur D. Little, Inc., *Wine/America*, vol. 3: *Wine and the Consumer* (Arthur D. Little, Inc., 1972), p. 5.

15. "Coke's View: Things Go Better with Wine," *Wines and Vines*, September 1977, p. 40.

16. Arthur D. Little, Inc., *Wine/America*, vol. 3: *Wine and the Consumer*, p. 50.

17. Ibid., p. 5, and Arthur D. Little, Inc., *Wine/America*, vol. 1: *The U.S. Wine Market*, p. 30.

18. Alfred Fromm, "An Expert Evaluates the Industry," *Wines and Vines*, November 1981, p. 28.

19. R. R. Cant as quoted in "What Does the American Consumer Want?" *Wines and Vines*, September 1974, pp. 56, 57.

20. Arthur D. Little, Inc., *Wine/America*, vol. 3: *Wine and the Consumer*, p. 18.

21. Ibid., pp. 7–9.

22. "The First Color Breakdown of Table Wine Marketings," *Wines and Vines*, December 1979, p. 28.

23. Used to the hard knuckles campaigning of the soft drink industry, Coca-Cola was surprised to find that the Bureau of Alcohol, Tobacco and Firearms did not allow the use of direct brand comparisons in advertisement. After threatening to pursue a legal challenge based on the First Amendment, Coca-Cola backed down.

24. "Selling It Like It Is," *Wines and Vines*, September 1972, p. 23.

25. "A Wineman Tells It Like the Market Is," *Wines and Vines*, March 1971, p. 19.

26. "1980 Market: 490 Million Gals.?" *Wines and Vines*, November 1972, p. 18. The Wells Fargo economists deserve a prize: per capita consumption reached 3.2 gallons, and total sales in 1980 totaled just under 480 million gallons. Again, this estimate is for *all* wines.

27. "1974 Forecast: 380 Million Gals.," *Wines and Vines*, January 1974, p. 17.

28. See "The Grapes of Wrath," *Dun's Review*, July 1972, pp. 35–37, 82, for a less-than-sanguine view of vineyard syndications. In the early 1970s, federal tax regulations allowed an almost complete expensing of vineyard development costs against other earned income. After the tax code change, these expenses were amortized across the expected life of the vineyard, generally thirty years.

29. Louis Gomberg, "The Five-Faced Winery Picture," *Wines and Vines*, September 1980, p. 43.

30. There is no exact record of new wineries. According to data reported in *Wines and Vines*, California had 231 bonded wineries in 1967 and 470 in 1980. Yet the difference of 239 is probably somewhat less than the total of new wineries established, since some both began and ended business during this period, while other older wineries included in the 231 closed their doors.

31. Napa County Agricultural Commissioner, *Annual Report*, 1967 and 1980. The gross value of grapes in 1967 was 5.8 million; by 1980 it was 49.8 million.

32. "Judgment of Paris," *Time*, June 7, 1976.

33. Although the Napa notice of intent was the first received by the BATF, the BATF chose to hold the Napa hearings second, on the rationale that Napa's formal petition was received after the filing of a formal petition by a group of growers in the Augusta area of Missouri. It was generally assumed that the BATF had decided to use the Missouri hearings as a test case, where fewer individuals were involved and less money was at stake in the outcome. See "Napa Hearing in March," *Wines and Vines*, December 1979, p. 18.

34. Rex Davis, "New ATF Proposals for 'Seal' Wine; Appellations," *Wines and Vines*, December 1976, p. 25.

35. Ibid.

36. Ibid., p. 26.

37. August Sebastiani as quoted in *Wines and Vines*, January 1977, p. 16.

38. "The BATF Hearings: No Meeting of the Minds . . . Yet," *Wines and Vines*, March 1977, pp. 20–23.

39. A detailed discussion of the 1978 regulations can be found in James Seff and John Cooney, "The Legal and Political History of California Wine," in *The University of California / Sotheby Book of California Wine*, ed. Doris Muscatine, M. A. Amerine, and Bob Thompson (Berkeley: University of California Press; London: Sotheby Publications, 1984), pp. 412–46.

40. *Wines and Vines*, March 1979, p. 22.

41. "The BATF Hearings: No Meeting of the Minds . . . Yet," *Wines and Vines*, March 1977, p. 23.

42. "Napa Valley Appellation Hearings before the Bureau of Alcohol, Tobacco and Firearms," April 28, 1980, p. 60.

43. John Gay, "Napa Valley Appellation Hearings before the Bureau of Alcohol, Tobacco and Firearms," April 28, 1980, p. 58.

44. Howard Thompson, "Napa Valley Hearings before the Bureau of Alcohol, Tobacco and Firearms," April 29, 1980, p. 25.

45. Robert Mondavi, "Napa Valley Appellation Hearings before the Bureau of Alcohol, Tobacco and Firearms," April 28, 1980, p. 42.

46. Stephen Higgins, "Napa Valley Hearings before the Bureau of Alcohol, Tobacco and Firearms," April 29, 1980, p. 70.

47. "Napa Valley Viticultural Area," Bureau of Alcohol, Tobacco and Firearms, 27, CFR, Part 9, p. 2.

48. Robert Louis Stevenson, "Napa Wines," in *The Silverado Squatters,* (1883; Lewis Osborne: Ashland, Ore., 1972), pp. 23–24.

49. "Mondavi, Rothschild Join in New Wine Venture." *Wines and Vines*, May 1980, p. 16.

Select Bibliography

Bottled Poetry draws primarily on three types of sources: serial publications, oral histories, and archival materials, such as minute books and Bureau of Alcohol, Tobacco and Firearms records. Of these, serial publications have perhaps been the most important, giving continuity to the roughly half a century covered. The three major serials are not listed in the bibliography by author or article citation, since they have been fully referenced in the notes; however their importance should be acknowledged.

Wines and Vines, a monthly magazine that bills itself as "the authoritative voice of the grape and wine industry since 1919," provides an excellent overview of industry trends and concerns. Generally the May or April issue was devoted to an annual review of industry statistics, and the industry news section in each issue allows the historian to track wine and grape prices and to follow the actions of industrywide trade associations. The *Wine Review*, which began publication in 1933, just prior to Repeal, was a serious competitor to *Wines and Vines* until 1950, when it combined with *Wines and Vines*. The third serial publication is the *St. Helena Star*, a local newspaper published each Friday in St. Helena. Available on microfilm, the *Star* is an especially fruitful source for the decade of the 1930s as the Napa Valley wine industry reemerged from Prohibition.

Oral histories proved a second and invaluable source of information on Napa winemaking and grape growing. Any historian of California winemaking owes a tremendous debt to Ruth Teiser and her colleagues at the Regional Oral History Office at the Bancroft Library at the University of California at Berkeley. These histories, presently funded by M. Shanken Communications, not only capture the recollections of a now departed generation of winemakers, they benefit from Teiser's intimate knowledge of the California industry and her resulting ability to structure the interview by asking penetrating questions. A second set of shorter, but valuable, oral histories have been recorded by the Napa Valley Wine Library Association and are contained in four volumes published by that group.

Archival material represents a third source of information on the California wine industry. Of the various archival materials reviewed, probably the Bureau of Alcohol, Tobacco and Firearms records of inactive wineries have the broadest potential for other researchers. Held by the Shields Library of the University of California at Davis, these records of several hundred defunct wineries from the 1930s and 1940s provide an uneven but rich source of specific detail, generally from the viewpoint of the government regulators.

Archival Material

Bureau of Alcohol, Tobacco and Firearms Collection, Special Collections, Shields Library, University of California at Davis

Bartolucci, Andrea, 1934–42, box 100
Beaulieu, 1920–31, box 047
Beringer Brothers, 1933–34, box 084
Bicceglia Brothers, 1935–39, box 099
California Wine Association, 1921–25, box 023
Churchill, M., 1933–35, box 110
Covick, 1922–40, box 064
Cresta Blanca, 1942–50, box 104
Fawver, 1920–24, box 009
Gagetta, 1933–41, box 038
Garetto, J., 1935–39, box 127
Italian Swiss Colony, 1948, box 041
Larkmead Vineyards, 1941–48, box 115
Lombarda, 1930–42, box 121
Madonna Winery, 1941–45, box 018
Martini, L., 1931–47, box 048
Mont Helena Calistoga Wine Company, 1933–35, boxes 035 and 044
Mont La Salle Vineyard, 1926–50, box 033
Montelena, 1934–37, boxes 035 and 117
Mount Eden, 1922–43, box 118
Napa Valley Grape Products, 1943–48, box 089
Oakville Winery, 1936–48, box 017
Prosperity, 1942–46, box 050
Salmina, 1922–41, box 059
Sunny Hill, 1934–39, box 066
Sunny St. Helena Wine Company, 1939–43, box 069
Sunny St. Helena, 1937–46, box 066
Tubbs, 1936–48, box 001
Tubbs, Merrit Reid, 1921–49, box 067

Materials held by Gomberg & Fredrikson, San Francisco

Gomberg, Louis, R. *The Gomberg Report*. San Francisco: L. Gomberg, various dates, 1949–65.

Premium Wine Producers of California [later Academy of Master Wine Grow-
    ers], minutes, taken and reproduced by Louis Gomberg, 1955–65.

Materials held by Napa Cooperative Winery, St. Helena

Napa Valley Cooperative Winery minutes, 1934–65.

Materials held by the Napa Valley Vintners' Association, St. Helena

Napa Valley Vintners' Association minutes, 1949–65.

*Materials in the library of the Bureau of Alcohol, Tobacco
and Firearms, Washington, D.C.*

"Napa Valley Hearings before the Bureau of Alcohol, Tobacco and Firearms in
    the Matter of Proposed Regulatory Definitions of Appellation of Origin."
    Monday, April 28, 1980, and Tuesday, April 29, 1980. Napa.

Printed Material

Abruzzini, Fred. Interview by Charles Carpy. June 20, 1978. In *History of Napa
    Valley: Interviews and Reminiscences of Long-Time Residents*, vol. 3. St. Helena:
    Napa Valley Wine Library Association, 1981.
Adams, Leon D. *The Wines of America*. Boston: Houghton Mifflin, 1973. 3d ed.
    New York: McGraw-Hill, 1985.
———. *California Wine Industry Affairs: Recollections and Opinions*. Interview
    by Ruth Teiser. 1986. Berkeley: Regional Oral History Office, Bancroft
    Library, University of California, 1990.
Amerine, Maynard A. "An Introduction to the Pre-Repeal History of Grapes
    and Wines in California." Paper presented at the second annual meeting of
    Library Associates, University Library, University of California, Davis, 1969.
———. *The University of California and the State's Wine Industry*. Interview by
    Ruth Teiser. Berkeley: University of California, Bancroft Library, Regional
    Oral History Office, 1972.
———. Interview by Robert Travers. July 9, 1983. In *History of Napa Valley:
    Interviews and Reminiscences of Long-Time Residents*, vol. 4. St. Helena: Napa
    Valley Wine Library Association, 1985.
Amerine, Maynard A., and Maynard A. Joslyn. *Commercial Production of
    Table Wines*. Berkeley: California Agricultural Experiment Station, College
    of Agriculture, University of California, 1940.
———. *Table Wines: The Technology of Their Production*. Berkeley: University of
    California Press, 1951.
Amerine, Maynard A., and H. Phaff. *A Bibliography of Publications by the Fac-
    ulty, Staff, and Students of the University of California, 1876–1980, on Grapes,
    Wines, and Related Subjects*. Berkeley: University of California Press, 1986.
Amerine, Maynard A., and Vernon L. Singleton. *Wine: An Introduction*. 2d ed.
    Berkeley: University of California Press, 1972.

Amerine, Maynard A., and A. J. Winkler. *Composition and Quality of Musts and Wines of California Grapes*. Berkeley: University of California, 1944. *Hilgardia* 15, no. 6.

Arthur D. Little, Inc. *Wine/America*. 3 vols. Privately printed. Arthur D. Little, Inc., 1972.

Balzer, Robert L. *California's Best Wines*. Los Angeles: Ward Ritchie Press, 1948.

Bancroft Library. Regional Oral History Office. *California Wine Greats: Pioneers in Building the Wine Industry of California*. California Wine Oral History Project. New York: M. Shanken Communications, 1984.

———. *California Wine Pioneers: Profiles of the State's Wine Industry Leaders*. San Diego: M. Shanken Communications, 1991.

Bank of America. *California Wine Outlook: An Economic Study Prepared by Bank of America*. San Francisco: Bank of America, 1973.

Bank of America National Trust and Savings Association. *Outlook for the California Wine Industry*. San Francisco: Bank of America, 1970.

Bartolucci, Louis. Interview by Gunther R. Detert. August 1980. In *History of Napa Valley: Interviews and Reminiscences of Long-Time Residents*, vol. 3. St. Helena: Napa Valley Wine Library Association, 1981.

Benson, Robert. *Great Winemakers of California: Conversations with Robert Benson*. Santa Barbara: Capra Press, 1977.

Bentley, Iris. *Wine with a Merry Heart*. New York: Comet Press Books, 1959.

Biane, Philo. *Wine Making in Southern California and Recollections of Fruit Industries, Ltd*. Interview by Ruth Teiser. Berkeley: Regents of the University of California, 1972.

Bioletti, Frederic T. *A New Method of Making Dry Red Wine*. Berkeley: Agricultural Experiment Station, 1906.

———. *Grape Culture in California: Its Difficulties, Phylloxera and Resistant Vines, Other Vine Diseases; Improved Methods of Wine Making*. Berkeley: Agricultural Experiment Station, 1908.

———. *The Principles of Wine-Making*. Berkeley: University of California Agricultural Experiment Station, 1911. Bulletin 213.

Blout, Jessie S. *A Brief Economic History of the California Wine-Growing Industry*. San Francisco: Bureau of Markets, California Department of Agriculture, 1943.

California. Agricultural Experiment Station. *Reports of Experiments on Methods of Fermentation and Related Subjects During the Years 1886–87*. Sacramento: J. D. Young, supt. state printing, 1888.

———. Board of State Viticultural Commissioners. *Statements and Extracts from Reports of the Board of Viticultural Commissioners, Prepared Specially for Distribution at the New Orleans World's Fair, A.D. 1885*. Sacramento: J. J. Ayres, supt. state printing, 1885.

———. California Journal of Development. *California — Wine Land of America*. San Francisco: California State Chamber of Commerce, 1935.

———. State Board of Public Health. Bureau of Food and Drug Inspection. *Regulations Establishing Standards of Identity, Quality, Purity and Sanitation, and Governing the Labeling and Advertising of Wine in the State of California*. Sacramento: California State Printing Office, 1942.

————. Wine Advisory Board. *The Wine Guide*. [Sacramento?]: Wine Advisory Board, [1948?].

————. *Wines and Wine Serving*. [Sacramento?]: Wine Advisory Board, [1948?].

"California Wine: Everybody Wants In." *Forbes*, December 1, 1968, pp. 70–77.

"Campaign to Create Connoisseurs." *Business Week*, August 10, 1963, pp. 82–83, 86.

Carosso, Vincent Phillip. *The California Wine Industry, 1830–1895: A Study of the Formative Years*. Berkeley: University of California Press, 1951.

Cella, John B. *The Cella Family in the California Wine Industry*. Interview by Ruth Teiser. 1984. Berkeley: Regional Oral History Office, Bancroft Library, University of California, 1986.

Colburn, Frona Eunice Wait (Smith). *Wines & Vines of California: A Treatise on the Ethics of Wine-Drinking*. San Francisco: Bancroft Company, 1889.

Conaway, James. *Napa*. Boston: Houghton Mifflin, 1990.

Cook, James A., and Thomas Kishaba. "Nitrogen Fertilization of Unirrigated Vineyards in the North Coastal Areas of California." *American Journal of Enology* 8, 3 (1957): 105–12.

Crahan, Marcus E. *California and Its Place among the Wine Nations: A Talk Given before the Los Angeles Westerners, August 20, 1948*. Los Angeles: H. H. Boelter, 1949.

Crawford, Charles M. *Recollections of a Career with the Gallo Winery and the Development of the California Wine Industry, 1942–1989*. Interview by Ruth Teiser. 1989. Berkeley: Regional Oral History Office, Bancroft Library, University of California, 1990.

Critchfield, Burke H. *The California Wine Industry during the Depression*. Interview by Ruth Teiser. Berkeley: Regional Oral History Office, Bancroft Library, University of California, 1972.

Cruess, William V. *A Half Century in Food and Wine Technology*. Interview by Ruth Teiser. Berkeley: Regional Oral History Office, Bancroft Library, University of California, 1967.

Daniel, John, Jr. "Notes on the History of Napa County Viticulture and Winemaking." Recording, November 23, 1969. In *History of Napa Valley: Interviews and Reminiscences of Long-Time Residents*, vol. 1. St. Helena: Napa Valley Wine Library Association, 1974.

Davies, Jack L., and Jamie Peterman. *Rebuilding Schramsberg: The Creation of a California Champagne House*. Interview by Ruth Teiser and Lisa Jacobson. 1989. Berkeley: Regional Oral History Office, Bancroft Library, University of California, 1990.

Detert, Gunther. "Historical Materials on Far Niente." In *History of Napa Valley: Interviews and Reminiscences of Long-Time Residents*, vol. 4. St. Helena: Napa Valley Wine Library Association, 1985.

Deuer, George. Interview by Bernard Skoda. June 19, 1974. In *History of Napa Valley: Interviews and Reminiscences of Long-Time Residents*, vol. 2. St. Helena: Napa Valley Wine Library Association, 1979.

Dieppe, William A. *Almaden Is My Life*. Interview by Ruth Teiser. Berkeley: Regional Oral History Office, Bancroft Library, University of California, 1985.

Draper, Jerome C. Interview by Gunther R. Detert. May 15, 1976. In *History of Napa Valley: Interviews and Reminiscences of Long-Time Residents*, vol. 2. St. Helena: Napa Valley Wine Library Association, 1979.

Farrell, Kenneth R. *Statistics Relating to the California Grape and Wine Industries*. Berkeley: University of California, 1961.

———. *The California Wine Industry: Trends and Prospects*. 1966.

Fisher, M. F. K. *The Story of Wine in California*. Berkeley: University of California Press, 1962.

Fluharty, L. W. *Standard Grape Costs*. Pamphlet. Berkeley: University of California Extension Service, 1939.

Forni, Charles. Interview by Elizabeth Martini. March 1974. In *History of Napa Valley: Interviews and Reminiscences of Long-Time Residents*, vol. 2. St. Helena: Napa Valley Wine Library Association, 1979.

Fromm, Alfred. *Marketing California Wine and Brandy*. Interview by Ruth Teiser. 1984. Berkeley: Regional Oral History Office, Bancroft Library, University of California, 1984.

"Golden Grape." *Newsweek*, December 18, 1967, p. 113.

Gomberg, Louis R. *California Prestige Wines Study Report*. San Francisco: Producers of California Prestige Wines, 1955.

———. *Analytical Perspectives on the California Wine Industry, 1935–1990*. Interview by Ruth Teiser. 1990. Berkeley: Regional Oral History Office, Bancroft Library, University of California, 1990.

Grgich, Miljenko. *A Croatian-American Winemaker in the Napa Valley*. Interviews by Ruth Teiser. 1992. Berkeley: Regional Oral History Office, Bancroft Library, University of California, 1992.

Haraszthy, Agoston. "Report on Grapes and Wine of California." In *Transactions of the California State Agricultural Society, 1858*, pp. 311–29. Sacramento: State Printer, 1859.

———. *Grape Culture, Wines, and Wine-Making: With Notes upon Agriculture and Horticulture*. New York: Harper & Brothers, 1862.

Haraszthy, Arpad. *Wine-Making in California*. 1871–72. San Francisco: Book Club of California, 1978.

Heintz, William F. *Wine Country: An History of Napa Valley: The Early Years, 1838–1920*. Santa Barbara: Capra Press, 1990.

Heitz, Joseph E. Interview by T. E. Wilde. June 19, 1980. In *History of Napa Valley: Interviews and Reminiscences of Long-Time Residents*, vol. 3. St. Helena: Napa Valley Wine Library Association, 1981.

———. *Creating a Winery in the Napa Valley*. Interview by Ruth Teiser. 1985. Berkeley: Regional Oral History Office, Bancroft Library, University of California, 1986.

Hilgard, Eugene W. *Report of the Viticultural Work during the Seasons 1883–4 and 1884–5, Being Appendix no. iv to the Report for the Year 1884. With Notes regarding the Vintage of 1885–6*. Sacramento: J. J. Ayres, supt. state printing, 1886.

———. *Reports of Experiments on Methods of Fermentation and Related Subjects during the Years 1886–87*. Sacramento: J. D. Young, supt. state printing, 1888.

Husmann, George. *Grape Culture and Wine-Making in California: A Practical*

Manual for the Grape-Grower and Wine-Maker. San Francisco: Payot, Upham, 1888.

Jones, Idwal. *Vines in the Sun: A Journey through the California Vineyards*. New York: Ballantine Books, 1949.

Jordan, Rudolf. *Quality in Dry Wines through Adequate Fermentations by Means of Defecation, Aeration, Pure Yeast, Cooling and Heating: A Manual for Progressive Winemakers in California*. San Francisco: Pernau Publishing, 1911.

Joslyn, Maynard Alexander. *Maynard A. Joslyn: A Technologist Views the California Wine Industry*. Interview by Ruth Teiser. Berkeley: Regional Oral History Office, Bancroft Library, University of California, 1974.

Kasimatis, Amand N. *A Career in California Viticulture*. Interview by Ruth Teiser. 1987. Berkeley: Regional Oral History Office, Bancroft Library, University of California, 1988.

Katz, Morris. *Paul Masson Winery Operations and Management, 1944–1988*. Interview by Ruth Teiser. 1990. Berkeley: Regional Oral History Office, Bancroft Library, University of California, 1990.

Knowles, Legh F. *Beaulieu Vineyards from Family to Corporate Ownership*. Interview by Lisa Jacobson. 1989. Berkeley: Regional Oral History Office, Bancroft Library, University of California, 1990.

Landfield, Jerome. *California—America's Vineyard*. San Francisco: Verdier Cellars, 1949.

Lanza, Horace O. *California Grape Products and Other Wine Enterprises*. Interview by Ruth Teiser. Berkeley: Regional Oral History Office, Bancroft Library, University of California, 1971.

Larsen, John W. *Vineyard Development Financing in California*. San Francisco: Wells Fargo Bank, 1972.

Leggett, Herbert Boynton. *Early History of Wine Production in California*. San Francisco: Wine Institute, 1941.

Levenstein, Harvey. *Paradox of Plenty: A Social History of Eating in Modern America*. New York: Oxford University Press, 1993.

Lider, James V. "Observations on Problems in North Coast Vineyards." *American Journal of Enology* 6, 1 (1955): 35–36.

————. *Sample Costs of Establishing a Vineyard of Standard Head Pruned Wine Varieties in the North Coast Counties, 1960*. Berkeley: Agricultural Extension Service, 1960.

Lider, Lloyd A. "Phylloxera-Resistant Rootstock Trials in the Coastal Valleys of California." *American Journal of Enology* 8, 2 (1957): 58–67.

————. "A Grape Rootstock Trail in the Napa Valley: A Nine-Year Progress Report of Three Stocks on Bale Loam Soil." *American Journal of Enology* 8, 3 (1957): 121–26.

Louis M. Martini Corp. *The Louis M. Martini Winery, St.Helena, Napa Valley, California, 1933–1983*. St. Helena: Louis M. Martini Corp., 1982.

"Lure of the Grape." *Newsweek*, January 24, 1955, pp. 96, 98–99.

Maher, Richard L. *California Winery Management and Marketing*. Interviews by Ruth Teiser. 1990–91. Berkeley: Regional Oral History Office, Bancroft Library, University of California, 1992.

Martini, Louis M., and Louis P. Martini. *Wine Making in the Napa Valley*.

Interviews by Lois Stone and Ruth Teiser. Berkeley: Regional Oral History Office, Bancroft Library, University of California, 1973.

Martini, Louis P. *A Family Winery and the California Wine Industry*. Interviews by Ruth Teiser. 1983–84. Berkeley: Regional Oral History Office, Bancroft Library, University of California, 1984.

Marvel, Tom. "The Great New Wine-Finds." *Vogue*, June 1958, pp. 136, 139.

McCrea, Eleanor. *Eleanor McCrea: Stony Hill Vineyards: The Creation of a Napa Valley Estate Winery*. Interview by Lisa Jacobson. 1990. Berkeley: Regional Oral History Office, Bancroft Library, University of California, 1990.

Melville, John. *Guide to California Wines*. Garden City, N.Y.: Doubleday, 1955.

Meyer, Otto E. *California Premium Wines and Brandies*. Interview by Ruth Teiser. Berkeley: Regional Oral History Office, Bancroft Library, University of California, 1973.

Mondavi, Peter. *Advances in Technology and Production at Charles Krug Winery, 1946–1988*. Interview by Ruth Teiser. 1988. Berkeley: Regional Oral History Office, Bancroft Library, University of California, 1990.

Mondavi, Robert. Interview by Ina Hart and T. E. Wilde. December 29, 1978. In *History of Napa Valley: Interviews and Reminiscences of Long-Time Residents*, vol. 3. St. Helena: Napa Valley Wine Library Association, 1981.

————. *Creativity in the California Wine Industry*. Interview by Ruth Teiser. 1984. Berkeley: Regional Oral History Office, Bancroft Library, University of California, 1985.

Moone, E. Michael. *Managing and Marketing at Beringer Vineyards and Wine World, Inc.* Interview by Lisa Jacobson. 1989. Berkeley: Regional Oral History Office, Bancroft Library, University of California, 1990.

Moulton, Kirby S., ed. *The Economics of Small Wineries: The Proceedings of Two Seminars at University of California, Davis, May 1979 and May 1980*. Berkeley: Cooperative Extension, University of California, 1981.

Muscatine, Doris, M. A. Amerine, and Bob Thompson, eds. *The University of California / Sotheby Book of California Wine*. Berkeley: University of California Press; London: Sotheby Publications, 1984.

Napa County Agricultural Commissioner. *Annual Report*. Napa: Napa County Agricultural Commissioner, 1922–82.

Nightingale, Myron S. *Making Wine in California, 1944–1987*. Interview by Ruth Teiser and Lisa Jacobson. 1987. Berkeley: Regional Oral History Office, Bancroft Library, University of California, 1988.

Olmo, Harold P. "Our Principal Wine Grape Varieties Present and Future." *American Journal of Enology* 5, 1 (1954): 18–20.

Ough, Cornelius. *Researches of an Enologist, University of California, Davis, 1950–1990*. Interviews by Ruth Teiser. 1989, 1990. Berkeley: Regional Oral History Office, Bancroft Library, University of California, 1990.

Parker, Tom. *Inglenook Vineyards: 100 Years of Fine Winemaking*. Rutherford, Calif.: Inglenook Vineyards, 1979.

Pellegrini, Angelo M. *Americans by Choice*. New York: Macmillan, 1956.

Perelli-Minetti, Antonio. *A Life in Wine Making*. Interview by Ruth Teiser. 1969. Berkeley: Regional Oral History Office, Bancroft Library, University of California, 1975.

Peterson, Dr. Richard G. Self-Interview. February 1976. In *History of Napa Valley: Interviews and Reminiscences of Long-Time Residents*, vol. 2. St. Helena: Napa Valley Wine Library Association, 1979.

Petri, Louis A. *The Petri Family in the Wine Industry*. Interview by Ruth Teiser. Berkeley: Regional Oral History Office, Bancroft Library, University of California, 1971.

Peyser, Jefferson E. *The Law and the California Wine Industry*. Interview by Ruth Teiser. Berkeley: Regional Oral History Office, Bancroft Library, University of California, 1974.

Priber, E. C. *The Vineyards in Napa County; Being the Report of E. C. Priber, Commissioner for the Napa District*. Board of State Viticultural Commissioners. Sacramento: A. J. Johnston, supt. state printing, 1893.

Ratner, Sidney, James Soltow, and Richard Sylla. *The Evolution of the American Economy*. New York: Macmillan, 1993.

Raymond, Roy, Sr. Interview by Robert Trinchero. In *History of Napa Valley: Interviews and Reminiscences of Long-Time Residents*, vol. 1. St. Helena: Napa Valley Wine Library Association, 1974.

Rossi, Edmund A., Jr. *Italian Swiss Colony and the Wine Industry*. Interview by Ruth Teiser. Berkeley: Regional Oral History Office, Bancroft Library, University of California, 1971.

————. *Italian Swiss Colony, 1949–1989: Recollections of a Third-Generation California Winemaker*. Interviews by Ruth Teiser and Lisa Jacobson. 1988–89. Berkeley: Regional Oral History Office, Bancroft Library, University of California, 1990.

Schmidt, Arthur H. "Sunny St. Helena Winery." In *History of Napa Valley: Interviews and Reminiscences of Long-Time Residents*, vol. 2. St. Helena: Napa Valley Wine Library Association, 1979.

————. Interview by Gunther R. Detert. March 21, 1981. In *History of Napa Valley: Interviews and Reminiscences of Long-Time Residents*, vol. 3. St. Helena: Napa Valley Wine Library Association, 1981.

Schoch, Ivan. "Varietal Vineyard Management." *American Journal of Enology* 6, 1 (1955): 40–43.

Schoonmaker, Frank. "California's Vintage Vale." *Holiday*, August 1952, pp. 103–7.

————. "American Wines." *Holiday*, September 1958, pp. 109–12.

Schoonmaker, Frank, and Tom Marvel. *The Complete Wine Book*. New York: Duell, Sloan & Pearce, 1934.

Seghesio, Eugene P. "Grape Growing in Sonoma County." *American Journal of Enology* 7, 1 (1956): 77–78.

Shear, Sherwood W. *California Grape Acreage, Production, Yields, and Acreage per Farm, 1930, by Varieties, Counties, and Districts: A Statistical Summary by S. W. Shear, August, 1932, Based upon Data from a Survey by the California Grape Control Board*. Berkeley: University of California Extension Service, 1932.

————. *Supply and Price Trends in the California Wine-Grape Industry*. Berkeley: California Agricultural Experiment Station, 1934.

Sisson, Robert L. "Yield and Quality Response of Some Respaced North

Coast Vineyards." *American Journal of Enology and Viticulture* 10, 1 (1959): 44–47.

———. "Sonoma County Wine Grape Management Study." Mimeo. Santa Rosa, Calif.: Cooperative Extension Service, 1954.

Skofis, Elie C. *California Wine and Brandy Maker: Elie C. Skofis.* Interview by Ruth Teiser. 1987. Berkeley: Regional Oral History Office, Bancroft Library, University of California, 1988.

"Spotlight on Business: From Our Own Vines." *Newsweek*, October 29, 1956, pp. 90, 92–94.

Stewart, J. Leland. Interview by T. E. Wilde. April 30, 1978. In *History of Napa Valley: Interviews and Reminiscences of Long-Time Residents*, vol. 3. St. Helena: Napa Valley Wine Library Association, 1981.

Stoll, Horatio F. *California's Important Grape Industry.* San Francisco: California Grape Grower, 1927[?].

Stralla, Lou. Interview by Jim Beard. February 2, 1972. In *History of Napa Valley: Interviews and Reminiscences of Long-Time Residents*, vol. 2. St. Helena: Napa Valley Wine Library Association, 1979.

Tchelistcheff, André. Interviews by Richard G. Peterson. July 7, 1972, and January 15, 1975. In *History of Napa Valley: Interviews and Reminiscences of Long-Time Residents*, vol. 2. St. Helena: Napa Valley Wine Library Association, 1979.

———. *Grapes, Wine and Ecology.* Interview by Ruth Teiser and Catherine Harroun. Berkeley: Regional Oral History Office, Bancroft Library, University of California, 1983.

Teiser, Ruth, and Catherine Harroun. *Winemaking in California: The Account in Words and Pictures of the Golden State's Two-Century-Long Adventure with Wine.* New York: McGraw-Hill, 1983.

Thompson, Bob, ed. *California Wine Country.* Menlo Park, Calif.: Lane Books, 1968.

Timothy, Brother. *The Christian Brothers as Winemakers.* Interview by Ruth Teiser. Berkeley: Bancroft Library, University of California, Regional Oral History Office, 1974.

———. Interview by Bob Trinchero. September 16, 1976. In *History of Napa Valley: Interviews and Reminiscences of Long-Time Residents*, vol. 2. St. Helena: Napa Valley Wine Library Association, 1979.

Wente, Ernest A. *Winemaking in the Livermore Valley.* Interview by Ruth Teiser. Berkeley: Regional Oral History Office, Bancroft Library, University of California, 1971.

Wente, Herman. "Grape Growing in the Livermore Valley, Past and Present." *American Journal of Enology* 7, 1 (1956): 69–71.

West, Charles Henry, and Gerald Pearce. *Economic Aspects of the Wine Industry in the United States.* Berkeley: N.p., 1935.

Wine Institute. *Dictionary of California Wine Types.* San Francisco: Wine Institute, 194[?].

———. *Guide Maps to California Wineries. Prepared for Wine Advisory Board.* San Francisco: Wine Institute, 1945[?].

Wines and Vines Yearbook of the Wine Industry, 1941–1942. San Francisco: Wines and Vines, 1942.

Winkler, A. J. "Better Grapes for Wine." *American Journal of Enology* 9, 4 (1958): 202–3.

———. "Varietal Wine Grapes in the Central Coast." *American Journal of Enology and Viticulture* 15, 4 (1964): 204–5.

———. *Viticultural Research at University of California, Davis, 1921–1971.* Interviews by Ruth Teiser and Joann Leach Larkey. Berkeley: Regional Oral History Office, Bancroft Library, University of California, 1973.

Wright, John H. *Domaine Chandon, the First French-Owned California Sparkling Wine Cellar.* Interviews by Carole Hicke. 1991. Berkeley: Regional Oral History Office, Bancroft Library, University of California, 1992.

Index

Compositor: G & S Typesetters, Inc.
Text: 11/13 Galliard
Display: Bernhard Modern
Printer: Edwards Bros.
Binder: Edwards Bros.